Sustainable Building Design

A twenty-first-century renaissance is emerging in architecture. After a century of building designs characterized by high energy demand, low quality lighting and poor thermal comfort, the fundamental questions must be asked again: is there a better path to designing the most energy-efficient, comfortable, functional and beautiful buildings for a sustainable future? While seeking solutions for the future, are there lessons to be learned from the best buildings of the past?

Sustainable Building Design explores outstanding buildings and building designs of the twenty-first century, with an emphasis on the artistry of masters of architecture who came before. By dissecting and analyzing great public buildings of the nineteenth and twenty-first centuries, efficient materials, techniques and methods are discovered. This book presents the reader with clues and suggestions that will reveal the secrets of these buildings and in doing so provides the reader with a thorough understanding of how these architectural masterpieces work.

Using photographs, drawings and diagrams which are painstakingly redrawn for consistency and clarity, based on a wide range of documentation, Vidar Lerum compares works of architecture from the nineteenth and twenty-first centuries. The reader is presented with a careful analysis of each building, providing a compelling sourcebook of ideas for students and professional architects alike.

Vidar Lerum is an Associate Professor at the Illinois School of Architecture at the University of Illinois, Urbana-Champaign, USA. He teaches design studios and design seminars at the undergraduate and graduate levels. His teaching experience includes design studios exploring the path to net zero energy building design, design seminars addressing minimalism in the age of conspicuous consumption and environmental control systems courses. Lerum's research focuses on energy performance, human comfort and user satisfaction in buildings. He is a licensed architect in Norway and a member of the Norwegian Society of Architects (NAL). He is also a Co-opted Committee Member of the CIBSE Heritage Group and an International Associate member of the American Institute of Architects (AIA).

'A must-read for architects in practice or education that brings home the sustainable reality of technics of physics that first matured during the nineteenth century, a reality that, with electronic assistance, still bears environmental fruit today. Vidar Lerum digs deep to shed light on the performance attributes of landmark buildings now more fully discovered.'

– Colin Porteous, Professor of Architectural Science,
Mackintosh School of Architecture, Glasgow, UK

'This book should be compulsory reading for all students of architecture and environmental systems engineering. By means of a unique combination of nineteenth century and twenty-first century case studies, Vidar Lerum convincingly demonstrates that the techniques often used in contemporary exemplar buildings for the improvement of energy efficiency were first tested in monumental buildings about 150 years ago. The modern case studies provide an incredibly detailed resource of information for all those seriously interested in Sustainable Design.'

– Neil S. Sturrock, Chairman of CIBSE Heritage Group, Senior Lecturer in
Building Energy Studies, Liverpool John Moores University, UK (1971–2012)

Sustainable Building Design

Learning from nineteenth-century innovations

Vidar Lerum

LONDON AND NEW YORK

First published 2016
by Routledge
2 Park Square, Milton Park, Abingdon, Oxon OX14 4RN

and by Routledge
711 Third Avenue, New York, NY 10017

Routledge is an imprint of the Taylor & Francis Group, an informa business

British Library Cataloguing-in-Publication Data
A catalogue record for this book is available from the British Library

Library of Congress Cataloging-in-Publication Data
Lerum, Vidar.
Sustainable building design : learning from nineteenth century innovations / Vidar Lerum.
pages cm
Includes bibliographical references and index.
1. Sustainable architecture. 2. Buildings—Technological innovations—History—19th century. I. Title.
NA2542.36.L46 2015
720'.47—dc23 2014046015

ISBN: 978-0-415-84073-6 (hbk)
ISBN: 978-0-415-84074-3 (pbk)
ISBN: 978-1-315-73626-6 (ebk)

Typeset in Avenir
by Keystroke, Station Road, Codsall, Wolverhampton

CONTENTS

FIGURES

ACKNOWLEDGMENTS

Twenty years ago, long before this book was conceived, seeds were planted. During a lecture series at Arizona State University, the late Professor Jeffrey Cook eloquently and enthusiastically talked about his research at the Natural History Museum in London. Many years later, during a pub lunch in Copenhagen, Sergio Fox shared his thoughts and insight on the performance of buildings by Andrea Palladio and Bartolomeo Francesco Rastrelli, a conversation which eventually led me to the Winter Palace in St Petersburg, Russia.

Five years of research leading up to the making of this book were funded in part by the Arnold O. Beckman Research Award from the University of Illinois Campus Research Board and a Creative Research Award from the University of Illinois College of Fine and Applied Arts. Special thanks go to David Chasco, Director at the Illinois School of Architecture, for his encouraging support for my research, and to my colleagues Botond Bognar and Ralph Hammann for sharing their enthusiasm for architectural photography.

There are so many architects, engineers, building owners, librarians, archivists and scholars with whom I have toured buildings and searched through archives over the past five years that it would be impossible to name them all. Nevertheless, that in no way diminishes my deep appreciation for their support. I sincerely thank each and every one of them.

Special thanks go to Alexey Bogdanov, Deputy Director of Operations at the State Hermitage Museum, and his secretary, Olga Korolkova, for providing access to the basement, the attic and the beautiful public rooms at the Winter Palace and to all the staff members who offered insights into the history of the building and its interior climate. Special thanks also go to Neil Sturrock, Chair of the CIBSE Heritage Group, for sharing his wealth of knowledge about the St George's Hall and other great nineteenth-century buildings in England.

A special note of thanks goes to Francesca Ford, Emma Gadsden, Grace Harrison, Trudy Varcianna, Ed Gibbons and Susan Dunsmore at Routledge for their expertise, understanding and patience during the process of making a book idea into the product you are now holding in your hand.

I am grateful to my family in England and in Norway for their genuine interest in and support for my research, generously hosting me en route to building sites in Europe. Special thanks go to my wife Lori, a thoughtful reader and a wise companion who never stopped believing in my work.

Introduction

This book is about the FUTURE of sustainable building design. It is also about the PAST, recognizing that advances in sustainable building design could be compromised if the best examples from the history of our common built capital are ignored.

The research leading up to Part III and Part IV of the book included a thorough investigation of some of the best performing buildings of the twenty-first century. Fourteen innovative buildings and two unbuilt projects were selected for inclusion in the book. A central theme is built on the realization that the best new buildings of the twenty-first century—and those still on the drawing board—while innovative and experimental, are at the same time reflecting an awareness of scientific principles and technological advances found in great nineteenth-century buildings.

It is a fascination with the creative and fruitful tension between the future and the past that drives the research agenda behind this book. A collage is created where images of innovative, high performance buildings of our time are projected on a background of tales of the most significant historic buildings still standing as beautiful, comfortable and functional examples of great architecture. The best buildings of the future, like those of the past, share a common devotion: to create comfortable built environments for human activity, while maintaining a sustainable relationship with the natural world.

Sustainable building design of the twenty-first century increasingly is incorporating technological advances in high performance materials, multi-functional assemblies and automated monitoring, sensing and control systems. Simultaneously, design strategies for sustainable buildings of the future are closely aligned with the basic scientific principles applied to great nineteenth-century buildings, discussed in Part II.

There is a new awareness of the energy efficiency of buoyancy-driven ventilation in buildings, including an understanding of the need to eliminate devices and contraptions that introduce significant pressure drops in the passageways of air. Similarly, there is a growing interest in the properties of the building itself that can serve as multi-functional designs, such as the double-glazed skylights pulling air out of the building while bringing daylight into the interiors without compromising energy performance and thermal comfort.

Thermal mass is again recognized as an integral concept in sustainable design strategies, as exemplified by exposed concrete ceilings and structurally integrated hydronic heating and cooling. There is an emerging interest in the hygroscopic properties of materials and the role that moisture exchange can play in decreasing energy demand when coupled to constructions with high thermal storage capacity. The diurnal and seasonal stability of the indoor climate at the Winter Palace, housing one of the largest and most impressive art collections in the world, cannot be comprehended without an awareness of how the baroque lime-plastered interior surfaces and the heavy mass behind them aid in stabilizing the air temperature and humidity, passively and as integral to the architecture, without the need for energy expenditure.

As one delves into the fertile ground between the future and the past, sincere interest in advanced building designs leads to an understanding of the necessity to learn from the past, to question the present and to build a sustainable future. The following chapters offer a window into the wealth of knowledge embedded in some of the most valuable segments of our built capital.

PART ONE

1

The age of science and technology

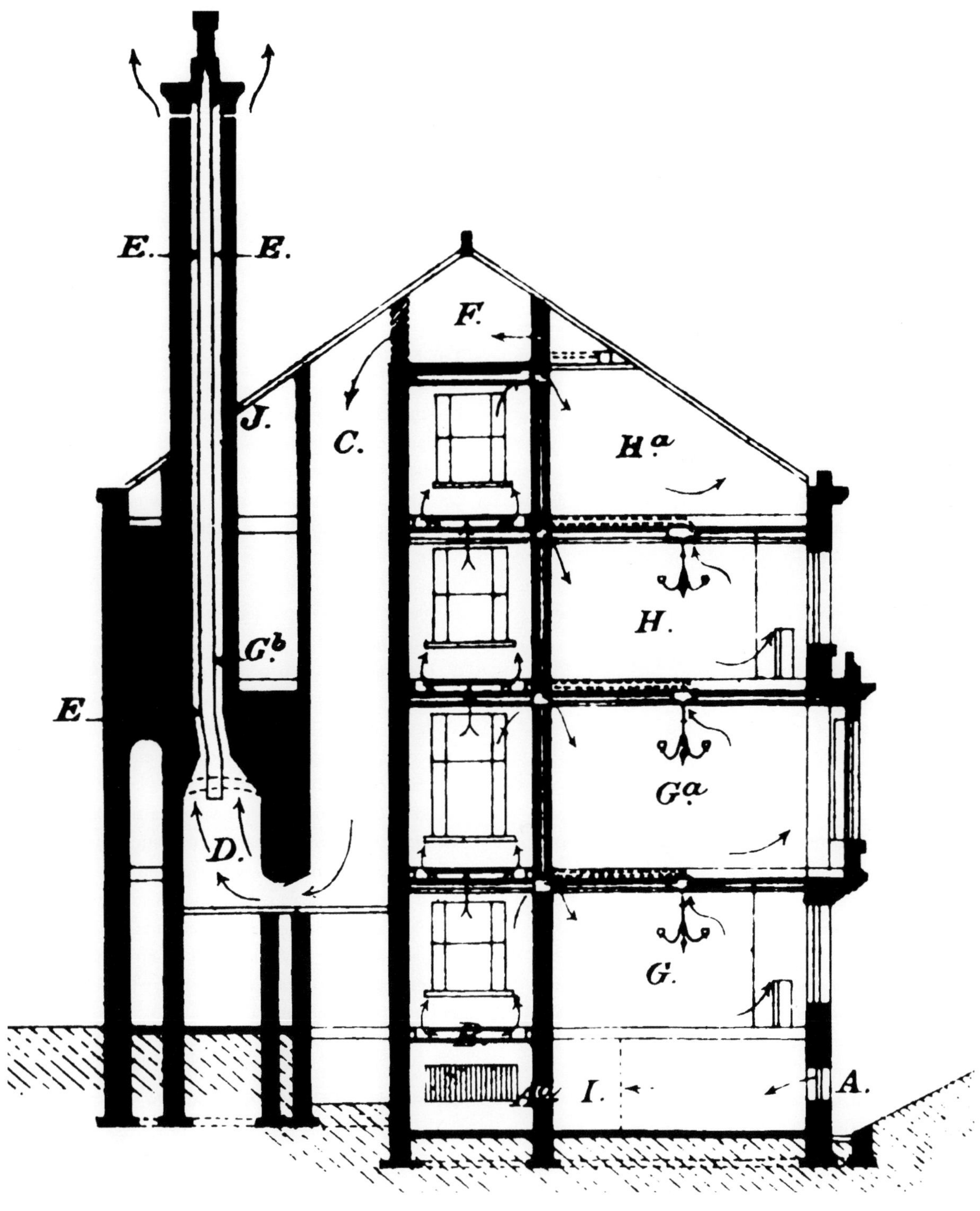

1.1 Section of Dr. Hayward's house in Liverpool, showing how the air flow is driven by an aspirated chimney

In the early morning hours on the 22nd of April, 1871, a small group of interested gentlemen met at Dr. Hayward's house "The Octagon" in Liverpool. The task at hand was to make observations and take measurements of parameters characterizing the thermal comfort of the interior as compared to the ambient climate conditions. They were now preparing a book where they would report on their findings (Drysdale, 1890).

John James Drysdale and John Williams Hayward, medical doctors taking an interest in how improvements in warming and ventilation could benefit public health, had built their houses as experimental laboratories of thermal comfort, installing hybrid comfort systems with hot air for warming and ventilation, assisted by traditional fireplaces. At Dr. Hayward's house, air circulation was driven primarily by a smoke chimney above the kitchen fire.

The following quotation is indicative of the scientific methods by which they approached the subject:

> Mr. Summers entered the fresh-air chamber with a Casella's anemometer to register the velocity of the primary ingress of the air into the house, and commenced observations at 7:27 AM. Dr. Drysdale and Mr. Footner entered the foul-air chamber – Dr. Drysdale, with a Biram's anemometer, to register the velocity of the air entering the foul-air chamber from the different rooms of the house, and commenced observations at 7:31; and Mr. Footner, with a Casella's anemometer, to register the velocity of the air passing out of the foul-air chamber through the downcast shaft, and he commenced observations at 7:45. Mr. Fletcher entered the breakfast room with a thermometer and his own anemometer, to register the temperature and velocity of the air passing up the upcast by means of a small hole through the brickwork at Gb, and commenced observations at 7:48. Mr. Harrison placed himself outside at the top of the kitchen chimney, with three thermometers, to register the temperature of the issuing smoke and foul air, and commenced observations at 7:45. Mr. Higginson placed himself by the Perkins's stove, to observe the temperatures of the warming apparatus. Dr. Hayward went about the house, to take the readings of the thermometers in the central lobbies and rooms and to superintend the lighting of the fires and gases.
>
> (ibid., p. 126)

THE FIREPLACE

Drysdale and Hayward's application of central warming and ventilation systems in their private residences was a rarity, even in the late nineteenth century. The open fireplace was the most commonly used means of creating thermal comfort in homes and offices (Figure 1.2). A nineteenth-century semi-detached English home, with two main rooms on each floor over three floors and a basement, would typically be equipped with eight fireplaces, each with its own dedicated smoke flue built into a load-bearing masonry wall.

The fireplace had become such a familiar feature in any building that one rarely thought about how it actually worked and what it offered in terms of conditioning a room: it not only could warm up a room by radiant and convective heat, but the air required for combustion was pulled into the room from the outside through cracks and openings around windows and doors. The fireplace, therefore, was a system that met the requirements for both warming and ventilation. This system warmed the space by convection and it warmed people in the room by radiant heat. As a ventilation device, the fireplace moves air out of a room by utilizing the motive force of heat. When in use, it refreshes the air in the room, improving indoor air quality by pulling vitiated air up the chimney along with the smoke.

SEASONAL MODES OF OPERATION

Since the open fireplace was primarily seen as a warming device, it was not actively used outside the cooler seasons. It could, however, still work as a ventilation system if the flue was kept open. As needed, operable windows were used to increase the ventilation rate, especially when the ambient air temperature allowed for space cooling by natural ventilation. The method of space

1.2 Fireplace, Glasgow School of Art, by Charles Rennie Macintosh

conditioning by means of fireplaces, which at first glance appears to be a very simple comfort system, is in fact quite sophisticated. When equipped with a mechanical damper inside the smoke flue and combined with operable windows, it is a system that has the ability to adapt to seasonal variations in the ambient climate conditions by switching between a summer and a winter mode.

WARMING THE AIR

However, the method of warming and ventilating by fireplaces has its limitations, particularly when applied as a comfort system in the large and elegant rooms of palaces and concert halls. The continuing need for servants to bring firewood, coal or coke into elegant rooms and to take out ashes from fireplaces could easily become a nuisance in a large ballroom or a great hall. Furthermore, open fireplaces were not particularly efficient, especially if they were left unattended at night with open smoke flues now pulling heat out of the room.

The hot air system, therefore, was seen as a major leap forward in the development of warming and ventilation technologies. For a while, several alternative systems evolved side by side: the "calorifer," the hot air stove or the "Amosov stove" were all variations on the same theme, expressions of the enthusiasm for designing one system that would provide space heating and ventilation without the limitations and disadvantages of the fireplace.

WARMING BY AIR

The first hot air stoves were typically placed in the basement below the rooms to be heated and ventilated. Air was pulled in from the outside and warmed by circulating in channels surrounding a firebox. Smoke from the fires was led up through smoke flues built into masonry walls. By placing the smoke flues adjacent to the hot air channels, heat from the smoke assisted in the upwards movement of the conditioned air supplied to the spaces above.

As precursors to the Industrial Revolution, prototypes of the steam engine were tested in the early 1700s. Thomas Newcomen installed his first commercial steam engine in 1712, but it was not until the last quarter of the eighteenth century, with the inventions of James Watt and Matthew Boulton, that engine designs reached a thermal efficiency high enough to make a significant economic impact. Half a century later, steam engines would pump air and water out of mines, drive machinery in factories, and move trains and ships forward with speeds never seen before. Steam for the engines were provided by boilers, which in turn needed to be fed large quantities of fuel. Nineteenth-century Britain saw the output of coal from mines increase from 10 million tons in 1800 to 225 million tons towards the end of the Victorian era.

Improvements in the design of boilers and the piping needed to supply hot water and steam had an impact far beyond the mines, factories and transportation systems. Since water has a significantly higher heat capacity per unit of volume than air, hydronic systems presented themselves as attractive and efficient competitors to the hot air stoves. What followed was an evolution

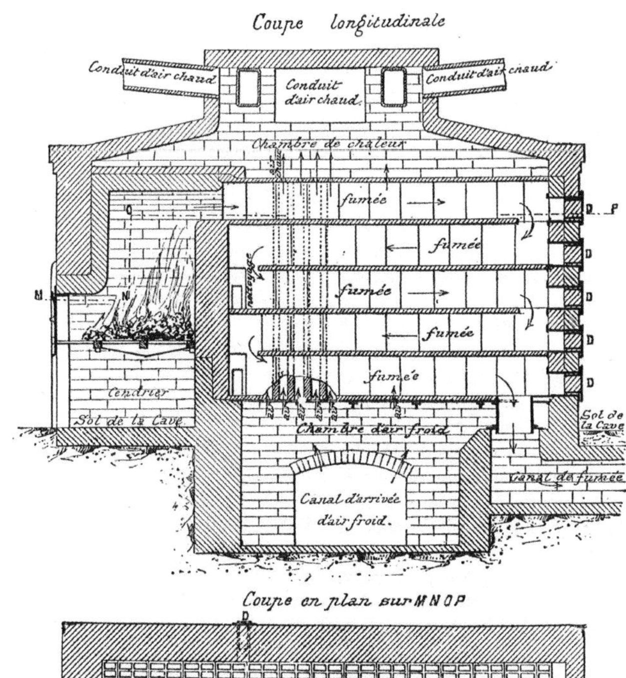

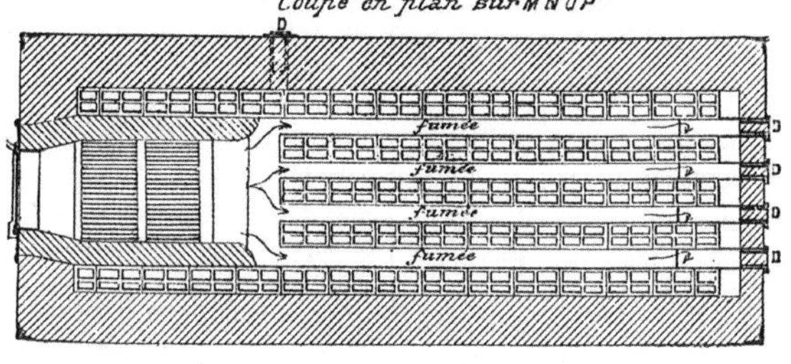

Fig. 4. — Calorifère Haillot.

1.3 Calorifère Haillot, plan and section

in radiator designs, first operating with hot water, then by steam. Heat could now be distributed to individual rooms in a building by the use of piping circuits and radiators.

But there were also disadvantages associated with using hot water or steam. Warm water distribution in large buildings required large diameter pipes, while the steam system presented specific problems associated with the return of condensing water. In response to these challenges, the Perkins family of engineers developed the high pressure hot water system, which permitted higher heat flow rates with smaller diameter pipes.

While any hydronic heating systems could deliver heat to a space quicker and more efficiently than the air stove, to the eye of the architect, these radiator systems were not as elegant as a quiet and nonintrusive air system. Additionally, the higher efficiency of heat delivery was offset by the lack of effective provision for improvements in air quality by ventilation.

AIR AND WATER OR STEAM: THE PLENUM SYSTEM

Several improvements in early nineteenth-century hydronic heat delivery systems came about as a result of technological advancements in boiler design, radiator design, and the design of piping, fittings and other hardware associated with the steam engine-driven economy. Taking advantage of this development, the next logical step was to bring the hot water system to the air system. During the second half of the nineteenth century, high pressure boilers were installed in the basement of large buildings, delivering high pressure hot water or steam to heating coils placed in warming chambers. Fresh air could now be filtered, humidified and heated more efficiently in dedicated large volume compartments, transported horizontally through underfloor tunnels and delivered to the spaces above through architecturally integrated ventilation shafts. The plenum system was born.

One advantage of the plenum system was that the boilers could be centrally located while several warming chambers could be decentralized, responding to the need to condition the spaces above. At the Winter Palace in St Petersburg, 84 "Amosov stoves" were installed in the basement, each needing 24-hour attendance (see Chapter 3). The new arrangements kept the fuel storage and the operation of the boiler at one location and, as a consequence, reduced heat loss in extended masonry tunnels as passageways for warm air.

Like the hot air stove systems, early plenum system designs were based on buoyancy-driven air circulation, aided by the motive force of heat in smoke flues, aspirated chimneys and "smoke towers." With the development of the plenum system, ventilation and warming were again provided by one unified system. The elegance of this display of unity, however, was at times overshadowed by some advantages lost in how water was moved to the basement.

WARMING AND VENTILATION: INSEPARABLE ENTITIES?

While the new all-air plenum systems represented a major improvement over earlier means of warming and ventilation, they also had their limitations. In spaces with high heating demand but less need for ventilation, such as a library or an art studio, the problems soon became apparent. The high demand for heating in a tall space with large single pane windows could only be met either by increased air flow rates or by higher air supply temperatures, leading to an inefficient system unable to provide optimal indoor comfort. Art students in studios with large north-facing single pane windows would suffer from extremely low surface temperatures. Librarians would complain about draughts, and books suffered from the dryness of the air and the dust from the tunnels below the floor.

In some cases, the solution to the problems was to reintroduce the hot water or steam radiator as a complementary system. Radiators represented an intrusion into the interior and a compromise to the elegant simplicity of the all-air system, but by separating the need for heating and ventilation, the two systems could be optimized, resulting in improved comfort and higher fuel efficiency.

In the advanced designs of the twenty-first century, we are once again witnessing a departure from the all-in-one forced air system to more sophisticated and diverse installations for efficient delivery of human comfort in buildings.

HOW TO MOVE AIR

Mechanical "fanners," moved by human labor, beasts of burden, or water wheels, had existed for centuries. But it was not until the last quarter of the nineteenth century that the technology of moving air was perfected. Air, of course, is capable of moving by its own force, governed by the laws of physics, without applying

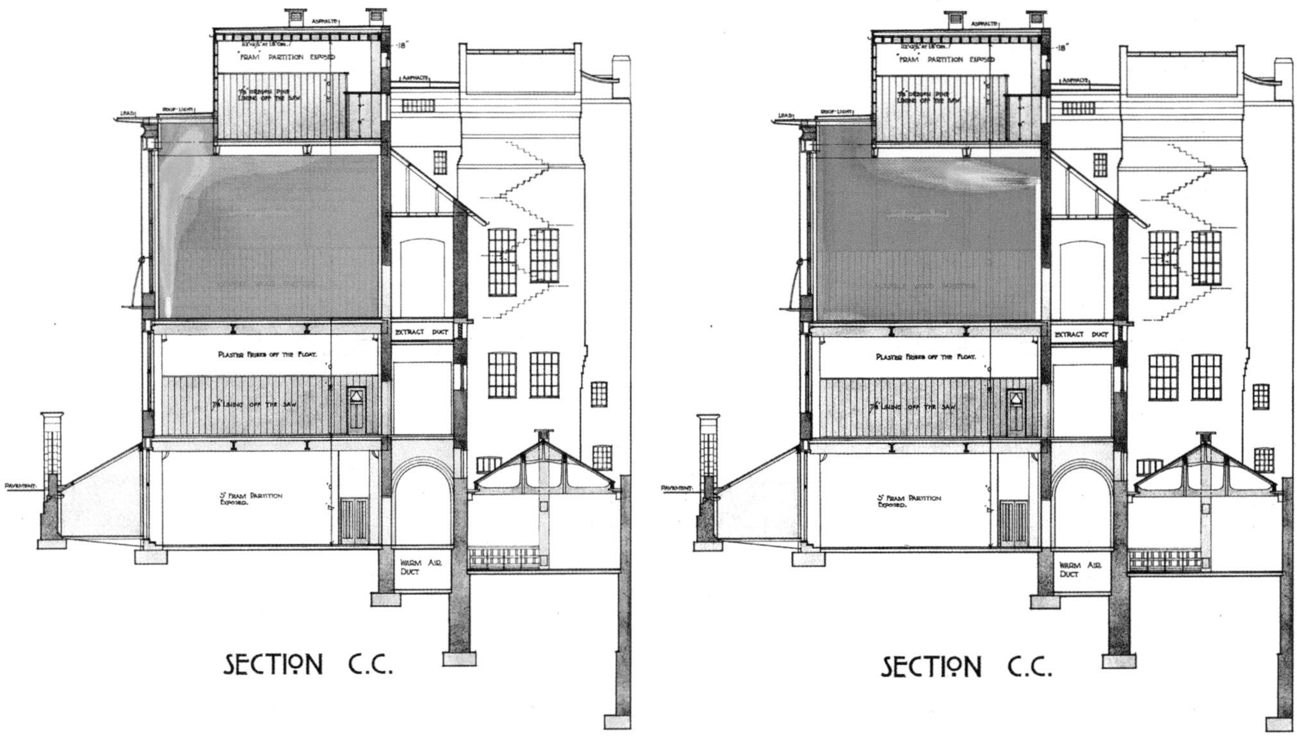

1.4 Images from CFD simulations showing airflow and temperature distribution with original warm air system (right) and after installing radiators (left), superimposed on Section C. C., from 1910 set of drawings by Charles Rennie Macintosh

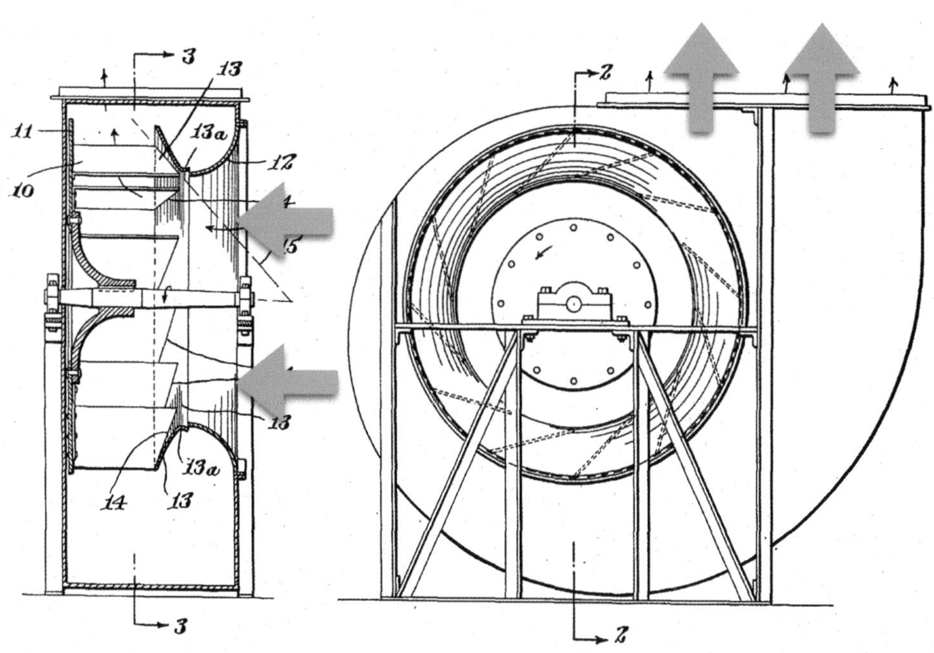

1.5 Airflow diagram showing axial air intake and radial air supply. Centrifugal fan by the B. F. Sturtevant fan company

1.6 Section diagram of the Kelvingrove Art Gallery and Museum, Glasgow, showing the airflow pattern with the warm air system in ventilation mode and heat recovery mode

mechanical force. The early plenum systems of warming and ventilation, therefore, made use of the motive force of heat to move air through buildings. Like the fireplace, the first air systems were predominantly buoyancy-driven designs based on the principle that hot air rises. As needed, wood fires or gas flames were introduced into chimneys to aid the force of buoyancy. By maintaining a considerable indoor–outdoor air temperature difference, the "chimney effect" was maintained, even on a warm summer day.

The mechanical fan, driven by a steam engine or an electric motor, changed the rules of the game. Now, with the centrifugal fan, it was possible to pull in air from the side, along the axis of rotation, and push air out in a direction tangential to said axis. Enthused by this new invention, designers of ventilation systems realized they were no longer limited by the laws of nature. Air could now be moved sideways and downwards, arrogantly defying what the Greek philosopher Aristotle had said about air's final destination being an upwards movement.

This game change, however, did not come without a dramatic increase in the use of energy to power the fans.

HEAT RECOVERY

On a cold winter night, an all-air warming system would operate at high airflow rates while, at the same time, the requirement for ventilation was minimal. Nineteenth-century warming and ventilation systems would typically pull in fresh air with no means of recovering the energy used to heat the air. One can imagine how much energy from burning coal would be wasted when the Great Hall at the Kelvingrove Art Gallery and Museum (Figure 1.6) had to be warmed up before a concert on a wintery morning. In typical warming and ventilation mode, fresh air was pulled in through two air intake towers, one on each side of the great hall. Conditioned air was delivered to the galleries through wall vents from walkable air tunnels below the floor. Vitiated air would typically leave the building through air exhaust turrets connected horizontally to glazed attics above the perforated glass ceilings at the top side galleries.

Constructed at the very end of the nineteenth century, the Kelvingrove Art Gallery and Museum was equipped with two powerful centrifugal fans pulling air from the air intake towers and supplying air through the underfloor tunnel system. By placing the tunnels vertically at two different levels, each fan could supply air in two directions tangential to the axis of rotation.

Large double-acting wooden doors were installed at the ground floor level of the air intake towers. When these doors were opened, fans at the base of the towers would pull air from the interior of the galleries instead of pulling cold air from outside. With the installation of this simple but ingenious arrangement, heat recovery was introduced, effectively saving tons of coal each year.

2

Architecture of Modernity

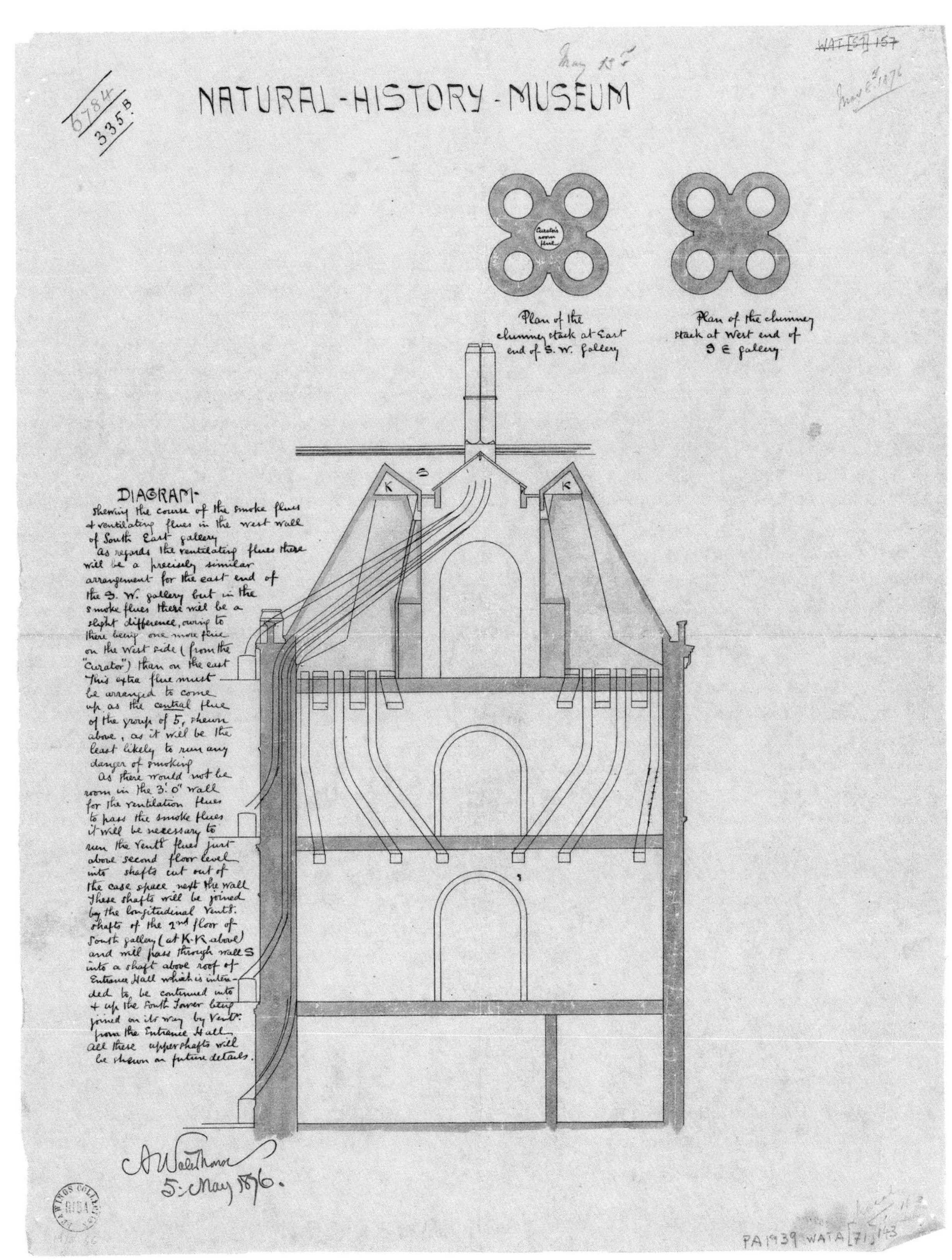

2.1 Alfred Waterhouse: Diagram showing the course of smoke flues and ventilating flues in the west wall of the South-East gallery of the Natural History Museum, London

The term modern architecture is most commonly used synonymously with a style called twentieth-century Modernism. Le Corbusier's *Towards a New Architecture* (Le Corbusier, 1923) was a defining text in the development of the Modernist architectural style. The possibility of eliminating the load-bearing wall and replacing it with the movable interior wall and the lightweight exterior curtain wall was clearly rooted in technological development. The new architecture of the twentieth century could not have been realized without the invention of the reinforced concrete flat plate slab carried by "pilotis" (Le Corbusier's term for columns). The concept of architectural design driven by technological invention was, however, not a phenomenon limited to the twentieth century.

Modernity is characterized by the development of scientific methods to gain knowledge of the natural world through empirical observation, leading to technological innovation. By embracing new technology associated with energy, power, construction and movement, and adapting it to architecture through building integration, architects of the nineteenth century were genuinely modern in their approach. Alfred Waterhouse and other leading architects of the time, assisted by skilled engineers, implemented new technological inventions in materials and methods of construction as well as new developments in the warming and ventilation of large buildings. The architecture emerging from their drawing boards was a modern architecture in its essence, while still resting on a foundation of classical ideas of form, proportions and style.

The new architecture that emerged from the end of the twentieth century was again freeing itself from stale rules of form generation. Developing designs for a sustainable relationship between the built and the natural environment, architects and engineers are embracing technological invention while staying true to the basic elements of site, orientation and form in response to sun, light, wind, water and earth.

TOWERS AND TURRETS

Methods for warming and ventilation developed for new public building types in the nineteenth century represented an opportunity for architectural expression of environmental systems. Many prominent architects of the time, such as Charles Barry, George Gilbert Scott, Alfred Waterhouse and William Henman, enthusiastically embraced this opportunity. Their buildings were enriched with towers and turrets, often justified as necessary features inseparable from passive and active comfort systems. While Charles Barry was uncomfortable having to work with David Boswell Reid, a medical doctor, as the warming and ventilation expert for the new Palace of Westminster, he quickly embraced Reid's suggestion to build three large towers for the supply and exhaust of air (Chapter 6).

In the heavily polluted nineteenth-century city of Glasgow, Scott designed the new university campus at Gilmorehill with a central "ventilation tower" rising above the main entry on the banks of the River Kelvin. At the Kelvingrove Art Gallery and Museum on the opposite side of the river, Smithson and Allen added two utilitarian air intake towers nested among the several more architecturally sculpted and decorated towers (Figure 2.2)

This was not an entirely new phenomenon. The trend had been preceded by a long tradition of well-crafted, architecturally designed smoke chimneys. As the trend continues into the twenty-first century, architects and engineers are developing elements of innovative architectural expression, such as the solar chimney at Manitoba Hydro Place (see Chapter 16) and the perforated stainless steel screen at the San Francisco Federal Building (Lerum, 2008). At the Hilton Foundation, a series of downdraught air supply towers work in tandem with operable clerestory windows at the top of the atrium, forming a buoyancy-driven natural ventilation system.

THE BASEMENT

Le Corbusier did not specifically include the basement in his *Towards a New Architecture*, but the Villa Savoy, where his principles were applied, show a building floating above the ground, held up by "pilotis." In this most important of his early work, the basement is non-existent. In the process of transformation from an "old" to a "new" architecture, the basement, a foundation stone

2.2 Kelvingrove Art Gallery and Museum (left), and Glasgow University, Gilmorehill (right)

of the nineteenth-century approach to comfort systems engineering, was lost.

In this context, it is of interest to note the role of the basement in some of the most significant works of architecture of the twenty-first century. Not unlike the Villa Savoy, the Glass Pavilion at the Toledo Museum of Art seems to "float" in a park, surrounded by beautiful mature trees. The 1.5-ft-thick flat roof appears to be carried by curving double skin walls made exclusively from sheets of glass, rendering the floor as an extension of the ground beneath the canopies of the trees. It would not be possible to achieve this serene simplicity of design, however, without a full basement buried in the ground below the main floor. Even with the central mechanical plant removed to a remote building, space in the basement is still needed for the supply and return ducts serving heating, cooling and ventilation to the spaces above.

THE THICK SERVANT WALL

A century before Louis Kahn introduced the organizational concept of "servant" and "served" spaces, Alfred Waterhouse had devised a similar arrangement. At the Natural History Museum in London, he used a rhythm of narrow and wide galleries to organize the northern exhibition halls (Chapter 11). The idea was to use the narrow galleries as "laboratories" for the scientists and their research assistants. Examples of ongoing research would be placed in display windows facing the wide galleries where the public would be served the latest findings in natural science. Similarly, thick masonry walls would not only serve a load-bearing function, but would also house smoke flues, ventilation shafts and other "mechanical" features. In his hand-written notes on a section drawing signed and dated 5 May 1876 (Figure 2.1), Waterhouse describes the arrangement of vertical flues and shafts inside the 3-ft-thick walls and how these were to be connected to longitudinal (horizontal) ventilation shafts and vertical chimneys in the attic above.

Renzo Piano takes a similar approach at the Nasher Sculpture Center (Figure 2.3). The building is conceived as a series of parallel spaces defined by six thick walls, which emit a sense of solidity and mass with their Travertine surfaces. Upon closer inspection, however, the walls present themselves as containers for structural, mechanical and electrical services. Along with narrow floor grilles at the base, these walls enable the architect to create beauti-

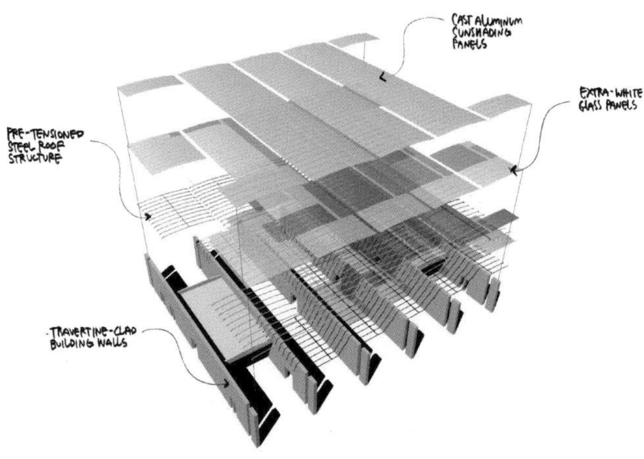

2.3 Nasher Sculpture Museum. Exploded axon by Renzo Piano Building Workshop

ful, serene spaces devoid of ductwork, piping and suspended ceilings.

THE ATTIC

One of Le Corbusier's "Five Points of a New Architecture" was the principle of a flat roof replacing the sloped roof above a loft or attic (Le Corbusier, 1923). By introducing the roof garden or deck, the flat roof could be made into a utilitarian space, while protecting the concrete slab beneath. This concept eliminated the loft or attic above the top floor of the building, effectively taking out one of the most important links in the chain of features associated with a buoyancy-driven natural ventilation system.

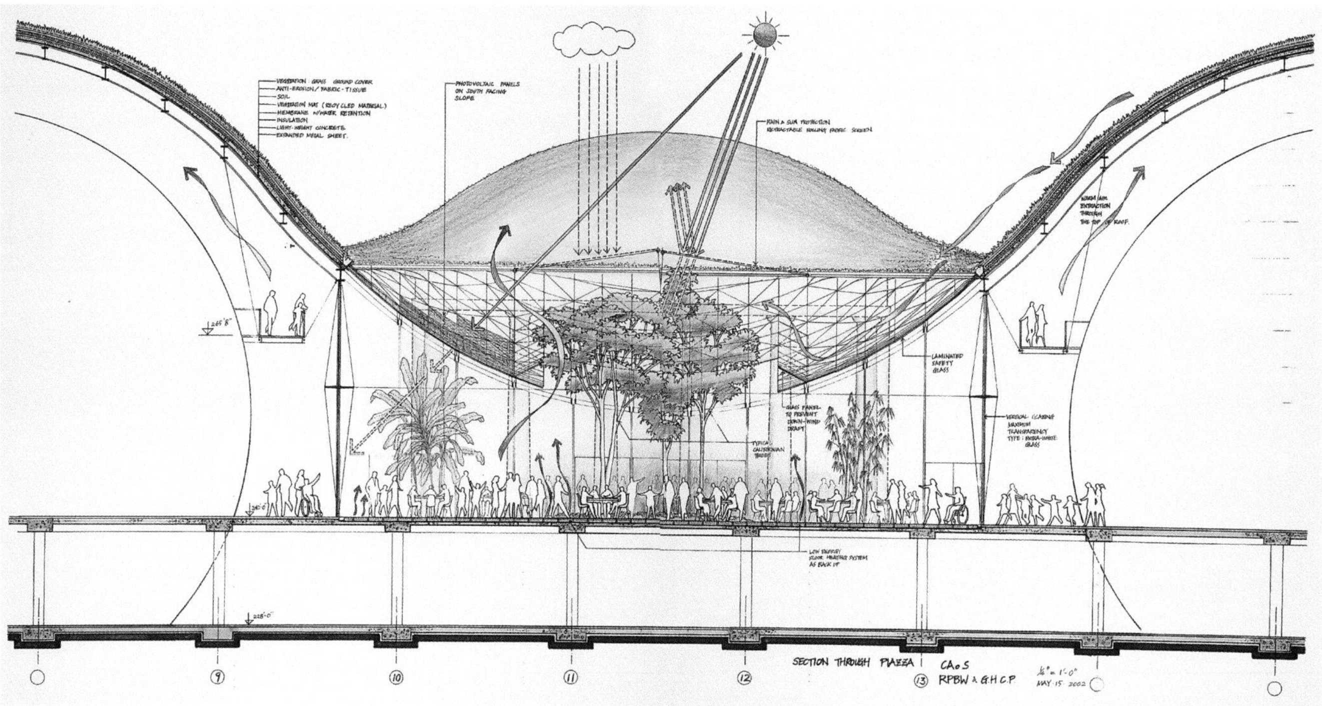

2.4 California Academy of Sciences, by Renzo Piano Building Workshop. Section diagram

At St George's Hall, large skylights were built above glass ceilings, forming volumes of air that would heat up to temperatures well above the outside air, thus acting as solar chimneys pulling vitiated air from the spaces below (see Chapter 7).

At the California Academy of Sciences (Figure 2.4), the architect Renzo Piano with consulting engineers ARUP built an enclosure for the tropical rainforest as a globe residing below the exterior envelope formed by the undulating vegetated roof. Lights necessary for the life of the tropical plants are placed in the "attic" space above the glazed rainforest globe. The heat generated by the lights drives the air from the main floor up into the "attic" void and out through the operable skylights, effectively reducing the energy used to power electrical fan motors.

THE SKYLIGHT

Gas lamps for illuminating streets and building interiors had been available since the early 1800s, but it was not until the last quarter of the nineteenth century that a practical and longer-lasting incandescent lightbulb was made. Even with artificial lighting readily available, daylight was still appreciated. Then, as now, illuminating interiors by daylight not only saves energy but also improves productivity by an increased sense of well-being. Since the application of glass in buildings, windows placed in walls were used to bring light into homes, offices, and multi-story factories, hospitals, and prisons. In the new types of assembly halls, exhibition spaces and galleries of the Victorian era, the skylight provided the same service.

The concert hall at the municipal buildings in Reading (Figure 2.5) is beautifully lit by a curved daylight aperture of iron and glass continuing all around the ceiling. Above the curved glass is an attic space with large skylights inserted in the sloped, slate-covered roof. Narrow openings between the panes of glass let air through to the attic, where gas flames were lit to aid the natural buoyancy of the air.

Similar designs incorporating a skylight forming a "suction chamber" above a perforated ceiling were used in the Winter Palace (see Chapter 3) and at St George's Hall (see Chapter 7).

2.5 The municipal buildings in Reading: "The lighting arrangements are similar to those of the House of Commons. In this case, instead of the glass ceiling, the architect (Thomas Laison) has contrived a glass cove all around the hall below the ceiling. Behind this are placed the gas-lights, which, communicating with the external air by means of properly constructed flues, not only carry off the products of combustion from the gas, but assist materially in the ventilation of the hall." (*The Times*, May 29, 1882)

SIMPLY SOPHISTICATED

The concept of a dynamic façade, responding to the changing impact of the ambient conditions outside as well as the needs of the users inside, is not new. Influenced by Le Camus de Mézières' book, *The Genius of Architecture* (1992), Sir John Soane lectured

2.6 Typical apartment building façade, Versailles, France. Diagram illustrates four window system modes, from all closed to all open

to his students at the Royal Academy about the advantages of the "french window."

Figure 2.6 shows a typical urban façade in Versailles, France, with residences on three floors above retail spaces at the street level. As we can see from the sketch (by the author), the dual modes of the shutters and the windows (open or closed) generate four variations. If we add curtains on the inside (open or closed), movable louvers in the shutter frames (open or closed) and the diurnal shift from light outside to light inside, this simple system can be changed among 32 possible variations by human interaction (2 × 2 × 2 × 2 × 2 = 32).

The "french window," besides being functional, beautiful and energy-efficient, also provides active solar control by protecting the interior from solar gain before the sun's rays reach the glass.

THE RESPONSIVE FAÇADE

In the second opening scene of the PBS series *Downton Abbey*, the camera catches the transition from light to dark as window shutters are opened by an unseen servant. Opening and closing of window shutters was an important part of the servants' morning and evening routine.

At Highclere Castle, designed by Charles Barry, wooden shutters are divided into four panels for each window. Except for secondary rooms such as storage rooms in the towers, the shutters are painted glossy white. They fold and store neatly into the sides of the deep window openings in the thick masonry walls.

Window shutters such as these, typical of the nineteenth-century country houses, serve other functions in addition to controlling light. The confined air space between wood and glass forms an additional layer of thermal insulation. Although most beneficial on a winter night, they would also protect furniture and fabric from ultraviolet light if left in the closed position on a bright summer day. If the window was open and the shutters closed, heat from solar gain could be vented out before reaching the spaces inside.

On a beautiful summer day in 2012 (Figure 2.7), half of the more than 50 windows on the south side were left in the closed position.

ADAPTIVE PERFORMANCE

At the Arab World Institute in Paris, designed by Jean Novel, a curtain wall is installed on the entire south-west-facing façade above the ground floor. The façade is framed by the white volumes forming the passage of entry into the plaza.

On closer examination, the curtain wall is the exterior layer in a double-skin system where light-controlling apertures are placed between the exterior double-glazed skin and the removable glass panels facing the interior.

Like the mechanics of a film camera, the openings in the aperture were designed to open and close, thus regulating the amount of light admitted to the building's interior. The electrically

2.7 Highclere Castle, south façade

powered mechanical system required to regulate the openings is quite complex. Placed in a narrow cavity between layers of glass, the mechanism is not readily accessible for maintenance and repair.

Figure 2.8 (top right) shows a floor-to-ceiling height panel with 73 openings. Although the mechanism is no longer functioning, the play of light as reflected on the floor enlivens the interiors by creating continuously changing patterns of light and shade as the sun moves across the sky. By creating associations with geometric patterns in Islamic art and architecture, a cultural layer is added to a functional and beautiful design.

The Men's and Women's Portal Spas, designed by the architecture firm Worksbureau, form the gateway to the King Abdullah Financial District of Riyadh (Figure 2.8). The program is divided between two distinct building volumes framing the main Park as it flows into the Wadi pedestrian artery. Seen as geologic formations rising from the land, they form great shade porticos beneath long cantilevered masses.

The guest experience is choreographed on three levels as episodes of varied light and character: from sifted light in the atria, or dim relaxation of treatment, to the brighter vaults of the upper pools.

The buildings are dematerialized by an ethereal perforated metal rainscreen, a performance-driven jacket with dynamic "tessellate" shading. The skin transforms the interior and exterior character with time and seasons. The performance-driven adaptive portions of the façade are built with three layers of perforated steel panels. One layer is stationary while the two other shift laterally to control the ratio of transparency and opacity.

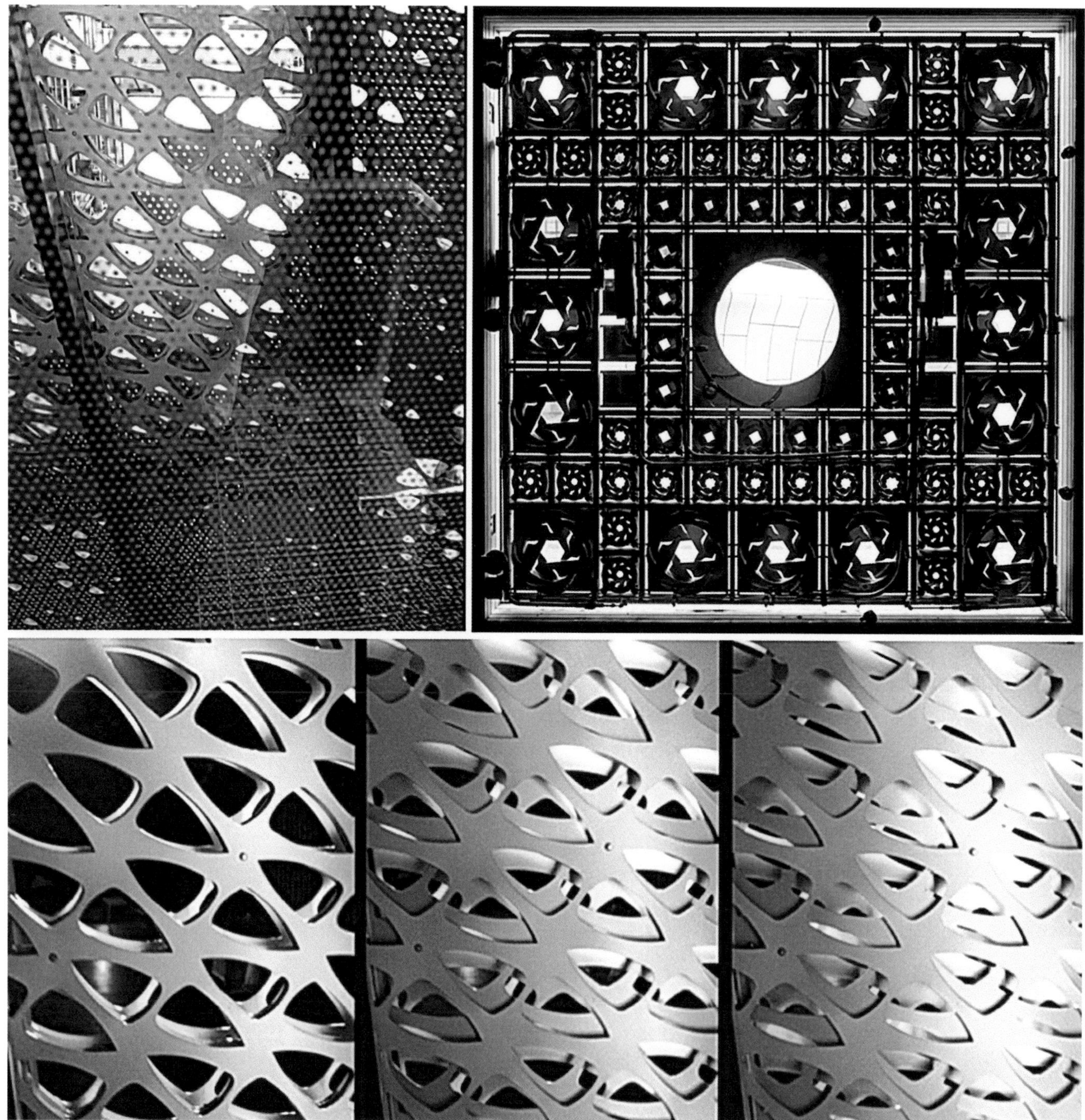

2.8 Arab World Institute by Jean Nouvel, interior view of building skin (upper right). KAFD Portal Spas by Worksbureau, environmentally responsive shade system

The gear used to move the panels includes rods and wheels, transforming linear motion into rotation, which generate complementary shifts in the position of the peripheral panels around the stationary panels in the center of the assembly.

The finely detailed geometry of the openings contribute to a sensation of continuously changing patterns of light and shade, not unlike the shade created by tree canopies as the sun moves across the sky.

PART TWO

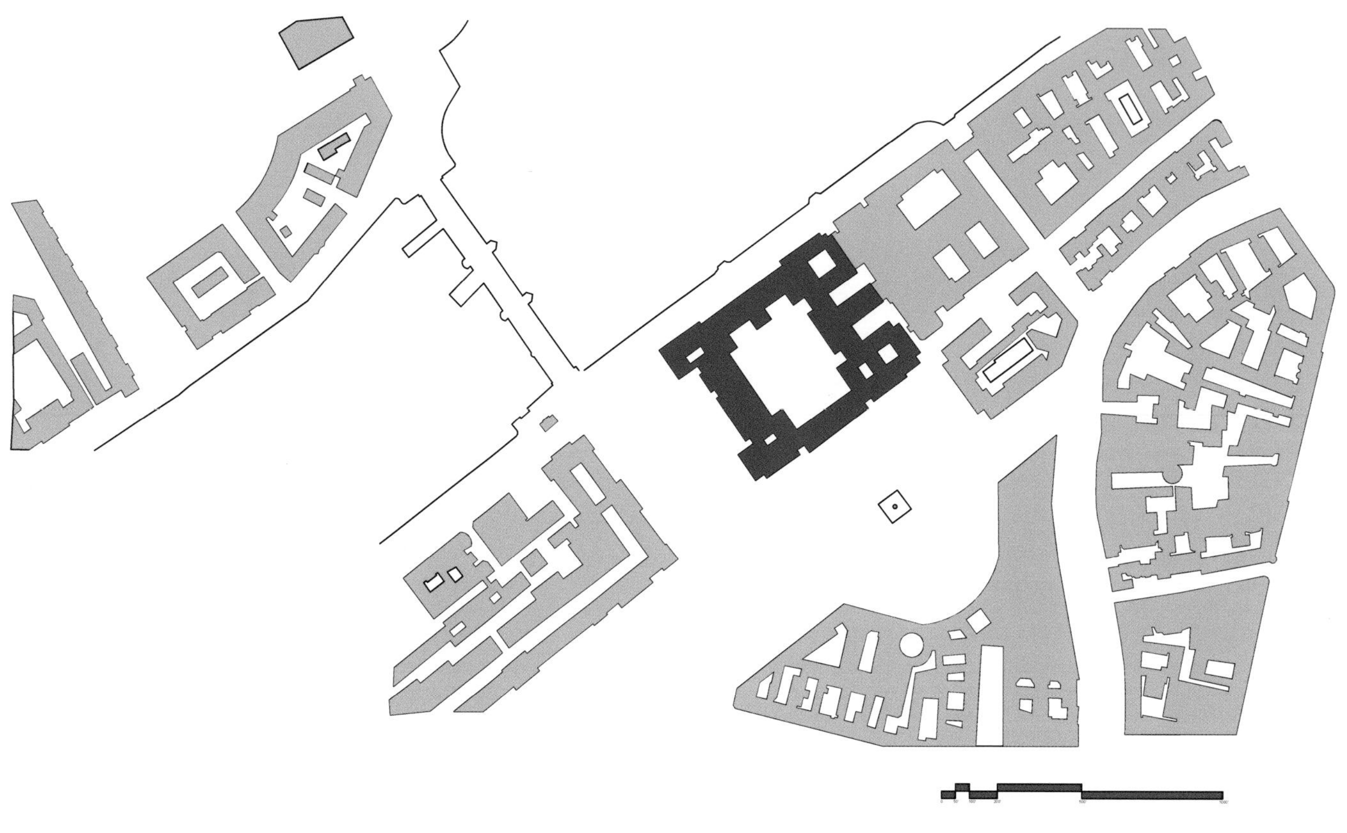

3

The Winter Palace

LOCATION: ST PETERSBURG, RUSSIA

BUILT: 1756

ARCHITECT: BARTHOLOMEO RASTRELLI

60°N

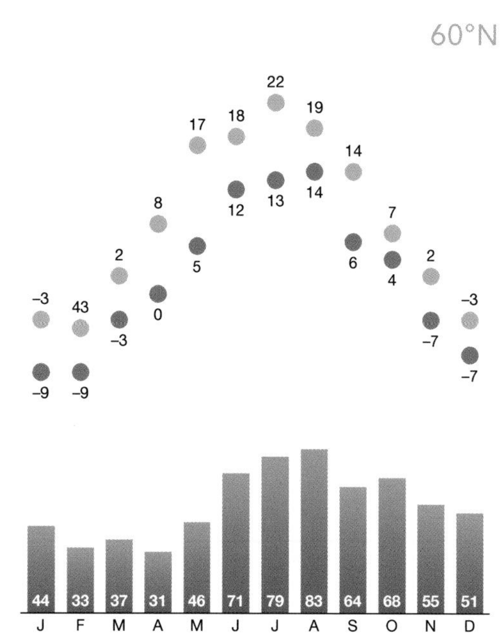

3.1 The Winter Palace. Main entrance on Palace Square

Source: Vidar Lerum.

WHERE EAST AND WEST WERE SET TO MEET

It was at the mouth of the River Neva that Peter the Great decided to build a new city. The lands were low and wet, so the river delta was in many ways not the most favorable place to build what was to become the most important city in Russia. Peter the Great, however, saw the task at hand in a larger context. The new city was, in his view, an instrument to make a grand plan possible. That plan was to turn Russia around, to face the world to the west.

Several years before St Petersburg was officially founded, Peter had traveled through Europe in search of ideas and technology. He traveled, sometimes incognito, on learning missions and head-hunting adventures. What he brought home to Russia was not only the new ideas and the knowledge about new methods of production, but he also made agreements for artists, intellectuals and skilled workers to leave their country for a new life and a fresh start in the service of Tsar Peter I, who was to become the Emperor Peter the Great.

Among the artists whom Peter had attracted to St Petersburg was Bartolomeo Carlo Rastrelli, an Italian sculptor, who had moved to Paris from Florence. While working as a sculptor in Paris, where he had executed many funerary monuments, one can imagine how he was approached by Peter's head-hunters and how he might have become excited about the promise of making a contribution to the new Russia.

Carlo brought with him his son, Bartolomeo Francesco Rastrelli, who was born in Paris in 1700. As a man of artistic heritage, the young Rastrelli set out to become an architect. During his first years in Russia, which coincided with Peter the Great's last years on the throne, he made several study trips back to France and to Italy to train as an architect.

THE ARCHITECT AND THE TSARINA

From the beginning of Bartolomeo Francesco Rastrelli's career in the mid-1720s until the mid-1790s, Russia was governed mostly by female rulers. Peter's wife Catherine I ruled for two years (1725–1727). With brief intermissions, she was succeeded by Anna Ivanovna (1730–1740), Elizabeth I (1741–1762) and Catherine II (1762–1796). The rules of these four tsarinas were separated by three emperors whose reign ended abruptly: Peter II (1727–1730) supposedly died after having fallen ill from a hunting expedition but was probably murdered. Ivan IV, the child emperor (1740–1741) was killed during an attempt to escape from imprisonment. Peter III reigned for eight days in 1762 until his wife Catherine the Great had him killed.

It was during this post-Peter the Great period dominated by female rulers that Rastrelli built his career as an architect. By the time Elizabeth I came to power, he had positioned himself to become her Court Architect.

Was the young Rastrelli a member of the group known as Gentlemen of the Bedchamber? That might well have been the case. A handsome and well-educated man, he was three years younger than Anna Ivanovna and nine years older than Elizabeth I, Peter the Great's granddaughter. By the time Elizabeth was succeeded by Catherine the Great, however, Rastrelli found himself serving a client 29 years younger. Catherine, who preferred young lovers, demoted Rastrelli from his position as court architect, supposedly because she did not favor his Italian Baroque architectural style.

Rastrelli might have pleased the female rulers of Russia at his time, but that was not to shape his legacy. For Bartolomeo Francesco Rastrelli was a brilliant man, an architect who mastered to the fullest the art and technology of building.

THE ARCHITECT AND THE MATHEMATICIAN

When Bartolomeo Francesco Rastrelli returned to Russia from his architectural studies abroad, he found that another young man had joined the club of intellectuals in St Petersburg. Daniel Bernoulli, the son and nephew of the famous Bernoulli brothers from Switzerland, had been hired as a professor of mathematics.

Rastrelli and Bernoulli were of the same age, both born in Western Europe in 1700. St Petersburg was still a town of modest size, so it is likely they must have met. One can easily imagine a conversation between the two highly intelligent men.

DANIELIS BERNOULLI Joh. Fil.
Med. Prof. Basil.
ACAD. SCIENT. IMPER. PETROPOLITANÆ, PRIUS MATHESEOS SUBLIMIORIS PROF. ORD. NUNC MEMBRI ET PROF. HONOR.
HYDRODYNAMICA,
SIVE
DE VIRIBUS ET MOTIBUS FLUIDORUM COMMENTARII.
OPUS ACADEMICUM
AB AUCTORE, DUM PETROPOLI AGERET, CONGESTUM.

ARGENTORATI,
Sumptibus JOHANNIS REINHOLDI DULSECKERI,
Anno M D CC XXXVIII.
Typis Joh. Henr. Deckeri, Typographi Basiliensis.

3.2 Ventilators, chimneys and sculptures on the roof of the Winter Palace (right). The cover of Daniel Bernoulli's book on hydrodynamics (left)

Naturally, Rastrelli would strike up a conversation about the latest trends in architecture. He would speak eloquently about his grand schemes for the new St Petersburg, the "Venice of the North." But Bernoulli was already so deeply involved in his investigations into what he called "hydrodynamic" that he hardly could respond to Rastrelli's ideas. Instead he kept talking about how he had discovered that water does not always come out of a hole in a water pipe. He had found that under certain conditions relating to velocity and pressure of water, air would be sucked in through a hole in a water pipe. It was through his hydrodynamic experiments that he came to a deeper understanding of the behavioral patterns of smoke in chimneys:

> Therefore, it is the same for smoke ascending as for water descending; but . . . the latter flows through the orifice . . . more quickly, the larger it is, and the lower it is positioned; therefore, also, the smoke will travel through the chimney more quickly, the more the fire is kindled in the furnace, the higher the chimney is carried, and the more it diverges facing upward, if only it does not diverge too much; experience confirms each of these. I myself learned in addition that if the chimney be perforated somewhere, it is not at all so that smoke attempts an exit through that opening, but rather that air rushes in with a great impetus, and, mixing itself with the smoke, it rises through the chimney, and not otherwise than as we indicated that the air rushes into the pipe. So indeed the smoke ascends certainly in a lesser amount, or at least with more difficulty, as the fire slackens.
>
> (Bernouilli, 1738, pp. 55–56)

Magically, these two seemingly opposing sets of thoughts and ideas, those of the artful construction of space in buildings versus those of dynamic flows of air and water, came together. As Bernoulli went on to publish his revolutionary book on hydrodynamics, Rastrelli positioned himself to become the architect of the marvelous Winter Palace. Knowingly or not, in his design for the great palace on the banks of the Neva, he applied Bernoulli's principles, integrating hundreds of channels inside the walls and a thousand chimneys on the roof.

3.3 The Winter Palace ballroom, with fireplace

FIREPLACES AND DUTCH STOVES

Before the fire in 1837, there were two main "systems" for heating and ventilation in the Winter Palace: fireplaces and Dutch stoves. Sergio Fox describes how each room with a fireplace was served by three channels built into the thick masonry walls and connected to chimneys or vent hoods on the roof. While one channel served as a smoke chimney, the one next to it was used to replenish air consumed by combustion. The proximity of the fresh air channel to the smoke chimney caused the incoming air to be preheated. The third channel, with a grille near the ceiling, served as an exhaust duct for vitiated air.

Peter the Great and his "prime minister" Menshikov traveled to Europe to learn about modern technology and trades. For a while Peter worked incognito as a shipbuilder in Holland because he wanted to learn how to build ships from the leading ship building nation at the time. Peter was a practical man (today we might call him a modern progressive man) who was skilled in many crafts. It is said that when he ordered something to be done, he also provided all the necessary details about how it was to be done.

So Peter learned about Dutch stoves and introduced them to Russia. In the beginning, the tiles (*kakkel*) came from Delft in Holland, but also from Meisen in Germany and Åbo or Turkuu in Finland. Later, Russia built their own production facilities for *kakkel*.

The stoves were superior to the open fireplaces in many ways: you could keep a fire going all night long, they were more fuel-efficient, and they added beauty to the interior. But like fireplaces, they required the transportation of wood or coal into the finest rooms and the removal of ashes, which also meant that low-level servants had to be allowed into the finest rooms where only the nobles had access.

And then there was the danger of fire. So after the devastating fire of 1837, it was decided that the entire palace should be heated and ventilated by a warm air system.

IN THE THICKNESS OF THE WALL

A rather curious item in the State Hermitage Museum's art collection is a recently restored sculpture of an ancient man protecting his child. The sculpture (badly damaged) was recovered from a cavity inside a thick wall! How and why it was placed inside the wall is not known. It was discovered when a crew punched a hole in the wall because they needed to insert an electrical panel there.

As they peered into the hole, they looked straight into the eyes of the caveman. I inspected the place where the sculpture was hidden and found that this particular cavity wall was more than 1.5 meters thick! Without these thick masonry walls, the heating and ventilation system could not have functioned as well in the first place and would certainly not survived the test of time. The system of channels inside thick walls is still the living backbone of the modern air conditioning system that serves the palace today.

FORTOCHKA

The *fortochka* is a Russian version of a ventilated double-glazed window system. While fixed panes of glass are installed in most of the frames, some frames are operable, allowing fresh air to enter the room.

When two sets of operable window frames are placed high and low in the window assembly, they can be arranged in multiple configurations. This provides straightforward direct ventilation, allowing the entry of fresh air. If the inner operable frame near the floor and the outer operable frame near the ceiling are shut, the in-flowing air is preheated by the use of solar radiation before entering the interior space.

The distance between the outer and inner glazing is normally between 150 and 200 mm, but was increased to 300 mm in Maria Alexandrovna's residence to allow for the installation of a warm air system.

VAULTED CEILINGS REFLECTING LIGHT

As one walks through the beautiful interiors of the Winter Palace, one is presented with the most astonishing examples of Rastrelli's mastery of daylighting design. Light enters the spaces through apertures in the exterior walls and the ceilings, openings that are carefully placed and sculpted to make the most use of available light from the sky dome outside.

Daylight in buildings serves multiple purposes. Research shows that daylight elevates the mood and enhances productivity. When natural light can replace light from candles, oil lamps,

3.4 Lime-plastered vaulted ceilings carry daylight while stabilizing air temperature and relative humidity

gas flames or electric light bulbs, energy is saved more than once, not only by eliminating the energy used to produce light, but also by reducing the need for mechanical cooling because the internal heat gains are reduced.

And above all, the spaces flooded by natural light are just simply beautiful. That is certainly true for Rastrelli's Winter Palace.

MIRRORING DAYLIGHT

In a large building like the Winter Palace with its thousand rooms, every space cannot afford the luxury of being evenly lit from two sides. The Grand Staircase is located at the northern corner of the palace. Daylight enters the space from large windows facing the River Neva.

Although the quality of the north-western light is very good, the space is unevenly lit. So Rastrelli placed similarly shaped and sized windows on the opposite interior and installed mirrors where there otherwise would be glass. This technique of mirroring and multiplying daylight is used throughout the most prominent public rooms in the Winter Palace. In the richly decorated Grand Staircase, the effect is stunning (Figure 3.5).

HYGROSCOPIC PROPERTIES OF MATERIALS

The State Hermitage Museum holds one of the largest art collections in the world, more than three million pieces. Many of the most significant objects of art from this collection are on display in the Winter Palace. In spaces that do not lend themselves to modern forced air conditioning systems, how is it possible to provide optimal interior climate conditions to prevent the valuable works of art from deteriorating?

When searching for an answer to that question, one must look long and hard at the hygroscopic properties of materials. A typical exhibition space in the palace may look like the one in Figure 3.6. The sculpted walls and ceiling vaults are made with lime plaster. The floors are covered with hardwood, often beautifully decorated with inlays.

Wood and lime plaster are materials with superb hygroscopic qualities. In his (2005) book *Water in Buildings*, Bill Rose demonstrates how much water is contained inside materials in traditionally constructed buildings. When the sixteenth-century architect Andrea Palladio was forced to use brick and plaster to build a villa because his favorite stone was not available nearby, he discovered how cool this new villa was in the summer. The improved environmental behavior came about as a result of the ability of the interior surfaces to interact with heat and moisture in the air.

The graph in Figure 3.6 illustrates a theoretical exercise on the question at task: Starting with a 21C/50%RH ideal state, relative humidity (RH) decreases as the temperature rises (red horizontal line). This causes the moisture contained in the plaster to migrate out of the walls and ceilings, a process involving evaporation. The heat required for the evaporating moisture causes the air to cool (sloped red line). At night the reverse process takes place. As the temperature drops, the RH increases, which causes the moisture to shift back from air to material, a process of condensation which releases heat.

As compared to non-hygroscopic materials commonly used in Modernist architecture, the interiors of the Winter Palace are interacting with the air, causing the temperature to fluctuate less, while stabilizing the relative humidity. The building is alive. It breathes.

SMOKE IN THE ATTIC

When attending a performance at the theater one evening in 1837, the Tsar received a note informing him that smoke had been detected in the attic of the Winter Palace. The message was not alarming enough for him to leave the theater before the performance had ended. But what at first seemed to be smoke coming out of a cracked masonry chimney soon turned into a devastating fire that would damage the entire palace before it was put under control.

Although the cause of the fire has not been determined, it is likely that it spread undetected for a long time through voids in the thick walls. During a hasty remodeling project four years

3.5 The Grand Staircase

earlier, wood was used to build the thick walls instead of masonry. Unused fireplaces with smoke stacks and ventilation channels that were left inside the walls now allowed the fire to spread from room to room and ultimately into the attic.

Rastrelli had designed the roof of the palace using wooden trusses. Once the attic started filling up with smoke, a mixture of air and combustible gases created an explosive atmosphere. At this point, the fire could not be controlled.

The Tsar realized that a palace in ruins would be seen as a sign of Russian weakness and political instability, but he also saw the potential for a publicity gain if the palace could be rebuilt quickly. He therefore ordered the palace to be rebuilt within one year. This enormous task would take a workforce of 6000 laborers, many of whom died on the job.

The wooden trusses were now replaced by steel trusses, using the newest technology and engineering skills available. The thick wall concept, including hundreds of channels and chimneys, was, however, kept but rebuilt with mostly non-combustible materials. The entire basement structure with its cavernous spaces was also left intact. This opened up the possibility of introducing an entirely new approach to heating and ventilation.

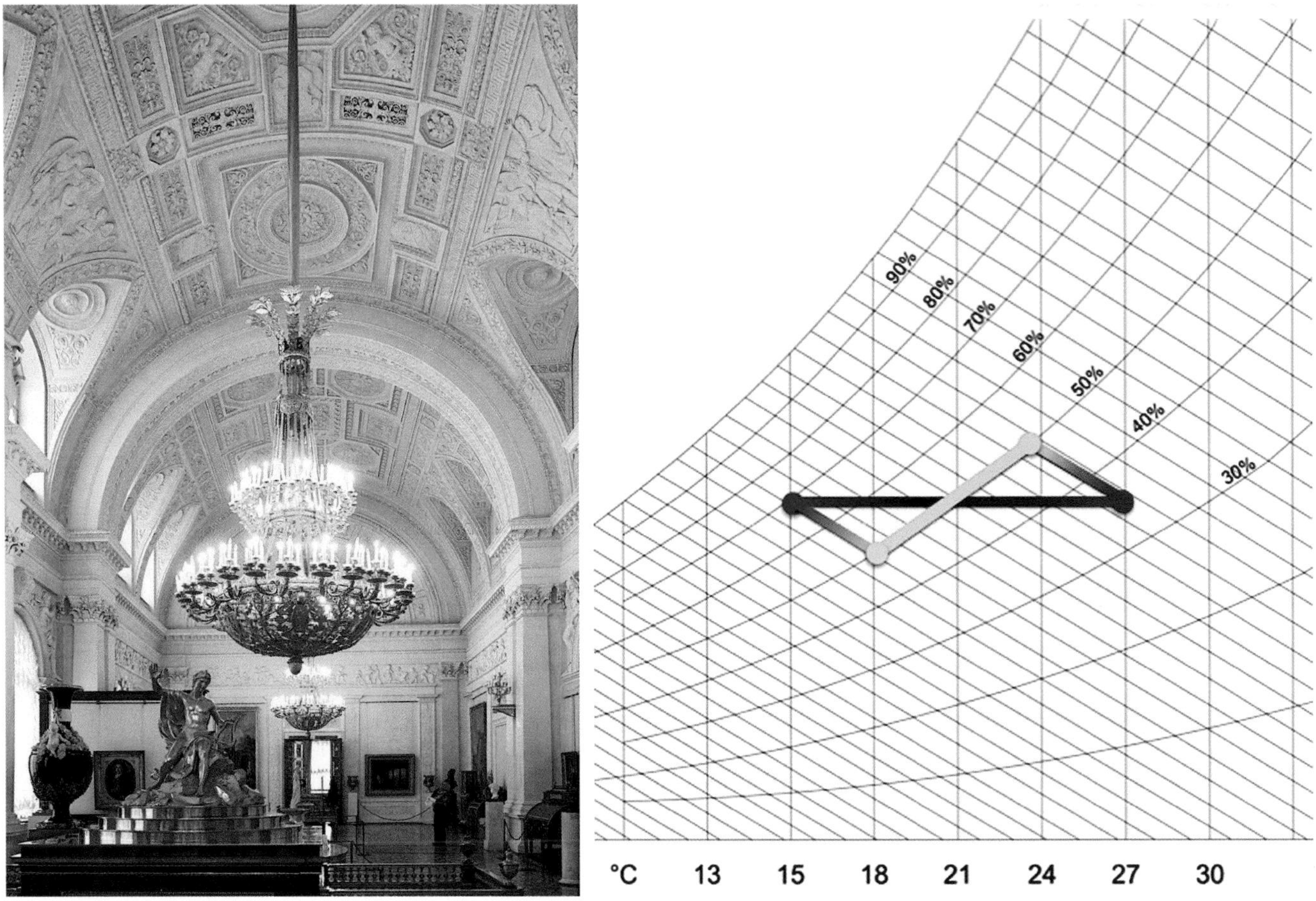

3.6 The dampening effect of the hygroscopic properties of lime plaster on diurnal air temperature fluctuations

GENERAL AMOSOV

A few years prior to the fire of 1837, General Nicolai Amosov had invented a warm air furnace: the Amosov stove. Smoke from the fuel burning in the combustion chamber was led through an intricate system of cast iron finned tubes where the heat was transferred to air passing through the warming chamber. Fresh air brought in from the outside was warmed before it was sent to the rooms above through channels in the thick masonry walls.

The new system was revolutionary. It was no longer necessary to keep open fires burning inside the populated rooms in the palace. No need for servants to bring in firewood and to take out the ashes. Instead, warm air magically heated and ventilated the palace quietly and invisibly.

As seen in an individual room in the palace, the new system could be characterized as central heating, but seen on the scale of the large palace, it was actually a decentralized system. Amosov built and installed 84 Amosov stoves, as indicated in Figure 3.7.The stoves came in two sizes, customized to the requirements of the rooms they served.

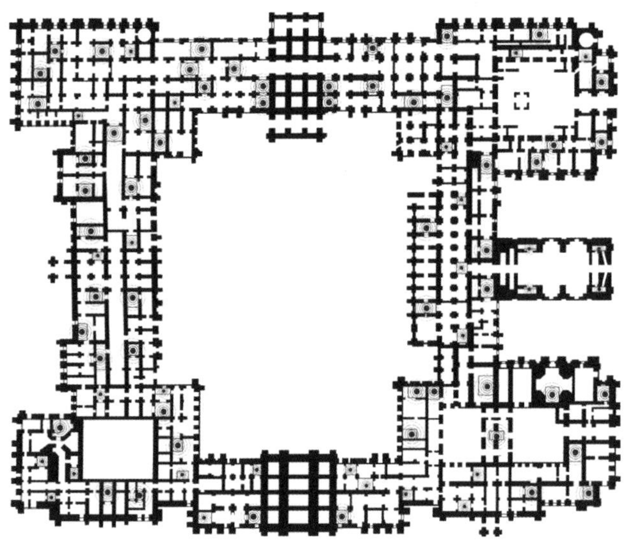

3.7 Plan diagram showing the placement of the Amosov stoves in the basement of the Winter Palace

3.8 Beautifully decorated vaulted ceiling with integrated air exhaust vents

Since the new system was designed to use the previously installed channel structure of the thick masonry walls, no major changes to the main interior space were necessary. The decentralized character of the Amosov system also offered the potential for energy efficiency. Since each stove could be fired or left disengaged, according to the actual time of use of the rooms it served, the system was in fact what we today call an on-demand heating system.

ATTIC PLENUM VENTILATION

To this day there are hundreds of beautifully designed brass grilles and vent caps to be found in the most prominent rooms of the Winter Palace. Cataloging these brass apertures would be a sizable task. The fact that they are still functional adds to their value as objects of utility and beauty.

When there was a need for additional ventilation from the grand halls, ventilation grilles were installed in the vaulted ceilings. The integrated design of these utilitarian devices was so skilled and artistic that one hardly notices their existence. Only after careful examination can they be detected—with great pleasure to a student of the art and technology of environmental controls in historic buildings.

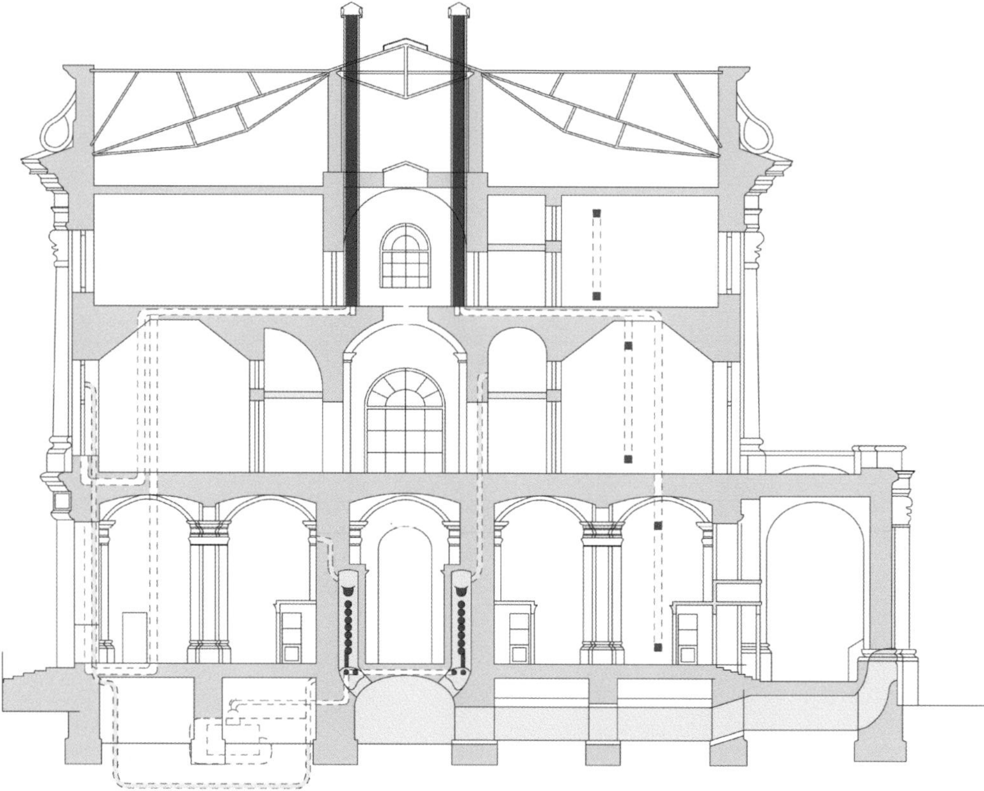

3.9 Heating and ventilation diagram, redrawn from a Winter Palace section drawing (project 1870)

THE CALORIFERE

With the introduction of boilers delivering hot water through a network of iron pipes, a new development in heating and ventilation supplemented the Amosov system. The sectional diagram in Figure 3.9, based on an illustration in Matsenkov (2011), shows heating chambers built into the walls of a central corridor. Identified by the staff as "calorifiers," these new installations warmed the fresh air coming in through the basement. The warm air was then distributed to the rooms by way of the vertical shafts and channels built into the masonry walls.

The section diagram also shows an actively warmed and ventilated double window system installed in Maria Alexandrovna's chambers.

As hot water systems supplemented and ultimately replaced the Amosov stoves, a large boiler room was built inside one of the smaller courtyards. This boiler room was located near the western corner of the palace.

To this day, the Winter Palace is still heated and ventilated by a hot water system, but the supply of hot water no longer depends on boilers on site. A district heating system serving the central areas of St Petersburg now brings the hot water, allowing the Amosov stoves and the boilers to be replaced by modern air handling systems, still using the old network of vertical masonry channels, attic ventilation, and hundreds of chimneys and vent hoods.

MARIA ALEXANDROVNA'S DOUBLE SKIN FAÇADE

After her marriage to Alexander II, Princess Marie von Hesse came to be known as Maria Alexandrovna. The young princess came to Russia after growing up in Southern Germany. She was not very pleased with the climate of St Petersburg and immediately started demanding improvements to her comfort during the harsh winter months.

Her residence occupied the south-west corner of the palace. It had a separate entrance onto Palace Square and Maria complained about cold air coming in when the door was opened. The result of her complaint was the first hot water radiator to be installed in the palace, placed under a window near the entrance. The hot water circulated through a small wood-fired boiler placed in the basement below.

The apartment, including the Blue Bedroom, has many windows, each with about 7.5 square meters of glass area. Even with double glass, the cold exterior walls contributed to an uncomfortable indoor environment.

Having given birth to eight children, her health was compromised and the Russian winters became even more intolerable. The solution her engineers came up with was a novel one: Since the palace already was equipped with Amosov stoves in the basement, warm air was coming up channels inside the thick masonry walls. The windows were modified to increase the distance between the two panes of glass to 300 mm and ducts were fitted into the window cavity, allowing warm air to be introduced near the top. As the air cooled while warming the glass, it fell by gravity into a duct opening in the window sill. This must have been the first actively heated and ventilated double skin window wall system ever known!

MICROCLIMATE IN THE COURTYARD

The cooling effect of leafy trees is a well-known phenomenon. This human experience from interacting with nature is so ingrained in our collective mind that one hardly reflects on it.

Trees not only provide summer shade but also take the heat out of the surrounding air. Photosynthesis uses water and sunlight to produce biomass and oxygen. Evapotranspiration cools the surroundings through the process of evaporation.

So when Princess Dagmar of Denmark became the Empress Maria Feodorovna in 1883, she designed a garden in the central courtyard of the Winter Palace. These trees are now tall. Along with a water fountain, they create a wonderful space that feels like an oasis as one enters from the rather bare Palace Square on a hot summer day.

3.10 The Winter Palace, the inner courtyard

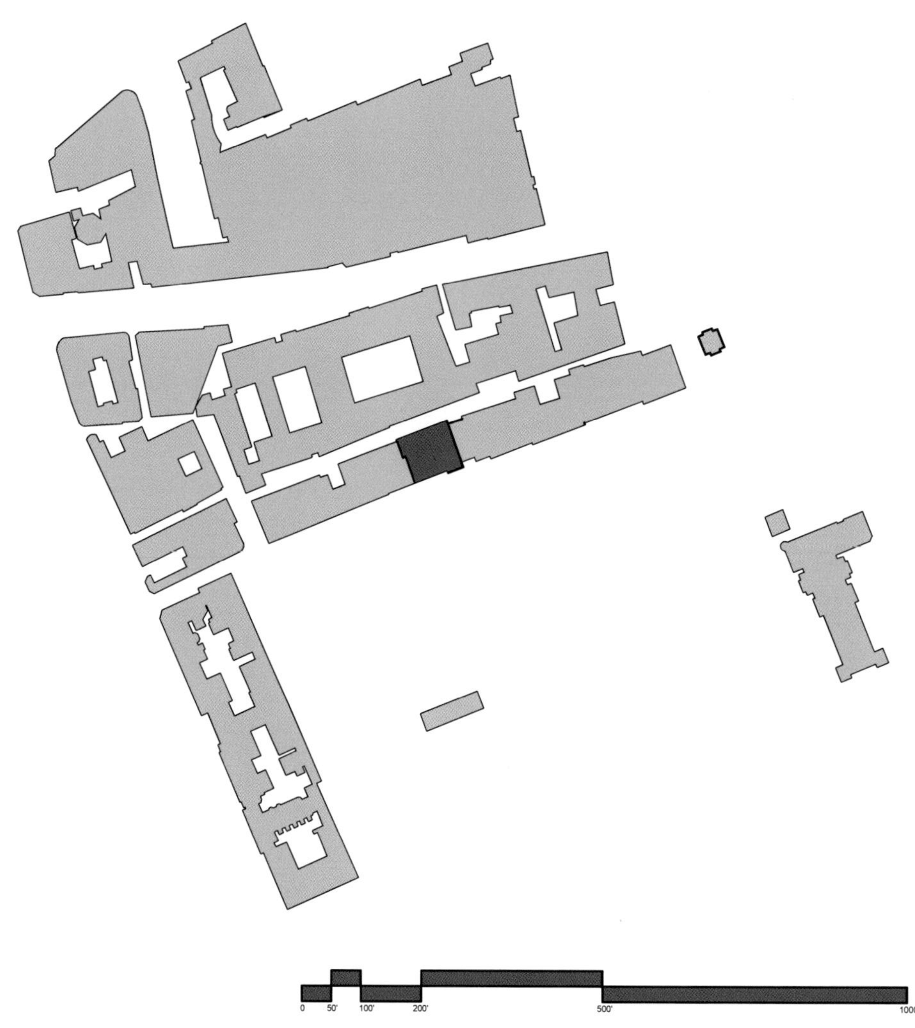

4

Sir John Soane's Museum

52°N

LOCATION: 12–14 LINCOLN'S INN FIELDS, LONDON

BUILT: 1813 (1792–1837)

ARCHITECT: SIR JOHN SOANE

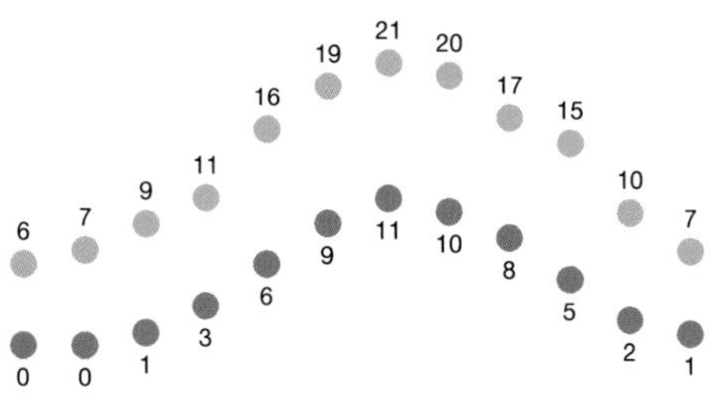

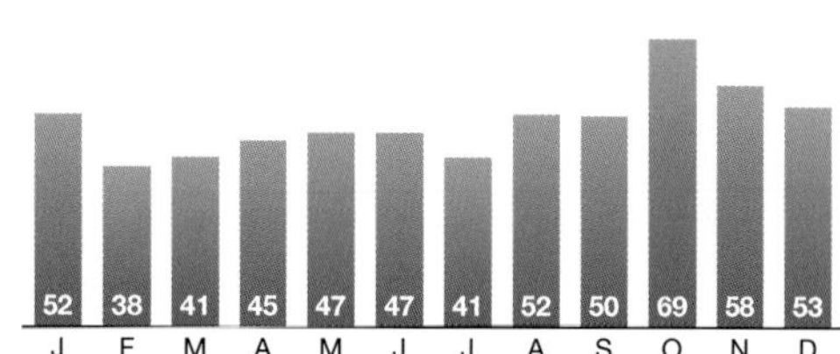

4.1 Sir John Soane's Museum, the glazed dome surrounded by linear skylights

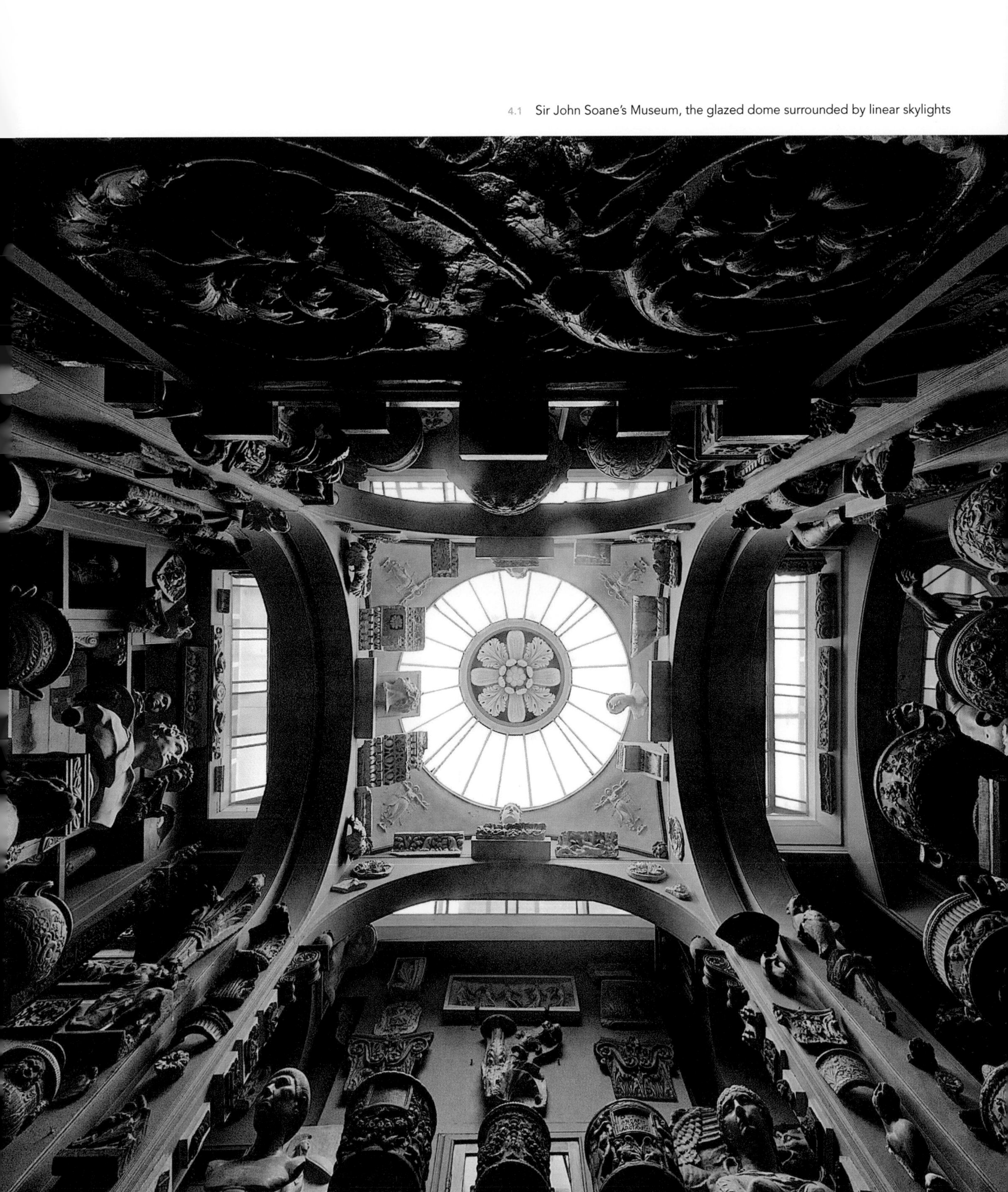

LIFE AND WORK AT LINCOLN'S INN FIELDS

From the time when he bought No. 12 in 1792 until his death 45 years later, Sir John Soane lived and worked at Lincoln's Inn Fields in London. He later purchased the house at No. 13 and joined it with No. 12. These two properties became Soane's architectural laboratory, soon housing his museum, a picture gallery, students' studio, office, library and home. Today a third building, No. 14, is added to what is known as Sir John Soane's Museum.

The son of a bricklayer, John Soan (he later added an e to his last name) had studied at the Royal Academy before setting out on the Grand Tour of France and Italy in 1778. When he returned to London, he was deeply in debt and needed to find a job. After a challenging period where income-producing work was scarce, he carefully built his career and soon became one of the most inventive and successful architects in England. He also was a respected Professor of Architecture at the Royal Academy and held a position at Public Works.

Soane's work at Lincoln's Inn Fields was truly revolutionary. Here he experimented with design strategies to bring daylight deep into internal spaces. He broke through walls and floors, creating spatial flows in ways typically associated with Modernist architecture of the twentieth century. He installed and tested warm air- and water-based heating systems. He completely rebuilt the façade of No. 13.

ADDING CHARACTER TO A MODEST STRUCTURE

For No. 13, the middle of his three buildings at Lincoln's Inn Fields, John Soane designed and built an armature that would completely change the character of his home and museum. The net distance between the south-east-facing window wall and the new façade was only 2–3 feet. The space created on the outside of the existing brick wall, therefore, could not have been used as a balcony space for outdoor living. But if the windows were of the French type, the added space could be seen as an extension of the indoor spaces of the rooms facing the street and the park.

The perspective drawing to the left in Figure 4.2 shows the new façade rendered with shadows. It illustrates how the play of light and shade generated by the new armature enhanced the façade as the sun moved across the sky on a bright summer day.

The addition is an outstanding example and a demonstration of how Soane mastered the translation of the message he delivered in his Royal Academy lectures into a three-dimensional physical construction.

In Lecture VII, he proclaims:

> [A] man of genius and superior intellect will create an interest, display as much talent, and show the powers of his art as effectually in small buildings, even in confined situations, as in works of great magnificence and expense.
>
> He points out to his students: "The British Coffee House [Figure 4.2, right] . . . shows more novelty and fancy and does as much honour to Robert Adam as the great structure he raised to contain the public records of Scotland."
>
> (Watkin, 2000, Lecture VII, p. 174)

A NEOCLASSICAL SUN BREAK?

In Lecture X, Soane again makes a reference to the British Coffee House design as he points out to his students how some "otherwise superb mansions" have façades of minimal architectural quality:

> This deficiency of invention, this want of mass, quantity, and contrast of light and shadow in the exteriors of these buildings, and the general poverty in the materials and their arrangement, may be traced in some of them to want of due consideration in making the fronts of buildings accord in their general character with the internal finishings. That variety at least can be produced in limited fronts, the exterior of the British Coffee House at Charing Cross, noticed in a former lecture, is a striking example.
>
> (Lecture X, ibid., p. 229)

4.2 Sir John Soane's Museum, façade renovation (left), compared to the British Coffee House (right) Soane made a reference to it in his Lecture VII (Plate 25)

Was the addition to the façade at No. 13 Lincoln's Inn Fields also a functional sun shading device, and, as such, a forerunner to Le Corbusier's "brise soleil"? A reconstruction of the façade by means of a simplified digital three-dimensional model proved that the shadows in the illustration are indeed generated from actual sun angles in accordance with the solar geometry at the location. The rendering represents shadows created on the façade on an early morning at or around the summer solstice.

Figure 4.3 illustrates shading patterns on the window wall behind the armature of the neo-classical façade. It is evident from this analysis that while the shading effect modestly reduces the solar gain during the heating season, it does not fully eliminate the unwanted summer heat gain. (Note that the façade is rotated 15 degrees towards the east from south.) It is therefore safe to conclude that when the windows, at a later point in time, were moved out to the new face of the building, extra space was added to the interiors without much negative effect in terms of solar control. The play of light and shade, however, was lost.

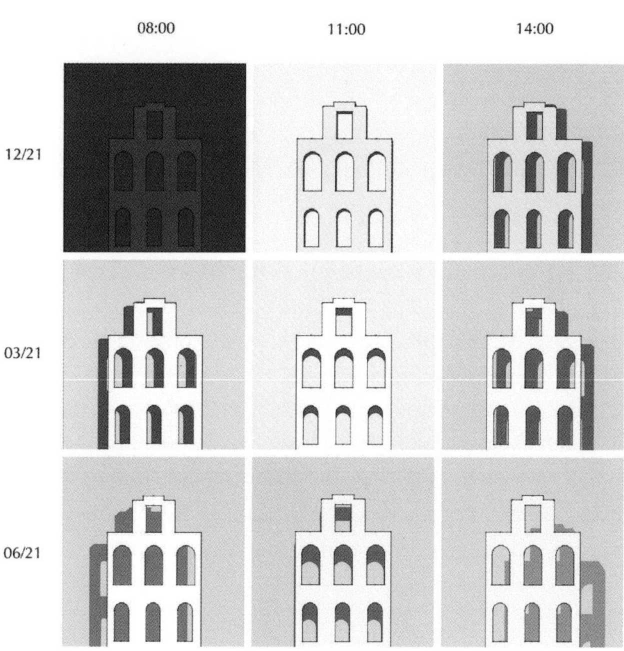

4.3 Sir John Soane's Museum, shading study

THE DYNAMIC FAÇADE

The rooms on the street façade are sufficiently lit solely by daylight coming in from the side, through traditional window arrangements. The façade is facing south, but rotated 15 degrees towards the east. The windows are tall and generous in size, reaching all the way down to the floor. In his Lecture VIII, Soane put forward his recommendations regarding the size and shape of windows for habitable spaces:

> The French mode of lighting rooms with windows down to the floor has of late been frequently adopted in this country, and certainly produces a cheerful effect. Our windows are likewise now made of larger dimensions than they were formerly and, being constructed so as to open in the middle, the general effect is much improved; more light and air are admitted thereby, and a more habitable appearance is given to the apartment.
>
> (Watkin, 2000, p. 183)

To compensate for the cold draft radiating from large single-pane windows, water-based central heating was installed with heat coming out of beautifully designed grilles set into the floor below the windows. If Soane installed windows that could be "opened in the middle," these did not survive. He did, however, install foldable wooden shutters that reside in the thickness of the wall on the sides of each window. When pulled shut and secured at night, the wooden panels created privacy, provided security and added an insulating layer to the windows.

While the exterior "sun breaker" was fixed and therefore needed no adjustment, the wooden panel system on the inside is similar to a modern dynamically changing device, with the exception that Soane's façade is operated by energy from human muscle, not by motorized systems that frequently fail.

WE MUST SEE THE FIRE

Towards the northern end of his properties, Soane started experimenting with innovative means of lighting and heating, installing skylights, clerestory windows, and hot air circulation. In the front, however, he kept the fireplaces. Soane made frequent references to the English climate, but also recognized the importance of respecting the cultural side of the equation:

> The ancient writers speak of the Heliocaminus as a favorite mode of warming their rooms and, according to Piranesi, there is an example thereof amongst the remains of Hadrian's Villa at Tivoli. This mode of warming rooms might suit hot climates and ancient customs, but in England it is not sufficient that our houses are well warmed: we must see the fire, or no degree of heat will satisfy us.
>
> (Lecture VIII, ibid., p. 180)

AN ACADEMY FOR THE STUDY OF ARCHITECTURE

In his Introduction to the reprint of the Royal Academy lectures, Watkin notes: "Contrasts of darkness and light, of expansion and constriction, constantly stimulate speculation as we follow what can seem as a path of initiation, or of an unfolding course of instruction" (ibid., p. 190).

As one enters the Museum today, one is struck by the sheer number of artifacts displayed in a rather complex spatial sequence of rooms within rooms. What makes this experience deeply joyful and educational is the organization of space and the mastery of light. Circulation is guided by light and the display of objects is carried out with such precision that one is not overwhelmed. As certain objects come into light, others fade into shadow. Even for a young person visiting the museum in the context of today's world dominated by digital imagery, the Museum truly is an academy. John Soane described his Museum as "an Academy for the study of architecture upon principles at once scientific and philosophical" (ibid., p. 48). See also *Civil Engineer and Architect's Journal*, vol. 1, 1837–1838, p. 44.

Figure 4.1 clearly illustrates one major design strategy applied by Sir John Soane at the Museum. He would open up walls between rooms and create "rooms within rooms" by supporting the floor above by columns set in from the perimeter of the room below. That allowed him to remove the connection between floor/ceiling and wall, thus opening up the flow of space, allowing the flow of light.

ADMITTING LIGHT FROM ABOVE

The museum and picture gallery (Figure 4.4) are located towards the northern end of the property. Here the building borders an alley. Soane blocked all windows in the northern wall, thus depending entirely on light being admitted from above in addition to some light coming in from the courtyards. He experimented with a variety of sizes and shapes of skylights, typically constructed with a double layer of glass.

In the picture gallery, he also installed clerestory windows on three sides. The abundant daylight flowing into the gallery is diffused to some extent by the richly decorated ceiling designed specifically for the room. It is important to note that this Gothic-inspired ceiling, like the floors in the museum, is pulled back from the walls. This design move allows the windows to extend all the way to the original ceiling. As a design strategy, this approach is quite modern. It treats the new decorative ceiling as a unique architectural element placed in the space as an object attached to but simultaneously separated from the plane of the original ceiling.

4.4 Sir John Soane's Museum, linear skylight and tall clerestory windows in the picture galley

LUMIÈRE MYSTÉRIEUSE

In the Museum, sculptures and other three-dimensional objects of art are displayed and illuminated by daylight with astonishing precision. At first sight, one could think that the foo dogs (Figure 4.5, right) must be lit by electric light. They are not. Daylight is provided from two sides: from the back through the one-sided skylight facing a courtyard and from the front by daylight seeping through a grille in the floor from a skylight at the top of the building. The Egyptian-inspired display (Figure 4.5, left) is also illuminated from light entering through a floor grille above.

In his daylight design, Soane was influenced by Le Camus de Mezieres' book, *The Genius of Architecture, or, The Analogy of That Art with Our Sensations* (1780). Lecturing to architecture students at the Royal Academy, he spoke of the mysterious light:

> The architect will do well to examine and reflect on the different modes adopted by painters of introducing light into their studios. The "lumière mystérieuse", so successfully practised by French artists, is a most powerful agent in the hands of a man of genius, and its power cannot be

4.5 Sculpture exhibits at the basement level illuminated by daylight from above

> fully understood, nor too highly appreciated. It is, however, little attended to in our architecture, and for this obvious reason, that we do not sufficiently feel the importance of character in our buildings, to which the mode of admitting light contributes in no small degree.
>
> (Lecture VIII, Watkin, 2000, p. 184)

CIRCULATION OF AIR AND WATER

Soane was familiar with the new advances in central heating and ventilation systems that were on the market in the early 1800s. These new technological inventions had existed side by side for decades and Soane tested them out at Lincoln's Inn Fields. For the first time since the Roman radiant heated wall and floor system, thermal comfort could again be provided without the use of a fire in the room.

The most common systems at the time were the warm air stove, sometimes identified as the calorifer, the low pressure warm water system, the steam heating system and finally the pressurized high temperature Perkins system. There is evidence Soane tried them all.

In his essay on heating methods and their impact on Soane's work, Todd Wilmert (1993) explored the connection and interdependence of the new heating technology and Soane's spatial flow design.

Were the advances in heating technology the inspiration leading to Soane's spatial experimentation, or were these systems introduced because they were necessitated by the opening up of walls and floors?

It is fair to say that the innovative spatial arrangements in the Museum and Picture Gallery could not have been heated and ventilated by traditional means. But even with the most advanced systems of the time, providing thermal comfort in these spaces was no small task.

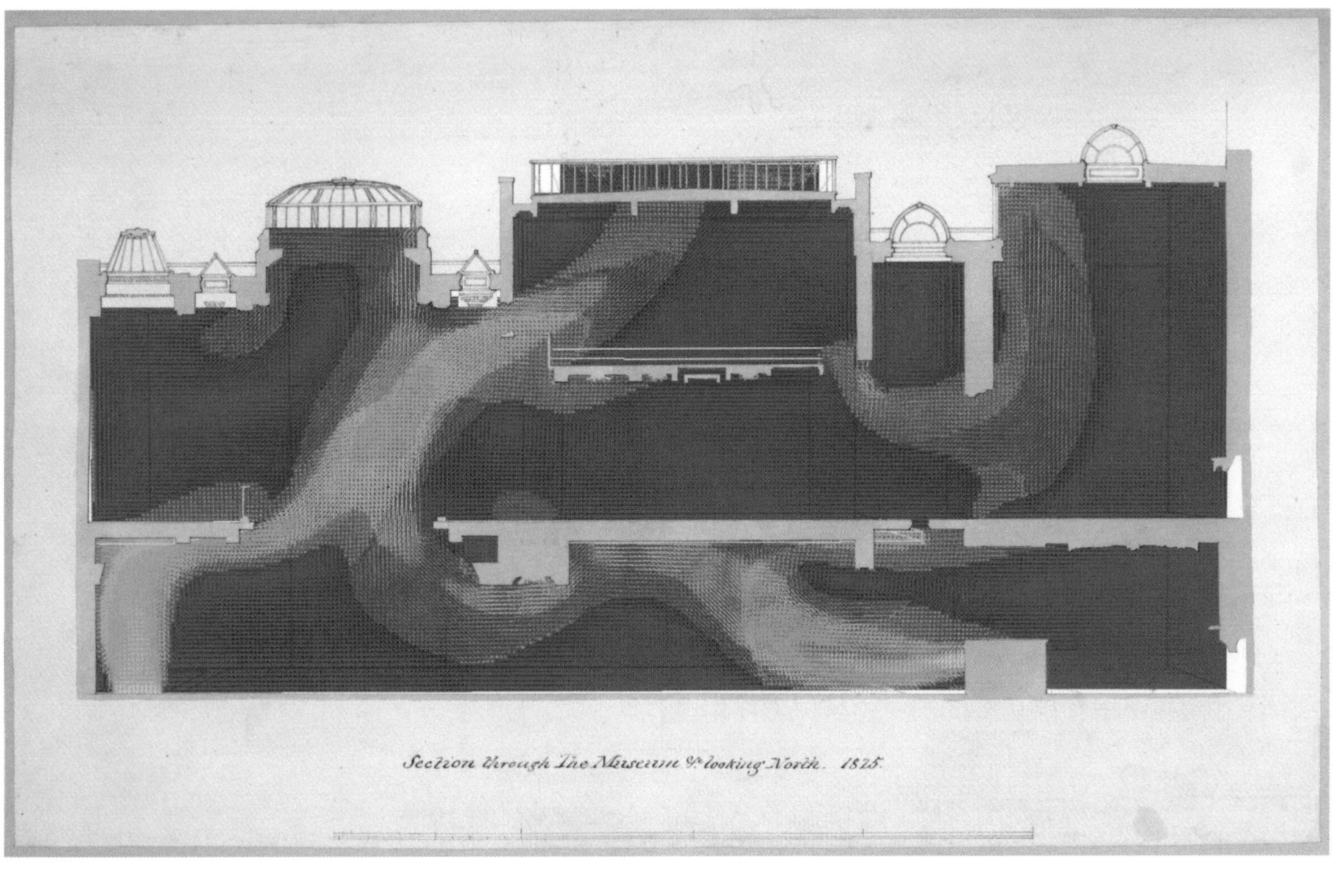

4.6 CFD simulation diagram showing air temperature and airflow distribution, superimposed on section drawing by Sir John Soane

Richardson addresses this problem in his book, *A Popular Treatise on the Warming & Ventilation of Buildings . . .*

> The Soane Museum . . . presents great difficulties to procuring a circulation of warm air within it, as has been sufficiently proved by the repeated failures of the various systems which from time to time had been introduced there for the purpose; among them was one of steam, and one by the common method of heated water.
>
> (1856, p. 54)

At this author's laboratory at the University of Illinois, computational fluid dynamic simulations were carried out on a simplified three-dimensional model of the museum and gallery spaces. The results (Figure 4.6) provide clear indications of the complex task at hand. On a winter day, there are eddies of slow-moving cold air creating discomfort, while the radiant effect of the skylights added insult to injury.

HEATING AND VENTILATION

Among the many systems that Soane tested and installed at Lincoln's Inn Fields, the most successful of them all was the Perkins system. Although these systems have been replaced, evidence of the early nineteenth-century thermal comfort technology can still be found in the Museum.

Richardson (1856) provides a detailed explanation of the most recent heating system used by Soane:

> There are 1,200 feet of pipe in the Soane Museum: it is divided into two circulations, one of which warms the picture-room and the two rooms beneath. The other, which has the largest circulation annexed to it, first warms the office in which the expansion and filling tubes are placed; the pipe then traverses the whole length of the museum, then passes through the breakfast room under the long skylight, intended to counteract the cooling effect of the

> glass; it then passes through the floor into the lower room, forms a coil of pipe of 100 feet in the staircase, and returns to the furnace, passing in its course twice round the lower part of the museum; a coil from this circulation is likewise placed in a box under the floor of the dressing room, which, by an opening in the floor and the side of the box, admits a current of warm air into the room above.
>
> (ibid., p. 55)

By using the pressurized hot water tubes in the air supply heating chamber, a hybrid system was developed where ventilation air was pre-heated without interacting with smoke from a fire, while thermal comfort was delivered more directly to the occupants by means of water tubes radiating heat.

NEWTON DEMANDS ON THE MUSE

In her book, *Newton Demands on the Muse,* Marjory Hope Nicolson (1946) discusses the influence that Isaac Newton's scientific explorations had on English eighteenth-century poets. Newton describes his experiments with prisms and the refractions of light in his book *Opticks*. Here Newton seems to develop a preference for the yellow color, towards the red end of the spectrum of visible light.

Soane was reluctant to show his museum on grey, overcast days when the light was dull. He would rather show his museum on sunny days, most likely because of his preference for yellow light, which he shared with the post-Newtonian poets. To Newton, the golden light of yellow was the most luminous and beautiful. James Thomson's poem *The Seasons* reflects the same obsession with color and light:

> Here, awful Newton! the dissolving clouds
> Form, fronting on the sun, thy showery prism
> And to the sage-instructed eye unfold
> The various twine of light, by thee disclosed
> With golden light enliven'd, wide invests
> The happy world. Attemper'd suns arise,
> Sweet-beam'd, and shedding oft thro' lucid clouds
> A pleasing calm; while broad, and brown, below
> Extensive harvests hang the heavy head.

4.7 Sir John Soane's Museum, colored light from linear skylights

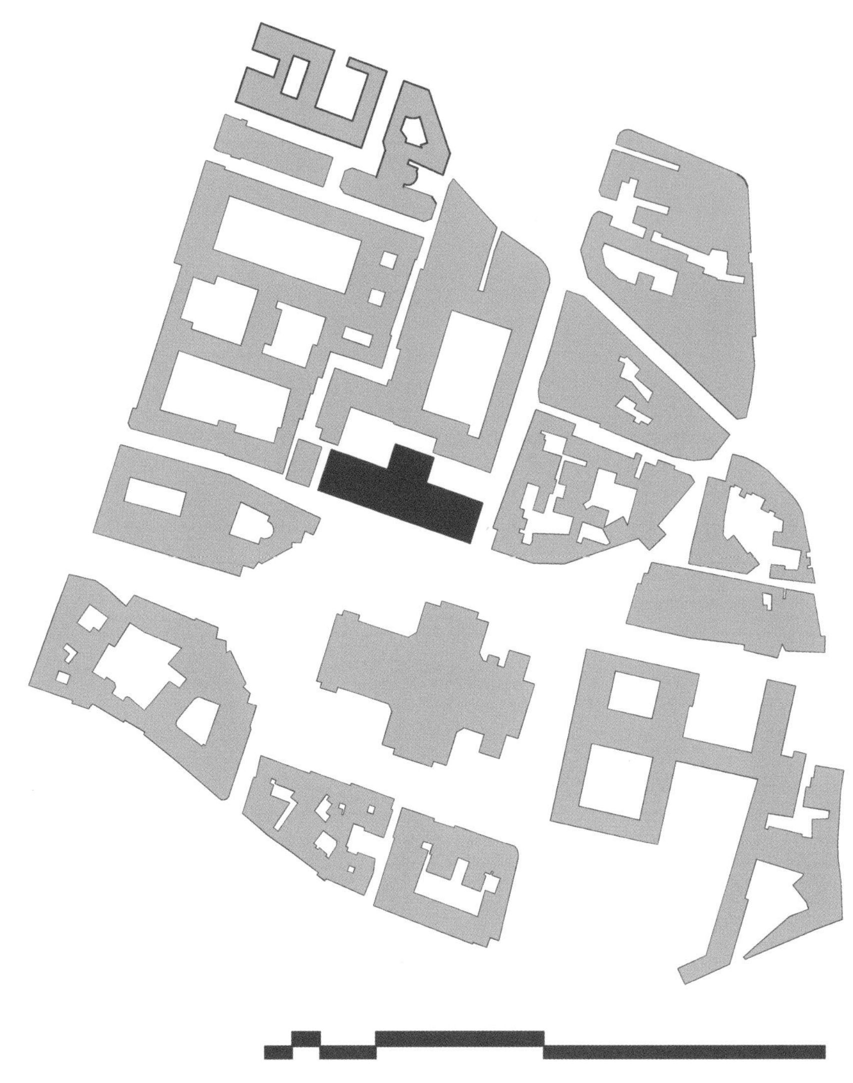

5

Bibliothèque Sainte-Geneviève

49°N

LOCATION: 10 PLACE DU PANTHÉON, PARIS, FRANCE

BUILT: 1850

ARCHITECT: HENRI LABROUSTE

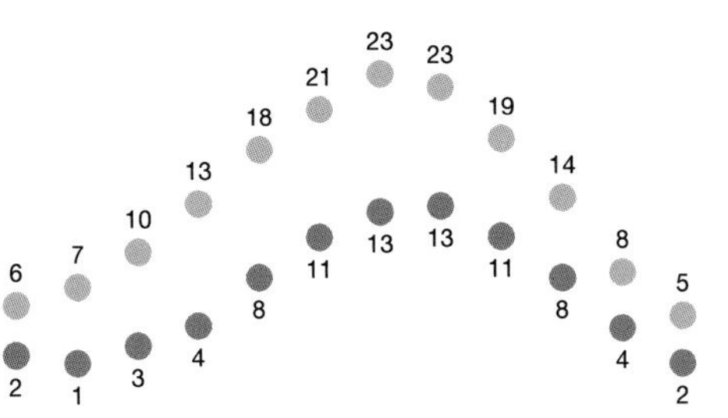

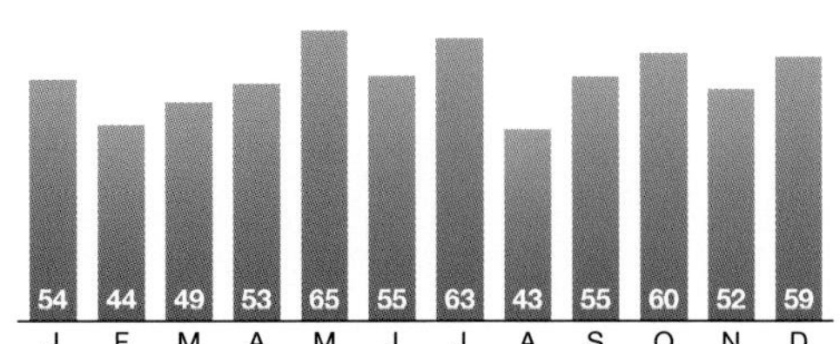

5.1 Bibliothèque Sainte Geneviève, interior view of the Great Reading Room

10 PLACE DU PANTHÉON

On an early Monday morning students line up on the sidewalk outside the Sainte-Geneviève library to get a seat at a desk in the grand reading room. One of the finest public buildings of the nineteenth century, Sainte-Geneviève has served the university and the public for 160 years. Writings and books from the Abbey of St Geneviève formed the initial foundation of its collections.

All the major functions of the library, entrance lobby, offices, archives and reading room, are contained within an elongated massive volume measuring roughly 85 meters in length, with a transverse section 20 meters wide and 20 meters high. Only the central staircase, including mechanical and other servant spaces, is positioned outside the main building form, to the north-east.

The library sits on the edge of Place du Panthéon with the main façade rotated 18 degrees west of due south. While daylight fills the reading room from clerestory windows on all four sides, it is the south-west facing façade that sees the sun. The library is shouldered by other buildings to the east and west and faces a narrow courtyard to the north.

Although it has been widely written about, the Bibliothèque Sainte-Geneviève still holds unanswered questions about its inner workings. Its calm and collected appearance towards the city does not reveal much, but there are some clues: a chimney is positioned at the north-western corner. Hidden from public view is a row of ventilation stacks on the northern half of the roof.

ENTERING THROUGH THE GARDEN

When Henri Labrouste was appointed architect of the Sainte-Geneviève library in 1838, it had been almost ten years since he returned to Paris from his Grand Tour of Italy. He may have envisioned the entry to his great library through a garden, but realized that the entrance would have to sit directly on the edge of a hard landscaped urban plaza. So he designed the entrance lobby in a manner that has been interpreted as a metaphor of a garden with tree tops rising above sculpture-lined side walls and a blue sky above.

5.2 Bibliothèque Sainte-Geneviève, entry sequence through the lobby

The laced iron girders resting on masonry pillars hint at what will be revealed later in the entry sequence. As one proceeds through the lobby, focus is on the top-lit grand staircase at the back.

5.3 Bibliothèque Sainte-Geneviève, "the Bridge"

THE BRIDGE

Visitors arriving at the second landing find a tall and wide space generously illuminated by daylight borrowed from the grand reading room as well as from clerestory windows facing east and west. As one looks back from the third landing, it appears that we have come up from under a bridge.

The vertical movement up into the reading room, therefore, can be seen as a procession from under and alongside a work of civic pride. The beautiful bridge with its pillars, arches, rich decoration and urban lamp posts is a reminder that after entering through a garden, one is still on the outside of the library's most important space: the grand reading room.

We are transitioning into a container of universal knowledge.

THE READING ROOM

The reading room, lit by large arched clerestory windows, exhibits its main compositional elements with great clarity. The 1.65-meter-deep perimeter zone with its masonry walls, pillars and roman arches is contrasted with a central line of iron columns and laced iron girders forming the paper-thin double-barreled vaulted ceiling. Bookshelves lining the perimeter walls below the windows, tiered by a gallery, stand 5.5 meters high.

The arrangement of windows, 19 bays on the long sides and 4 bays at the ends of the room, provides abundant diffuse light from the sky dome on a cloudy day. But on days with a clear sky, the sun could potentially create a discomforting asymmetry of direct beam light. How did the architect solve this problem?

The clue lies not only in the thickness of the perimeter masonry structure, but also in its proportions and the careful positioning of the windows.

PLAY OF LIGHT

Contrary to widely published claims (Middleton, 1982; Van Zanten, 1987; Hawkes, 2008), the armature of the masonry structure does

5.4 Bibliothèque Sainte-Geneviève, interior view of the grand reading room

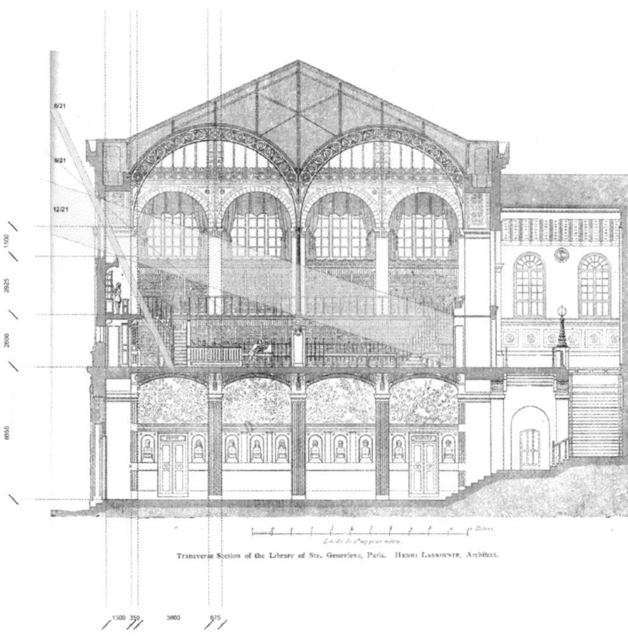

5.5 Bibliothèque Sainte-Geneviève, sun angle diagram

not fully prevent the sun's rays from entering the reading room. When designing for sun control, the architect had to take into account not only the geo-positioning of the building at almost 49 degrees northern latitude, but also the fact that the building is rotated 18 degrees west of due south. A cross-section analysis of sun angles at or around solar noon (Figure 5.5) shows how the sun would enter the interior at midday.

On the longest day of the year, only a faint narrow beam of light hits the floor near the southern wall. On the shortest day of the year, the sun reaches across the reading room and lights up the lower tier of the book-lined wall on the north side.

Images generated by a simplified digital model of the interior show that while the sun is constrained and controlled, it is not entirely blocked out. On sunny days the warm direct beam sunlight is allowed to create celebrated moments of light and shade.

SERVED FROM BELOW

The mechanical systems and installations are among the best-kept secrets of the Bibliothèque Sainte-Geneviève. A signature drawing of the building, the transverse section (Figure 5.5) shows the ground floor at street level and the reading room above, but provides not even a hint of the basement below.

Nearly a century after Labrouste made his first sketches for the design of his new library, Le Corbusier published his "Five Points of Architecture" in *Towards a New Architecture* (1923), a set of architectural principles which revolutionized the concept of a modern building. With the introduction of flat plate reinforced concrete slabs supported by "pilotis" (reinforced concrete columns), modern buildings could be laid out with free-flowing floor plans. The absence of load-bearing walls made it possible to develop the horizontal window and the curtain wall, which in turn eliminated the need for basement walls as foundations. In the Villa Savoye, the roof garden replaced the attic. Historically significant features of buildings: the thick exterior wall, the attic and the basement were removed. These features had traditionally played important roles in the approach to provide comfort in buildings through the use of shading, thermal mass, warming and ventilation.

At the Sainte-Geneviève, book storage was placed below the grand reading room and books were mechanically hoisted up from the archives. Fresh air was taken in from areas along the basement walls, heated in warming chambers by calorifers, supplied through vertical channels and delivered through grilles built into bookshelves placed between the central row of columns. I am using the term "calorifer" or "calorifere" as a device capable of warming air by means of water circulating in tubes or smoke circulating in air channels. See Figure 1.3 on p. 8.

Run-off from the roof was led through gutters to downspouts inside the hollow corner pillars. It was then led through channels cut into the basement floor and into an underground storm water drainage system below street level.

WATER AND AIR

Comparing early illustrations of the interior with the reading room as it stands today, we discover two later alterations that significantly changed the look and feel of the space. Radiators are now placed between the pillars in the central line of steel columns. The long wooden tables are placed perpendicular to the central axis. This was not always so.

We can see marks in the floor and on the pillars indicating that shelving for reference books was originally placed here. Located right above the built-in warm air channels were supply air grilles providing heating and ventilation for the comfort of the library patrons. We can only speculate on the reason for this major change. Water is a better medium for delivering heat than air. Despite its elegant application of modern technology, the central warm air system may have proved inadequate for maintaining thermal comfort in the reading room on a cold winter day.

SECRETS OF THE ATTIC

After conditioned fresh air is supplied to the interior, where does it go and how is it moved through the building?

The centrifugal fan, or fan blower, is known to have been used for ventilation as early as the sixteenth century. Dr. Reid installed four large blowers in the basement of St George's Hall in the 1850s and Phipson installed a large engine driven fan at Glasgow University 20 years later. But with low engine speeds and inefficient fan designs, architects and engineers still relied on natural forces in moving air through buildings.

Before the development of more powerful and efficient centrifugal fans towards the end of the nineteenth century, air movement through buildings depended largely on exploiting the buoyancy of warmer air. The systems, therefore, were arranged vertically with inlets at the bottom and exhaust at the top. At Sainte-Geneviève, the air was conditioned by passing through the "caloriferes" in the basement before it was sent upwards through channels or shafts in the central masonry spine. Since the air could

5.6 Bibliothèque Sainte-Geneviève, decorations and perforations in the ceiling of the grand reading room

5.7 Bibliothèque Sainte-Geneviève, interior view of the grand reading room

not be pushed by fan power, it had to be pulled from the top. This is where the importance of the attic becomes evident.

Since the power of a stack ventilation system depends not only on height difference from inlet to outlet, but also on temperature differential between the inside and outside air, the pulling force would be less efficient on hot days. This lack of power was compensated by the attic space being heated by the sun through a thin metal roof. Ten ventilation stacks above the roof pull the air out of the attic. So how did the air enter the attic from the reading room below?

The answer to this question cannot be found without a determined search. After careful inspection of the ceiling, several black painted grilles appear directly above the intersections of the laced iron girders (Figure 5.6). These grilles are found only on the northern half of the double vault. They are so well integrated into the overall design that they are almost invisible. Again we see the mastery of an architect who did not leave details of mechanics and technology unattended.

TRUTH IS FOUND IN SIMPLICITY

Henri Labrouste was most certainly aware of the works of Isaac Newton, who wrote: "Truth is to be found in simplicity and not in the multiplicity and confusion of things." With his design for the Bibliothèque Sainte-Geneviève, Labrouste arrived at a level of simplicity that is powerful, not because he avoided complexity, but because he had the ability to process tight urban site conditions, complex programmatic needs, high demand for thermal and visual comfort, and the opportunities of a new prefabricated fireproof structural system, into one integral comprehensive beautiful piece: the public library.

The fact that this artifact of civic pride serves its main purpose after 160 years of intensive use speaks to the accomplishments of its architect and the environment in which he created his masterpiece.

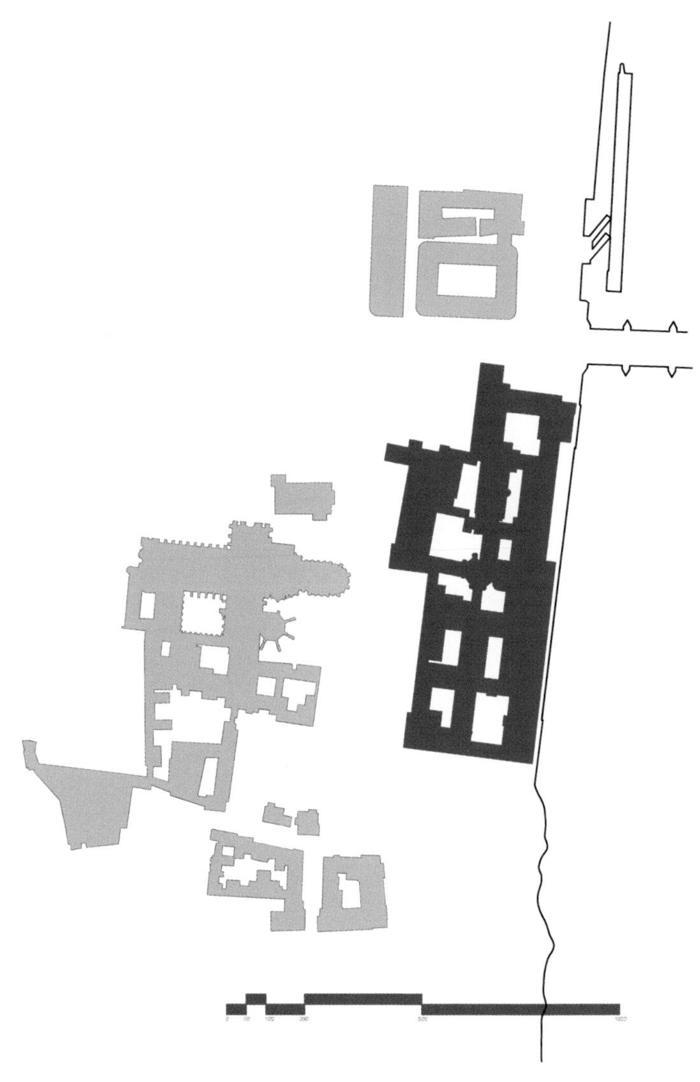

52°N

6

The Palace of Westminster

LOCATION: CITY OF WESTMINSTER, LONDON, UK

BUILT: 1852 (1840–1870)

ARCHITECT: CHARLES BARRY (1795–1860)

VENTILATOR: DAVID BOSWELL REID (1805–1863)

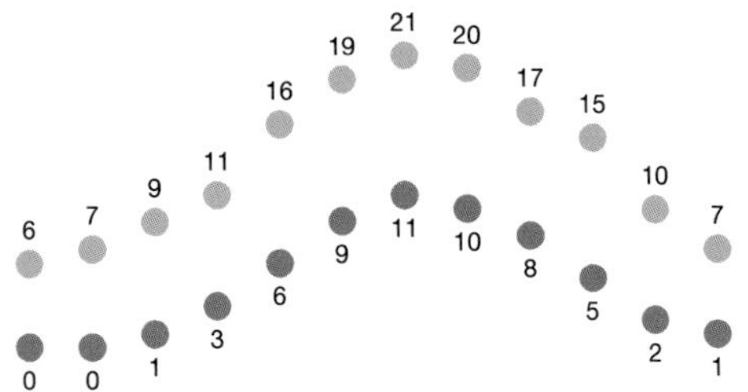

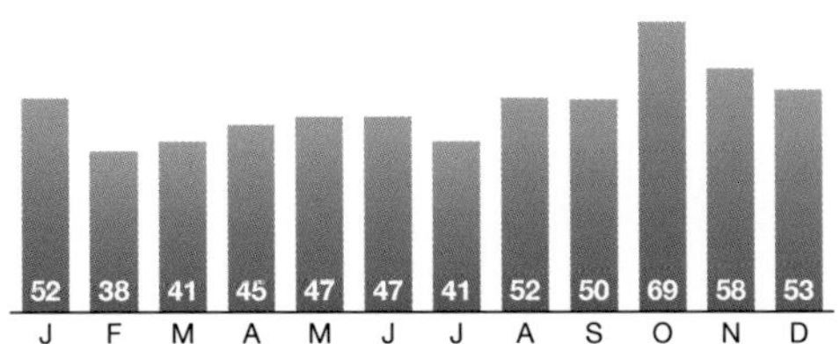

6.1 The Palace of Westminster, with Victoria Tower (left) and the Central Ventilation Tower

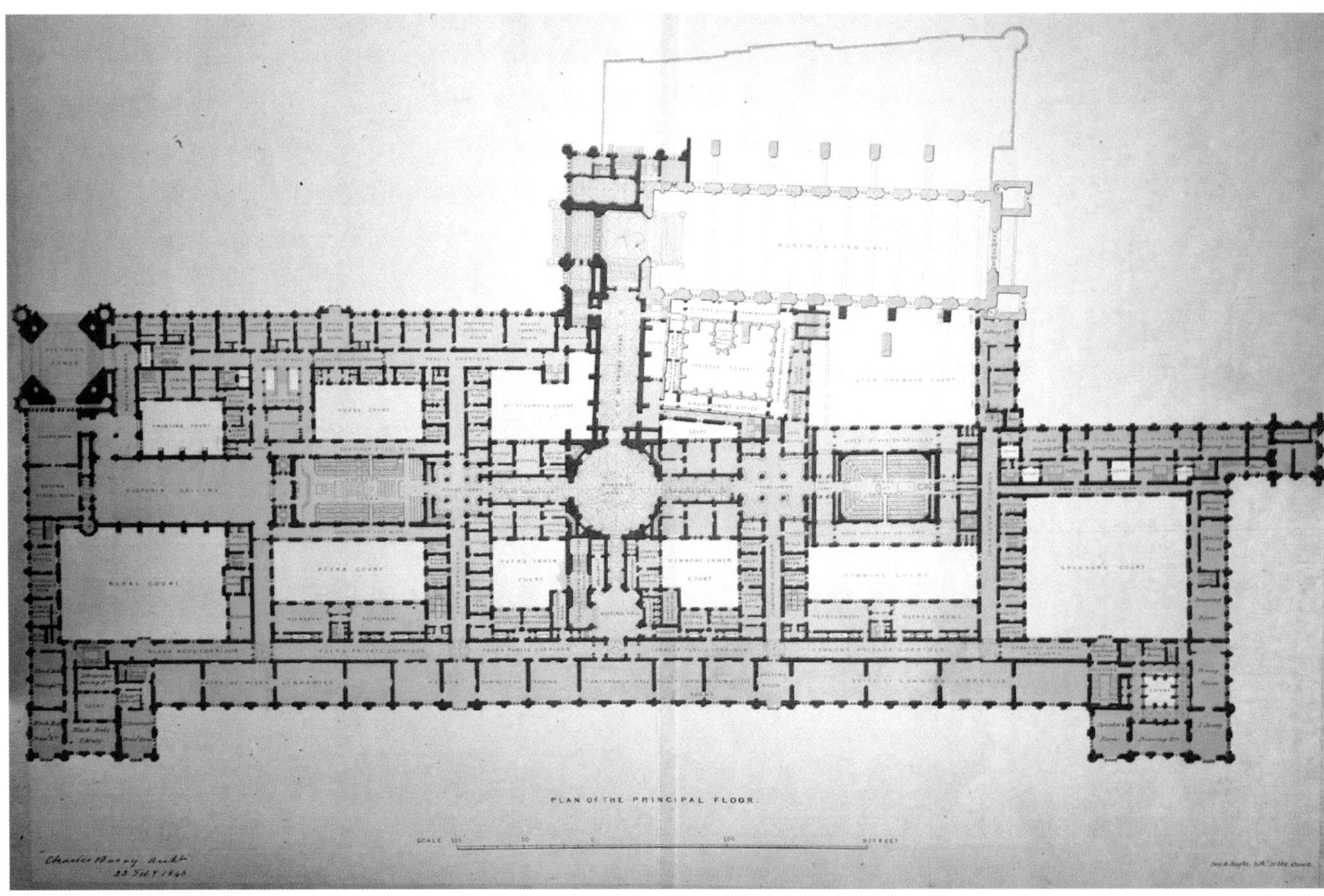

6.2 Palace of Westminster. Plan drawing by Charles Barry Archt, 23, Feb. 4 1843, Parliamentary Archives, HC/LB/1/114/28.

BARRY WINS THE COMPETITION

After the devastating fire at the old Westminster Palace in 1834, temporary provisions were hastily constructed for the Members of Parliament to continue their legislative work while preparations were made for new buildings at the site. Under the direction of Sir Robert Smirke, architect at the Office of Works, the Painted Hall and the White Hall were repaired for the Houses of Parliament to reconvene in February 1835.

The only structures to survive the fire were Westminster Hall, the Cloisters of St Stephen's, the undercroft of the Chapel of St Mary and the Jewel Tower. The task at hand, therefore, was to construct new buildings for the Houses of Parliament entirely from the ground up. The building program soon amounted to more than 1100 rooms.

Among the first tasks for the Members of Parliament to consider after the fire of 1834 was the forming of a commission charged with organizing an architectural competition. After reviewing 97 entries, the commission announced that the competition had been won by Charles Barry.

The 41-year-old architect was at the time finishing up work on the major reconstruction of Highclere Castle (see Figure 2.7). His proposal for the new parliament buildings was a quadrangle with three bars parallel to the River Thames and rooms organized around two series of courtyards (Figure 6.2). In accordance with guidelines developed by the House of Lords, his design was in a Perpendicular Gothic style, a style that at the time was seen as embodying conservative values, in opposition to the neo-classical style which carried associations with revolution and republicanism in the United States.

In developing the competition design, Barry was aided by Augustus Pugin, who continued to work with him on the project. Pugin's contribution is seen mainly in the Gothic detail of the interiors, but he also had a hand in the design of towers, vanes and spires.

WHAT THE DOCTOR ORDERED

Three weeks before Charles Barry's wife Sarah laid the foundation stone near the north-east corner of the site, Dr. David Boswell

Reid had been appointed as the "ventilation engineer" for the New Houses of Parliament project. Who was he, and how did it happen that he was selected as an important member of the design team?

An assistant to the Professor of Chemistry at the University of Edinburgh, later to became a medical doctor, Reid had established himself as one of the leading experts on thermal comfort and indoor air quality, including new methods of heating and ventilating large buildings. He had been in charge of the design for heating and ventilating the temporary House of Commons and he was to become a leading member of the Health of Towns Commission.

But the now famous architect Charles Barry, who was ten years older than Reid, did not welcome him as a member of his team. He thought Reid did "not profess to be thoroughly acquainted with the practical details of building and machinery" (Port and the Paul Mellon Centre for Studies in British Art, 1976). What could have developed as a productive collaboration started out on the wrong foot and soon became a major headache.

Dr. Reid would soon be presenting his requirements for air tunnels, ventilation shafts, for vacuum chambers in the attic and plenums in the basement, none of which generated much enthusiasm on the part of the architect. When Reid proposed large towers to be included in the design, however, Barry became more responsive. The need for two tall towers for a fresh air supply, positioned at the north and south ends of the project, and a tower for smoke and vitiated air exhaust in the middle, was in agreement with Barry's composition which would include the Victoria Tower, the Central Tower and the Elizabeth Tower. As much as Barry welcomed the opportunity to justify his tall towers by assigning utility to their purpose, he was reluctant to accept the other remedies recommended by Doctor Reid.

DR. REID'S LABORATORY

Considering the immense power of the London elite and the political climate of the time, it was not without difficulty that a young Scottish academician with no formal training in the construction industry attempted to find a place at Charles Barry's table. But was he unfit for the task as Barry had suggested, and was he a charlatan as Lord Derby declared (Disraeli *et al.*, 1982, p. 109. n.2)?

David Boswell Reid had established himself as a successful teacher of practical chemistry in Edinburgh. When the university was unable to meet his needs for a well-equipped chemistry lab, he built his own in 1833. The next year, during a meeting of the British Association in Edinburgh, he invited the participants to visit his laboratory. Among the visitors were several Members of Parliament. Their field trip to Reid's classroom was instrumental in establishing his reputation in London.

The ground plan of Dr. D. B. Reid's premises shows the sheer size of his well-equipped laboratory. As a chemist, he understood the need to remove smoke, gases and odor from his working environment. Naturally, he employed the motive power of fire to pull bad air out of the building, thus allowing fresh air to be drawn in by the slightly lower pressure created by the pulling force of the chimney.

After he was hired to consult on the heating and ventilation of the temporary House of Commons, he built several smaller chambers and a larger assembly room at his laboratory where he used smoke experiments to learn about the behavior of air under changing temperature fluctuations and humidity levels. The scientific approach he took to understanding the principles of air movement and his enthusiasm is exemplified by a story told by his son, published in an article in *The Lancet* (April 1903).

Reid's son, who for 30 years was the chief surgeon of the Geelong Hospital in Australia, had built a 5-ft-long glass model of a hospital ward "employing the motive power of a spirit lamp placed rather higher than the ceiling and at the foot of a glass chimney." Smoke was used to illustrate air movements. Dr. Reid, the son, then refers to his father:

> I had seen Her late Majesty Queen Victoria with Prince Albert and accompanied by King Louis Philippe, Queen Marie Amélie, and Princess Clementine looking at the working of a similar model in my father's experimental room while listening to his explanations.

THE HOUSE OF COMMONS

In his book, *Illustrations of the Theory and Practice of Ventilation* (1844), David Boswell Reid explains in great detail his design for the temporary House of Commons and the theory behind his design. Figure 6.3 shows a principal transverse section of the installations for heating, cooling and ventilation.

There were many old sewer lines on the premises, one of which, the drain from the Old Palace Yard, represented a major source of foul air. Dr. Reid installed a network of underground ventilation pipes to remove the odors from the sewers ((a) in Figure 6.3). This system was not an essential part of the ventilation system for the building, but used the motive power of the large chimney to remove foul air and burn ill-smelling gases. The main purpose of the chimney was to pull air from the ventilation chamber in the attic ((B) in Figure 6.3) above the new ceiling that Reid had designed.

The suspended ceiling, which had sloping glass panels along the sides, not only created a "vacuum chamber" to pull air out of the building, but also improved comfort by preventing cold air from descending on the Members of Parliament from the single pane clerestory windows. Here, Dr. Reid benefited from what he had learned about convective air loops in tall spaces during his lab experiments.

It is worth noting that Reid saw the construction of a large chimney separated from the building as a necessity rather than an ideal solution. He knew that pulling air back down, against its "final cause" as Aristotle had explained in his general account of the four causes (Wicksteed and Cornford, 1929), demanded extra power. In the new construction he would prefer building air exhaust towers or chimneys on top of the building and to integrate them into the architectural design.

Air entering the heating chamber in the basement was filtered, humidified as needed, cooled by blocks of ice, or heated by hot

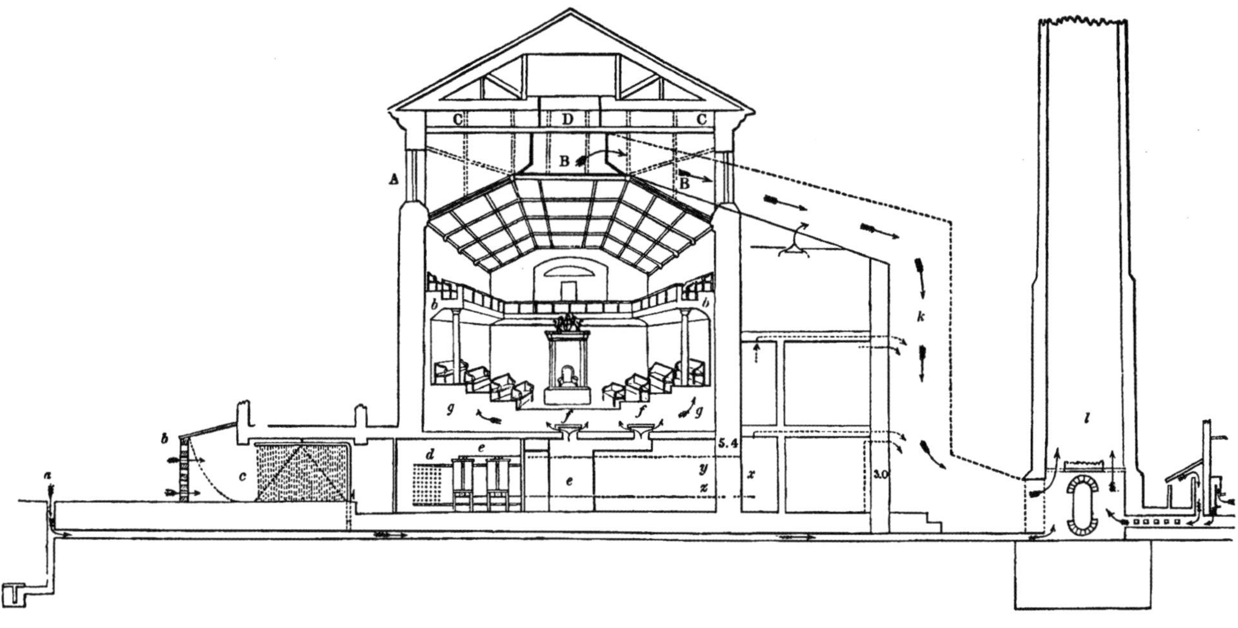

6.3 David Boswell Reid, House of Commons, section diagram

water coils before entering an equalizing chamber below the floor in the assembly hall. Deflectors were designed to distribute the supply air evenly. Separate air channels served the galleries above.

Experimenting with diffuse air supply systems, Reid had the floor perforated with thousands of holes covered with a horse-hair cloth. He understood the advantages of diffuse air supply to improve comfort by avoiding drafts, but later found that air should be supplied through holes in stair risers and perforated "skirting board" wall panels rather than perforated floors where dirt from shoes could be mixed with the incoming air from the equalizing chamber below.

AIR CONDITIONING

For the temporary House of Commons, Dr. Reid devised what we today would call a variable air volume (VAV) system. Dampers in the air extract duct leading from the ventilation chamber in the attic to the ventilation chimney could be operated to vary the air flow rate. Additionally, there were control mechanisms to vary the air temperature and the relative humidity of the conditioned air supply.

Dr. Reid explains how he designed three modes of operation of the air supply channels and warming chamber. (1) Fresh air could be supplied through filters directly to the vertical channels leading to the equalizing chamber above. This mode was used as a night ventilation cooling strategy, but could also be used to cool the space when the parliament was in session on a warm day. (2) By opening and closing doors, the entire volume of air could now be heated before entering the space above. (3) As needed, warm and cold air could be mixed to generate the desired air temperature as conditions changed in the debating chamber below:

> The House is heated to 62° before it is opened, and maintained in general at a temperature between 63° and 70°, according to the velocity with which the air is permitted to pass through the House. This velocity is necessarily regulated by the numbers present on a given space, the temperature to which the air can be reduced in warm weather, and the amount of moisture which it may contain, when the quantity may be excessive. Some members are much more affected by an excess or deficiency of moisture, than by alterations in temperature.
>
> After dinner, other circumstances being the same, the temperature should be diminished, the velocity increased, and the amount of moisture in the air reduced, when practicable. During late debates, as they advance to two, three, four and five in the morning, the temperature should be gradually increased as the constitution becomes more exhausted, except in cases where the excitement is extreme.
>
> (Reid, 1844, pp. 294–7)

THE ASPIRATED CHIMNEY

Technology for movement of air by fanners (humans operating primitive forms of fans) had been known for centuries. In the 1840s, mechanical fans were being developed, but their practical implementation was still in its infancy. Motive power generated by heat was, therefore, the primary means of moving air through buildings.

In a traditional open fireplace, smoke moving up the chimney draws with it air from the room, thus providing heating and ventilation simultaneously. This device is so familiar that its dual function is often not considered and simply taken for granted. Vertical shafts and channels built next to chimney flues in masonry construction could be heated by the smoke and therefore could function as separate ventilation tubes. It was this same principle that was developed into the "aspirated chimney."

Figure 6.4 shows plans, section, elevation and details of a spire constructed to pull smoke and vitiated air out of the building. Smoke was collected from a multitude of fires and led through large channels horizontally and vertically until it was channeled up through the center of the spire. Ventilation shafts thermally coupled to but physically separate from the smoke channels would benefit from the motive power of the heat.

In the end, the Central Tower could not serve its purpose as the only means to extract foul air from the Houses of Parliament.

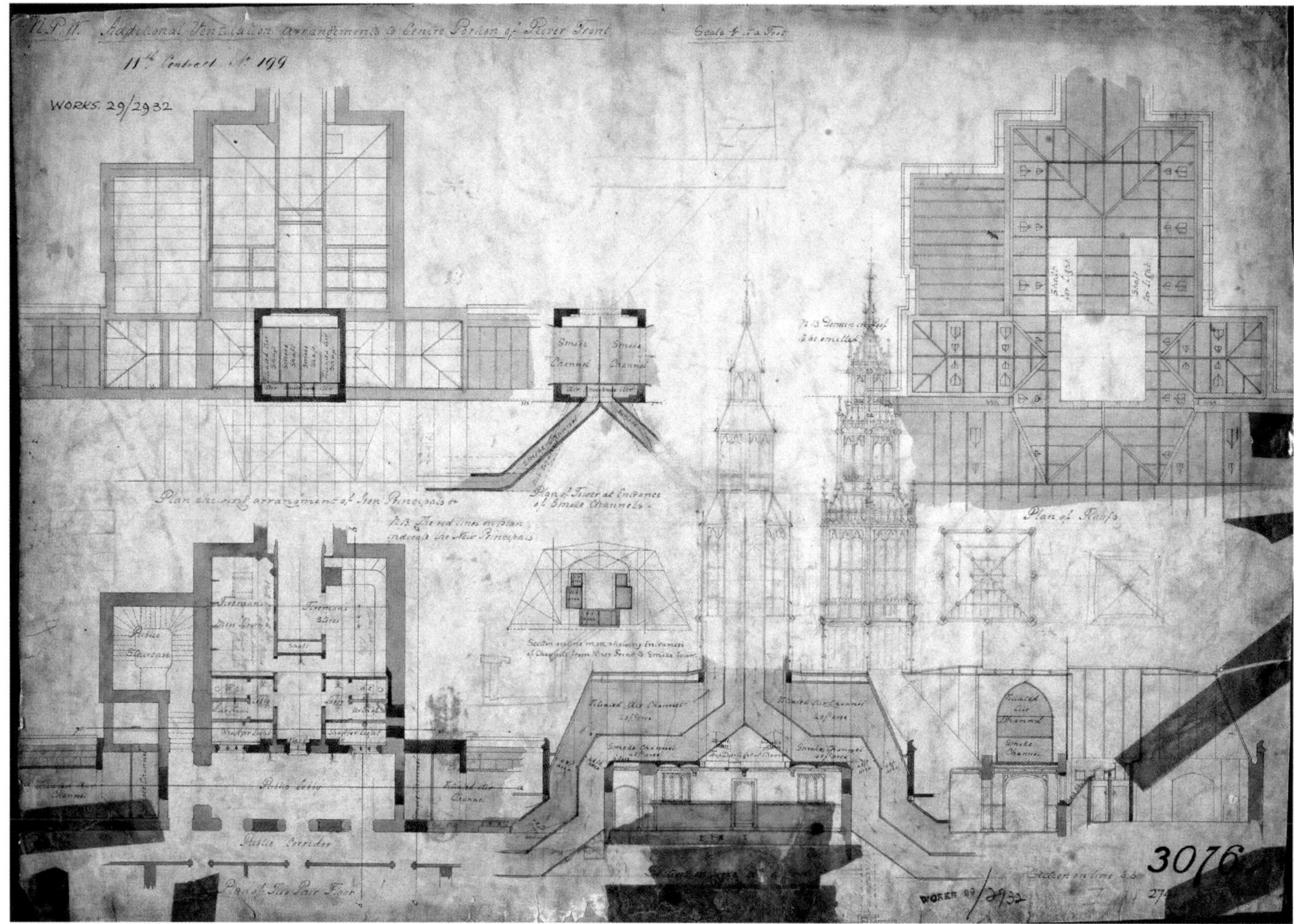

6.4 Plan and section diagrams with designs for a ventilation tower: "Additional Ventilation arrangements to Central Portion of River Front." Parliamentary Archives, ARC/PRO/WORK29/2932.

Several spires, most likely of Pugin's design and engineered by Barry's assistant, Alfred Meeson, can be seen to this day standing alongside the masonry towers so characteristic of the Westminster Palace profile. Appropriate to their purpose, they are made from iron and painted black.

BIG BEN

The Elizabeth Tower, also known as the Clock Tower, was Pugin's masterpiece. It served as a clock tower, but was also functionally justified as a fresh air intake tower. The outside air at street level was at times of very poor quality and it was commonly thought that the air at a higher elevation would be cleaner and better suited for human health:

> When a great fall takes place in the barometer, the drains, the river, and the surface of the ground exhale bad air to such an extent, that the entire atmosphere, on every side of the houses, is loaded with impurities. Gas-liquor on the surface of the river is an occasional source of offense . . . Emanations from the grave-yard at St Margaret's Church are occasionally very offensive . . . The smell of gas-works on both sides of the river occasionally affects the atmosphere on every side of the House . . . The entire surface of the streets has occasionally been found to present a surface of decomposing impurities not capable of being easily controlled by the action of lime-water . . . In some cases, where the most extreme complaints have been made, as to the state of the atmosphere, they have been connected to barges laden with manure, and to drains exposed during the progress of the works of the New Houses.
>
> (Reid, 1844, pp. 297–299)

The drawing (Figure 6.5 right) shows a fresh air shaft descending the whole length of the Elizabeth Tower to supply heating

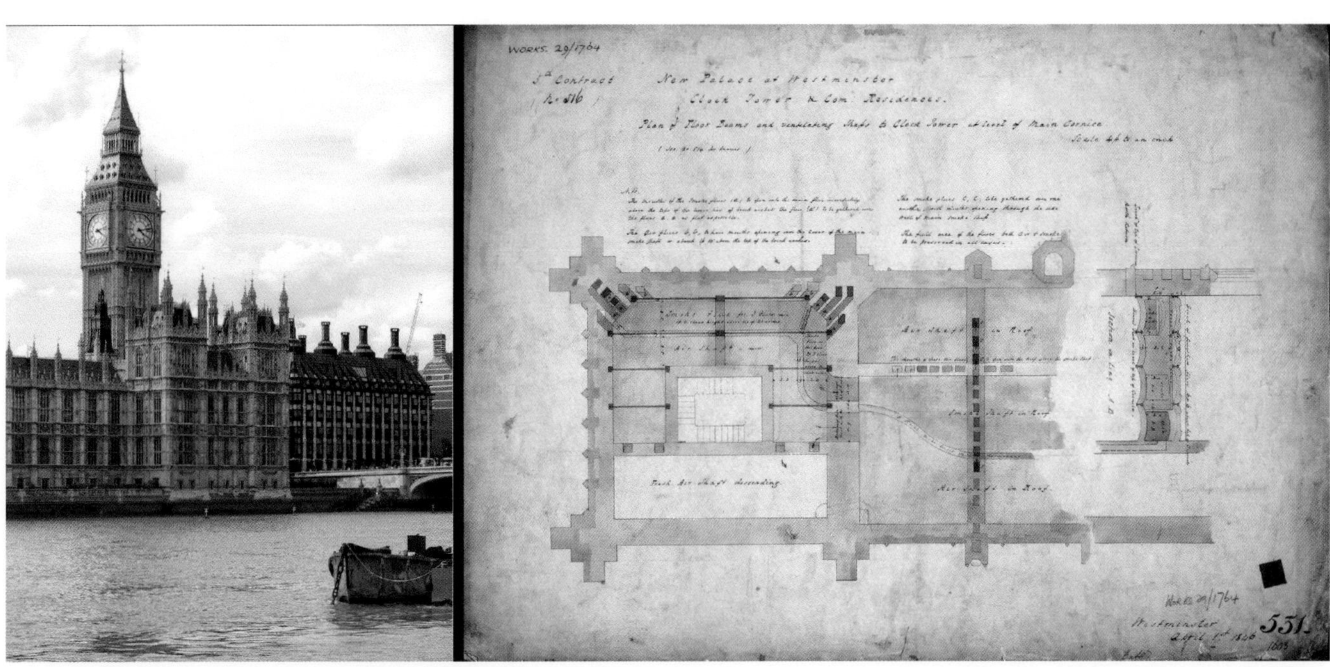

6.5 The Elizabeth Tower as seen from the River Thames, with "Plan of Floor Beams and Ventilating Shafts to Clock Tower at level of Main Cornice." Parliamentary Archives, ARC/PRO/WORK29/2999.

chambers in the basement. Additionally, the lower part of the tower was used for the vertical movement of vitiated air and smoke by an air shaft and a smoke flue connected to horizontal channels in the attic leading to an aspirated chimney disguised as a spire. Big Ben, therefore, served as an object of utility, as well as standing tall as a beautiful clock tower.

NO FURTHER BUILDING SHOULD BE PERMITTED

The stressful relations between Barry and Reid reached a climax in connection with the design of the Central Tower, originally proposed by Reid as the most important means of evacuating vitiated air from the building. Attached to a statement presented to the Rt Hon. The Viscount Canning on April 30, 1846, was a sheet of drawings explaining the difficulties of providing sufficient quantities of ventilation channels. Reid discusses ways to improve on the situation, even suggesting that several spires could be designed to alleviate the lack of capacity in the central tower. Anticipating a negative response from Charles Barry, or no response at all, Reid found it necessary to emphasize the graveness of the situation by issuing an ultimatum. The introductory text to the drawing (Figure 6.6) reads:

> Fig. 6 embraces the example referred to; the others are explanatory of Fig. 6, and illustrate some of the difficulties which have occurred in connection with the ventilating channels around the Central Tower, in consequence of which Dr. Reid is desirous of any discharge that can be obtained there such as is suggested below. Other examples might be mentioned, that equally demand attention, and in respect to which Dr. Reid considers that no further building should be permitted till the circumstances detailed in the statement referred to are taken into consideration.

With this submission, Dr. Reid's tenure as ventilation engineer at the New Houses of Parliament came to an end. He was formally

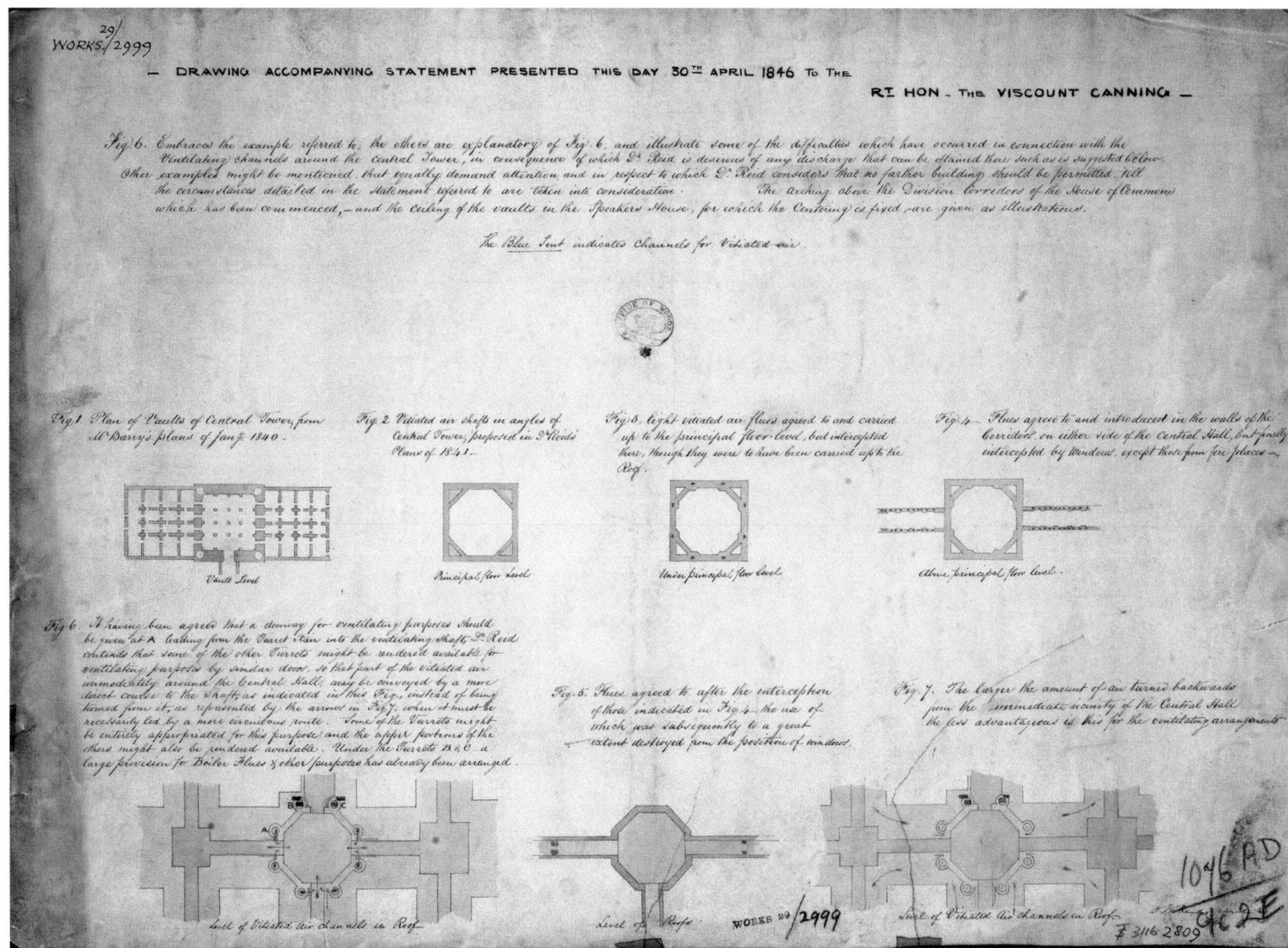

6.6 David Boswell Reid: "Drawing accompanying Statement Presented This Day 30th April 1846 to the Viscount Canning." Parliamentary Archives, ARC/PRO/WORK29/1764.

dismissed in 1852 after an extended process leading to a settlement where Reid received a substantial monetary compensation, acknowledging his invaluable contribution.

THE LEGACY

Charles Barry will be remembered as the architect who designed the buildings for the Houses of Parliament at the new Palace of Westminster, buildings that for years to come will be seen as the essential symbol of democracy and parliamentarian rule in Great Britain. The Lords Chamber was completed in 1847 and in 1852, the year Reid's dismissal was final, the Commons Chamber was complete and Barry was rewarded with a knighthood.

The construction of the New Houses of Parliament, however, was not complete until 30 years after the foundation stone was laid. The final cost was way over budget and the immense task of designing such a large structure with a complex program asking for more than 1100 rooms had taken its toll on the architect. Barry died in 1860 before he could see his masterpiece in the state of final completion that we admire today.

Dr. Reid went on to become a leading member of the Health of Towns Commission and, responding to a request from the young architect Harvey Lonsdale Elmes, successfully designed the most advanced heating and ventilation system of its time at St George's Hall in Liverpool (see Chapter 7).

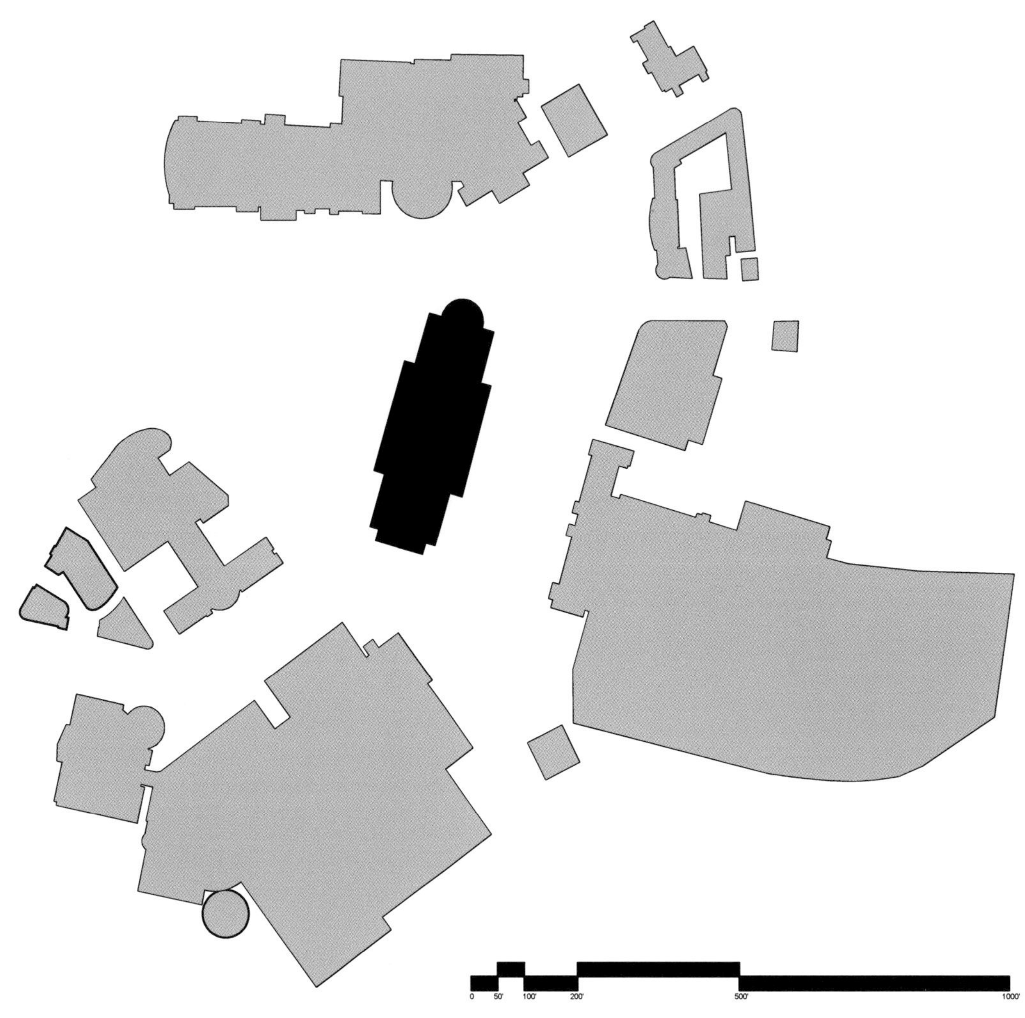

53°N

7

St George's Hall

LOCATION: LIME STREET, LIVERPOOL, UK

ARCHITECT: HARVEY LONSDALE ELMES

HEATING AND VENTILATION BY DAVID BOSWELL REID

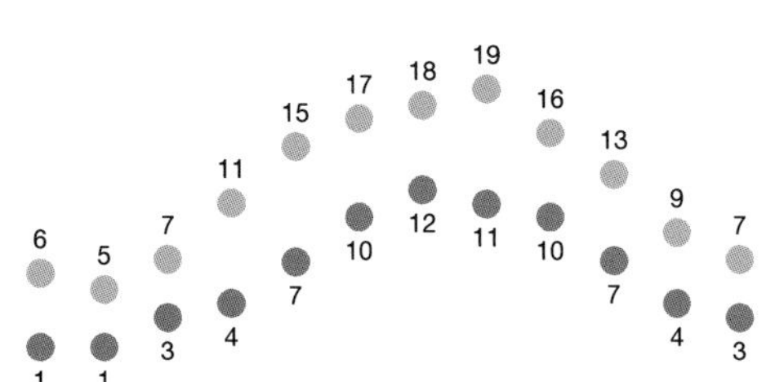

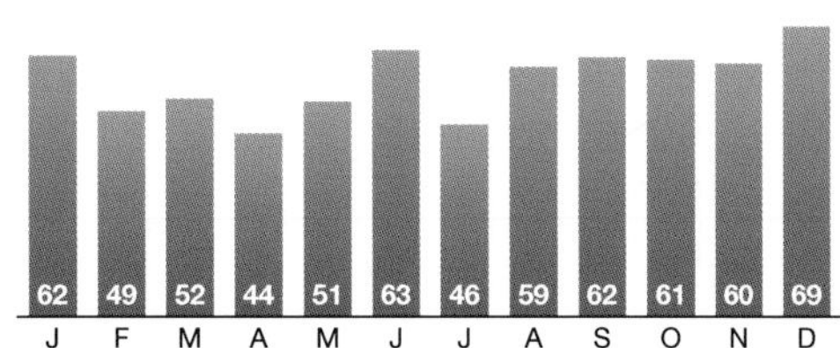

7.1 St George's Hall, north façade

A YOUNG ARCHITECT GOES TO SEE THE DOCTOR

Son of the London architect, James Elmes, a close friend of Sir John Soane, the young Harvey Lonsdale Elmes was sent to study at the Royal Academy, where Soane was a Professor of Architecture. At the age of 22, the young Elmes joined his father as a partner in his architecture firm. Soon after, he found himself the winner of an architecture competition for St George's Hall in Liverpool, a large and prestigious project for a civic building in the rising maritime mercantile city in the north-west.

Elmes' competition entry was chosen as the winner from among 75 submissions. In addition to building a new grand concert hall, Liverpool corporation also saw the need to build Courts of Assize. The competition for this project was again won by Elmes, this time competing with 88 other entrants.

Harvey Lonsdale Elmes was just graduating from his studies in architecture at the Royal Academy when the devastating fire destroyed the old Palace of Westminster. He must have followed closely the efforts by Sir Robert Smirke to hastily construct new temporary assembly halls for the Houses of Parliament.

It is in this setting that Harvey Lonsdale Elmes went to see Dr. David Boswell Reid.

The young architect was eager to learn about Dr. Reid's experiments with heating and ventilation. He followed closely as the work at the temporary House of Commons progressed and he visited Dr. Reid's testing facilities at his chemistry laboratory, which at this time had been expanded into a research facility for experimental studies of the movement of air and smoke under changing environmental conditions (Reid, 1855).

A TEMPLE OF CULTURE AND CIVIC PRIDE

Upon the recommendation of the architect, Liverpool corporation appointed Dr. Reid as consulting engineer for heating and ventilation for St George's Hall in 1841. The two projects for a large public hall and for the Courts of Assize had at this point in time been joined into one building, which program had grown to be quite extensive. In addition to a Great Hall to accommodate events where several thousand people were in attendance, space was required for the Crown Court, the Civil Court, two entrance halls, offices and cells for juries, judges and prisoners, and galleries for the public attending the trials.

After the two projects were joined, Elmes had produced a more developed scheme for a large, monumental building in the neo-classical style. Influenced by Soane, and mentored by C. R. Cockerel, also a friend of his father's, he set out to build what would become "perhaps the finest neoclassical public building in England" (Curl, 1990).

When the projects for the Great Hall and the Courts of Assize were still conceived as separate buildings, a grand scheme was developed for a public plaza. To this day, St George's Hall stands as the centerpiece of this civic urban space which now serves as the gateway to the UNESCO World Heritage site, Liverpool Maritime Mercantile City.

THE MONUMENTAL VENTILATING TOWER

Other significant buildings forming this public square would be the Lime Street Station (Richard Turner and William Fairburn, 1849), with its adjoining London and Northwestern Hotel (Alfred Waterhouse, 1879) and the William Brown Street Cultural Quarter which incorporated the beautiful Picton Reading Room (Cornelius Sherlock, 1879).

A tall columnar monument, similar to an unexecuted design by Sir Robert Smirke for national monuments to commemorate Waterloo and Trafalgar, was introduced as a central element of a design by Elmes for the new Daily Courts. A functional justification for this monument was to have the column work as a smoke chimney pulling vitiated air and smoke from the buildings surrounding it by way of underground smoke tunnels. As this scheme was abandoned, however, Dr. Reid had to reconfigure his early heating and ventilation concepts for St George's Hall.

7.2 Cockerell and Elmes: St George's Hall, print perspective

7.3 Elmes: Elevation showing the proposed new Daily Courts

WORKS LIKE MAGIC

Upon the first encounter with St George's Hall as it stands today, beautifully renovated and restored, one is struck by the stoic calmness of its urban presence. There are no apparent architectural or mechanical expressions of the advanced systems designed and built to make this complex conglomerate of public spaces work as a comfortable environment for human activity.

Several of the most prestigious public buildings of the mid to late nineteenth century, in which new methods of heating and ventilation were introduced, are characterized by their towers, spires, chimneys and turrets. Prominent architects such as Charles Barry, Alfred Waterhouse and Sir George Gilbert Scott had assigned functions of fresh air supply or discharge of smoke and vitiated air to the towers that were so integral to their designs. At St George's Hall, however, there are no architectural expressions of this kind.

The building just works—like magic.

AN ACTIVE, ATTENTIVE AND OBSERVING DISPOSITION

In the Introduction to his *Diagrams of the Ventilation of St George's Hall* (Reid, 1855), Dr. Reid emphasized the importance of appointing a person with the right qualifications to take charge of the maintenance and daily operations of the warming and ventilation system that he had designed. The person to be considered for the position as director of operations should know practical chemistry and should have "attended to questions of natural philosophy, architecture, apparatus and machinery." An "active, attentive and observing disposition" was also required.

Reid found his man in William Mackenzie. At the annual meeting of the Members of the Institution of Mechanical Engineers (Great Britain) in 1863, Mackenzie presented his report. It was now 12 years since the Courts had been completed. The Great Hall had been in active use for eight years.

Three plates with diagrams accompanied Mackenzie's report, one of which was based on Dr. Reid's "Diagram No. 37" (see Figure 7.5 on p. 70). This is a section through the Civil Court, looking towards the south. This drawing represents the typical sectional organization of the building to the north and south of the Great Hall. The courtroom is positioned within a tall, rectangular volume in the center of the building, flanked by the east portico to the left and the offices and meeting rooms to the west.

There are two main fresh air intakes positioned at the podium of the east portico, at the bottom of which were installed spray fountains for cleaning the air by removing dust particles and other impurities. The fresh air passed through large vaults under the portico to arrive at four "fanners" arranged around a steam engine. From here, the air was conditioned in warming chambers, distributed laterally through three main air tunnels, and delivered to the occupied spaces by diffusors at or near the floor.

Vitiated air was extracted from the occupied spaces through four combined smoke flues and ventilation stacks placed at the corners of the main building volume. It is important to note, however, that fresh air could also be supplied directly to an occupied space, as needed when natural cooling by outside air was called for.

What Reid had constructed was a hybrid natural ventilation system powered by the pulling force of chimneys and vacuum chambers at the top, and aided by the push force of fans on the supply side.

THE THERMAL POWER OF MASS

Three parallel underground vaults run the length of the east side of the building (Figure 7.4). The thick masonry walls and vaulted ceilings represent an enormous amount of thermal mass. The large interior volume of these vaults makes the supply air move slowly, creating perfect conditions for passive exchange of energy between the mass and the air. Since the massive vaults are thermally coupled to the earth around and below the building's foundations, the masonry surfaces will tend to reach a temperature near that of the ground.

As a rule of thumb, ground temperature at or below 6 feet below ground level (deep well temperature) is equal to the average annual air temperature. For Liverpool, this temperature is just above 10° C or 50° F. Mackenzie states in his report (Mackenzie, 1863) that the temperature of water supplied from the city mains did not reach

7.4 Massive basement vaults with air supply channels

above 54° F or 12° C, even in summer. Therefore, city water could be circulated through the coils in the warming chambers to provide additional cooling. This form of early air conditioning was, however, rarely used since the pre-cooling of incoming fresh air by thermal mass exchange was sufficient in most situations.

The arrangement for fresh air supply at St George's Hall is an elegant, effective (and free once the vaults are built) way of pre-conditioning the air by ground coupling, delivering the air supply below ambient air temperature in the summer and above ambient air temperature in the winter.

Marks on the stone-retaining walls below the air intakes indicate that there may have been stairs providing access from the east portico to the building's "underground," suggesting that spaces under the portico were used as air raid shelters during World War II.

AIR CONDITIONING THE GREAT HALL

The annotated copy of Dr. Reid's "Diagram No. 37" (Reid, 1855) explains the arrangements for heating, cooling and ventilation in and around the Great Hall (Figure 7.5). The applied colors are in accordance with a color scheme used by Reid: shades of "lake" (red or pink) for the conditioned air, green for fresh air supply and shades of blue for vitiated air exhaust.

Since the barrel-vaulted ceiling of the great hall reaches a height near the very top of the upper parapets, the four main vertical shafts in the corners could not be used to ventilate this part of the building. Instead, a large vitiated air chamber is built above the ceiling. Warm air entering the "vacuum chamber" from the hall below generates a lower pressure.

It is evident from the sectional diagram in Figure 7.5 that the significant height difference from the vaults in the basement to the "vacuum chamber" on the roof, combined with the temperature difference between the outside air and the vitiated air in the chamber, represents a considerable force pulling air through the building.

Heating is provided in four different ways. Two hot water boilers send hot water to warming chambers where the air is heated as it passes through heating coils made from pipes 4 inches in diameter. Two steam boilers deliver steam to steam coils mounted inside the warm air channels and other special steam coils. When the building is warmed before it is occupied on a cold winter morning, the steam coils would work in tandem with the hot

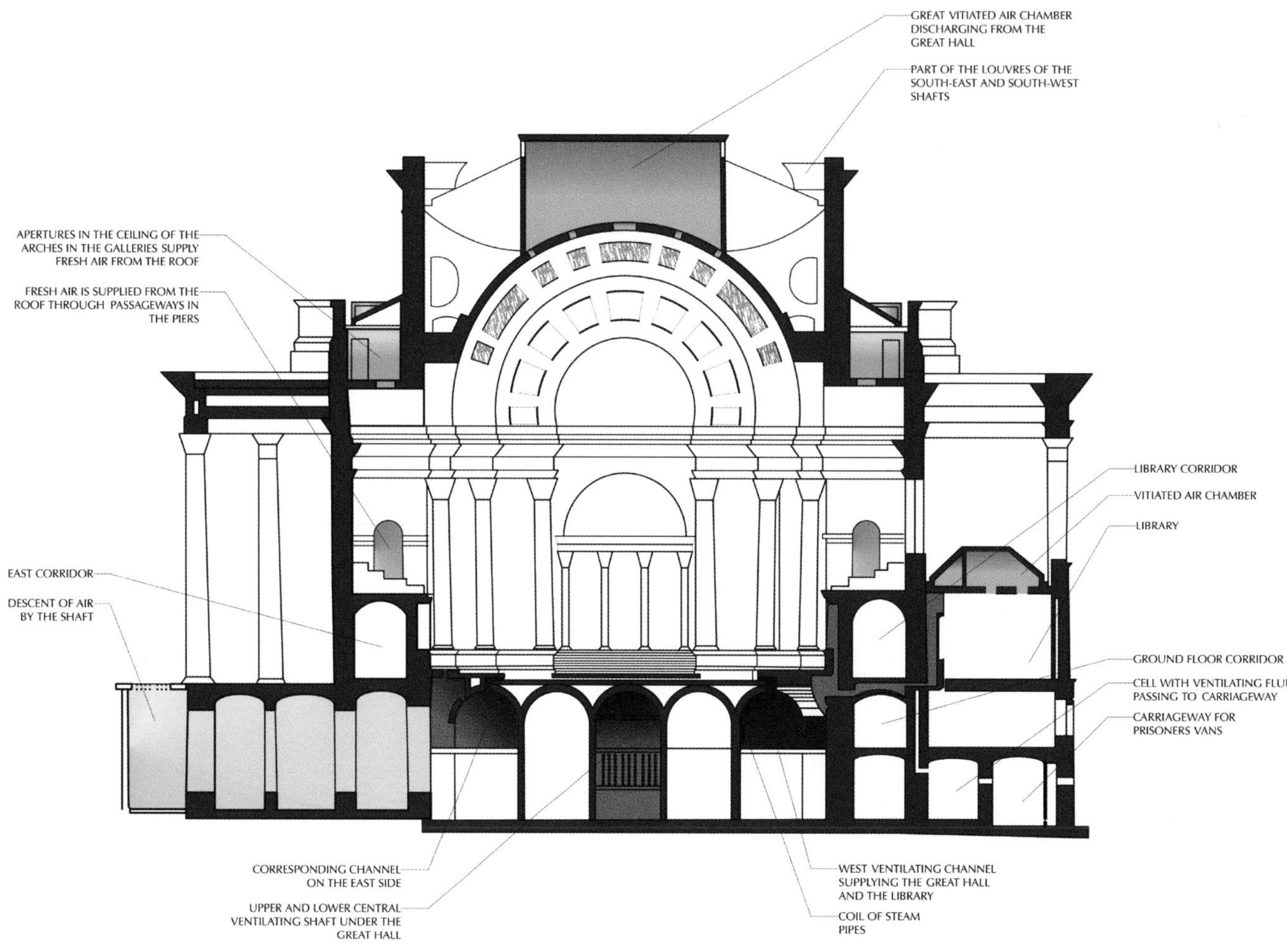

7.5 Ventilation, warming, and passive cooling system, redrawn from Reid (1855)

water coils. They could also act as air temperature boosters if heat was needed in a specific space at any time. Steam could also be injected directly into the air supply to provide humidification to the air. This combination of hot air coils, steam coils and steam injectors (jets) was a design responding to two problems commonly associated with central warm air systems: if the supply air temperature was too low or the air flow insufficient, the system could not heat the building fast enough, but if the temperature was too high, the air would become too dry, particularly if no provisions were made for recirculation when the building was in unoccupied warming mode.

Offices and meeting rooms were heated by fireplaces. Smoke from chimney stacks in masonry walls was moved laterally through tunnels and fed into smoke channels in the four corner stacks. Corridors and stairwells were used to supply air to these rooms. The prisoners' cells were warmed from the adjacent corridor and ventilated through channels inside the walls leading to a vitiated air chamber above the library (lower right portion of Figure 7.5).

CONTROLLED AIR DISTRIBUTION

Five parallel tunnel vaults are aligned with the long north–south axis of the building, some of which are separated into two chambers, one stacked on top of the other, by intermediate floors. A steam engine driving four "fannes" was located at the very center, at the same level as the lower floor of the tunnels. The "fanners" were large axial fans 3 meters in diameter. When in operation, air was pulled in axially from the side and expelled tangentially. Figure 7.5 shows the placement of the fan wells, now covered with plywood. This arrangement allowed for air to be supplied laterally in four directions.

A system of doors in the air supply tunnels, described as "valves" by Dr. Reid (Reid, 1855), was designed to direct and redirect the airflow through the underbelly of the building in order to supply air, as needed. Mackenzie (1863) notes that the three centrally located tunnels could carry cold fresh air, "tempered" air warmed only by hot water coils, and "warm" air warmed by hot

7.6 St George's Hall, interior view of side gallery of the Great Hall

water coils and boosted by steam coils. The system, therefore, was not only a variable air volume (VAV) system, but also a variable temperature system.

A set of doors to control lateral air flow was combined with strategically placed doors and hatches to channel air flow vertically. The lightweight doors were made of painted canvas on wooden frames to make sure they could easily be operated by manpower. The light weight also avoided the effect of thermal mass, which could have a negative impact on the performance of the air tunnels. The walls and ceiling vaults of the tunnels, therefore, were plastered with a lime plaster and pumice mix to obtain a low heat capacity characteristic.

BREATHING

The Great Hall (Figure 7.6) could hold up to 3000 people. With an additional 1000 seated in the concert hall at the north end, the courts in session and the smaller "apartments" occupied, the building could theoretically house 5000 people simultaneously. Reid, therefore, designed the heating and ventilation system to deliver upward of 50,000 cubic feet of air per minute (cfm). Based on his research, he had arrived at a design demand for air supply of 10 cfm per person.

Much like a person's body, the building would breathe. In normal operations mode it would exhale through the upper lungs:

the vacuum chambers for vitiated air typically located between the ceiling and the roof. It would inhale from the air supply tunnels below through various nostril designs. Stair risers were perforated to allow for diffuse supply of air low in the space. In the Great Hall, air is also supplied from grilles in the floor and from openings concealed by the statues.

During a well-attended event taking place in the Great Hall, guests from the higher levels of society would be seated in front while members of the lower classes would be standing in the back. This created a situation in the room where the people density would vary greatly. Each person's metabolism and clothing value would also differ. What was needed for comfort was not the same in the front as in the back of the room. This realization led Dr. Reid to design a system where colder air was supplied at one zone while warmer air would comfort the audience in the other zone.

The system was also adaptive to users' need on a timeline. Before an event, the space could be warmed up by supplying hot air and recirculating the air back to the warming chambers below. When the event started, warmer and cooler air could be supplied to various zones with various air flows. When the space heated up as a result of 3000 bodies emitting heat, fresh air could be supplied from designated air intakes on the roof.

THE GALLERIES

Circulation through the galleries along the east and west sides of the Great Hall was facilitated by arched openings in the massive pillars. The portion of the pillar closest to the exterior wall is hollow, allowing for air to be introduced at one level above the main floor of the hall. Even higher, under the larger arches spanning from one pillar to the next, square grilles at the apex were used to supply cooler, fresh air from above when the hall heated up.

Airflow patterns generated by the fan-assisted natural ventilation system created stratification in the tall spaces of the building. To compensate for the rising temperatures at the gallery levels, fresh air was introduced here first, then to descend towards the main floor and there to replace vitiated air rising towards the barrel-vaulted ceiling in the center.

Reid developed a sophisticated system for controlling temperature and airflow. There is an air supply grille behind the judge's chair, allowing the judge individual control over his local climatic environment.

THE ARTFUL DESIGN OF APERTURES FOR AIR AND LIGHT

The barrel-vaulted ceiling of the Great Hall (Figure 7.7) was one of the largest in Great Britain. Beautifully decorated and designed as integral to a complete Great Hall interior, it also serves as a perforated curved screen for the removal of vitiated air. The grilles communicate directly with the "vacuum chamber" created above the ceiling and below the roof.

Square grilles were used for fresh air supply when cooling by outside air was beneficial to maintaining proper air quality and thermal comfort during events attended by large audiences.

The building was originally illuminated by gas lamps. The combustive gases from the gasoliers in the Great Hall created plumes of vertical air currents aiding the ventilation scheme without polluting the air where the audience was seated or standing.

THE COURTS

The rooms for the Civil Court and the Crown Court were heated and ventilated in a similar fashion to the Great Hall. Conditioned air was supplied through perforations in stair risers and wall panels. The prisoners' dock was used as an air supply plenum in order to provide the opportunity to vary the air flow rate according to the various levels of people density in the room.

In situations where cooling by natural ventilation was called for, fresh air was supplied from the roof through the square grilles behind the arches, as shown in Figure 7.7.

There was, however, one significant difference in the way the courts were ventilated. Since the ceilings over the courtrooms did not rise as high as the vaulted ceiling above the Great Hall, the courtrooms could communicate with the four ventilating shafts

7.7 St George's Hall, vaulted ceiling with integrated decorative air exhaust vents

placed at the corners of the main building volume. Gas flames or jets were placed inside the shafts and near the top, which allowed for a finer control over the power of the shafts to pull air through the rooms.

This scheme also freed up the ceiling from having to be perforated with air exhaust grilles, which in turn allowed the architect to make better use of the courtroom ceilings for admission and distribution of natural light.

Daylight was provided disproportionately at one end of the courtroom: over the judge's desk. The abundant use of skylights could be implemented without too much draft from cold glass surfaces because the space above was covered with a glass roof, thus effectively creating a double pane skylight system.

7.8 St George's Hall, view of the attic with skylight placed directly above glass ceilings

BREATHING MACHINES WITH EYES TO THE SKY

Attic spaces above the courts, the Great Hall and the smaller Concert Hall work as "vacuum chambers," vitiated air plenums that help the building breathe. In some of these attic spaces, natural light was supplied to the rooms below through glass ceilings and skylights.

Without any source of mechanical heating, these "attic greenhouses" would typically maintain an interior air temperature well above the ambient air temperature, even on a cloudy day with predominantly diffuse sky radiation. On a sunny summer day, the elevated indoor air temperature in the attic spaces would help maintain the indoor/outdoor air temperature differential necessary for the air to be pulled through the building passively by natural forces.

Under the skin of a calm, well-proportioned neo-classical architecture, St George's Hall reveals a complex machinery designed to make the building come alive as if it is breathing, tuned to the power of heat and the natural movements of air.

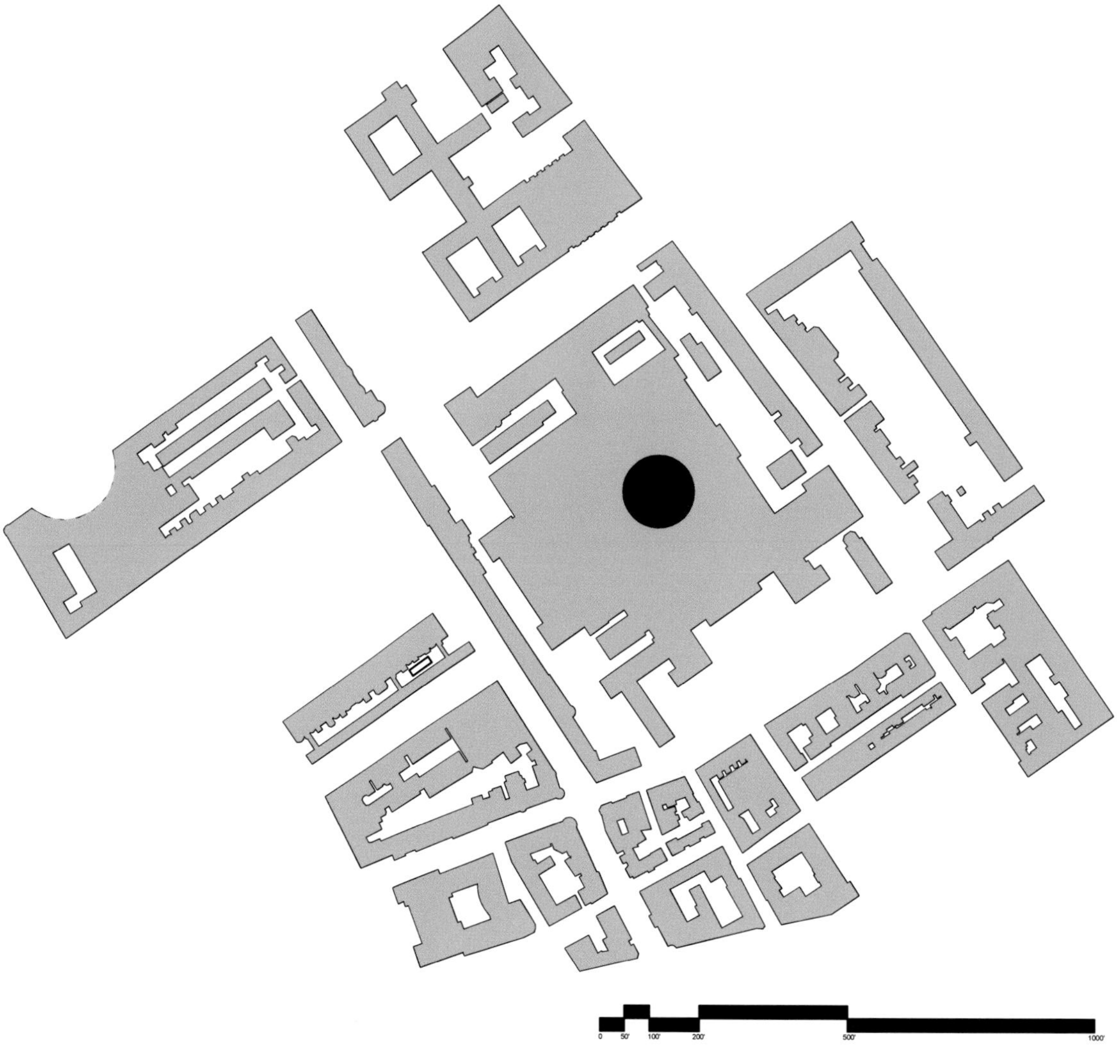

52°N

8

The British Museum Reading Room

LOCATION: GREAT RUSSELL STREET, LONDON

BUILT: 1857

ARCHITECT: SYDNEY SMIRKE

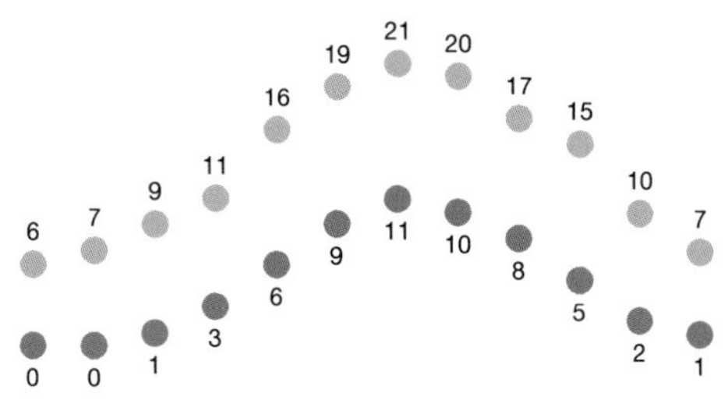

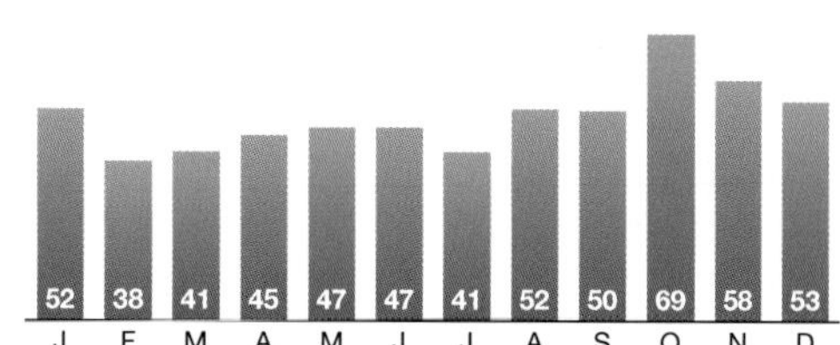

8.1 Exterior view of the British Museum Reading Room. Renovation of the Great Court by Foster + Partners

LITTLE SID

In the spring of 1855, *The Builder* and *The Illustrated London News* both reported on the work in progress on the new reading room at the British Museum. Since the work was taking place inside the quadrangle of the new museum buildings, the work was out of sight and therefore not known to the public. As seen from the sketch published by the *Illustrated London News* (Figure 8.2), what was being constructed was a marvel, not only due to its enormous height, but to the innovative use of modern materials and construction methods by the architect Sydney Smirke. A dome comparable in size with the Pantheon and the dome of St Peter's in Rome was being built with iron ribs supporting thin brick shell segments.

Sydney Smirke was the young brother of Sir Robert Smirke, the architect of the new British Museum. Declining health had forced Sir Robert to retire in 1845. By that year his design for the museum was mostly complete, but the enclosed quadrangle was left empty with little or no useful functions assigned to it.

Nineteenth-century England experienced exponential growth on many fronts. With the conversion of coal into energy for heat and motion came the growth of coal mining, of manufacturing, of transportation and of population in urban areas. From these phenomena grew new public institutions of learning, government and culture. At the British Museum, the number of books in the collection grew along a similar exponential curve. The Keeper of Printed Books, Mr. Panizzi, soon realized that the new buildings would not have the capacity to hold the entire book collection. The capacity of the existing reading rooms were challenged by hundreds of readers lining up daily to get a seat at a reading desk.

In 1852, after debating several alternative schemes for expansion, the trustees approved of Panizzi's plan to build a new circular reading room in the quadrangle. After consulting with Sydney Smirke, the trustees commissioned him as the architect of the new reading room and libraries at the British Museum. It would take another two years before Parliament voted to fund the project. Meanwhile, Panizzi and Smirke were busy developing plans for the new building.

8.2 The New Reading Room at the British Museum, in Course of Construction. Engraving by C.W. Sheeres

PROFESSOR HOSKING'S PROJECT AND PANIZZI'S PLAN

Some years before Sydney Smirke's assignment as the architect of the new reading room, William Hosking, Professor of Architecture and Engineering Construction at King's College, had developed a project for a circular, domed building at the center of the quadrangle (Figure 8.3, left). In 1850, Hosking decided to publish his project in *The Builder*, since "the original design (of the British Museum) now in effect being completed, and its author having retired from practice, . . . while available space in the most convenient position, . . . remains unoccupied" (*The Builder*, 1850).

The main purpose of the new building, modeled after the Pantheon in Rome, was to improve circulation by connecting the four wings of the museum to a central hall, which was intended

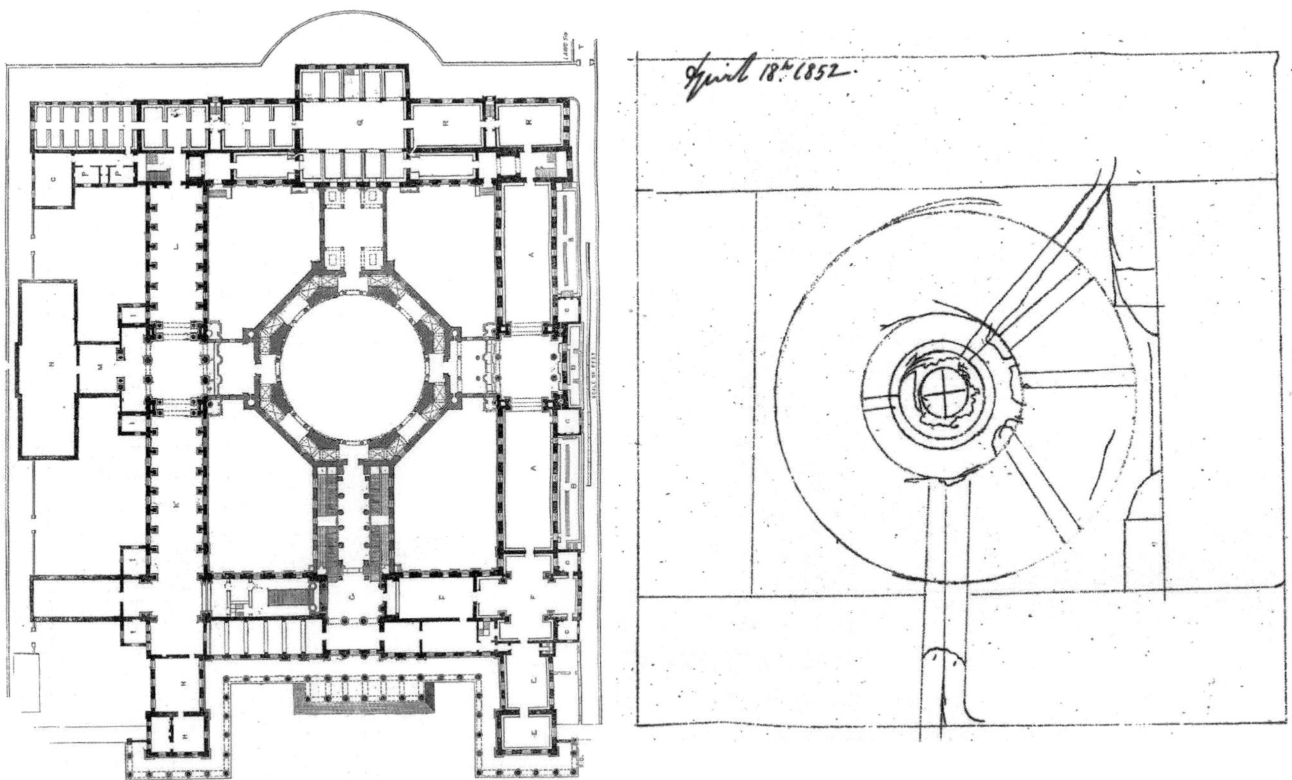

8.3 Professor Hosking's Project (left), and Panizzi's first sketch for the 1857 Reading Room, made on 18th April 1852 (right)

as a gallery for the exhibition of the most precious objects in the museum's collection.

When Mr. Panizzi presented his plan to the trustees two years later, he submitted a sketch showing a circular reading room placed in the center of the quadrangle similar to Hosking's project (Figure 8.3, right). In a detailed presentation ahead of the inauguration in 1857, *The Times* stated that while Mr. Smirke was the "architect of the trustees," he had always shown himself ready to carry out the plan of the "original designer," Mr. Panizzi. Years later, when Mr. Lowe in a speech to the House of Commons named Mr. Panizzi "the architect" of the reading room, Smirke set the record straight. In a letter to the editor of *The Times* in 1866, he wrote:

> Briefly the facts are these: Some years ago the late Professor of Architecture at King's College suggested building a circular, domed hall for sculpture in the quadrangle. Some years afterwards, Mr. Panizzi suggested building a flat, low circular reading room in the same place. The trustees did me the honor to consult me, and I quite approved of Mr. Panizzi's suggestion, but proposed a dome and glazed vaulting, to give more air to the readers and more architectural character to the interior. This grew, on maturer consideration, into the much larger dome as erected. The whole of the building was subsequently carried out from my drawings and under my direction as architect.

HEATING AND VENTILATION

Smirke's design for the new building (Figure 8.4) shows the circular domed reading room at the center of a rectangular building containing the book stacks, all constructed with fireproof materials. Access to the reading room for patrons is from the south through the main museum lobby. Librarians access the archives outside the new building through a corridor at the north end. There is also a connection to the King's Library and reading room to the east.

The new building was provided with a central air system for heating and ventilation. There had been complaints about the systems (or lack thereof) for heating and ventilating the existing building. In 1838, the Keeper of Printed Books complained about dry air and dust from the hot air stoves constructed on the Sylvester principle. The engineer John Sylvester (1798–1852) had carried out large-scale works related to heating and ventilation. Although the air temperature was not supposed to exceed 70–80° F, the Keeper complained that the system was "prejudicial

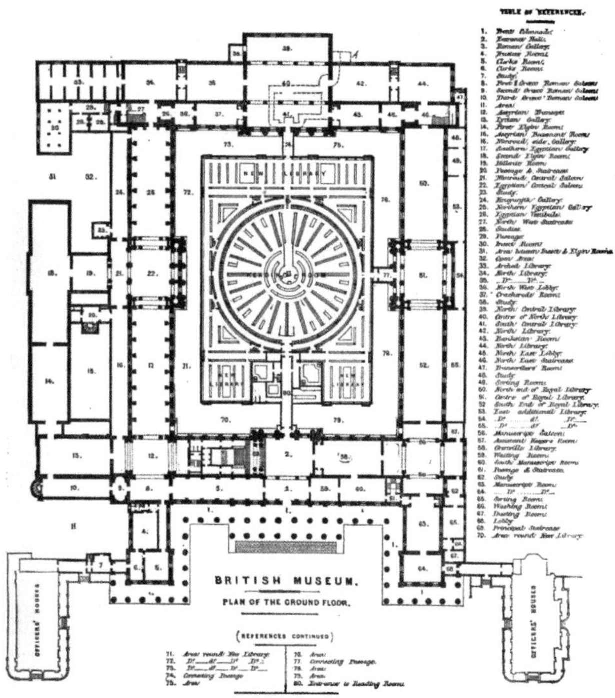

8.4 Plan of the Ground Floor (1844)

to health, and injurious to the manuscripts" (Harris, 1998). Angier March Perkins later replaced Sylvester and introduced his system of heat distribution by hot water at high pressure.

The new building was designed to be supplied with warm air for heating and ventilation from a 6-ft-high plenum below the reading room. Fresh air intake was through a 50–60-ft-tall tower on the north side of the museum, away from dusty city streets. Sprays were installed inside the tower to purify and cool the air.

In heating and ventilation mode (in winter), the air passed over and under the boilers, through a heating chamber, and was then forced into the air supply plenum ("the spider") by a fan with a 16 ft diameter. In ventilation only mode (in summer), the air could pass freely to the "spider" without being hindered by any pressure loss of passing through the boiler room, warming coils and fan.

Air entered the reading room above the readers' heads through channels inside the dividing walls of the desks. Similar channels were installed at the center of the circulation desks. Air could also be supplied through grilles at the ends of the readers' desks.

AIR RISES—AND FALLS

At the oculus of the dome, a decorative glass ceiling is installed below a lantern with operable clerestory windows for the exhaust of vitiated air. As in the Pantheon, the dome would carry light from the oculus to the space below, but in the reading room additional daylight was provided by 20 large windows.

The shell of the dome was constructed of a thin layer of brick, clad on the outside with copper and covered on the inside with a thin decorative skin. The inner and outer skins were installed at a distance from the centrally positioned brick layer, forming two cavities. The assumption was that the outer cavity would act as an insulating layer of air protecting the interior from the ambient temperatures. The inner cavity was designed to carry vitiated air upwards from the top of the windows to the lantern above the glass ceiling. These assumptions did, however, not always hold true. In the winter, when significantly lower outside air temperatures occur, the brick layer would represent a reservoir of thermal mass colder than the interior. If the pressure differential between the interior and the lantern was not sufficient to pull the air upwards, the air in the inner cavity would start to descend, potentially creating drafts falling on the patrons' heads.

COMFORTABLY SEATED

The original heating and ventilation system was installed by Messrs Haden of Trowbridge. The system was much praised at first (Harris, 1998). The interior photograph in Harris (1979) shows the screen between the tables where warm air entered above the readers' heads. Air was also supplied through grilles at the end of each row of desks. The elegant desks were carefully designed with fold out shelves for reference books and niches for writing supplies so that the leather desk surface could be kept free of clutter. Each reader's workspace measured 4 feet and 3 inches wide.

In addition to the heat provided by warm air, hot water pipes were installed under the desks, thus providing an additional source of radiant heat and doubling as a foot warmer.

Although Haden's system was advanced for its time, it did not live up to Smirke's high expectations. In 1859, he made a recommendation to the trustees to fit blinds to the windows in the reading room. His proposal was accepted, but the complaints did not go away entirely.

In his book, *A History of the British Museum Library, 1753–1973,* Harris writes:

> The matter which caused the most complaints was the prevalence of draughts in the Reading Room. Smirke recommended in October 1860 that the space between the double sashes of the windows should be heated by coils of hot water pipes, to deal with the problem caused by the chilling of air in the Reading Room because of the large expanse of windows.
>
> In 1863 Smirke was authorized to fit heating pipes between the windows. Then Watts complained about the bad effect on the health of the staff caused by the draughts at the center of the room. Three of the five seats there were particularly exposed to drafts, and he believed that people had actually died in consequence.
>
> [Panizzi] believed that the complaints about the draughts had been exaggerated, and he ordered hot water pipes to be fixed around the lantern of the dome to deal with the problem. On the whole these measures worked, and in 1875 the pipes which supplied the coils under the windows of the reading room were replaced, and moved from their former exposed position on the outer walls to the space between the external and the internal skylights over the gallery surrounding the Reading Room.
>
> (Harris, 1998)

UNDERSTANDING AIRFLOW

The dissatisfaction of patrons and librarians with the thermal comfort of the reading room, as reported by Harris, may or may not represent the majority of users. In the most comfortable buildings, there is always the potential for a dissatisfied user. However, this statistical fact does not prevent us from attempting to find a deeper understanding of the issues raised.

One can assume with certainty that, with the large expanse of windows combined with a brick layer of the dome that was cold, cool air would descend along the surface of the dome, thus causing a column of warmer vitiated air to rise up towards the lantern in the center of the space. This could explain why there were complaints about drafts near the perimeter of the circular reading room.

Another source of cold air descending could have been the grilles seen at the apex of the window niches. If these grilles were

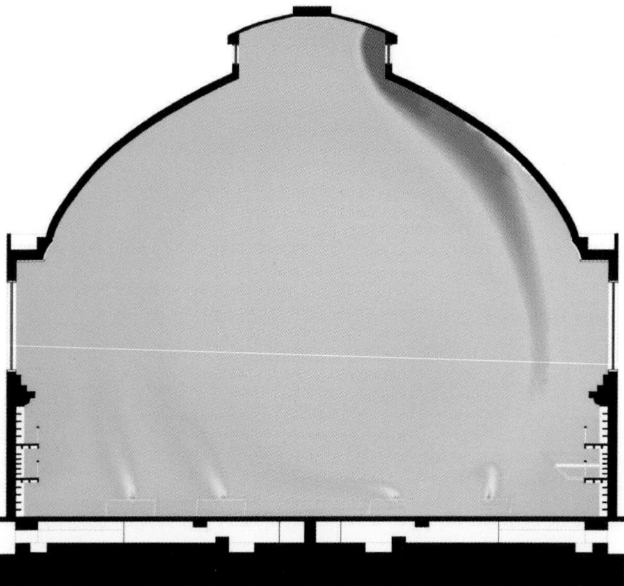

8.5 CFD diagram showing airflow and temperature distribution in the reading room

connected to the outside via vent hoods, as indicated by Forster's section drawing (Hawkes, 1996), fresh air could descend from the grilles when the space was in cooling mode on a warm summer day. The airflow pattern inside the reading room would then follow a similar pattern as seen in St Georges Hall (see Chapter 7).

But why was there a sense of draft at the center of the space where the reference librarians worked? Computational fluid dynamics computations performed at the University of Illinois at Urbana Champaign using a simplified three-dimensional model of a section of the domed space produced results that can be used to explain this phenomenon. Figure 8.5 shows simulated airflow patterns and temperature distribution on a winter day in a typical meteorological year. While warm air predominantly escapes out through the lantern, colder fresh air may enter at the same time, depending on the air temperature, wind speed and wind direction. Therefore, during certain conditions, a column of descending cold air might have targeted the very center of the reading room, causing the attendants to ask for the installation of porters' chairs (Harris, 1998). This finding is in line with what the author found while performing experiments at the central, top-lit space of the Nature Center in Nuuk, Greenland (Lerum, 2008).

SUSTAINABLE DESIGN

Quickly after the new building's inauguration in 1857, the success of Sydney Smirke's design was indisputable. Two years later, following in the footsteps of his father and brother, he was elected Royal Academician, joining a select group of only 40 members (*The Illustrated London News*, 1857).

Sydney Smirke's design for the reading room and library (book stacks) encompassed an internalized building with few openings. The exterior limits of the rectangle was pulled back 27–30 feet from the façades of Sir Robert's museum building on all four sides, allowing light to enter through the void between the two structures. There was, therefore, no need for an "external architecture," a cost-saving feature used by Panizzi to convince the trustees to vote for his plan.

A century and a half later, when the library at the British Museum had been moved to the British Library, the part holding the book stacks was demolished, leaving the reading room at the center of a renovated courtyard. Sir Norman Foster's triangulated glass roof created an inviting public space for circulation while adding valuable space for exhibitions and information.

The restored reading room remains the architectural jewel of the British Museum. Much appreciated and loved by the public, it stands as a prominent example of sustainable design: a space that lasts for centuries, accommodating new and unforeseen needs—an object of timeless beauty.

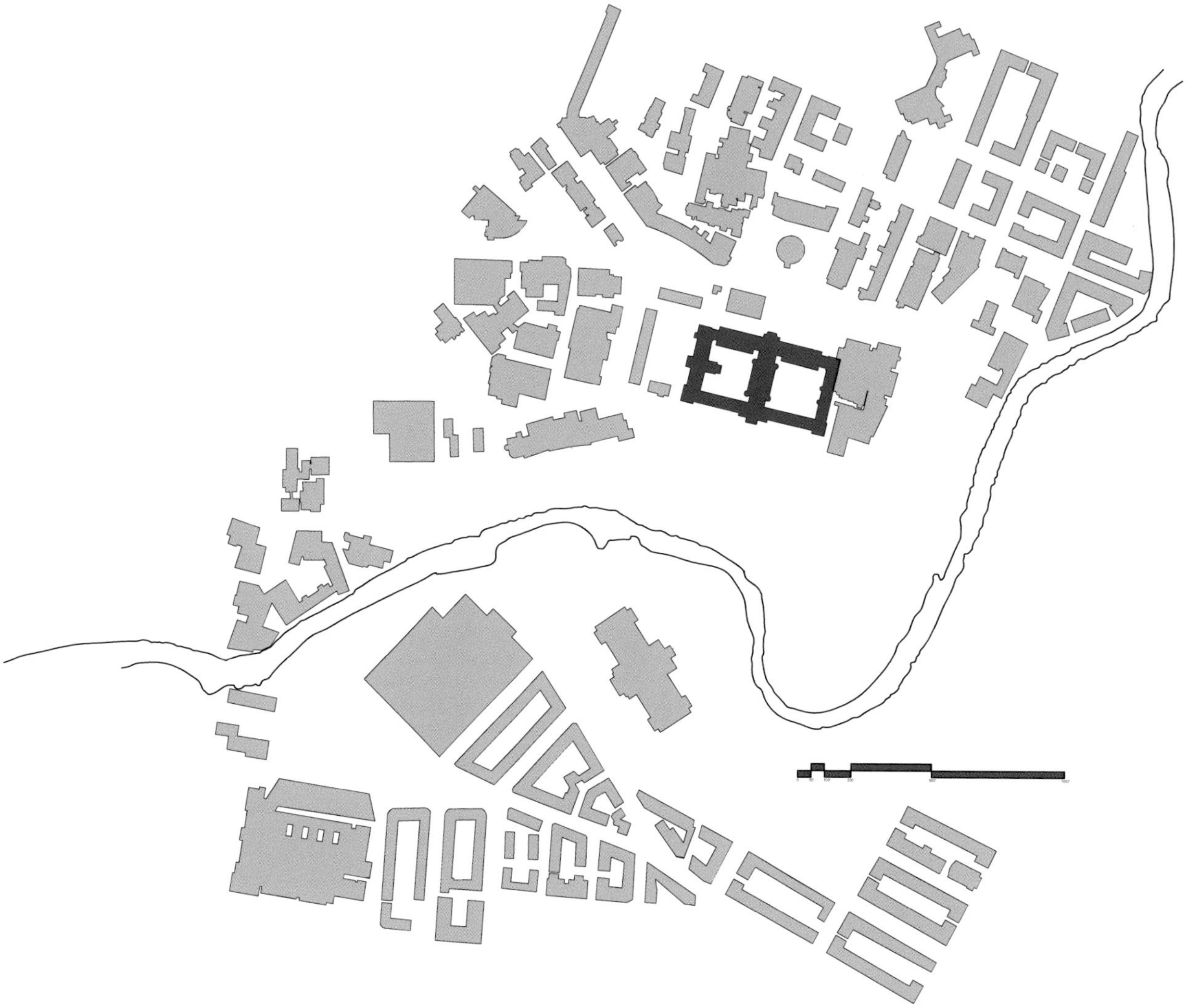

9

56°N

University of Glasgow, Gilmorehill

LOCATION: UNIVERSITY AVENUE, GLASGOW, UK

BUILT: 1870

ARCHITECT: SIR GEORGE GILBERT SCOTT

ENGINEER: WILSON W. PHIPSON

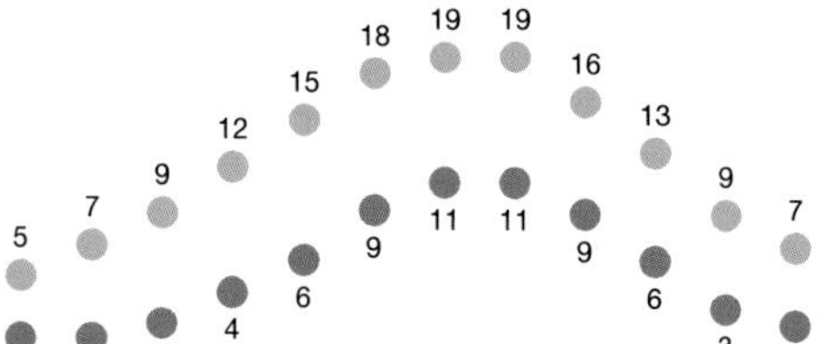

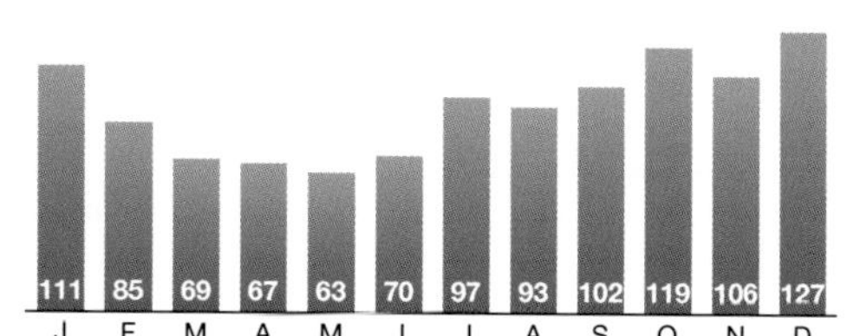

9.1 Central Ventilation Tower at University of Glasgow, Gilmorehill

GILMOREHILL

In the early 1850s, four hundred years after it had been founded, the High Street buildings occupied by the University of Glasgow were no longer suitable for a growing institution of higher education. As Glasgow was buzzing with economic activity brought on by the Industrial Revolution, increasing urban density, an expanding population and severe air pollution had all contributed to the deterioration of the neighborhoods around High Street in the city center. It was decided to build an entirely new university campus at Gilmorehill, a terrace in the landscape on the north-west side of the town, overlooking the River Clyde.

Except for the chapel, the two wings connecting it at the NW and SW corners, and newer additions on the east side, the original Gilmorehill campus has not changed much since its inauguration in 1870. The long and narrow buildings on the south and east sides of the campus green house classrooms, laboratories and offices. Along with the library and museum to the north, a rectangular quadrangle was formed. This inner courtyard is intersected in the middle by the Bute Hall, which is elevated off the ground and supported by a vaulted arcade.

On an axis with the Bute Hall, marking the main entrance at the center of the south façade, stands the tall "ventilation tower," designed by the architect George Gilbert Scott and completed by his son, John Oldrid Scott.

GEORGE GILBERT SCOTT'S PLAN

Scott's plan for the new campus was to form a rectangular courtyard defined by classroom and laboratory wings on the south and east sides, and the museum and library on the north side. By 1870, teachers accommodations had been built west of and outside the quadrangle, but the chapel was still unbuilt. Therefore, a masonry wall closed the inner courtyard towards the west. Buildings housing the chemistry laboratories and the anatomy department were added adjacent to the main campus buildings to the east, which allowed for the exclusion of these buildings from the overall heating and ventilating arrangements designed by Phipson.

Pavilions with a square footprint were placed at each corner of the rectangle, housing the larger classrooms, two or three stacked on top of each other and seating up to 300 students.

The overall dimensions of the new university campus were 530 feet by 300 feet (160 × 90 meters), excluding the chemistry and anatomy buildings.

Narrow buildings, only 40 feet (12 meters) wide, with large, tall windows, allowed the rooms to be lit by daylight as a general rule. The 12-meter structural module was carried through to the museum and library, but here the total width of the building was doubled by adding a 6-meter-wide bay on each side.

At the high northern latitude of Glasgow at 56°N and in a climate dominated by overcast skies, however, additional lighting was needed for early morning and late afternoon classes. Gas lighting was installed to satisfy this requirement.

Even without taking the complex ventilation requirements for the anatomy and chemistry departments into account, the campus plan represented a significant challenge to the heating and ventilating engineer. Various rooms and departments would operate in significantly different modes during winter or spring and fall, during daylight hours or times of day that required artificial lighting, in rooms with complex occupancy schedules, and spaces with diverse functional requirements.

PHIPSON'S CONTRACT

The engineer Wilson W. Phipson had won the commission to design systems for heating and ventilating the campus buildings. After reviewing proposals from three experts on heating and ventilation, Sir George Gilbert Scott recommended that Phipson's plan should be adopted.

Phipson's contract with the University is preserved at the historical archives at the University of Glasgow (Figure 9.3). This contract defines the client as a group of 25 professors, all listed with their names and titles. At the time the contract was signed, the university was still an institution governed by all tenured professors.

The contract went through several iterations, adopting a multitude of changes, which can be seen as a proof of how actively

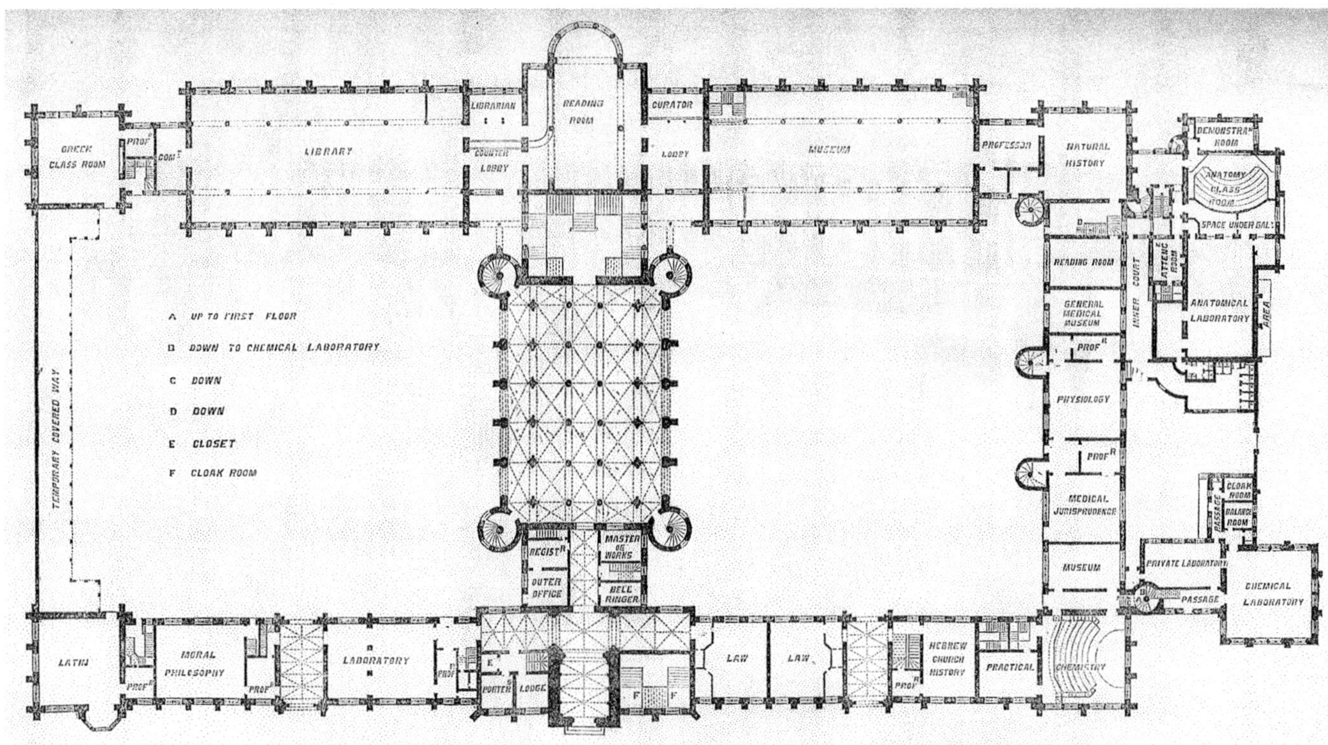

9.2 George Gilbert Scott: University of Glasgow, Gilmorehill, Ground Floor Plan

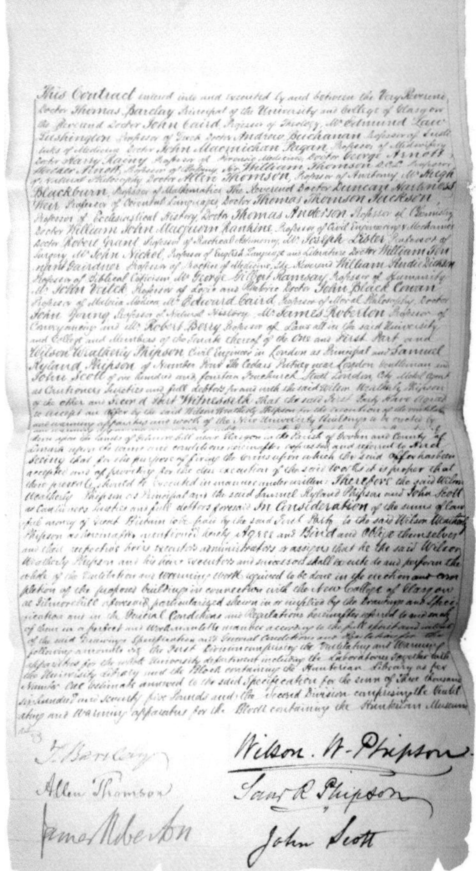

T. Barclay
Allen Thomson
James Roberton
Wilson W. Phipson
Saml R. Phipson
John Scott

9.3 The University of Glasgow's contract with Wilson W. Phipson

involved the collegium of professors were in the planning and the design of the new campus. Among themselves, they selected a sub-committee, the Building Committee, consisting of four of the most esteemed faculty members.

THE BUILDING COMMITTEE

The Building Committee was chaired by Dr. Allen Thomson, Professor of Anatomy, with Professor of Natural Philosophy William Thomson (Lord Kelvin), Professor of Mathematics Hugh Blackburn and Professor of Civil Engineering and Mechanics (William John) Macquorn Rankine as members. This was no ordinary building committee. All four members were internationally acclaimed scholars, ranking at the top among their peers.

Allen Thomson (1809–1884) reorganized the University's Medical School, improving the facilities as well as the standards of teaching. As Convenor of the New Buildings Committee, he helped organize the operation to move the University from High Street to Gilmorehill. On 6 June 1866, he cut the first sod at the new site.

William Thomson, 1st Baron Kelvin (1824–1907) was one of the most famous scientists of his age. He was as famous for his inventions as for his academic work. He published more than 600 scientific papers during his lifetime and earned international acclaim for proposing an absolute scale of temperature now known as the Kelvin Scale, and for his pioneering research in the fields of mechanical energy and heat. He was equally well known for his work on planning the Transatlantic telegraph cable and his invention of the Kelvin Compass and sounding machine.

Hugh Blackburn (1823–1909) studied at Trinity College, Cambridge, where he became a lifelong friend of William Thomson, later Lord Kelvin. At Cambridge, he invented a pendulum with a double suspension, later known as the Blackburn Pendulum, to demonstrate harmonic motion. In 1849, he was appointed to the Chair of Mathematics at Glasgow, succeeding William Thomson's father James.

(William John) Macquorn Rankine (1820–1872) has been described as "the father of engineering science" in the UK, in recognition of his achievements as a theoretical scientist and as an educator. He worked as a civil engineer and published papers on practical engineering subjects and then on molecular physics and thermodynamics. As the University's Chair of Civil Engineering and Mechanics, he proclaimed his intention to teach theory, practice and the application of theory to practice. Rankine worked closely with Glasgow shipbuilders on radical improvements to the design of vessels and their engines.

A PRESCRIPTIVE SET OF DESIGN CRITERIA

Members of the Building Committee, being well versed in the fields of civil and mechanical engineering, physics, the theory of heat and work, and mathematics, did not leave it to the contracted expert in heating and ventilation to start working on his commission without providing detailed guidelines for the system design. In his presentation of his design ten years later, Phipson relied heavily on the work of "General Morin" (Morin, 1863), who frequently made references to Dr. Reid's work (Reid, 1844). It is safe to assume that the building committee members were familiar with Morin's two volumes on "Méchanique Practique."

Instead of defining performance criteria for typical rooms and functional spaces in the buildings, the Building Committee ventured into developing a detailed set of rules for the system design. This prescriptive approach, however, can in hindsight be seen as possibly restricting Phipson's creativity and ultimately causing some problems with the system's efficiency and performance.

After lengthy investigation, the committee came to the following conclusions:

1. The foul air should be removed through outlets as near as possible to the place where it is produced, e.g. passages under desks and seats.
2. The total area of orifices of such outlets should be about 1/5 square foot per sitting, or 28 square inches.
3. The total area of the orifices of the inlets for fresh air should be about double the area of those of the outlets for foul air, or 2/5 square foot per sitting.
4. The inlets for fresh air should be at a high level and distributed round the circumference of the rooms.
5. The fresh air should be supplied both hot and cold, and each class-room be provided with means of mixing it.
6. The total supply of air to the class-rooms should be 6/10 cubic foot per sitting per second.
7. The sectional area of the channels and conduits for carrying away foul air should be 1/20 square foot per sitting.
8. The final outlets of the foul air should be so placed that none of it should return to the building.
9. The fresh air should be drawn from some place where the air is always pure.
10. The fresh air should be forced in by one or any required number of suitable machines.
11. The foul-air conduits should lead to chimneys in suitable positions, provided with furnaces capable of being lighted, the area of the furnace grate being 15/1000 square foot per sitting.

9.4 The Central Ventilation Tower, with elevation of the spire re-drawing from a drawing by John Oldrid Scott

12. The hot part of the fresh air should be heated by hot-water tubes, and that the most efficient position for such tubes was in the vertical passages in which the current of air ascends.

(Proceedings, 1878)

THE VENTILATING TOWER

The central tower rising above the main entrance on the south side of campus, the "ventilation tower," is in many ways the most vital architectural element in Scott's composition. Seen from far away, the tower signifies the importance and position of one of the most prestigious learning institutions in the UK. It was also a sign of the willingness of the new merchant class in town to support the development of new knowledge through research. Seeing how the theoretical studies of men like Lord Kelvin and Professor Rankine had been applied to commercial and military endeavors proved that their aid in funding the new university campus was a wise long-term investment.

The university was moving from its High Street location, which was characterized as having a noxious atmosphere. The

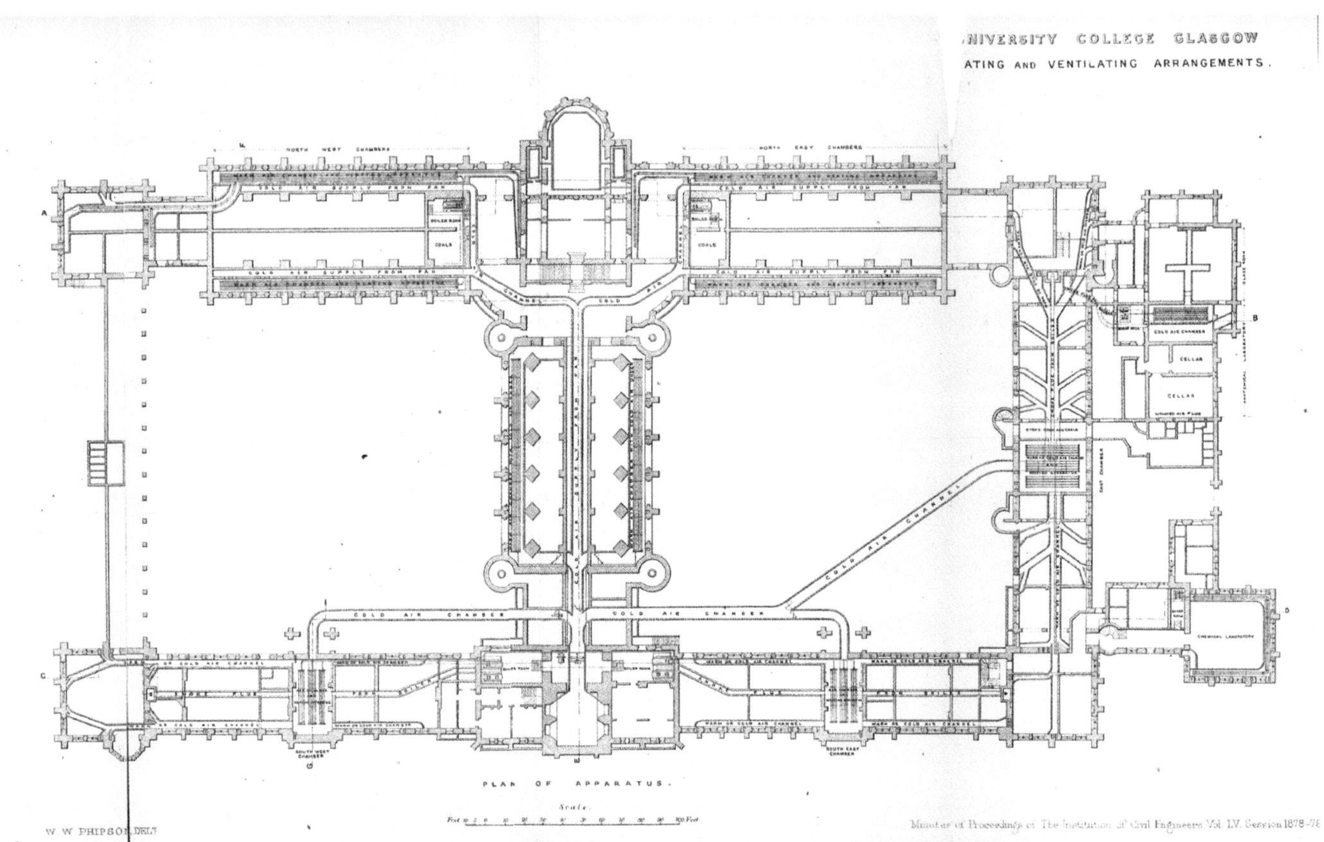

9.5 W. W. Phipson: University College Glasgow, Heating and Ventilating Arrangements, Plan of Apparatus

fast-growing, coal-based economy of Glasgow was rapidly causing the air quality to deteriorate, with smoke, dust and coal particles saturating the air. It was therefore decided that the air should be "drawn from some place where the air is always pure." The architect and the engineer took this requirement as an encouragement to build a very tall tower. For the ventilation system design, however, it meant that all the air supplied for heating and ventilating the entire campus had to come from one place: the ventilating tower.

In hindsight, one can ponder whether fresh air intakes could alternatively have been placed in the heavily vegetated slopes between the Gilmorehill plateau and the River Kelvin. But then the practical justification for the tower would have been lost.

HEATING AND VENTILATING ARRANGEMENTS

At the base of the central ventilating tower, Phipson placed a large fan. Phipson had adjusted the numbers provided by the Building Committee and found that the total air flow through the system should be no less that 1.8 million cubic feet per hour. To move this amount of air at a velocity of 12 ft per second, he decided to install a screw fan, which he argued was "of no more complicated form of construction than the ordinary rotary fans, but are less liable to get out of order" (Proceedings, 1878). Based on the most current knowledge obtained from the literature, Phipson sized the diameter of the fan at 7 feet 6 inches and the power of the steam engine driving the fan as 7 HP.

During the discussion following Phipson's presentation at the annual conference of the Institution of Civil Engineers, it was argued, however, that the choice of a screw fan was a bad one due to the "slip of the screw" rendering the fan to fail at producing the pressure difference required to move large quantities of air through long underground tunnels.

Phipson decided to decouple the air moving equipment (the centrally located fan) from the apparatus conditioning the air. Three large warming chambers were placed in the south and east wings in addition to separate air chambers in the library, the museum, the anatomy building and the chemistry department (Figure 9.5).

Cold air chambers were placed adjacent to each "warming chamber and heating apparatus," which allowed decentralized temperature control by mixing hot and cold air. This system of a central air intake and decentralized air warming stations meant that long underground tunnels would carry air that was not conditioned. Therefore, the air supply could potentially be saturated with humidity from condensation on surfaces inside the tunnels and exposed to contamination from old leaking sanitary sewers buried under the campus green.

Phipson does not discuss alternatives to the centrally located fresh air intake, but the lengthy discussion after his presentation did bring to light the disadvantage presented to him by the fact that the architectural design was largely complete before the engineer was on board.

ASPIRATED CHIMNEYS

By pushing the air into the air supply channels using a powerful fan, Phipson had introduced a system based on creating a slightly higher air pressure inside the building relative to the ambient conditions. This principle of stronger push than pull would lead the vitiated air to "find its way" out through the designated air exhaust channels, but also through cracks and openings in and around doors and windows, thus reducing uncomfortable drafts.

Where the requirements for air exhaust was extraordinary high, such as at the corner pavilions where three large classrooms were stacked vertically, the "aspirated chimney" was introduced. Smoke from the boilers was led horizontally through pipes in the basement and then up smoke stacks at the center of the chimneys. Channels for vitiated air surrounded the hot smoke pipe, causing the velocity of the upwards air movement to increase.

HOT AND COLD

The Building Committee had specified that "the fresh air should be supplied both hot and cold, and each class-room be provided with means of mixing it" (Proceedings, 1878). The reasoning behind this design criterion becomes clear in light of how classrooms were scheduled.

On a cold winter morning, the room had to be heated before the students arrived. Early morning classes frequently required gas lighting, which introduced additional heat and combustion to the space. Phipson's design provided for classrooms typically heated to 53° F at the beginning of a winter morning class, arguing that it was detrimental to the students' health if the difference between outside and inside air temperature exceeded 20–25° F. Then, as the classroom filled up with up to three hundred students, a

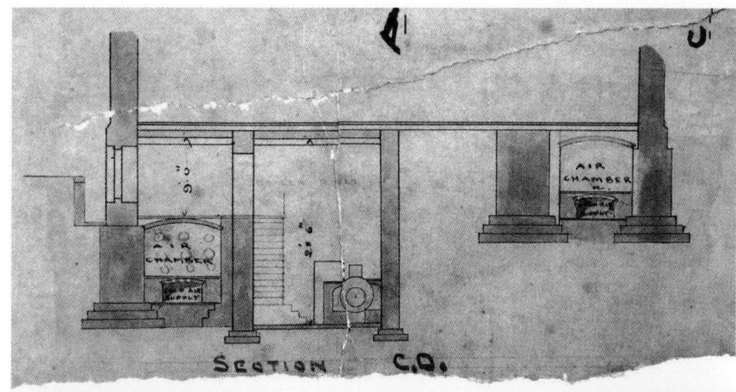

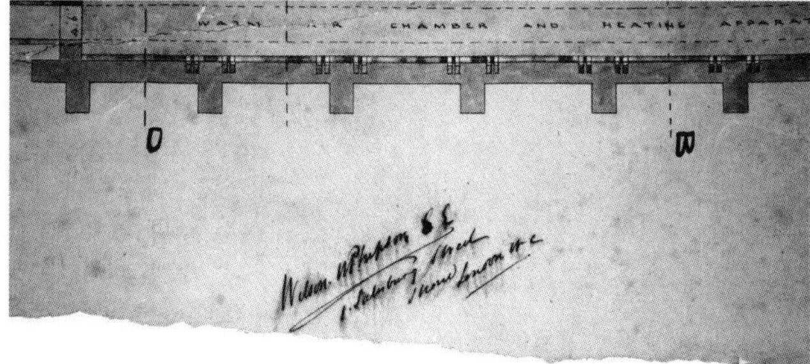

9.6 Phipson's signed drawings showing details of ventilation arrangements

considerable amount of heat was added to the space by warm bodies and hot gas lamps. Now, as the ventilation requirement increased, large quantities of fresh air were needed. This air, however, was often still warm because there is a considerable thermal lag in a system where the air passes through channels embedded in the masonry structures of basements and walls.

As seen in Figure 9.6, Phipson arranged for dual hot and cold air channels to be built at the basement level. The mixing of hot and cold air could take place here, but since two or three classrooms were stacked above, it was not always possible to regulate the temperature for each room individually. Densely populated classrooms, therefore, could quickly become too hot. At the time, an indoor air temperature between 60 and 65°F (15–18°C) was considered comfortable, while the hot air supplied typically reached 90–109°F (32–43°C) (Proceedings, 1878).

SMOKE IN THE CLASSROOM

Phipson's presentation of his paper at the annual conference of the Institution of Civil Engineers was followed by lengthy discussions, which continued over three days. One of the participants in the discussion was James Thomson, Lord Kelvin's older brother. After his studies, James had been a practicing engineer before he became a tenured Professor of Civil Engineering and Mechanics at the University of Glasgow in 1873, following in the footsteps of William Rankine. Since he had arrived at Gilmorehill after the construction was completed, he was not invested in the design.

The Building Committee had specified that air was to be supplied high, near the ceiling and extracted low, preferably under the students' seats. But James Thomson pointed out that the supply air openings typically were placed "half-way up the walls," since openings for the extract of combustion exhaust from the gas lamps had to be added near the ceiling. This change in the design turned out to alter the patterns of air movement and air distribution significantly. Professor Thomson illustrated this phenomenon by referring to an experiment he had conducted:

> In several of the classrooms the hot ventilation air comes in by openings about half-way up the walls and goes away in great part by passing clear over the heads of the occupants to wall-head outlets, without ever coming down for the use of the occupants, the cooler air tending to stagnate around them in the lower half of the room.

Professor Thomson went on to say that if 750 cubic feet of air were delivered, per hour and per sitting, as indicated by Phipson, professors and students would not make the complaints they did of deficient and faulty ventilation. He continued to describe how he had produced smoke in a classroom by burning cotton waste and jute fibers in a pan held up above the lecture table:

> The smoke arranged itself as to form a well-marked thin stratum, which remained persistently at the level of the inlet orifices for the warm air, and the result was obvious, that the warm ventilation air was floating like a canopy over the region to be occupied by the students and professor, and passing away by the wall-head outlets, while the original cold air remained stagnant in the lower part of the room.

When the wall-top outlets were closed, the smoke would descend slowly, allowing for an air exchange rate of well below 1 ACH, which was not satisfactory.

THE MUSEUM AND THE LIBRARY

Mr. Imray followed up on Professor Thomson's remarks and pointed out what to him was obvious, that the plumes of warmer air rising from the bodies and the gas lamps created an upwards movement in the space. The natural system of distribution of air in a space, therefore, was to supply fresh air low and place the outlets high, contrary to the principle applied, not successfully, by Phipson. Imray had extensive knowledge of the dynamics of air, having worked with Dr. Reid on many projects 30 years earlier.

Another problem associated with combining heating and ventilation in one centralized system was clearly demonstrated

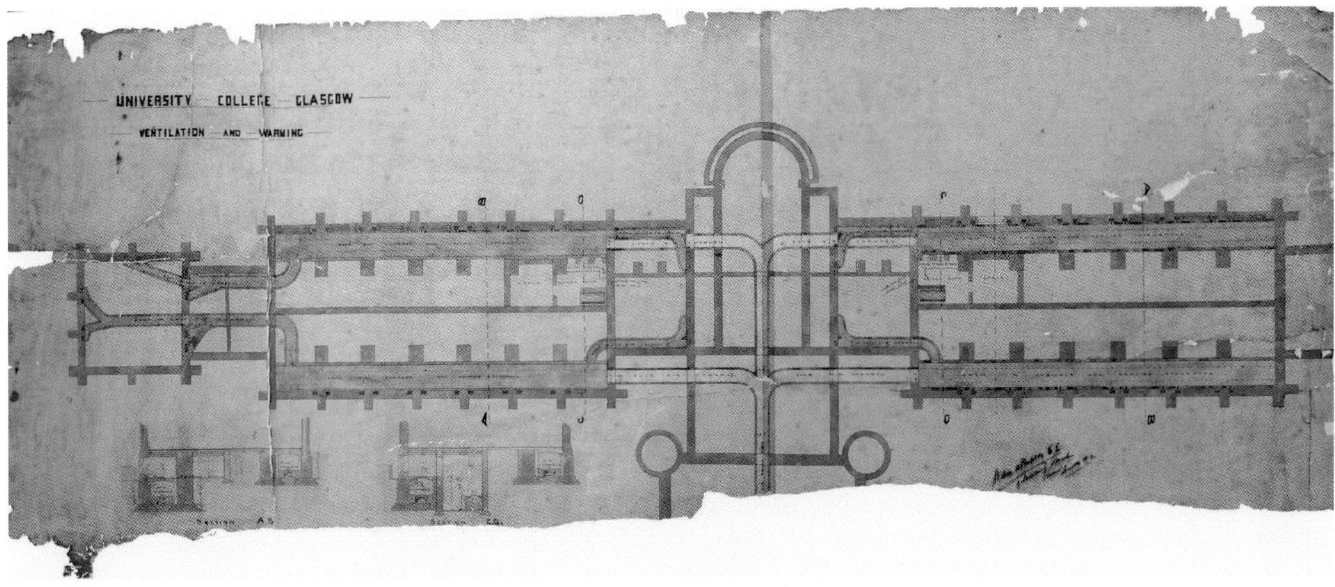

9.7 W. W. Phipson: University College Glasgow, ventilation and warming

in the museum and the library. Since there was no provisions for recirculating the air, large quantities of hot and dry air had to be introduced to warm high volume spaces, even at times when there was practically no requirement for ventilation. The museum and library spaces, therefore, were severely over-ventilated, which led to complaints about the dryness of air and dust.

Phipson acknowledged this problem at the conference in 1878 and suggested that low occupancy spaces, such as a museum or library, should be treated differently from high occupancy classrooms and assembly halls. In this regard, he seemed to be in agreement with the engineers in attendance who had proposed that heating specifically tailored to individual rooms should be provided by the high pressure hot water Perkins system.

THE LEGACY

After collaborating with Sir George Gilbert Scott at the Glasgow University project, Phipson moved on to work with other well-known architects, such as Alfred Waterhouse (see Chapter 11), where hybrid systems were developed with emphasis on the diverse heating and ventilation requirements of spaces with varying functional characteristics.

A detailed plan diagram obtained from the University of Glasgow archives (not dated) suggests that a "re-organization of warming arrangements" were proposed after some years had passed. A new blower powered by an electric motor was to be installed at the base of the ventilation tower, with filters on two sides, each serving to clean the air from two fresh air passages

9.8 Vaults supporting the Bute Hall

built into the central tower. Hot water pipes were proposed, circulating between the boilers and the classrooms, using the underground fresh air tunnels as raceways. New radiators were proposed, placed under windows in the classrooms, which would warm the rooms without introducing large quantities of hot air when ventilation was not called for. Fresh air was supplied directly to the Bute Hall through two vertical channels, with warming coils installed at the outlets in the space itself.

On August 20, 1872, *The Times* reported that "Her Majesty has been pleased to confer the honour of knighthood on Mr. George Gilbert Scott."

He was chosen an Associate of the Royal Academy in 1852, and admitted to his full honours of that body in 1860. Mr. George Gilbert Scott is the author of several professional works of high merit, including A Plea for the Faithful Restoration of our Ancient Churches, and a book on Secular Domestic Architecture. It is, however, in his capacity of architect of the National Memorial to the late Prince Consort in Hyde Park that the honour of knighthood has just now been conferred upon him.

(*The Times*, August 20, 1872)

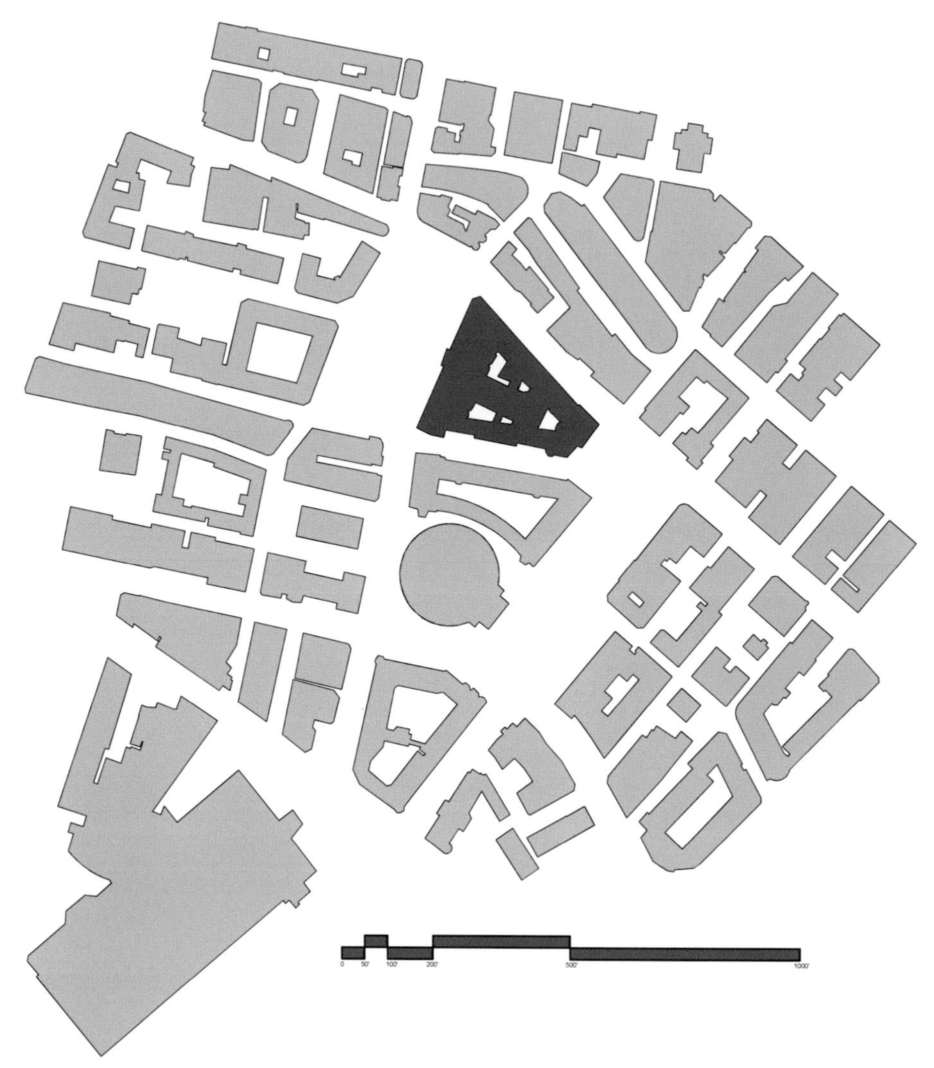

53°N

10

Manchester Town Hall

LOCATION: ALBERT SQUARE, MANCHESTER, UK

BUILT: 1876

ARCHITECT: ALFRED WATERHOUSE

ENGINEER: HADEN & SON

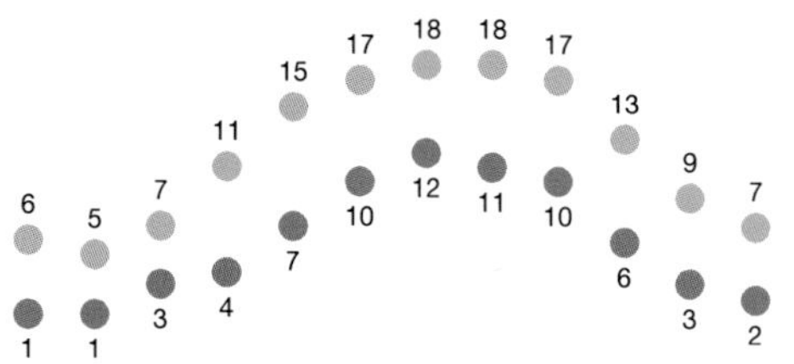

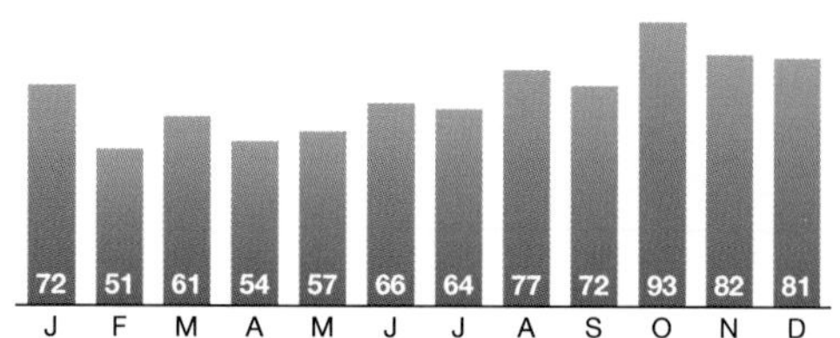

10.1 Manchester Town Hall, façade on Albert Square

ALBERT SQUARE

> Manchester and Salford, with half a million of inhabitants, lie in a plain of almost unbroken surface, the ground sloping upward from almost all the outskirts, but so gently that the city cannot well be seen from any eminence through an atmosphere thick with smoke.
>
> (*The Times*, 1875)

The original Manchester Town Hall stood on King Street. It had served the people of Manchester since 1825, when the town was governed by Police Commissioners. After the town was awarded city status in 1853, the services administered by the City Corporation grew, along with the economic development of Manchester. Soon the city was operating gas works, maintaining streets and sanitary sewers, and offering services for health and public safety.

When a decision was made to show off Manchester's civic dignity with a new town hall building, the desire was not only to build a new Great Hall accompanied by state rooms for the city council and its committees, but indeed to provide space for a multitude of administrative departments.

A site near the Infirmary was first considered for the new town hall, but the final decision fell on an open patch of land in the city center, used as a municipal depot. While the location adjacent to the newly constructed Albert Square was advantageous, the size and shape of the triangular site represented a challenge, considering the many functions and the amount of floor to be accommodated by the design.

THE COMPETITION

The significance and complexity of the task at hand led the city to launch a competition for the architectural design of the new Manchester Town Hall. Two prominent architects, Mr. G. E. Street, R. A., RIBA Fellow, and Professor Donaldson, Past President of the RIBA, were consulted to help organize the competition and to judge the entries to be submitted.

As the first stage of the competition attracted 136 entries, Street and Donaldson traveled to Manchester to begin their work as referees. They established a set of criteria which not only addressed the artistic qualities of the design, but also included evaluation of the practical aspects as well as choice of materials, methods of construction and cost. Their first report was submitted to the city corporation with a short list of the ten best projects. When the names of the architects were revealed, the referees found that two of the competitors had submitted more than one project. It was therefore decided to invite eight architects to enter the second stage of the competition.

Alfred Waterhouse loved the challenge of fitting a complex program onto a challenging site. He had competed with G. E. Street for the commission to design the law courts in London (1867) and lost. The popular opinion of him was as an architect who favored practicality over form. And it was because he scored highest on the requirements for "general arrangements and convenience, simplicity of plan and facilities of access, light, ventilation, and cost" that his Manchester Town Hall competition entry was ranked as number one.

Judged under the head of "excellence of elevation," however, he came in fourth behind Speakman and Charlesworth, J. O. Scott, and Worthington (Waterhouse, 1876). Not without protests, the Corporation appointed Alfred Waterhouse as the architect upon the recommendation of the two competition referees.

DESIGN DEVELOPMENT

In their second report to the Corporation, which was kept secret because they had been challenged to critique in writing the other second stage projects, Street and Donaldson also pointed out weaknesses with Waterhouse's submission. One strong objection was the simple treatment of the façades of the inner courtyards, which were rendered plain, almost without architectural features. Since the single-loaded corridors, 750 feet in length on each floor, were facing the courtyards, the interior façades would be in public view.

Waterhouse responded that his design decisions were based on limitations of the allotted budget. When the Corporation

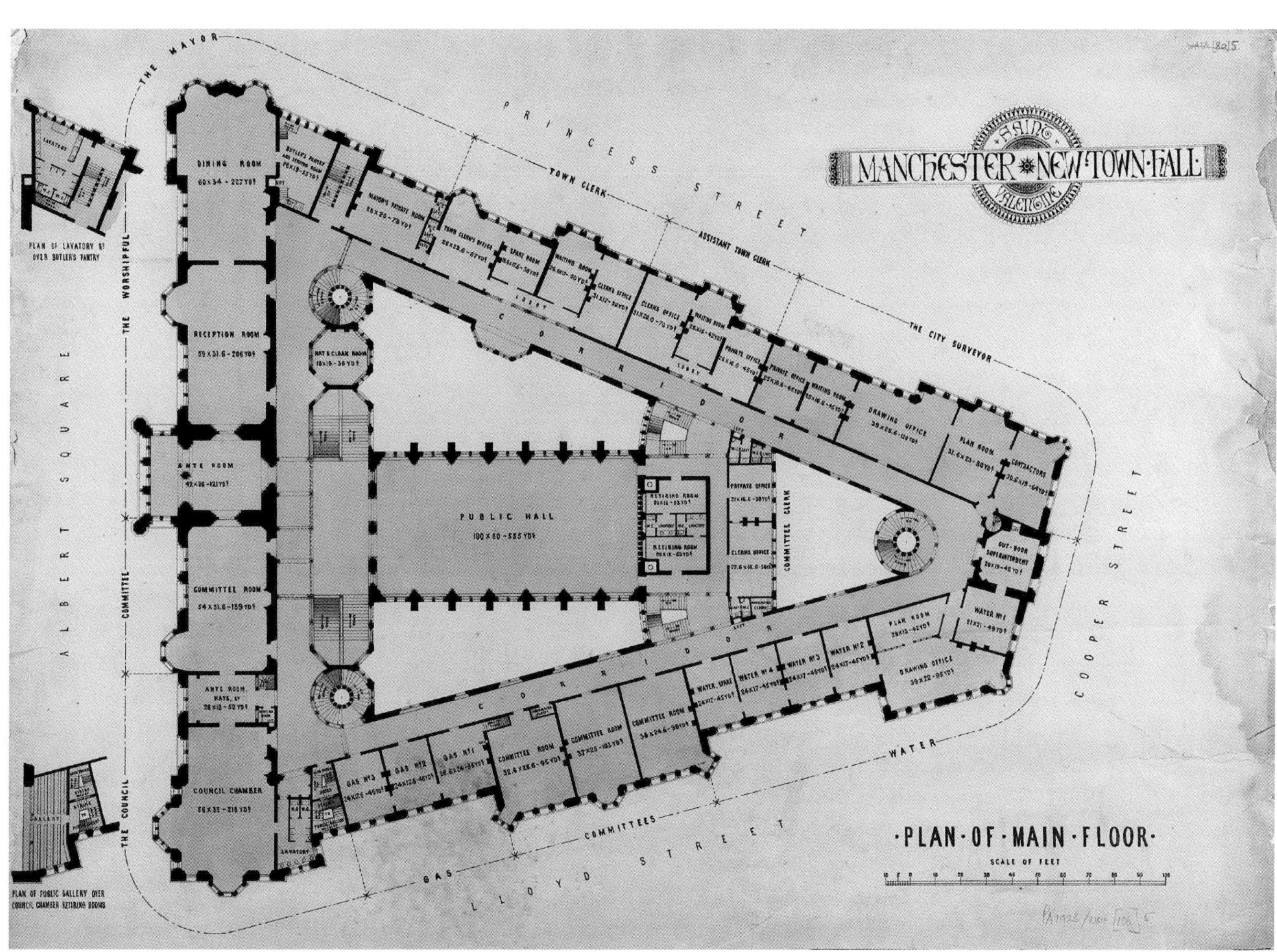

10.2 Alfred Waterhouse: Competition Design, plan of the main floor

agreed to spend additional funds, he redesigned the inner façades, including bay windows and panels of light colored, almost white, glazed tile to reflect the daylight.

Along the west side facing Albert Square, he placed the main entrance, the lobby and reception spaces, with state rooms for the city council and committee meetings on the first floor above. A 286-ft-tall bell tower stands symmetrically in the middle of the Albert Square elevation, with corner pavilions projecting one floor above the general height of the building (see Figure 10.1).

In his description of the tower, Waterhouse pointed to a passageway around the tower, 178 feet from the ground, "from whence half of South Lancashire can be seen on a Sunday morning early."

The asymmetrical shape of the triangular site led the architect to shift the axis of the Great Hall sideways from the axis of the main entrance. He then designed the grand staircase as an antechamber facilitating the shift.

Three circular stairwells with spiral staircases were introduced, one at each corner of the triangle. Along with two aspirated chimneys connected to the boiler house, these three stairwells were assigned dual functions, not only for the circulation of people, but also as conduits for the movement of air.

COURTYARDS

When Waterhouse described the views from the passageway around the central tower "on a Sunday morning early," he alluded to the fact that on any other day, even the tallest tower in Manchester would not reach above the polluted and smoke-saturated air. This may have influenced the decision not to use any of the towers for air supply. Instead, the air in the courtyards was perceived as somewhat cleaner than the air in the city streets. In addition to serving as light shafts, the courtyards therefore were also used to supply fresh air to the building. Defined by the building, controlled by gates and constructed with well-drained paved surfaces, the courtyards could be kept clean and free of the filth of a nineteenth-century city street.

Waterhouse had introduced bay windows to break up the straight single-loaded corridors and to provide incentives for informal conversation. Hot-water coils were located under oak benches in the bays and fresh air supplied through apertures in the thickness of the floor construction.

Exit doors from the three circular stairwells open up into the courtyards. At these locations, fresh air could be supplied to the bottom of the stairs, connecting with all office floors above.

The police department was located on two floors (the ground floor and the basement), tucked in under the Great Hall, at the east end of which one finds a coal storage room and the heating plant with three hot water boilers.

10.3 Manchester Town Hall, view of courtyard

10.4 Manchester Town Hall, view of the roof, with main clock tower and aspirated chimneys

WARMING APPARATUS BY MESSRS HADEN & SON

The entire building is warmed by a central hot water system designed and installed by Messrs Haden and Son. Thousands of feet of large-diameter hot water pipes were installed for this purpose, integrated into floor cavities, behind grilles, below windows and under bay window benches. To secure a means of additional heat, and for thermal and psychological comfort, this central system of warming was complemented by radiant heat from large open fireplaces in committee rooms and offices. Tall, circular radiators were installed at the base of the three spiral staircases.

A hybrid warming system combining the advantages of central hot water heat distribution with the tradition and well-known technology of the open fireplace offered relative simplicity of design and installation while having the ability to handle diverse demands represented by a complex building program. Adjusting to diurnal, weekly and seasonal schedules, heat could be supplied in a controlled manner responding to the demands of each individual space. As a general rule, all occupied spaces were warmed and ventilated, including the corridors, lobby areas and staircases.

ASPIRATED CHIMNEYS

The two tall ventilating shafts framing the central tower in Figure 10.4 were built as "aspirated chimneys," designed to carry smoke and air exhaust, as explained by Waterhouse:

> For the warming of the building, three hot-water boilers (one always being kept as reserve) are placed in a large sub-basement. The smoke from the furnaces passes through two wrought iron tubes placed within ventilating shafts, with an intervening air-space for the extraction of vitiated air.
>
> (Waterhouse, 1876)

Since the ventilation system at the Manchester Town Hall is based on the principle of pulling out vitiated air by the motive power of heat rather than pushing in fresh air by the employment of fans, it was necessary to ensure that there was enough power in the system all year round.

In a natural ventilation system of this kind, the temperature differential between indoor and ambient air, in addition to the

10.5 Manchester Town Hall, view of spiral staircase, looking up

difference in height between inlet and outlet, plays a major role in keeping the air moving. Therefore, as long as the boilers were in operation, they would boost the force of ventilation. As the demand for hot water decreased, however, the system still relied on the height difference as the constant factor in the equation. By making the ventilating chimneys reach well above the rooftops, they would keep pulling air through the building even on warm summer days, while preventing smoke and vitiated air from reaching the fresh air inlets.

The main purpose of the ventilating towers were to pull vitiated air from the Great Hall, but they could also be used to ventilate the corridors. This could have led to difficulties associated with the "retiring" rooms. By pulling air from the corridors, foul air and odors from the restrooms could be drawn in through the restrooms and into the corridors. This hypothesis provides the most likely explanation for the two metal ventilation shafts seen in Figure 10.4. Based on the characteristics of their material choice and fabrication method, they were probably installed several years after the building was completed.

SPIRAL STAIRCASES

The three circular staircases can be identified by the choice of colored stone:

> [T]hat at the Princess Street entrance being of the coffee coloured Shap granite, both shaft and steps, that at the Lloyd Street entrance, of dark grey from the North of Ireland, and that at the Cooper Street end of light grey Dalbeattie.
>
> (Waterhouse, 1876)

The architect and the engineers were well versed in the principles of thermodynamics. Realizing that tall stairwells would tend to promote upwards air movements, they used this principle actively and decided to make the stairwells function as vertical distribution channels for heat and fresh air.

The circular void at the center of the stairs seen in Figure 10.5 served two functions: the design facilitated vertical air movement but also allowed the treads of the stairs to be at least 11 inches deep for comfort and functionality, avoiding a problem commonly associated with shallow threads in spiral staircases.

The powerful radiators at the base of the stairs were complemented by lanterns at the top. Operable clerestory windows were installed around the perimeter of the lanterns. This arrangement made it possible to operate these warming and ventilating shafts in two modes, responding to seasonal variations.

MOVING PEOPLE AND AIR

The configuration of combined stairwells and ventilation shafts communicating with the corridors is illustrated in Figure 10.6, in which arrows showing air movement are overlaid on a longitudinal section by Waterhouse. The corridors communicated with the offices and committee rooms via open doors, supplemented by operable, louvered transom windows above the doors.

While people move up and down the stairs, the movement of air is always upwards. The movement of air between the rooms and the corridor, however, could go both ways.

In the winter, when the fireplaces were in operation and the central hot water system was active, warmed fresh air was supplied up the stairwells, warming the corridors and supplying the rooms with ventilation, as needed. Vitiated air would be pulled out of the rooms through the fireplace chimneys and through ventilation channels built into the masonry walls by way of perforated soffits.

In the summer, when the fireplaces and hot water systems were inactive, fresh air would come in through operable windows. By closing the air inlets at the base of the stairwells and opening up the clerestory windows around the lanterns, the upwards moving air in the stairwells would now pull vitiated air out of the rooms via the corridors.

This ingenious but simple design allowed the stairwells to supply preconditioned fresh air during the heating season and could be switched into air exhaust mode when heating was not called for.

THE GREAT HALL

Measuring 100 feet in length by 50 feet in width and 58 feet from the floor to the apex, the Great Hall, which has also been named the "central hall," the "public hall" or the "banqueting room," is of modest proportions compared to other contemporary public assembly halls, such as St George's Hall in Liverpool (see Chapter 7). It is, however, one of the most beautiful and beloved public spaces in Manchester.

Tall windows on both sides of the hall, elevated 12 feet from the floor, allow abundant daylight to enter the hall. Below the windows, but above an oak dado, 4 ft. 6 in. high, Waterhouse reserved space for a series of 12 pictures, illustrating the history of Manchester. His intention was that "these pictures, besides adding enormously to the interest of the hall, will act as ballast to the color of the ceiling above" (Waterhouse, 1876). The panels were completed by Ford Madox Brown in the early 1880s, painting directly onto the wall surfaces after heating and drying them, and then applying a varnish of wax for durability and ease of cleaning.

It was behind these panels that the warming and ventilation system for the hall was installed. Warm air was supplied through slats in the window sills, thus counteracting the downdraft from the single pane windows. The air was warmed by hot water coils installed in wall cavities behind the decorative panels.

But where did the fresh air enter the hall, and how was the vitiated air pulled out?

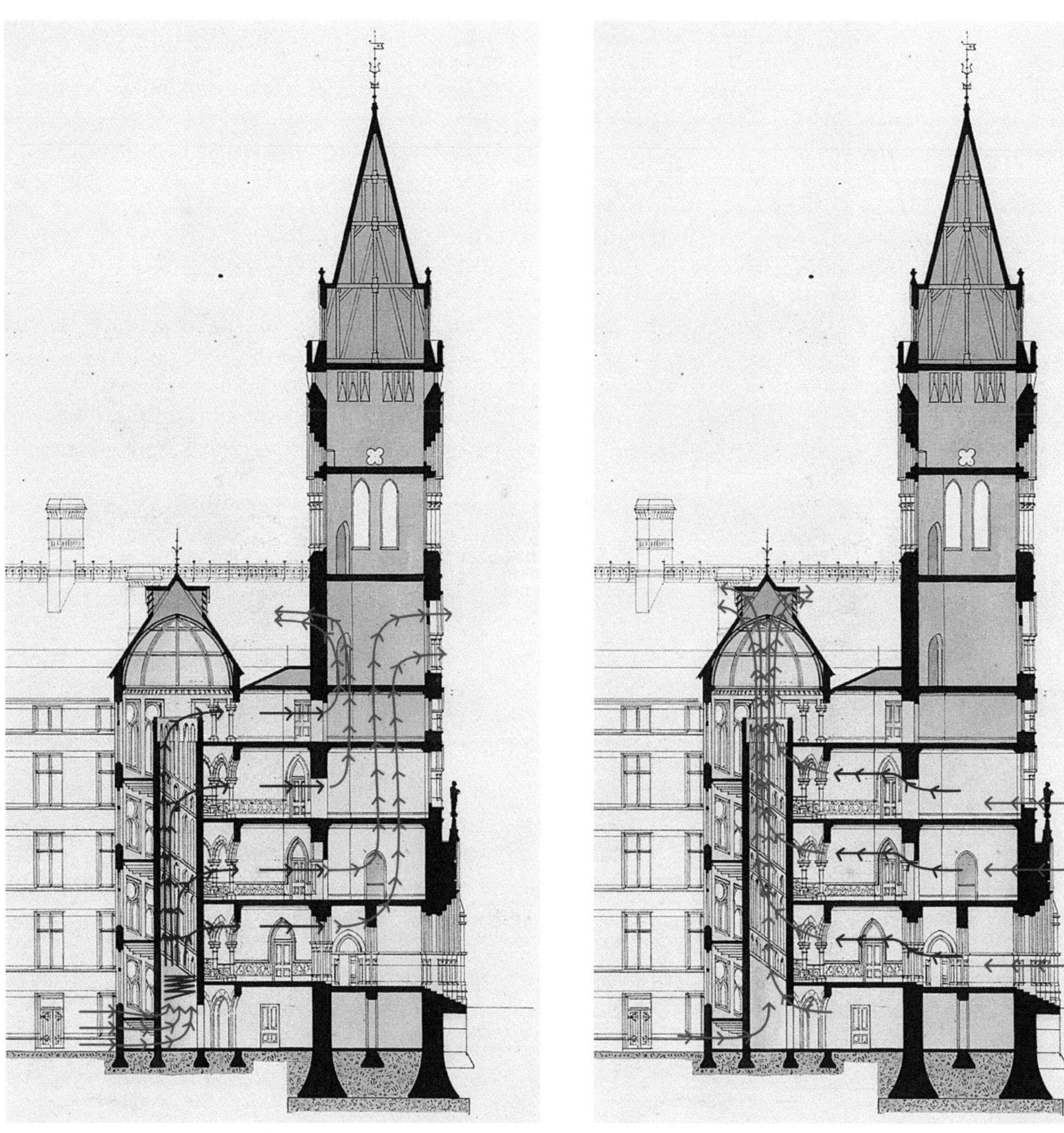

10.6 Diagram based on a longitudinal section drawing from the second competition design by Alfred Waterhouse

10.7 Manchester Town Hall, view of the Great Hall ceiling, with ventilation openings near exterior walls

VENTILATING STARS AND HUNGRY BEASTS

Figure 10.7, looking up at the vaulted ceiling of the Great Hall, exemplifies Waterhouse's mastery of the integration of structural systems, ventilation and decorative art in his architecture. The decorative panels pay tribute to cities in the United Kingdom and to countries of the world tied to Manchester through trade, as suppliers of raw materials or consumers of manufactured goods.

In his presentation at the meeting of the Royal Institute of British Architects in 1876, Waterhouse explains the roof construction in great detail. He continues:

> Below the more strictly constructional framing of the roof are massive curved and moulded ribs, the lower curve springing from the head of the clustered wall shafts; the upper one from the hammer beams, which terminate in grotesque heads, through the mouths of which pass iron tie-rods. The arches unite the principals together, the horizontal space between them and the walls being pierced with stars for the exit of vitiated air throughout the roof to the ventilation towers.

The arrangement of star-shaped openings for ventilation is so perfectly integrated that most visitors to the hall will not be aware of them. But if you happen to look up, what you see is a detail as carefully thought out as any other architectural element in the building.

ROSES BREATHING FRESH AIR

In his RIBA address, Waterhouse did not specifically explain how fresh air enters the hot water apparatus below the side windows of the Great Hall. This appeared to be an unsolved mystery until

10.8 Manchester Town Hall, view of courtyard, with air intake grilles concealed as rose windows

the author examined the building along with Neil Sturrock, Andy Haymes and Keith Roper in 2012. As we were looking at one of the exterior walls of the great hall facing the courtyard, the building revealed its secret.

The windows serving the floor below the Great Hall, occupied by the police department, extend above the floor line of the hall. What seem to be rose windows of the kind seen in the windows above, could not be windows since they were positioned above the ceiling of the police department offices. Upon closer examination, the "roses" were found not to be designed to let in light, but as nostrils breathing in fresh air (Figure 10.8).

The building does not actively advertise its mechanical systems, it just works, invisibly.

GLASS

When selecting glass for windows and skylights at Manchester Town Hall, Waterhouse used stained glass with utter care. Since a nineteenth-century factory town in a climate dominated with overcast skies experienced many days of dull light, emphasis should be placed on bringing as much daylight as possible into the interiors. Grey days, however, can be livened up by adding color, so Waterhouse decided to fill the windows "with white glass tenderly relieved by subdued color" (Waterhouse, 1876).

After Waterhouse had presented his paper at the RIBA meeting, he was asked by the President if "Mr. Waterhouse has been aided in his arduous task by the refined taste of a lady." This question is remarkable, since the official role of women in the world of nineteenth-century architecture was practically non-existent. It is therefore with interest one reads how the architect responded. Was he being modest and humble, or did he find a polite and culturally proper way to take all the credit for himself?

Waterhouse replied:

> With regard to the ornamental glazing, I may say, that though I am indebted for many things to the taste of my lady friends, they had nothing to do with the glazing, or it would doubtless have been much more satisfactory than it is.
>
> (ibid.)

STONE

From the Albert Square façade (Figure 10.1), the form of the town hall is seemingly very long and thin. It is when viewed from the Cooper Street end of the triangle, however, that the mass of the building becomes apparent. Waterhouse explains that what appears to be a stone building is essentially a brick building clad in Sprinkwell, a coal measure stone from quarries near Bradford, Yorkshire.

After having applied a multi-colored scheme to the Manchester Assize Courts, Waterhouse found that "all traces of color were obliterated in about three years after they were finished." This led him to apply a mostly monochrome material selection for the Town Hall. He was well aware of the "evil influences of the peculiar climate of Manchester," and made his material choices wisely.

In order to get the stone to bond in a satisfactory manner with the brickwork behind it, every horizontal bed of Sprinkwell coincides with a joint in the brickwork. The ashlar was set with alternate courses of 3, 6 or 9 inches in height.

The roofs are covered with dark gray slates from local quarries, relieved by patterns of light gray slates from the Lake District. The palette of stone on interior surfaces include White Rock, Bath, the blue Forest of Dean, grey Dalbeattie, gray Irish, salmon colored Rose of Mull and Peterhead, and red Inverness.

The corridors and halls are paved in marble mosaic, some with simple geometric patterns and borders in black and white, others with "mischiato die tutti colori," all laid by Venetian workmen (Figure 10.9).

10.9 Manchester Town Hall, view of corridor

MODERN MEDIEVAL

In their praise of the completed building, the referees of the competition, Street and Donaldson, expressed their admiration not only for the exterior as seen from the surrounding streets, but also for the design and arrangement of the inner courtyards, the corridors and the spiral staircases, which Street said was "the most charming part of the building" (Waterhouse, 1876).

Professor Donaldson congratulated Mr. Waterhouse "as a gothic architect – medieval architect, I should say," to which Waterhouse replied:

> I understood him to speak of Medieval architecture, as if that term described my building. Now, I hope when he sees the Manchester Town Hall completed, he will find the building essentially of the nineteenth century, and adapted to the wants of the present day.

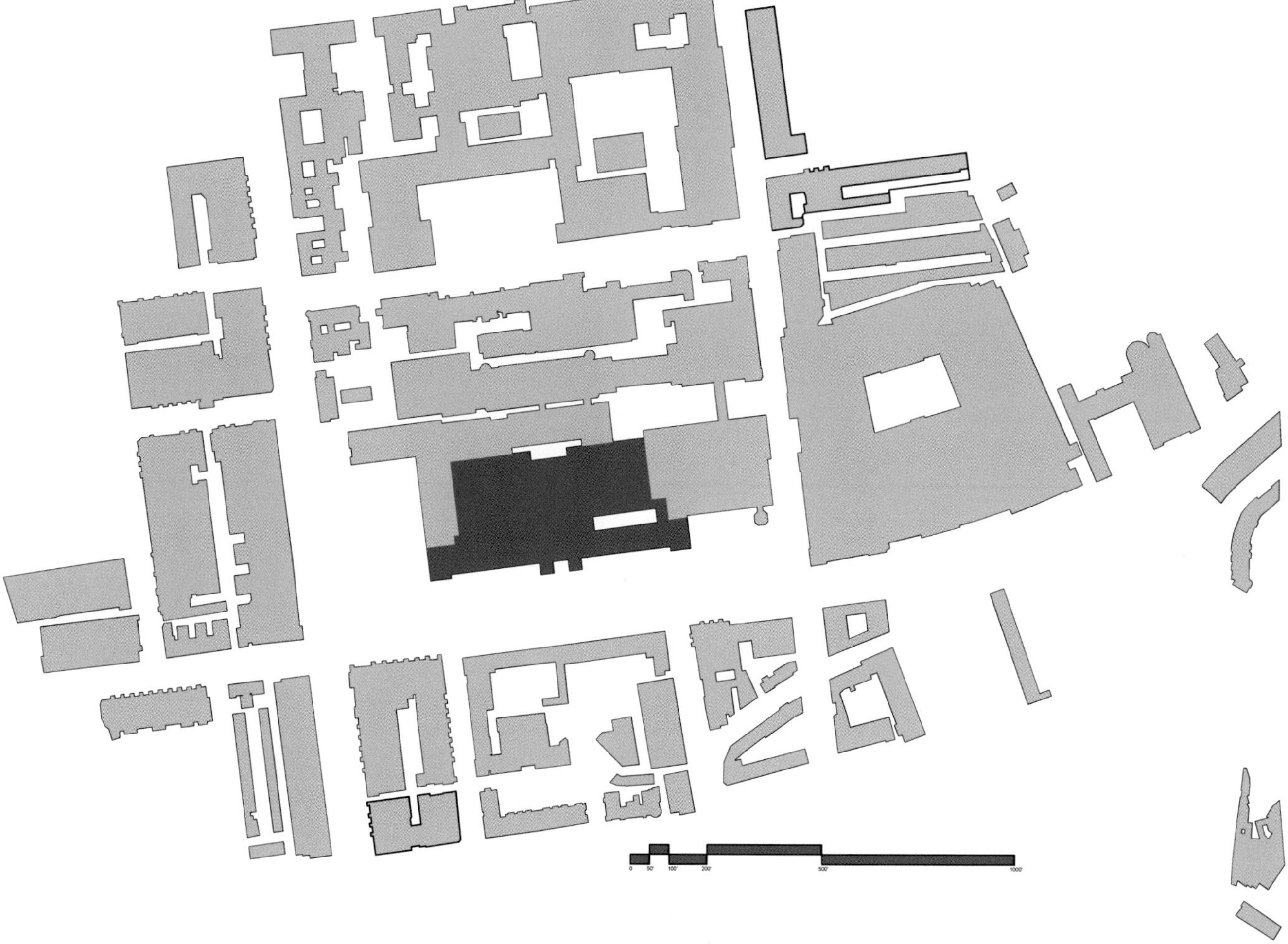

11

The Natural History Museum

LOCATION: CROMWELL ROAD, SOUTH KENSINGTON, LONDON

BUILT: 1881

ARCHITECT: ALFRED WATERHOUSE

WARMING AND VENTILATION ENGINEER: WILSON W. PHIPSON

52°N

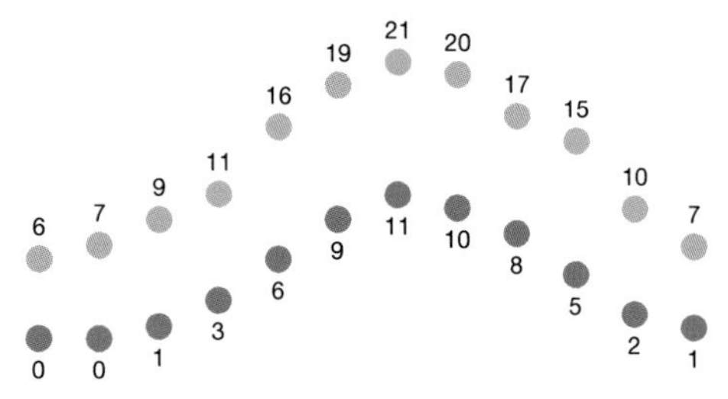

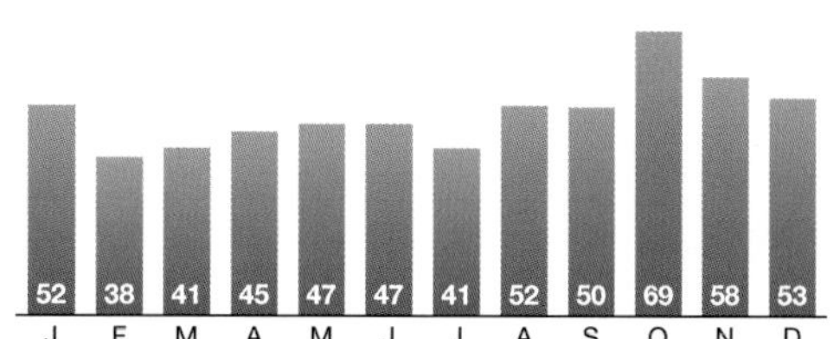

11.1 Natural History Museum, south façade with main entry

The International Exhibition of 1862 occupied a large site reaching from the Horticultural Gardens to Cromwell Road. After the Exhibition was over, an idea was floated that a portion of the Exhibition buildings could with advantage be converted into a museum of natural history. This idea, however, was abandoned when Parliament decided against preservation of any part of the buildings. They were accordingly entirely removed (*The Times*, 1881).

On approach to the Natural History Museum as it stands today, one is struck by how much lower the site is from the road. At the front of the building, along Cromwell Road, there is a considerable difference in height from the road to the grounds, enough to tuck in a basement with full height windows on the south side. To prepare for the International Exhibition, the entire site between the three roads had been excavated. The southern end of the site was set aside for the new museum of natural history, but no funding was set aside to fill it back in.

EXECUTING CAPTAIN FOWKE'S DESIGN

Captain Fowke (1823–1865), an engineer, an architect and a captain in the Corps of Royal Engineers, had been in charge of planning the International Exhibition. When it was decided to demolish the Exhibition buildings and a competition was held for the new museum of natural history, Fowke won the competition with a design for a building in the Renaissance style. After Fowke's sudden death in 1865 from a burst blood vessel, Alfred Waterhouse was appointed to carry on his work on the design for the new Natural History Museum.

Known for his knowledge-driven, practical approach to architectural design, and for his ability to successfully carry out large public projects, Alfred Waterhouse was found to be the right man to develop a project that had already been accepted as a preliminary design. It soon became evident, however, that Waterhouse would deviate from Fowke's style, a decision that did not go down well with the connoisseurs of the time. In 1871, the editor of *The Times* criticized Waterhouse's new design, "which will be Gothic, and thus, it is feared, a violent and dangerous contrast to the South Kensington buildings – a contrast which Captain Fowke had carefully avoided" (*The Times*, 1871).

Ten years later, at the opening of the new museum, Waterhouse indirectly responded to the criticism. As always, his argument is cool and factual:

> In designing the present building, Captain Fowke's original idea of employing terra-cotta was always kept in view, though the blocks were reduced in size so as to obviate, as far as possible, the objection to the employment of this material arising from its liability to twist in burning. For this and other reasons the architect abandoned the idea of a Renaissance building, and fell back on an earlier Romanesque style, which prevailed largely in Lombardy and through Rhineland from the tenth to the end of the twelfth century.
>
> (*The Times*, 1881)

He does not reveal, however, what the other reasons were that he alluded to.

BEASTS AND STUFFED ANIMALS

Later that same year, after the completion of the Natural History Museum, the government asked Parliament to set aside funds for a new War Office and Admiralty. This project had been delayed, it was argued, because of the great expenditures the nation had taken upon itself to build the new Law Courts and the Natural History Museum, to which *The Times* commented:

> The excuse may be accepted for what it is worth; but it seems hardly creditable to the richest country in the world that the administration of its Army and Navy should suffer because new houses are being built for its lawyers and its stuffed animals. It is to be hoped that there will be no further delay.
>
> (*The Times*, 1881)

11.2 Natural History Museum, animal sculptures

The elaborate use of creatures of the animal kingdom as inspiration for the ornamentation of the Natural History Museum was also criticized. This was originally Mr. Owen's idea, an idea that Waterhouse made a reality, with great joy. And again, there are reasons for the architect's decisions. Waterhouse explains in the *British Architect* in 1887, that the larger animals on the exterior of the south-west gallery are the wolf, the panther and the lion: "Those on the south-east are the extinct Machairodus (or scimitar-toothed lion), the great Palætherium, and the Mylodon."

The ornamentation, therefore, is not only the innocent play of an artist, but also a means of creating a didactic building. One of the lions, now retired, was posing for my grand-daughter in his secret garden during a recent visit to the museum (Figure 11.2, right).

In 1878, when the building was still under construction, "M.D." wrote in *The Times* criticizing the "sink tubes" and the "fake gargoyles," suggesting that the water could run down pipes inside the pilasters. Waterhouse replied that the voids inside the pilasters are, in fact, ventilation pipes and that he never would let water run inside concealed channels in masonry structures. He explained that the downspouts, made of galvanized cast iron, will be "speedily relieved from their present obtrusiveness" with help from the London atmosphere. About the gargoyles, he writes: "There is a misapprehension here. The gargoyles have a real and useful connection with the gutters, and they would come into operation and give timely warning whenever the down-spouts become by accident choked" (*The Times*, 1878).

SEA CREATURES AND CLIMBING MONKEYS

> The museum is the largest, if not, indeed, the only, modern building in which terra-cotta has been exclusively used for external facades and interior wall-surfaces, including all the various decorations which this involves.
>
> (Waterhouse, in *The Times*, 1881)

The terracotta-clad building is in fact constructed with a structural frame of cast iron. Brick is used in some places as infill, in others as load-bearing walls. Since the structural frame had to be protected for fireproofing, the architect could justify the terracotta interiors as a means to avoid the use of combustible materials.

The columns in the main galleries along the south front of the building are built with a cast iron structural core, around which there is a layer of brick and mortar. The terracotta cladding illustrates life in the ocean (detail shown in Figure 11.3, left). The crust of the water is shown on a row of terracotta moldings two-thirds up the columns, above which plants are growing out of the water.

The climbing monkeys receive, sometimes hands on, the affection of thousands of visitors to the museum, as can be seen on the polished head of the monkey in the lower left corner of the photograph (Figure 11.3, right). Each prototype piece of terracotta was carefully designed by the architect. Thousands were pre-fabricated offsite by a manufacturer that ended up breaking its back performing a task never before undertaken. Thanks to

11.3 Natural History Museum, terracotta sea creatures and climbing monkeys

the employment of such immense power of artistic and industrial energies, millions of visitors have enjoyed the presence of the climbing monkeys.

UTILITY AND BEAUTY

As he built a growing architectural practice, Waterhouse acquired an essential skill. A successful architect knows how to defend his design decisions by attaching vital functions to design elements that otherwise could be seen as pure artistry. Not unlike today's architects facing challenges from "value engineering," Waterhouse was at one time during the design process asked by his client to reduce the height of the two towers framing the main entrance on the south façade. Waterhouse responded that the towers were designed to hold two large cisterns for water to be readily available to suppress the flames in case of a major fire. He won the support of the Fire Brigade for making the cisterns so large that the towers could not be reduced.

The two 200-ft-tall towers facing south (see Figure 11.1) were also assigned a ventilating function, drawing vitiated air from the south galleries. Likewise, Waterhouse explains that the towering 165-ft-tall pavilion towers were used to ventilate the workshops below.

The main ventilating towers, however, were the two north towers (seen to the left in Figure 11.4). These were designed to ventilate the "index gallery" (the central hall) and the galleries running parallel to and east and west of the central hall. These strictly utilitarian towers were also seen as important architectural design elements. They are included in a perspective by Waterhouse, showing smoke coming out of one of the chimneys.

11.4 Natural History Museum, view of the roof

WARMING AND VENTILATION

Two engineering firms competed for the design and installation of systems for warming and ventilating the Natural History Museum. Messrs Haden of Trowbridge proposed a hot water system. Haden, who had installed a well-functioning hot water system at the town hall in Manchester (see Chapter 10), had a good reputation and was respected by the architect. The other contender was Wilson W. Phipson, who had designed the system for the new Glasgow University campus at Gilmorehill (see Chapter 9). Phipson proposed to use steam pipes rather than hot water to distribute heat through the building.

There was a concern that steam boilers were not as safe as hot water boilers, but Waterhouse still recommended Phipson's system. Boiler design had improved greatly and the steam pipe distribution system was expected to be more economical since more energy could flow through smaller dimension pipes. Phipson's bid was also slightly lower than what Haden could offer.

An early basement plan signed by Waterhouse in 1868 (Figure 11.5) shows a system of fresh air supply tunnels running below the center of each of the north galleries and otherwise under corridors in the east, south and west wings of the building. Access to this large drawing, rolled up and archived at a RIBA "out-store," has been limited. Contrary to published descriptions of air intakes facing north (Cook and Hinchcliffe, 1995), this drawing shows fresh air intakes located on the south side of the building. The direction of the air supply tunnels outside the walls of the building suggests that the air could have been supplied from grilles built into the retaining walls at Cromwell Road and at the curving driveway

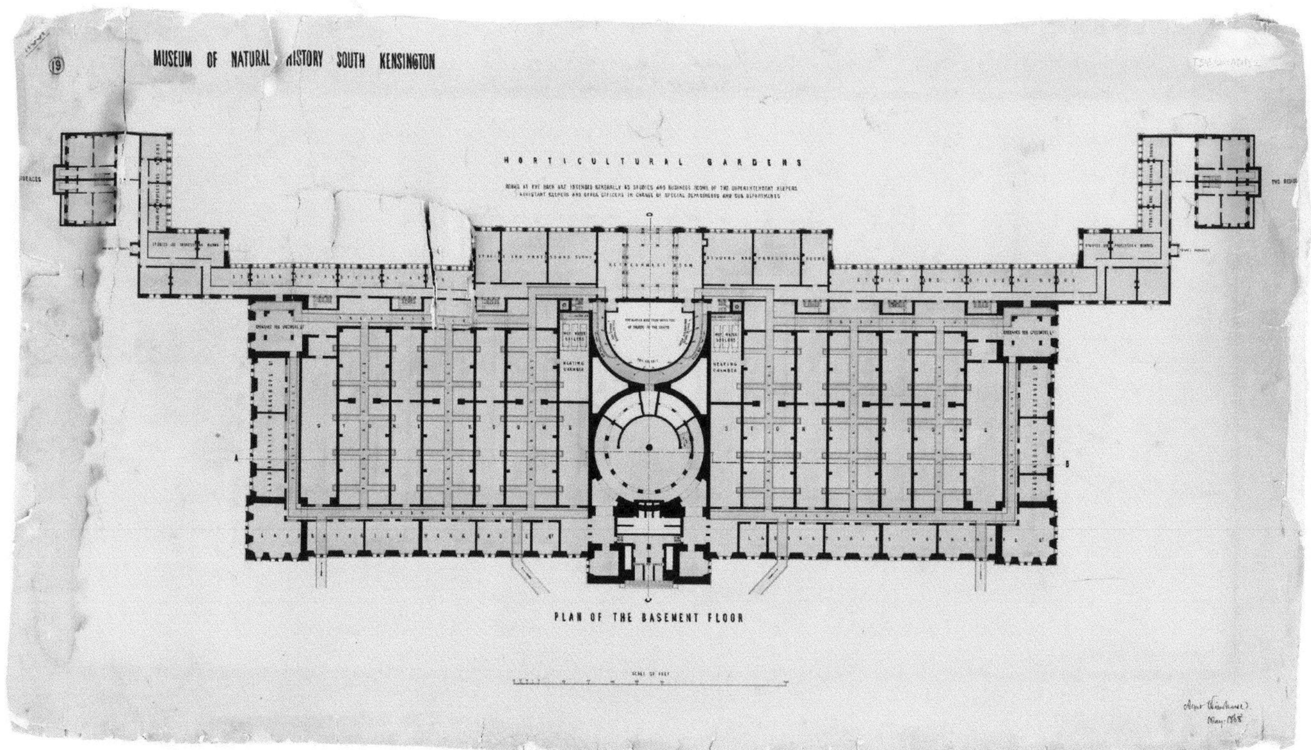

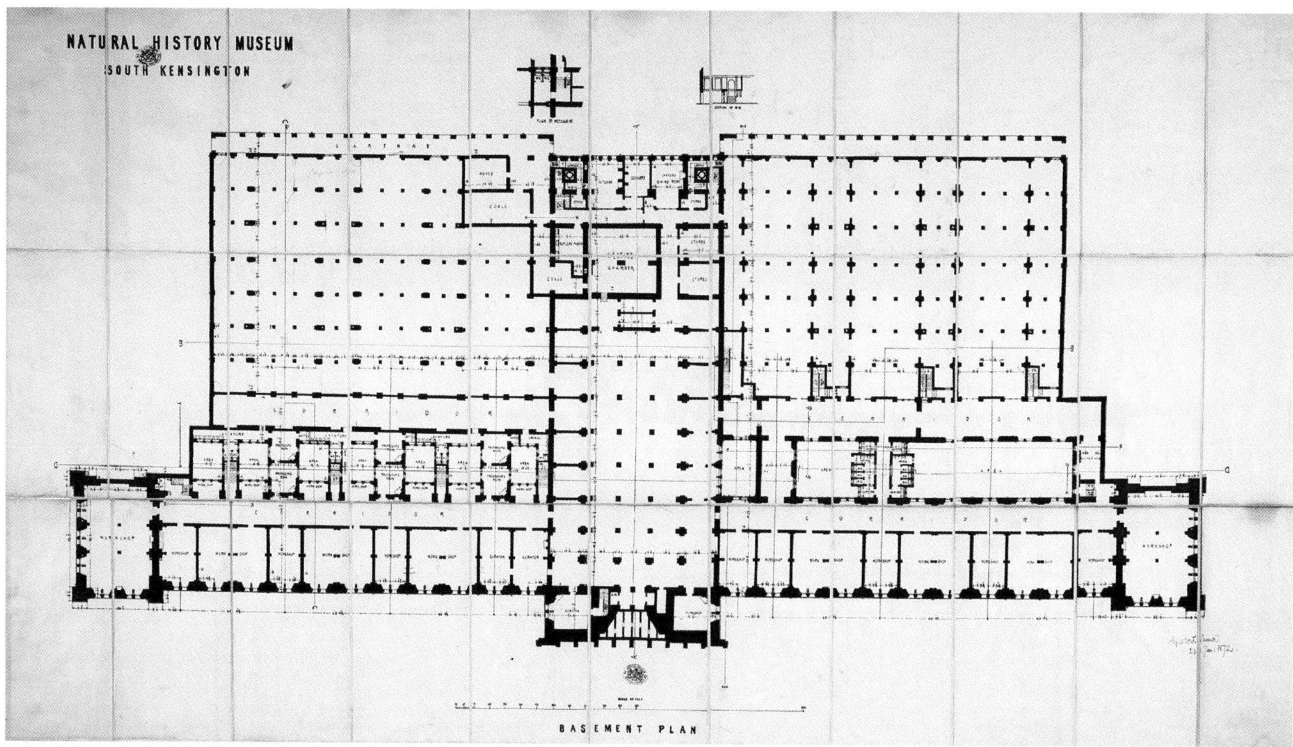

11.5 Alfred Waterhouse: Preliminary Basement Plan (top) and Basement Plan signed 24 Jan. 1872 (below)

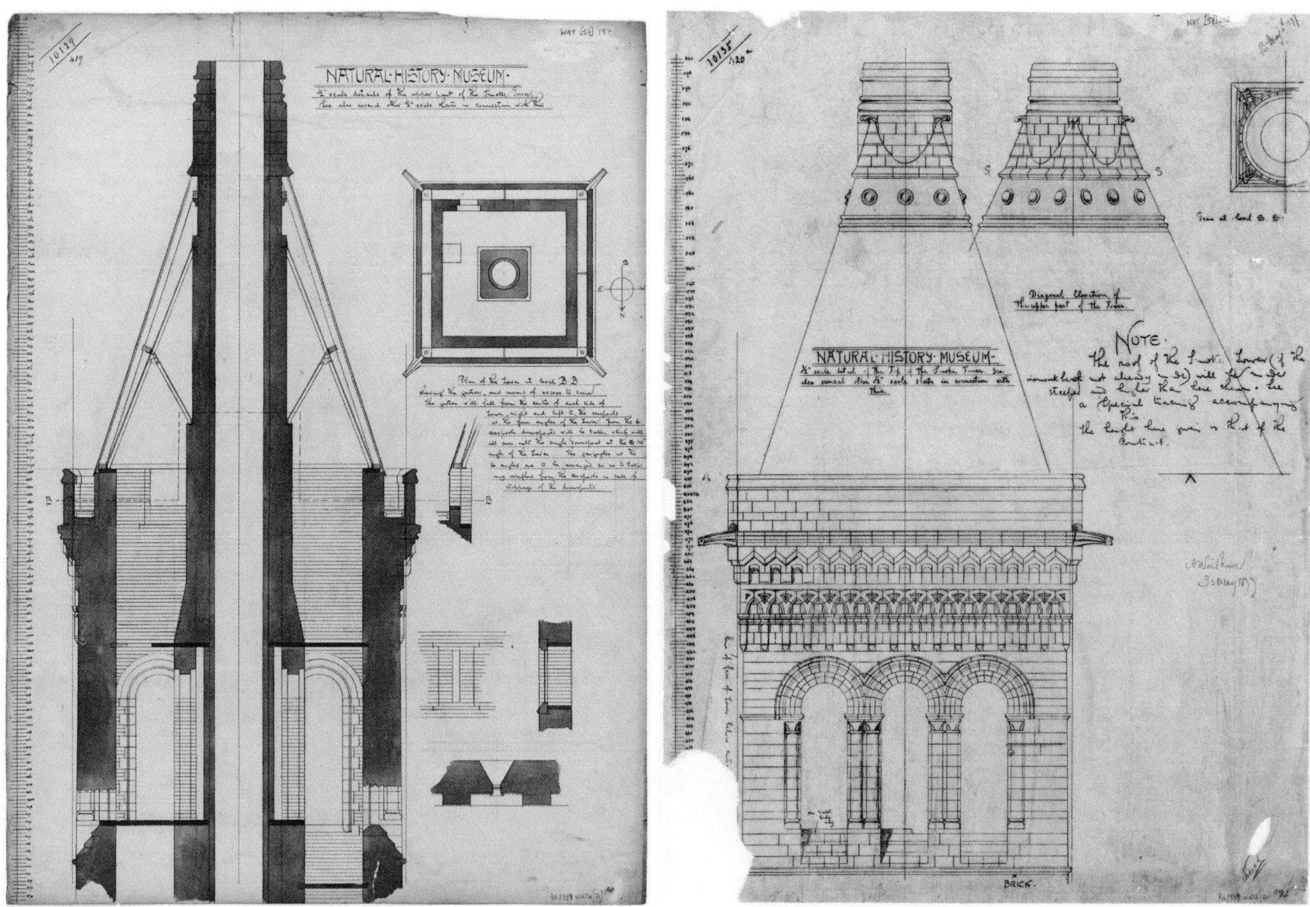

11.6 Alfred Waterhouse: Plan showing the gutter, and means of access to same & section of the upper part of the Smoke Tower (left), and Part plans & elevation(s) of the top of the Smoke Tower (right)

leading up to the main entrance. This hypothesis has not been verified.

The earliest drawing shows a symmetrical arrangement of two warming chambers with smoke from the boilers each feeding into one of the two aspirated chimneys. The later drawing, signed 1872 by Waterhouse (lower Figure 11.5), shows one centrally located boiler room where three steam boilers would be placed, two actively producing steam and one in reserve as needed for maintenance and repair.

THE NORTH TOWERS: ASPIRATED CHIMNEYS

The many detailed plan, section and elevation drawings of the north towers show that Waterhouse did not treat these utilitarian towers as unimportant. Despite their simplified design with less ornamentation than the front towers and the pavilions, the ventilation towers still received a great deal of attention. The elevation (Figure 11.6) shows the central smoke pipe projecting above the top of the tower. Below the roof are three ventilation openings on each side for the exhaust of vitiated air.

RISING SMOKE AND AIR

The smoke flue at the center of each ventilation tower is surrounded by a double mantle. The interior brick wall defines the inner cavity where vitiated air extracted from the galleries moves upwards, aided by the motive power of the heat emitted from the smoke pipe. Stairs with open risers wind around the inner core, allowing for additional air circulation.

Today the central mechanical room at the Natural History Museum houses a tri-generation CCHP plant where electricity is produced by a generator driven by a natural gas-powered engine. Waste heat from the engine supplements heating energy from boilers. Heat-driven absorption chillers are used for cooling. Combustion from the gas-powered engine and the boilers is carried out through the smoke pipe of the north-east tower, allowing this important architectural feature to serve a practical purpose even today.

WARM AIR DISTRIBUTION

Steam pipes were installed from the boilers to several "stations" where the incoming fresh air was warmed by passing through steam coils. According to Waterhouse, writing in the *British Architect* of 1878, there were 11 air warming stations installed in the fresh air tunnels. Steam coils were also installed under the main stairs at the north end of the central hall and at the main entrance to ensure that a sufficient volume of air was supplied to the index gallery at the right temperature.

A decentralized system of steam coils, as opposed to one or a few central warming chambers, increased efficiency, since heat loss in the main branches of the air tunnels was eliminated. After the air was warmed by a steam coil, cool unconditioned air would continue to flow in a lower chamber of dual air tunnels where the warm air was supplied in the upper chamber (Cook and Hinchcliffe, 1995).

The conditioned air was distributed to each room above through ventilation pipes built into the walls. The air supply to each gallery or thermal zone in the building was regulated by dampers on the side walls of the air supply tunnels. According to the *British Architect* in 1878, air to the south-east and south-west galleries was supplied through regulating valve gratings fixed in the skirting on each side.

In addition to the warm air system, two other methods of heating were employed. Smaller spaces were heated by steam radiators installed below windows, with fresh air supplied directly through the exterior wall. Similar to the arrangements at Manchester (see Chapter 10), some offices and conference rooms were heated by open fireplaces.

PULLING AIR THROUGH THE ATTIC

The main galleries at the front were ventilated through vertical ventilation shafts built into the walls. All shafts ended up in the attic where the air could move laterally towards the towers. Vitiated air from these two wings of the museum could also be discharged through six main extractors, placed in the sloping roof.

As seen in Figure 11.7, air was also communicated to the attic through wooden air ducts.

LIGHT IN, AIR OUT

Skylights were installed in the roof above the main galleries on the south side of the building. The beautifully designed ceiling is now to a certain degree obscured by the recently installed fluorescent tube light fixtures. The skylights are not operable, so air is discharged through grilles designed on a flower motif. The grilles communicate directly with the lateral air exhaust chambers in the attic.

SWITCHING TO SUMMER MODE

The warming and ventilation system relied on the pulling force of the vertical air distribution channels. No fans were installed in the basement. This system was designed to work with the tendency of warm air to rise, as a natural ventilation system, but aided by a mechanical system of heating.

During the winter months, the indoor to outdoor air temperature differential added to the power of the height difference between the inlet and the outlet in moving air through the building. During the summer months, as the effect of the temperature differential decreased, windows could be opened to let in fresh air directly, bypassing the tunnel system at the bottom of the building. This caused the pressure drop in the system to decrease, thus compensating for the loss of power due to the higher outdoor temperatures.

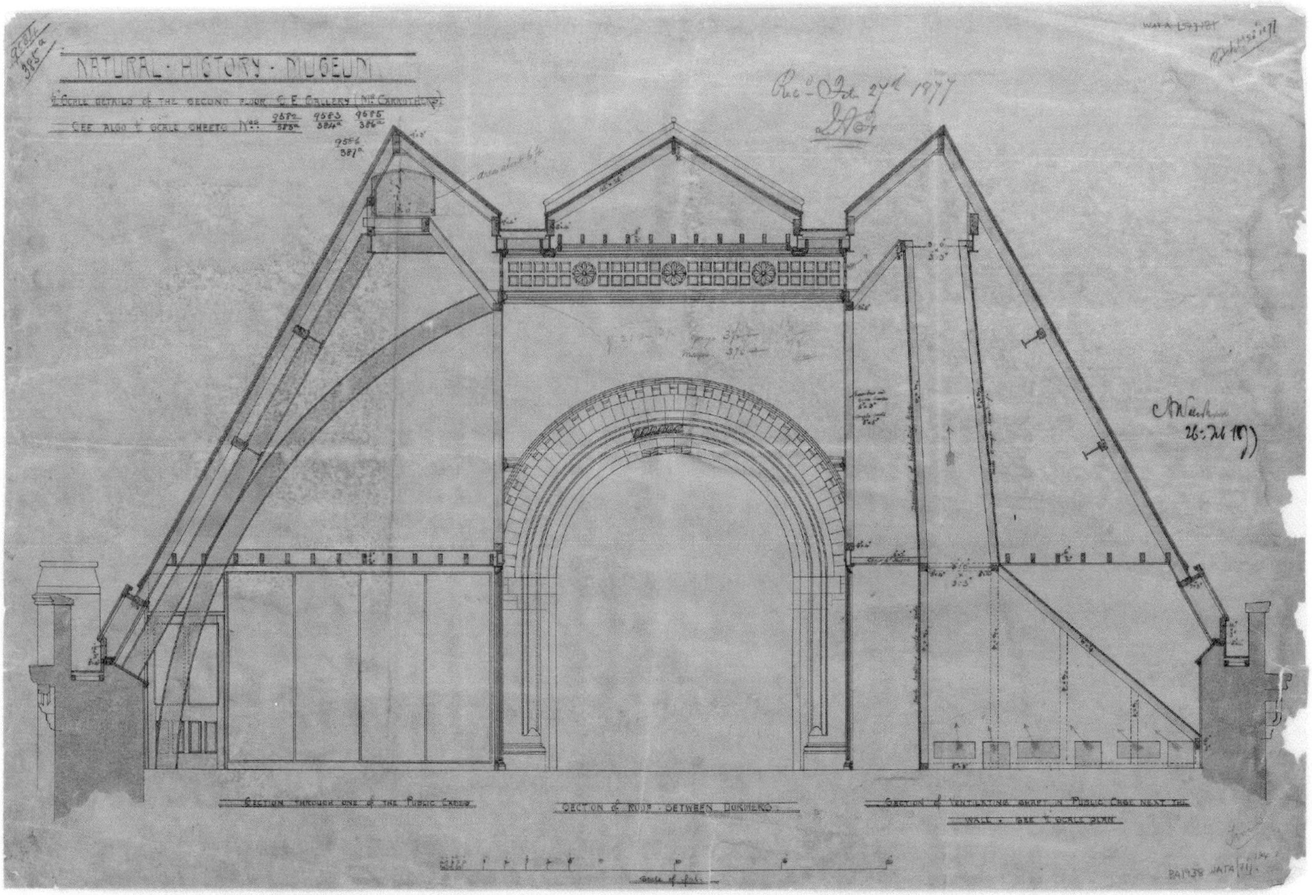

11.7 Alfred Waterhouse: "Section(s) through one of the Public Cases," signed 26 Feb. 1877

11.8 Natural History Museum, interior view of the great hall

VENTILATING THE CENTRAL HALL

The central hall or Index Galley was heated and ventilated through grilles under the main staircase at the north end. This large space was ventilated through a space located to the north of the central hall, between the hall and the two aspirated chimneys in the north towers. Vitiated air from the hall could also have been discharged through a conservatory on the top of the building, on each side of the hall. This could only have happened if there were openings in the balustrade at the top of the east and west walls. Today there is a low brick wall separating the glass-covered side galleries from the central hall, which may have been installed when storage cabinets were built up against the side walls of the top galleries.

When a new smoke detection system was installed recently, openings for the laser beams had to be made in the brick wall.

Immediately, as the hole was made, air gushed through the opening. A report from preliminary investigations indicated that the amount of air that could pass through the balustrade would be of a considerable volume (Fulcrum, 2011). A supplementary ventilation system is therefore under consideration, using this passage as a possible means of improving thermal comfort and air quality in the central hall, while building on the principles of controlled natural ventilation, possibly restoring the way the building would breathe, as originally designed.

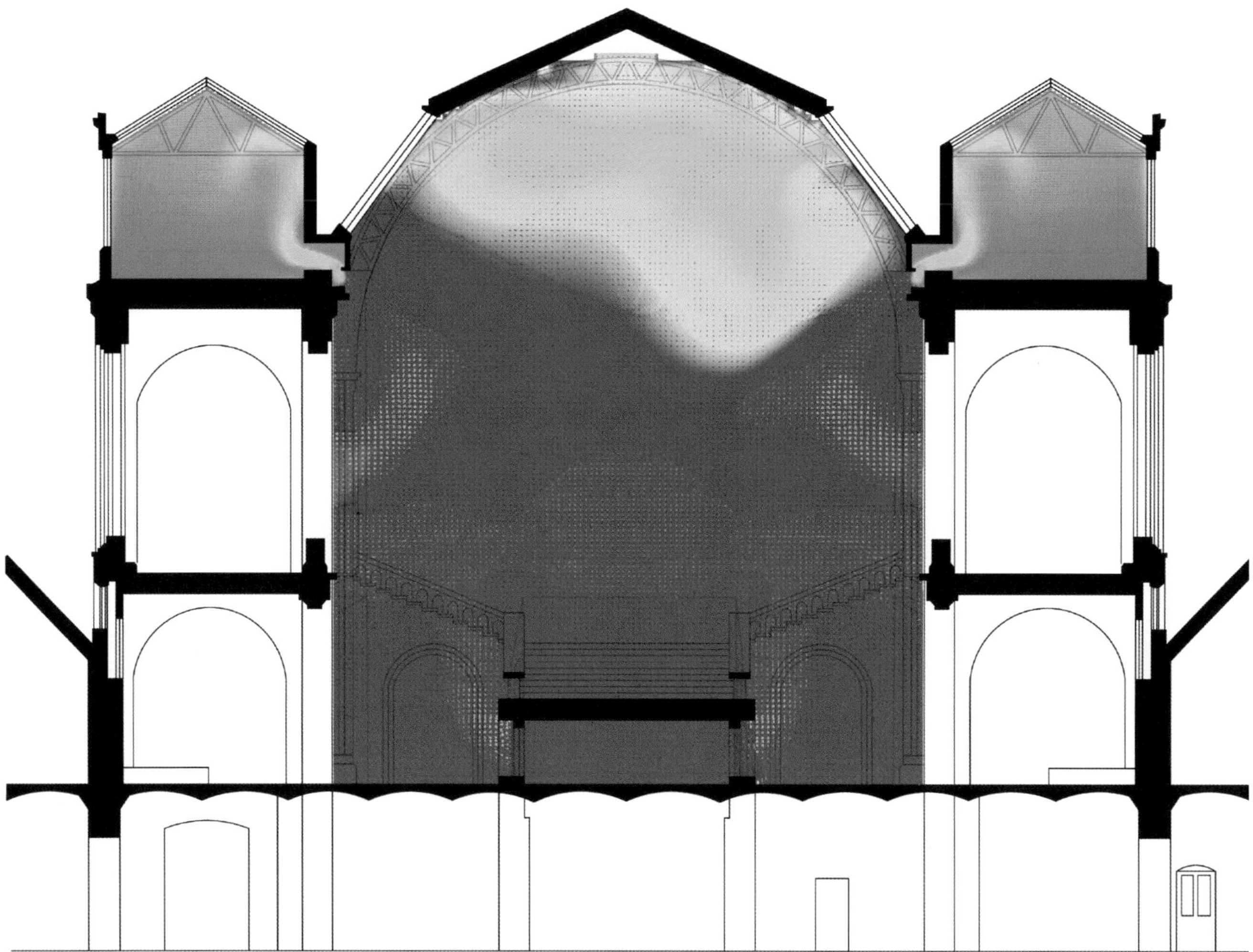

11.9 CFD simulation diagram showing airflow and temperature distribution in the great hall

SUSTAINABLE SYSTEMS RESTORATION AND INNOVATION

Could the glass covered side galleries work as exhaust plenums, pulling air out from the Great Hall? CFD modelling was undertaken at the University of Illinois UC in the summer of 2014 to investigate the potential for such a system to work as expected. Figure 11.9 shows a CFD simulation diagram showing airflow and temperature distribution in the main gallery. The simulation results indicate that the side galleries could in fact be used to increase the air exchange rate in the Great Hall, improving the indoor comfort for the visitors.

Over the years since the building was opened in 1881, the number of visitors to the museum has increased from roughly 1.5 million to 5.5 million per year. The overall goal of the project under way is to improve thermal comfort and air quality in the building, responding to the demands generated by an increasing number of visitors. The hypothesis is that if the original system could be restored and upgraded with the aid of new technology, the Natural History Museum could see a revitalization of its breathing, while operating with optimal energy efficiency.

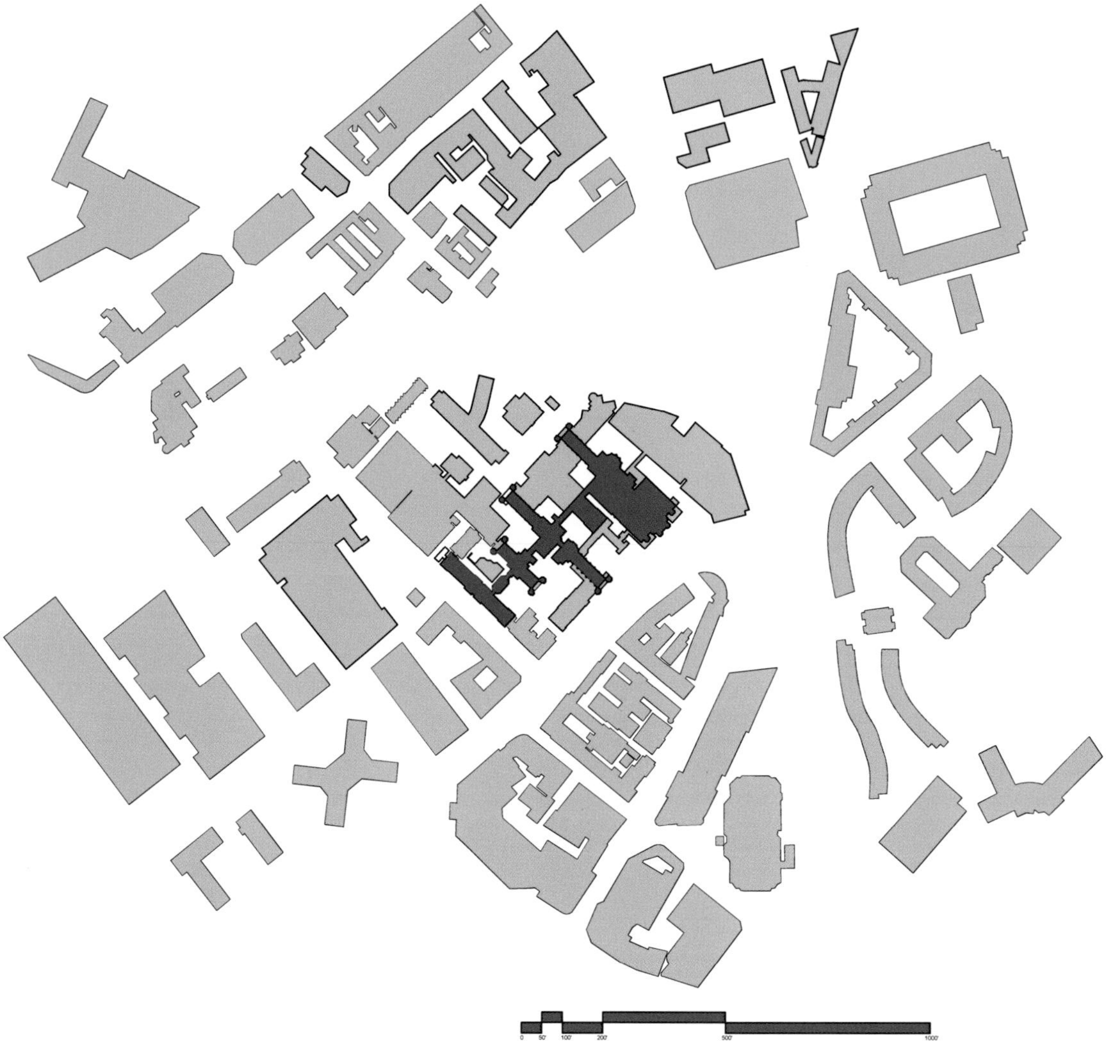

12

Birmingham Children's Hospital

LOCATION: 138–139 STEELHOUSE LANE, BIRMINGHAM, UK

BUILT: 1897

ARCHITECT: WILLIAM HENMAN

52°N

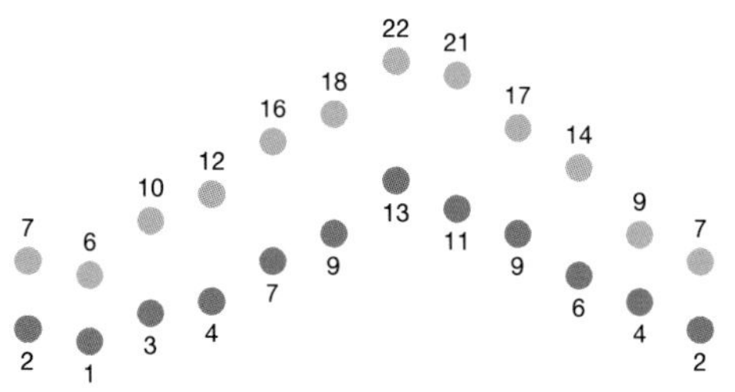

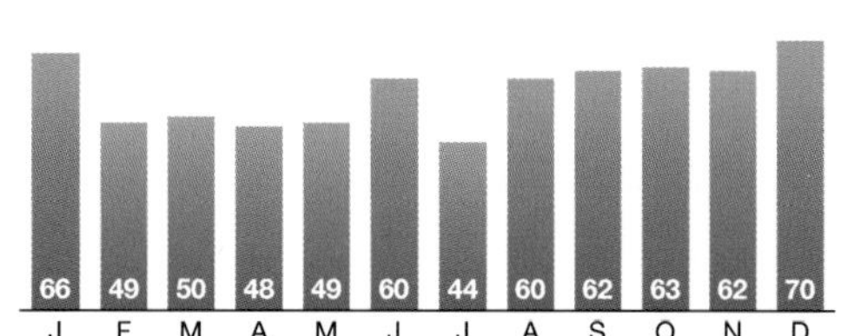

12.1 Birmingham Children's Hospital, view of the roof with ventilation turret (left)

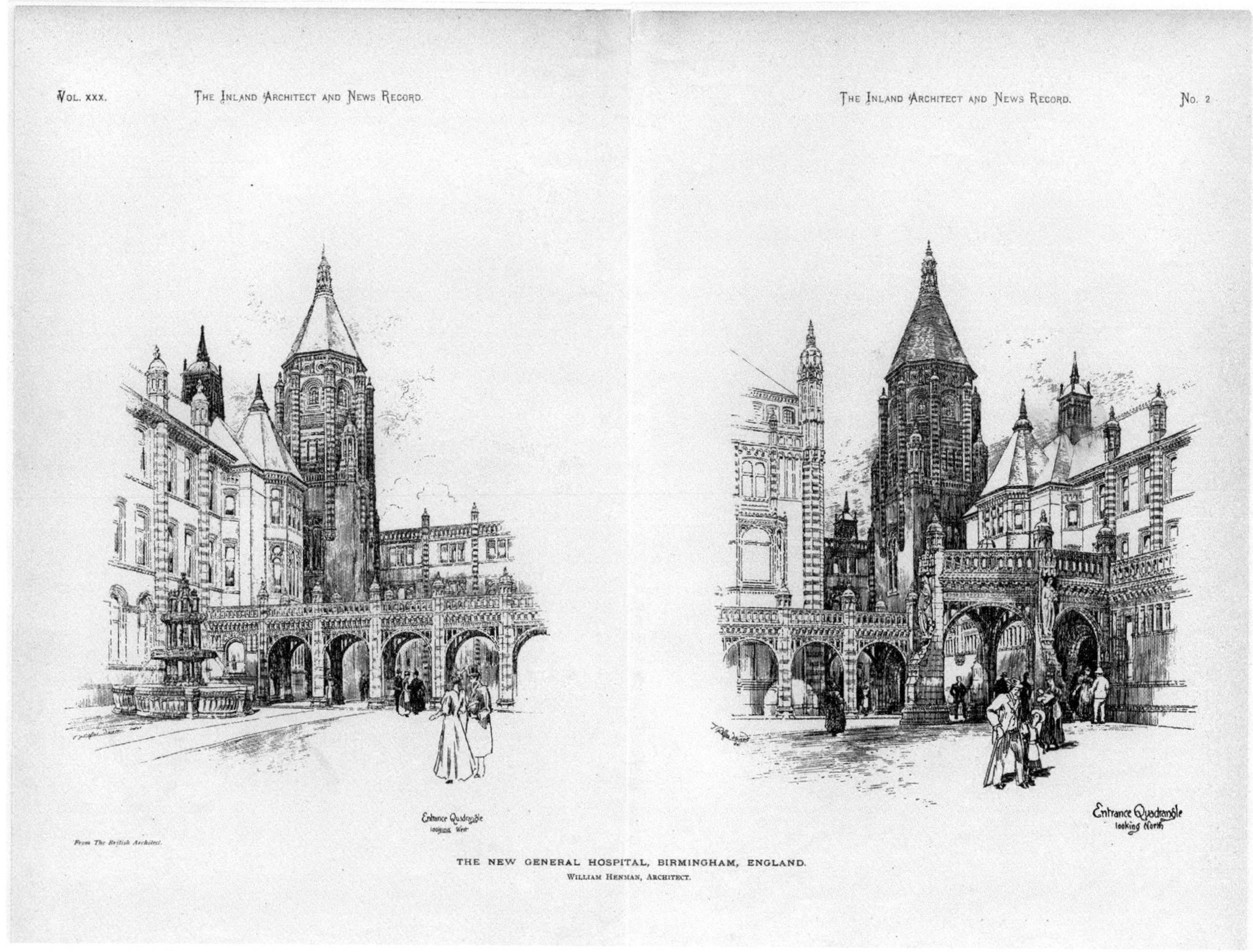

12.2 The New General Hospital, Birmingham, Entrance Quadrangle

A NEW BUILDING FOR THE OLD BIRMINGHAM GENERAL

On Tuesday, November 4, 1894, *The Times* reported that the Duke of York, accompanied by the Duchess, would lay the foundation stone of a new building for the General Hospital (now Birmingham Children's Hospital) in Birmingham. The old hospital, with 270 beds for in-patients and serving up to 60,000 out-patients a year, had outgrown its capacity and was in dire need of new accommodations.

The Times article is remarkably detailed in its description of the new building, which leads one to believe that the reporter relied heavily on information provided by the architect, William Henman. Earlier that same year Henman had read a paper on the subject of hospital design at a meeting of the Leeds and Yorkshire Society, a paper which was subsequently published in the *Journal of the Royal Institute of British Architects* (Henman, 1896).

William Henman (1846–1917) was not only a respected architect known for his advanced knowledge of modern hospital design, but also a scholar who wrote extensively on his research and design. At the age of 22, he had won the RIBA Silver Medal for his drawings of the Church of St. Thomas. He was awarded the Pugin Studentship in 1871, became an Associate of RIBA in 1882, and a Fellow in 1895.

Henman was the winner of the competition for the design of the new Birmingham General Hospital. By the time the foundation stone was laid, he had prepared an impressive set of drawings, accompanied by detailed specifications of materials, construction, structural systems, and a modern heating and ventilation system.

MISS NIGHTINGALE AND THE GUNMAKERS QUARTER

A central but fairly open site was chosen for the new hospital in the heart of the gunmakers quarter, along Steelhouse Lane and

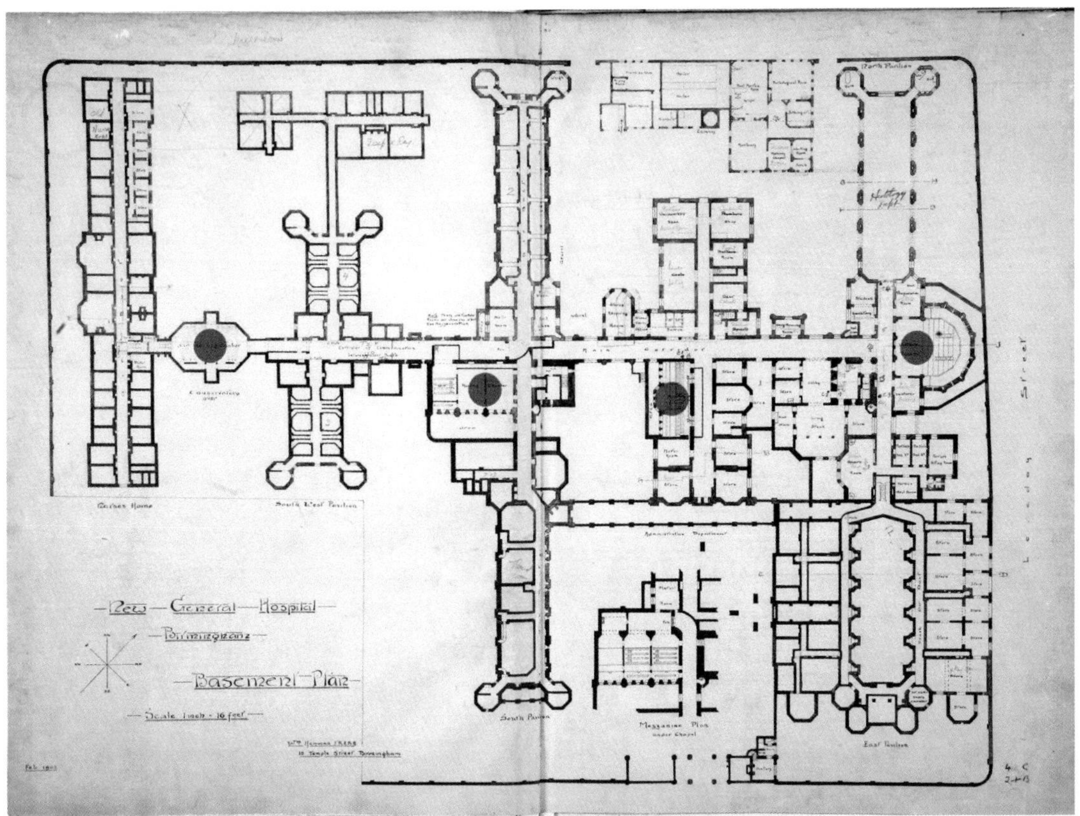

12.3 Red dots showing four main heating chambers, adapted from a plan drawing by William Henman, signed February 1902

in close proximity to the Law Courts and the County Court (Anon, 1894). The program asked for accommodation for 350 beds, with additional space for a large out-patient department, a lecture theatre, a chapel, a morgue, offices and a home for the nurses.

Henman's plan was laid out according to the "pavilion principle" with "Nightingale Wards" placed perpendicularly to and spaced out evenly along a central corridor. The central organizing spine of the project runs from the Nurses Home at the south-west end to the Lecture Theatre at the north-east end. There were originally ample landscaped open spaces between the wards, allowing sun and daylight to enter from windows on three sides. The wards on the street side had "sunrooms" or conservatories facing south-east where patients, on a good day, could take advantage of the healing properties of the sun's rays.

The administrative offices were located near the main entrance off of a public plaza where a separate entrance for out-patients was marked by a triangular porch. Each of the three piers was decorated with a terracotta figure representing Light, Air and Purity: three essentials to health (Henman, 1896).

The Nightingale Wards were, as the name indicates, attributed to Florence Nightingale, who wrote in great detail on the design of hospital wards. Her *Notes on Nursing for the Labouring Classes* (Nightingale, 1861) devotes the first chapter to the need for "pure air," the most important criterion for good hospital design. A later chapter is dedicated to light.

The wards design of the pavilion hospital did not, however, originate with Florence Nightingale. She was promoting an idea in evolution. George Goodwin, the editor of *The Builder* journal and an architect who was promoting the role of architects in improving public health, had written extensively on hospital design. He, in turn, was inspired by the work of Dr. John Robertson of Manchester, who had published an article on the construction and ventilation of hospitals in 1856.

HEATING AND VENTILATION BY PROPULSION

Towards the end of the nineteenth century, the technology of moving air by large centrifugal fans had been developed. Driven by electric motors, these fans made possible a shift from the extraction systems to a plenum system where the air was pushed into the building by propulsion. Henman aligned himself with William Key, an engineer based in Glasgow. At the Birmingham General Hospital, Key was responsible for the heating and ventilation arrangements, as well as the hot water supply. When Henman was hired as the architect for the new Royal Victoria Hospital in Belfast, he continued his collaboration with Key and further developed the plenum system there.

In his 1896 paper on hospital design, Henman discusses the pros and cons of "natural ventilation" vs "artificial" ventilation systems. He makes a clear distinction between the exhaust-driven extraction system and the supply-side plenum system where air is pushed in by propulsion. While a natural ventilation system is powered by a pressure differential created by the difference in height from inlet to outlet and the difference in temperature of the inside and outside air, these systems are turned into hybrid systems in the winter when the motive power of fireplaces assists in pulling air through the building.

An extraction system tends to create a negative pressure inside the building, pulling in air through operable windows. When these windows are closed, however, air is pulled from other rooms, through stairwells, doorways and elevator shafts. Henman points out how this "false air effect" prevents the supply of pure air to the patients while potentially transporting contaminated air from various sources. Of great importance was also the inability of an extraction system to control the quality of air supplied to the wards. Even if the air entered "fresh" through open windows, the dusty, dirty and dense urban environment of a manufacturing town in the late nineteenth century did not offer "pure" air.

In response to these challenges, Henman and Key designed a plenum system where temperature and air flow could be controlled in response to the needs of each individual space in the building. Heat was delivered by steam from a detached boiler house via a network of 35,000 feet of steam pipes to four heating chambers in the basement where the incoming air was cleaned, humidified or dehumidified, heated and distributed through horizontal air supply corridors and vertical channels built into the masonry walls.

AIR CONDITIONING

Outside air was supplied to the four heating chambers through sunken light wells along the buildings perimeter. Since the supply side (plenum) of the heating and ventilation system was installed in the basement, the air intakes were below ground. To reduce the chances of pulling in contaminated air, the wells were fenced in by masonry walls and located adjacent to landscaped gardens. Air intake louvers could be mechanically opened and closed (Figure 12.4).

Screens and filter curtains made with ropes were used to clean the incoming air by removing dust particles, soot and insects. The air was cleaned by allowing water to trickle down over the ropes. The ropes were held together with copper wire, which in addition to its structural function also had a disinfecting effect after reacting chemically with water.

In his paper on hospital design, Henman explains how humidification occurs in the winter and dehumidification can occur in the summer when the outside air is warm and humid. The idea that air can be dehumidified by passing it through a wet curtain made from ropes is counterintuitive and therefore less commonly understood. If the outside air was hot and dry, as in a desert location, the incoming air would be cooled but humidified. In the ocean-dominated climate of the British Isles, however, water molecules in the warm humid air could condense on the surface of the colder water trickling down the ropes, thus, in effect, dehumidifying the air.

Accordingly, ice could form on the ropes in the winter due to the cooling effect of evaporation. Therefore, steam coils were mounted on the outside of the rope curtains to prevent icing and to precondition the air supply. After passing through the rope curtains, the air was moved by fans over heating coils before being pushed into the air tunnels, which duplicated as corridors. The air then transitioned from the horizontal air tunnels into vertical channels inside masonry walls. Here, guillotine trap doors were used to regulate the airflow and smaller steam coils mounted behind the doors were used to control the air temperature, providing a way to adjust both temperature and airflow to the individual spaces above.

THE LECTURE THEATRE

The main lecture theatre (Figure 12.5) sits directly over the heating chamber at the north-east end of the main corridor. Air is supplied from below the staged seating and enters through grilles mounted in the stair risers. Similarly, air is supplied under the seats at the upper gallery through grilles in the floor.

Birmingham General Hospital was built as a teaching hospital. The lecture theatre, therefore, could be used for demonstrations

12.4 Birmingham Children's Hospital, warming chamber below the Lecture Theatre (left) and airflow control mechanism (right)

12.5 Birmingham Children's Hospital, interior view of the Lecture Theatre

using diseased human bodies to demonstrate dissections. To prevent odors spreading into the seating portions of the theatre, air exhaust grilles were placed near the floor on the wall behind the podium, as shown in Figure 12.6.

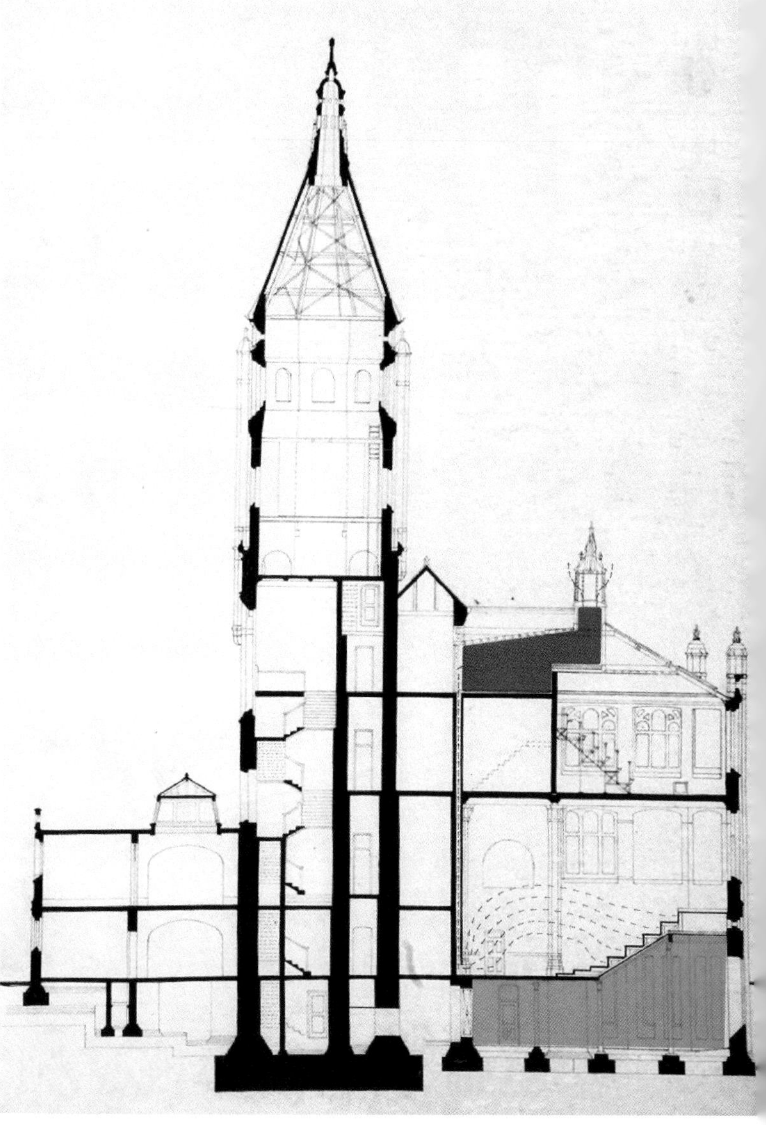

12.6 Airflow diagram showing the Birmingham Children's Hospital Lecture Theatre, adapted from a section drawing by William Henman

DUST EXPLOSION IN THE LECTURE THEATRE

As time passes, minor adjustments and major changes are made to the heating and ventilation systems in historic buildings. The changes are not always documented. Knowledge of the original systems was lost as key personnel retired and died. One day, as the ventilation grilles behind the podium were no longer functional, they were covered up with plywood panels loosely attached to the framing. The knowledge about this important part of the exhaust system for vitiated air was lost to history.

Many years later, as workers were doing masonry repairs on the upper floors, they found a channel in the wall. This, they thought, would be a fast and easy way to get rid of rubble and left-over material. So they threw it down the shaft, not knowing where it ended. What followed was a dust explosion in the theatre when the plywood panels broke loose and the content accumulated in the masonry channel emptied out into the theatre.

The tale of this dust explosion, when paired with careful examination of a section drawing by William Henman (Figure 12.6), leads us to understand how the original system worked:

Air pulled in from the light well, and conditioned in the heating chamber below the theatre, was supplied through grilles in the stair risers, thus delivering fresh air right where the audience was seated. Vitiated air was pulled out by the grilles behind the podium and up though channels in the masonry wall. The warmer and now contaminated air ended up in an exhaust chamber in the attic, which in turn was connected to a ventilation turret installed at the roof ridge.

LETTING THE AIR OUT

The results of the competition for the building of a new General Hospital in Birmingham were announced in March 1892. The winning entry was for a 346-bed hospital designed by William Henman. Alfred Waterhouse, who was a member of the competition jury, must have admired not only the extensive use of red brick and terracotta, but also the picturesque skyline of Henman's design dominated by towers, spires and turrets (Taylor, 1997). Decorative elements at the eaves of the roofs above the wards could lead one to think that these were functioning as ventilation hoods. This is not the case.

12.7 Birmingham Children's Hospital, air exhaust plenum in the attic

To fully control the exhaust of vitiated air from the spaces below, all vertical air extract channels were led to centrally located air exhaust chambers in the attic (Figure 12.7). At the mid-point of these horizontal channels were the ventilation turrets. The turrets were designed with a square footprint forming four equally sized sides. The air escaped through the grilles, which could be controlled manually. The design was such that changing wind speed and wind direction would not diminish the power of the chimney effect, allowing the air to leave the building.

STRUCTURAL COLUMNS CARRYING AIR

The out-patient department, the examination rooms and the offices for doctors and nurses were placed in extensions to the floor plate on both sides of the standard ward building. The Nightingale Wards occupied the two floors above, while the central space on the ground floor was used as a reception and waiting area. (It still is.)

To allow for a less restricted flow of space in the out-patient department, structural columns replaced the load-bearing masonry walls at ground level. The position of the columns correspond with the solid wall portions between windows in the wards above. This design feature solved the issue of spatial flow, but what about the flow of air?

The wards are supplied with air through channels in the masonry walls between windows, flowing into the wards through trumpet-formed apertures above the patients' beds (Figure 12.8). Vitiated air was pulled out through a grille in the wall near the floor under each bed and then let out through the ventilation turrets via the attic plenum (see Figure 12.7).

To maintain the same pattern of air circulation, Henman enlarged the diameter of the structural columns and made them

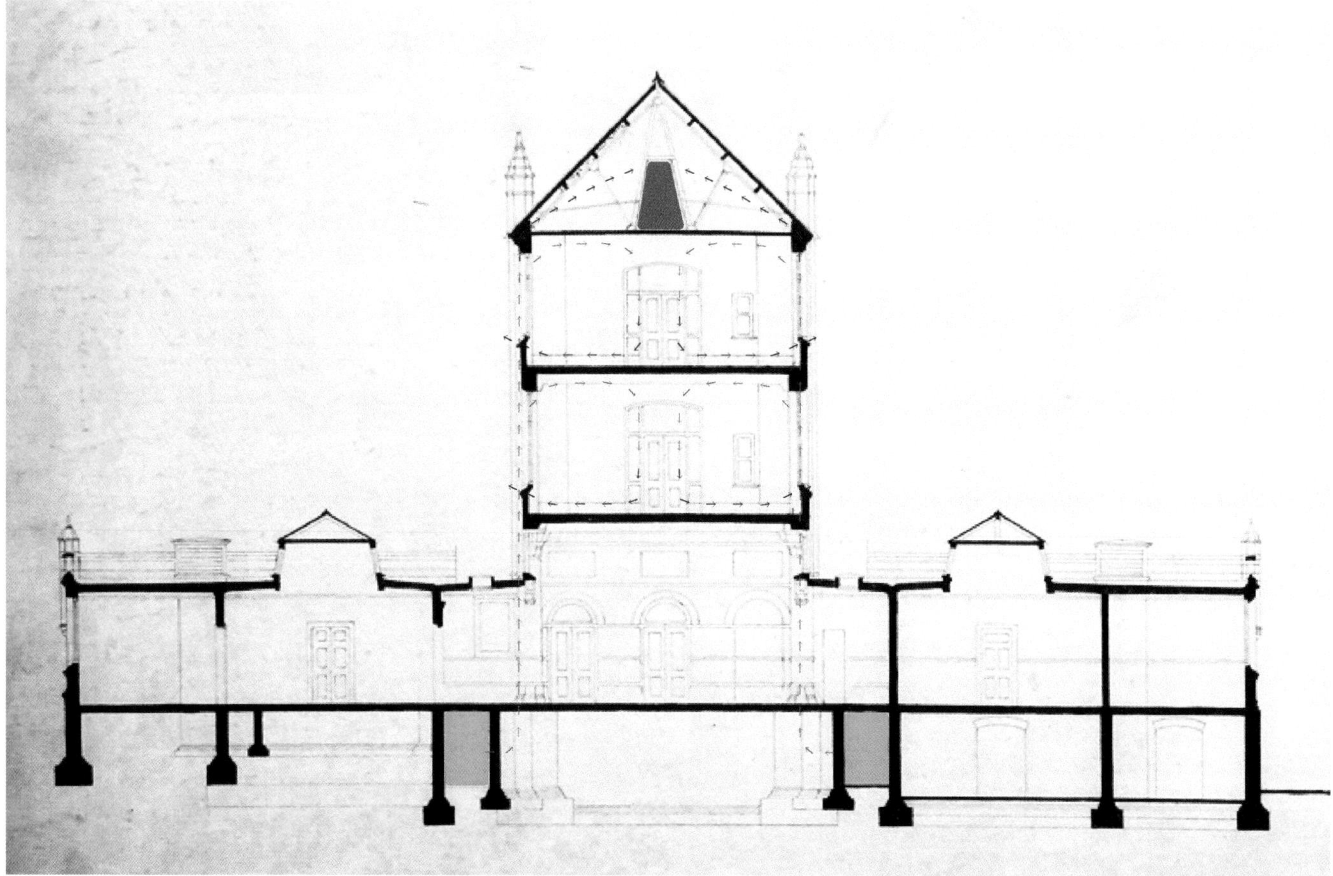

12.8 Airflow diagram showing the Birmingham Children's Hospital East Pavilion, adapted from a section drawing by William Henman

hollow. This allowed the columns to carry not only the load of the wards above, but also the air breathing into those same spaces.

WIND PIPES

A hundred years after the new Birmingham General was opened, the General moved out and the Children moved in. What was Diana Princess of Wales Children's Hospital in 1998 is now commonly known as the Birmingham Children's Hospital. Names change, but the buildings still serve a purpose. In the reception and waiting area of the out-patient department, wide beautifully decorated columns stand tall, magically hiding their inner secret. They still serve to make the wards above breathe, even if functions have changed and vital systems components have been replaced.

MOVING ON TO BELFAST

At Birmingham General, the architect William Henman and the engineer William Key introduced an innovative heating and ventilation system that eliminated the need to bring in coal and take out ashes from the wards, that did not require windows to be opened on a cold winter night, a system that made it possible to deliver air at a temperature and humidity to the spaces at a flow rate responding to the need of each space at any time.

Henman also introduced other innovative features, such as a sound insulating floor system without any voids where dust and dirt could collect. At the point where the central corridor connected to the nurses residences, he placed a conservatory where flowers could be grown for the beautification of the wards. Walking through the conservatory on their way home after a long day's work in the wards must have felt like a rite of cleansing passage for the nurses.

When he landed the commission to design a new Royal Victoria Hospital in Belfast, Henman and Key continued to innovate, introducing a revolutionary concept for the design of a modern hospital that represented a departure from the pavilion hospital.

PART THREE

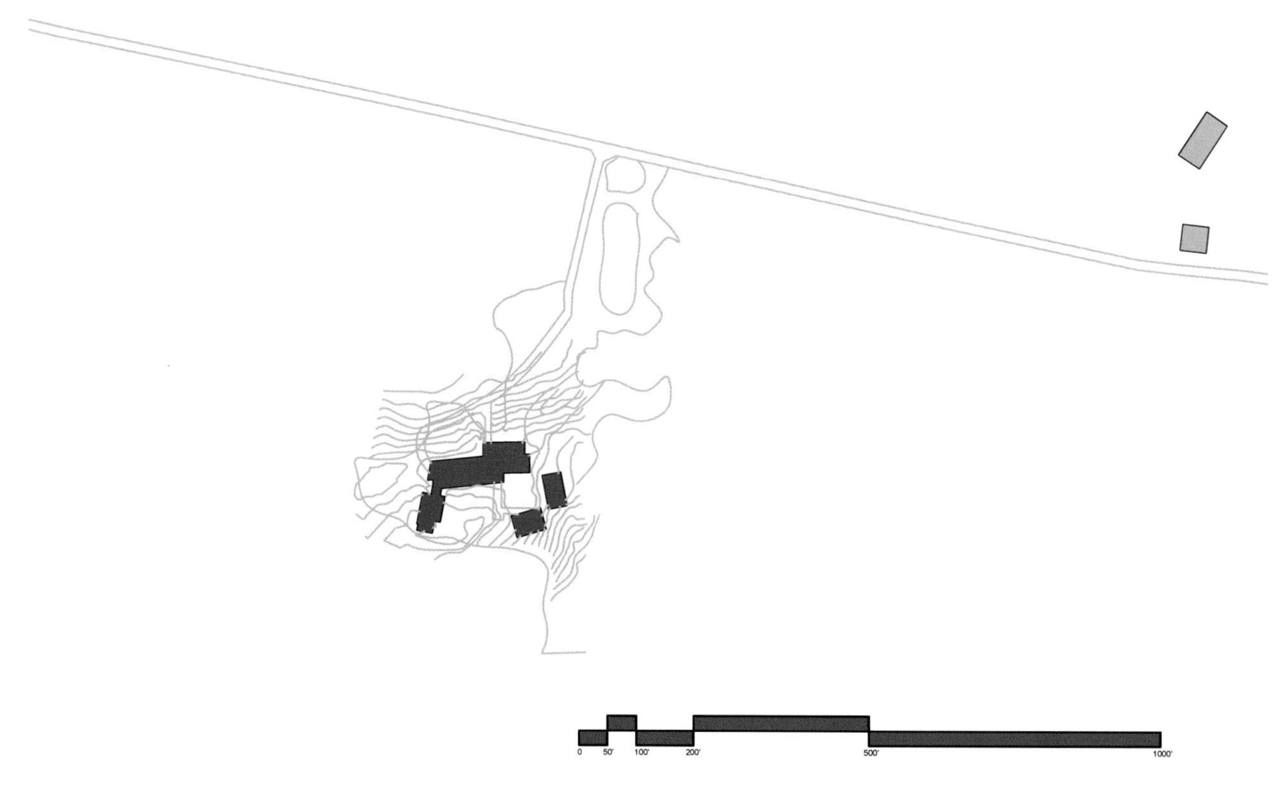

13

The Aldo Leopold Legacy Center

LOCATION: BARABOO, MADISON, WISCONSIN, USA

BUILT: 2007

ARCHITECT: THE KUBALA WASHATKO ARCHITECTS, INC.

LEED PLATINUM, ZERO ENERGY BUILDING, CARBON NEUTRAL

43°N

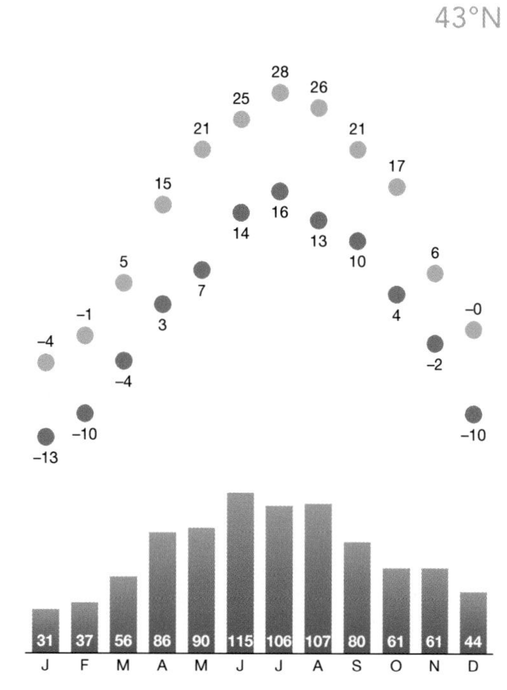

13.1 Aldo Leopold's Shack

A SAND COUNTY ALMANAC

> In 1935, Leopold purchased an abandoned farm north of the family's home in Madison, where Leopold was the nation's first professor of wildlife ecology. This "sand farm" along the Wisconsin River had been worn out by attempts to farm the fragile soils and by the twin specters of dust-bowl droughts and the Great Depression. The property truly had been reduced to its basic constituent, sand, with the only visible structure the farm's chicken coop, later known as "the Shack."
>
> (Leopold, 1949)

When transitioning from the nineteenth to the twenty-first century, nonchalantly leapfrogging the twentieth, the Aldo Leopold Legacy Center stands out as a symbol of how sustainable building design for the future is firmly rooted in lessons of the past. Aldo Leopold, the conservationist, forester, educator, writer and philosopher, was born in the late 1880s. The center celebrating his legacy was built in 2007, 120 years after his birth.

His best-known scholarly work, *A Sand County Almanac*, was written in the early morning hours in his office at the University of Wisconsin, based on research he did at his farm near Baraboo. Carefully observing nature as it unfolded around him, Leopold documented, analyzed and reflected upon nature: plant ecologies, the relationship between plants and animals, and most importantly, the relationship between humans and nature. His scholarly work was central to the development of modern environmental ethics. His concept of a Land Ethic describes the development of ethics as a three-step evolution where the first step deals with the relationship between individuals and the second step guides the relationship between individuals and society. Leopold then introduces a third step dealing with man's relationship to the land and to the animals and plants which grow upon it. He writes: "The extension of ethics to this third element in human environment is, if I read the evidence correctly, an evolutionary possibility and an ecological necessity" (ibid.).

SEEKING THE SUN

The Legacy Center was built as a cluster of buildings defining a landscaped area which in turn is divided into two parts: the welcome garden and the restored prairie. The main building has three wings connected by a circulation spine along the southern perimeter, forming a "thermal flux zone." Two separate buildings, the three season hall and the workshop, complete the cluster.

This simple but elegant principle of organizing the building program allows for the seasonal, diurnal and functional adaptation of the degree of thermal conditioning for each zone, effectively creating an on-demand thermal conditioning scheme.

The largest building volume, occupied by the administration wing, the entrance lobby and the exhibition space, is oriented along the east–west axis with a sloped south-facing roof. A large portion of the south-facing exterior wall along the circulation space is glazed, allowing for passive solar gains in winter when sun angles are low. Daylight flows across the thermal flux zone and enters the office area through glazed interior walls, supplementing the north light which enters the space through clerestory windows. Sliding portions of the interior wall open the office up to the sunlit circulation space, much like the arrangement often found in traditional Japanese temples.

PINE HARVEST

Aldo Leopold brought his wife and five children to the Sand County farm on weekends and over holidays and vacations. The only remaining building, a chicken coop, was rebuilt and upgraded to serve as their living quarters, which they sometimes shared with Leopold's graduate students. From 1935 until 1946, they planted about 3000 pine trees every summer.

Seventy years later, the forested areas were overcrowded, resulting in poor canopy development and an extremely low annual growth rate. Thinning could improve forest health, increase carbon sequestration and give the remaining trees an opportunity to live another 70–80 years. This thinning process provided raw material for the new buildings while honoring the symbolic importance of Leopold's land stewardship.

13.2 Aldo Leopold Legacy Center, garden view

13.3 Heavy timber structural columns from sustainable harvest (left), wood interior and stained concrete floors flooded with daylight from clerestory windows

While pine was predominantly used for structural lumber, cladding and siding, site-harvested cherry, maple and other woods were used as finish materials and for custom-built furniture.

REACHING NET ZERO

The path towards net zero energy use must start by reducing energy demand. Only by dramatically controlling demand through design is it realistically possible to achieve a level of annual energy use low enough to be matched by on-site energy supply. In a heating-dominated climate (4186 HDD versus 289 CDD), energy use is driven by the need for space heating, pre-conditioning of ventilation air and hot water supply.

Starting with a well-insulated and correctly oriented building, space heating is reduced by making use of direct solar gain through south-facing windows. Ventilation air is preconditioned through an expansive network of earth tubes. With an average annual temperature below 50° F (8° C), the incoming fresh air is warmed on a cold winter night and pre-cooled on a summer day. The building is cooled by natural ventilation when the ambient air temperature is favorable.

A geothermal loop minimizes the need for electric energy for auxiliary heating and cooling. Evacuated tube solar thermal collectors reduce the need for auxiliary energy for water heating.

The narrow building form allows energy savings by utilizing daylight to illuminate the interiors.

This carefully selected palette of "green" design strategies brings the specific energy demand to an EUI (Energy Use Intensity) of just above 50 kWh/m^2-Y. Over a typical meteorological year, electric energy produced by building integrated photovoltaic panels makes up for the energy used by the buildings after savings by design, making the Leopold Legacy Center a truly net zero energy building.

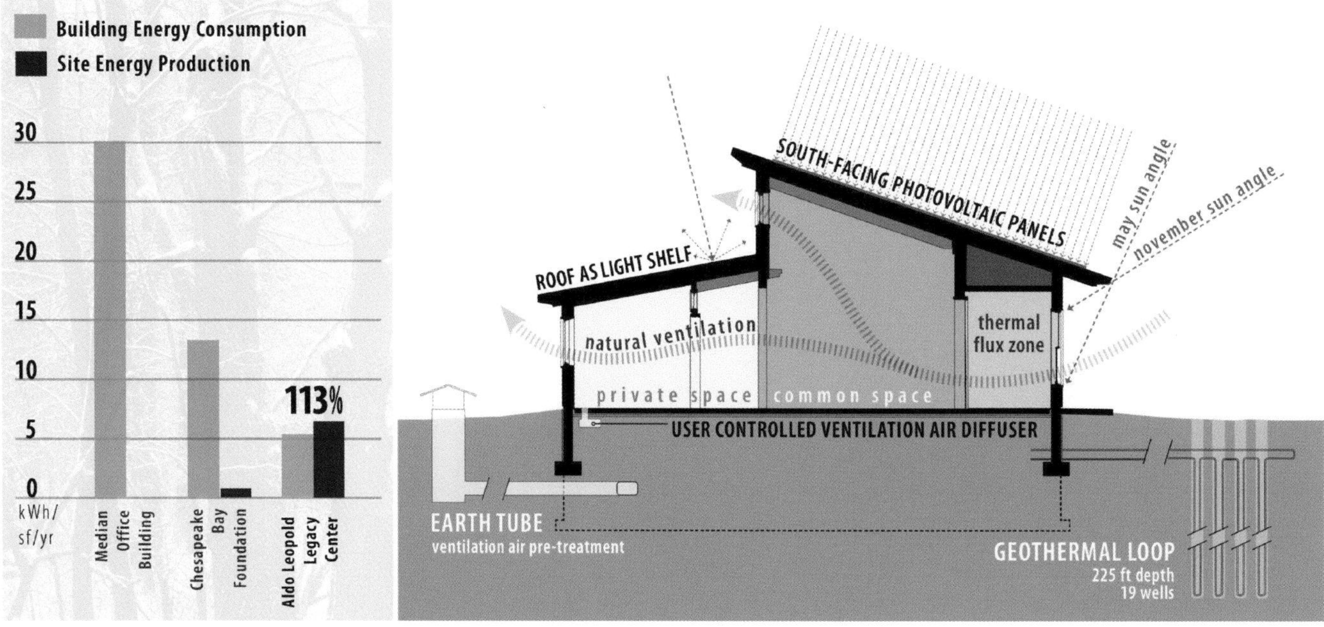

13.4 Aldo Leopold Legacy Center, diagrams showing energy balance (left) and environmental design strategies (right)

THE WATER CYCLE

Sandy soil lends itself to infiltration of rainwater and wastewater into the ground. Water from roof surfaces is channeled through a series of cascading steps in the central stone wall and fed back into the ground (Figure 13.5). A rain garden planted with native species filters the surface water captured from the roof. Storm water from roads and parking lots is filtered through permeable paving.

In the Center, waterless urinals, dual-flush toilets and water-conserving lavatories reduce water consumption by 65 percent, compared with a typical building. An on-site well provides potable water, and an existing septic system treats the wastewater.

13.5 Aldo Leopold Legacy Center, view from the south, showing water harvesting, solar power generation and solar water heating features

14

Great River Energy

LOCATION: MAPLE GROVE, MINNEAPOLIS, MINNESOTA, USA

BUILT: 2008

ARCHITECT: PERKINS + WILL

LEED PLATINUM (NC V 2.2)

45°N

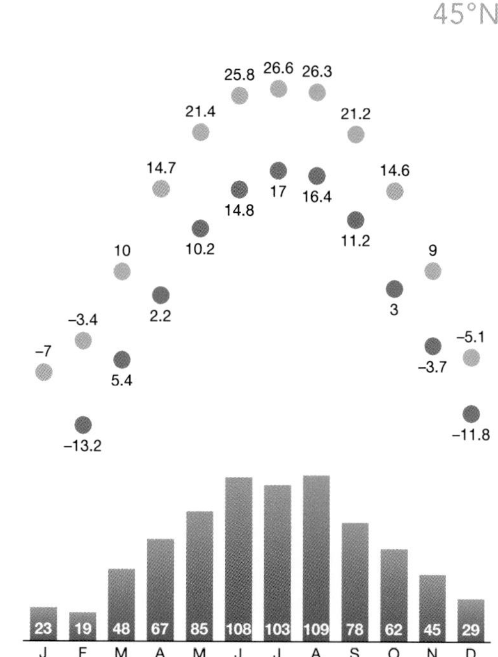

14.1 Great River Energy headquarters at sunrise

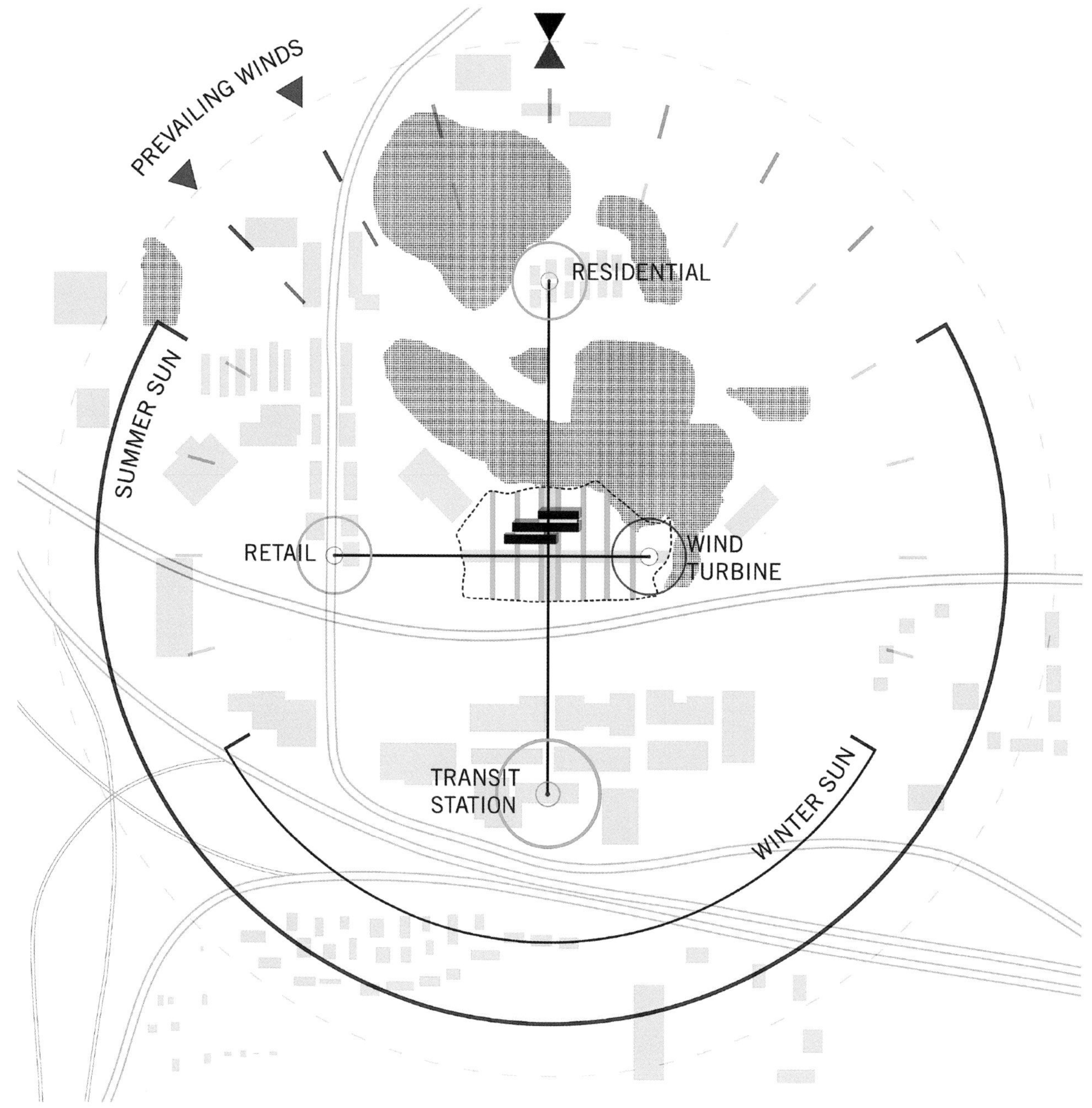

14.2 Great River Energy, site diagram

BY THE LAKE

Great River Energy, a non-profit public utility company, found a site for their new headquarters in Maple Grove, 15 miles north west of Minneapolis, Minnesota. The site is nested on the edge of a lake, just north of Interstate 94. Centrally located among retail and residential communities, easy access by car is complemented by the building's proximity to a transit hub to the south and a bike path that meanders at the lake's edge.

Placement and orientation take into consideration the sun's geometry and the characteristics of an open landscape exposed to wind. The building's form and massing hint at a design process where the potential for engaging sun, wind, water and earth has found a thoughtful architectural response. The sun warms the interiors on a cold winter day, the water cools the building in the peak of summer. The earth retains and processes storm water. Energy is produced on site from sun and wind.

14.3 Great River Energy, view of north façade

A BUILDING IN PLACE

While orienting the building squarely aligned with the cardinal directions, the overall massing is driven by the formation of three long and thin bars. The bars are placed parallel to each other with space for day-lit atria in between. By moving the bars sideways along the east–west axis, access to daylight is enhanced and more views towards the south and north can be enjoyed.

An important prerequisite for achieving openness and daylight was the relocation of the core. Functional elements traditionally found in the middle of a typical office building were instead moved out towards the east and west, thus forming end caps to the elongated bars. This design feature was enforced by making the east- and west-facing façades appear solid and opaque with only a few small windows accentuating the massiveness.

The north and south sides are mostly transparent, allowing for daylight from the side and views to the lake and surrounding landscape.

By developing the design according to accepted guidelines for environmental response, the building presents itself with great clarity, but stops short of expressing a more detailed dialog with the environment. There is a restrained approach to sun exposure, practically hiding photovoltaic panels from view and minimizing devices designed for sun control.

EFFICIENCY OF SPACE

Three parallel "bars" of office space are organized side by side with room for atria and circulation in between. The east-west-

14.4 Great River Energy, open office interior

oriented bars are shifted to increase views and daylight. An open office layout takes preference over private offices, contributing to more than 20 percent savings of programmed office floor area. By increasing the efficiency of space, an estimated $4.2 million in cost savings was achieved. The design team estimated the corresponding reduction in CO_2 emissions at 125 tons per year.

Efficiency of space is an important factor when assessing building energy performance. When Energy Use Intensity (EUI) is typically measured as annual energy use per unit of conditioned floor area, space efficiency is not taken into account. Increased efficiency of space, on the other hand, means that the people density in the building is higher. It follows that the energy use per occupant decreases accordingly.

In a wider view of sustainability in the building sector, efficiency of space is often neglected. It is a well-documented fact that while the EUI of residential buildings is decreasing, the amount of conditioned floor area per person has been increasing at such a pace that the energy savings from improved EUI are negated by overconsumption of space.

RELOCATING CORES, INVITING DAYLIGHT

Shifting traditional core functions such as storage rooms, utility rooms and archives to the end caps of the office floor "bars" opened up the centrally located spaces to daylight. On a reference design day, daylight harvesting provides 75 percent of the floor area in the building with a minimum of 25-ft-candles. Sun is allowed to penetrate deep into the building, while roof monitors with clerestory windows and sculpted ceilings distribute diffuse natural light.

HARVESTING SUN AND WIND, ENGAGING EARTH AND WATER

As with the building design, the systems design also responds to and works with natural sources of energy available at the site. The resulting Energy Use Intensity (measured) is 68 kBtu/ft^2-Y or 214 kWh/m^2-Y.

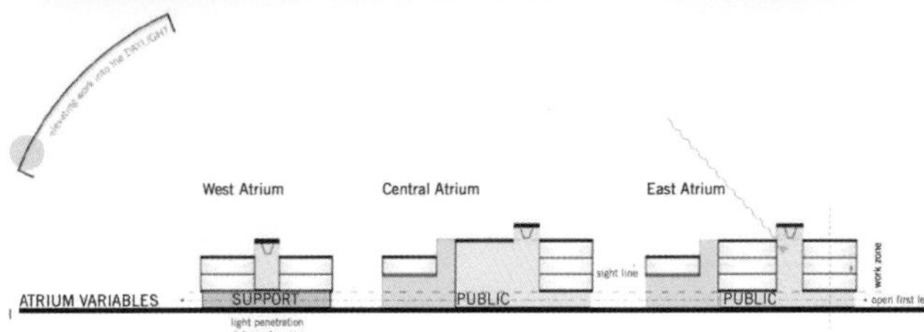

14.5 Great River Energy, view of atrium, with section diagrams

14.6 Great River Energy, renewable energy diagram

The client decided to purchase a used wind turbine, which was refurbished and installed at the site. The wind turbine was rated at 200 kWp capacity under optimal conditions. While measured site energy production data indicate that the turbine does not meet the target for electricity generation, it still provides 117,000 kWh in an average year. This translates to approximately 3.5 percent of the total building energy use.

A 72 kWp roof-mounted photovoltaic array delivers an additional 99,000 kWh in a typical year, bringing the amount of on-site renewable energy supply to a total of 216,000 kWh, or 6–7 percent of the total annual energy use. The building is prepared for a solar thermal system to be installed on the roof as well. This strategy was, however, not implemented.

Water source heat pumps use the lake as a source of heat in the winter and a source of cooling in the summer. The temperature is low enough at the deepest depths to make it possible to run a "water-side economizer" as a means of free cooling during shoulder seasons. This strategy works in tandem with low velocity under-floor air supply using a displacement system where air supply temperatures are significantly higher in cooling mode than traditional forced air systems.

Rainwater from the roof is piped into the ground. Bioswales are used for storm water management, processing all surface water on site.

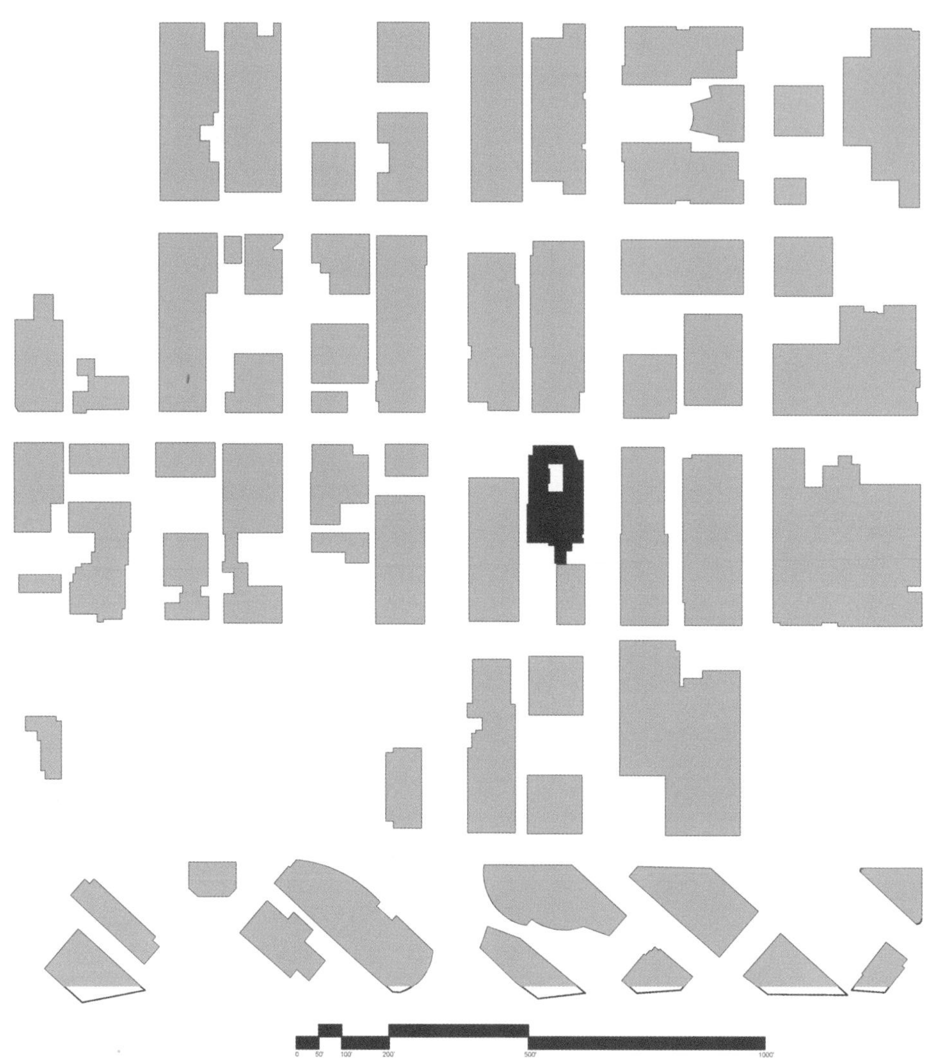

15

The Terry Thomas

LOCATION: SEATTLE, WA, USA

BUILT: 2008

ARCHITECT: WEBER THOMPSON

LEED GOLD (SHELL AND CORE)

LEED PLATINUM (INTERIORS)

AIA COTE TOPE TEN GREEN BUILDINGS 2009

48°N

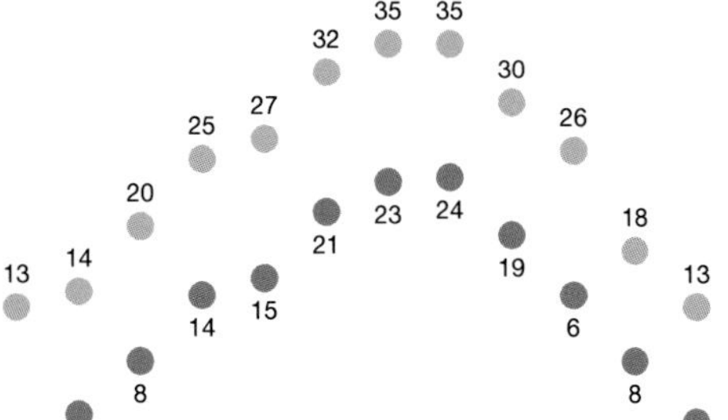

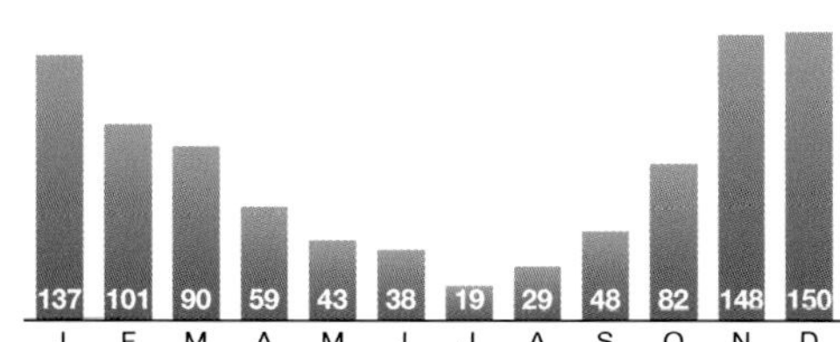

15.1 The Terry Thomas, view from Thomas Street

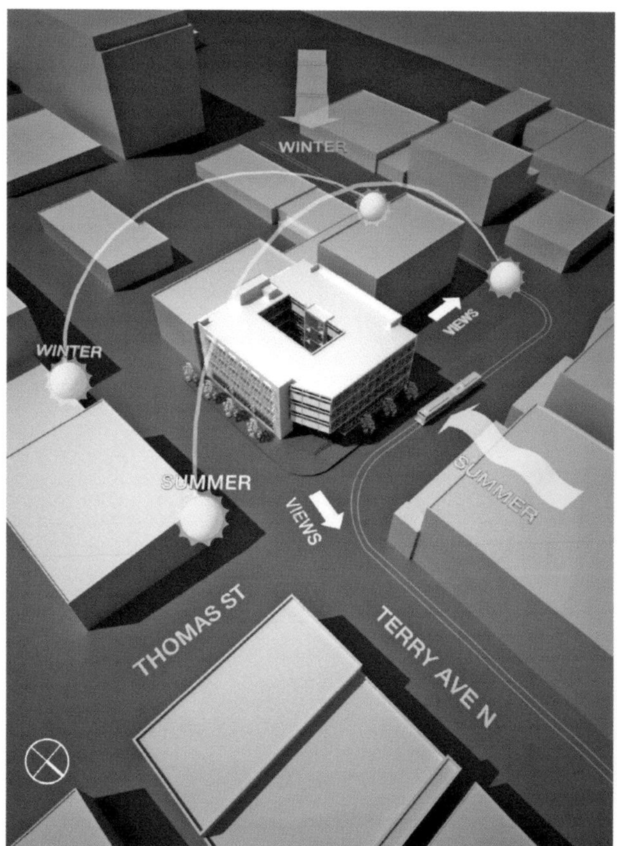

15.2 The Terry Thomas, sun wind and views diagram (left), view from Thomas Street (right)

PLACE SPECIFIC

The commercial mixed-use Terry Thomas building is named after its location at the north-east corner of Terry Avenue and Thomas Street in downtown Seattle. Within the urban context of a major city, the building design responds to site-specific environmental factors, such as wind, light, solar geometry and ambient air temperatures.

One enters the offices through the courtyard after passing under the building at the Terry and Thomas corner. The entry sequence is activated by the courtyard, which also serves as a community space and a design feature for optimal utilization of daylight in the offices. By optimizing the width of the floor plates and the height of the ceilings, the interior spaces are generously flooded by natural light and naturally cooled by cross-ventilation when the ambient conditions are favorable.

Unlike most commercial buildings, the Terry Thomas was designed to respond to the environment by switching between modes of operation: warmed by hydronic heat in winter, naturally ventilated all year round and cooled using high mass night ventilation in spring, summer and fall.

SHARING THE PERIMETER

With a few exceptions, the office floors are kept open at the perimeter, allowing daylight to enter and permitting airflow across the building. Depending on changing pressure differences, air flows from the street to the courtyard, and vice versa.

Space heating is supplied by floor-mounted radiators installed along the perimeter. By separating space heating from ventilation, less demand is placed on the air systems.

When the building is in outside air comfort ventilation mode, cross-flow is facilitated by motorized dampers. These are placed just below the floor slab decking, adjacent to steel ridge beams. Structural steel members have hexagonal cut-outs for cost efficiency and ease of systems integration, and to allow the free flow of air.

A HEALTHY AND PRODUCTIVE ENVIRONMENT

A typical open-plan office floor at the Terry Thomas is laid out with work stations placed perpendicular to the window walls. This

15.3 The Terry Thomas, interior view

15.4 The Terry Thomas, interior view

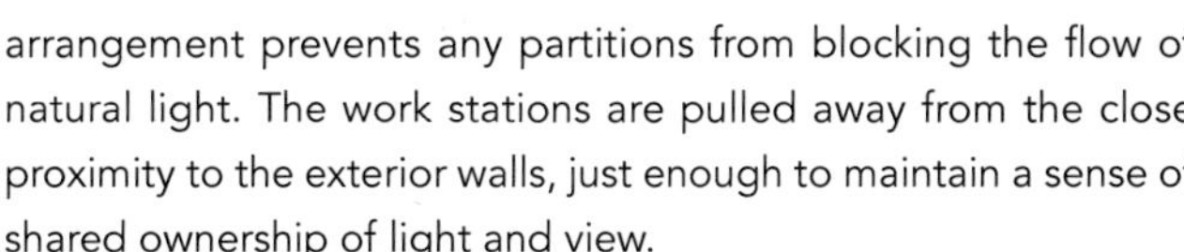

arrangement prevents any partitions from blocking the flow of natural light. The work stations are pulled away from the close proximity to the exterior walls, just enough to maintain a sense of shared ownership of light and view.

Supplementary electric lighting controls are designed to respond to the amount of daylight available at a typical work surface at any time. Circulation is organized along the middle of the floor plate, at the greatest distance from the windows. Zone controls allow for areas with sufficient daylight to operate without artificial light, as seen in Figure 15.4.

As the ambient air temperature, wind and precipitation allow, motorized dampers open and outside air flows across the space. This simple, yet functional and energy-efficient arrangement results in a healthy office environment, which in turn improves well-being and productivity.

The indoor air temperature typically swings between 22 and 27° C (71–81° F). In a typical year, the indoor air temperature range may be exceeded by 1–2° C during a few warm summer days, typically in the late afternoon.

RESPONSIVE ENVELOPE DESIGN

The design of the street façades and the walls facing the atrium addresses the need to take advantage of and to control environmental forces acting on the building from various directions. The ratio of the transparent to the opaque portions of the façade varies from one elevation to the next.

Stationary glass louvers are used as shading devices where that strategy is appropriate relative to how the sun angles change through the seasons. Exterior movable blinds are used for sun control on other elevations. Figure 15.5 explains how operable windows are used in sync with motorized dampers to allow for stack ventilation or cross-ventilation, depending on

15.5 The Terry Thomas, view from Terry Avenue (left), shading diagram (right)

15.6 The Terry Thomas, view of the courtyard

temperature and pressure differences due to changing ambient conditions.

Hydronic heating is supplied by radiators along the perimeter, with hot water pipes integrated with the structure below. Poured concrete slabs on top of steel decking provide sufficient thermal mass to counteract diurnal swings in the outside air temperature and variations in direct solar gain through vertical glazing.

PERFORMANCE

On the street side, retail spaces and a restaurant at the ground floor level engage the city. At the interior of the city block, a courtyard offers a semi-public gathering space for building occupants and visitors. Parking for cars and bicycles is available in a two-level underground garage. Shower facilities encourage bicycle use. The open exterior emergency stair is also an attractive means of vertical circulation, activating the courtyard and inviting the users to choose to walk between floors instead of using the elevator.

Based on metered energy use during a 12-month period following completion of construction, the 40,500 square foot building used 41 kBtu/ft^2-Y or 129 kWh/m^2-Y. During the period of documented data, electricity accounted for roughly 41 percent of the source energy mix, with 59 percent of the annual energy supplied by natural gas. After more than five years of active use, measures have been identified that could eventually improve the energy performance. Focusing on the annual natural gas usage, it is estimated that improved design of the air exchange grilles and motorized dampers with thermally insulated damper blades could lead to a significant reduction in gas usage.

The Terry Thomas is not only an energy-efficient LEED-certified building. It is a delightful urban structure, modest in scale but beautifully executed.

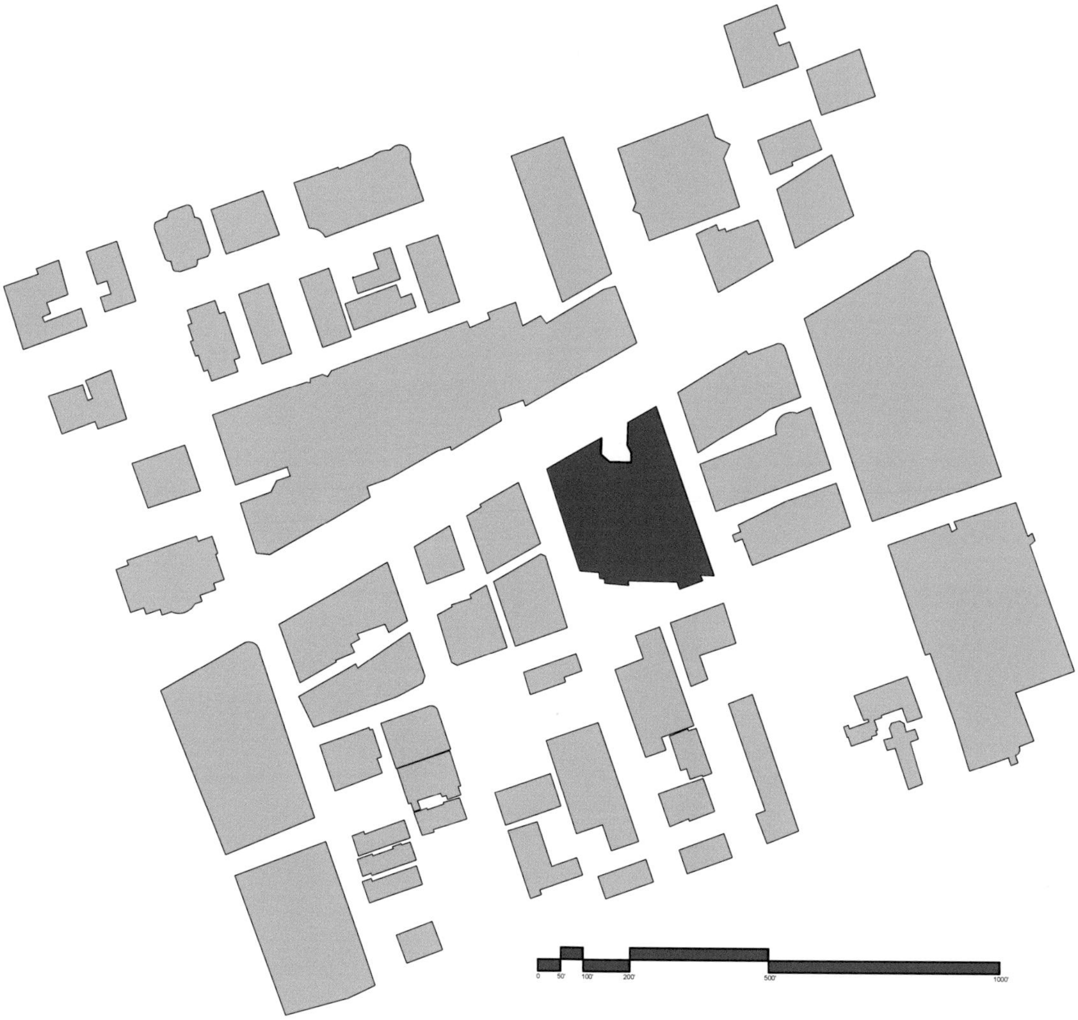

16

Manitoba Hydro Place

LOCATION: WINNIPEG, MANITOBA, CANADA

BUILT: 2009

ARCHITECT: KPMB ARCHITECTS, WITH SMITH CARTER ARCHITECTS

LEED GOLD

AIA COTE TOPE TEN GREEN BUILDINGS 2010

50°N

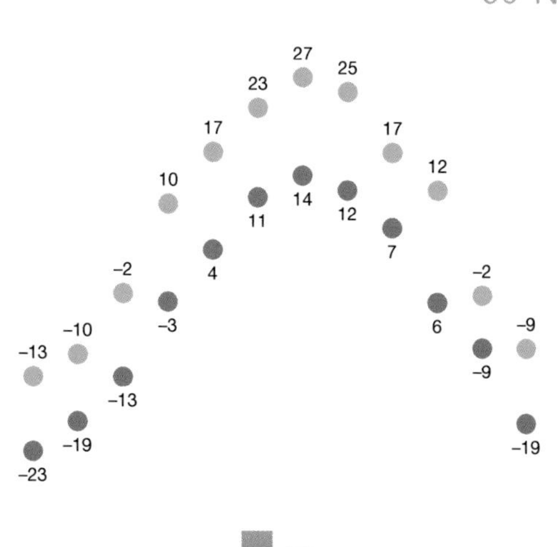

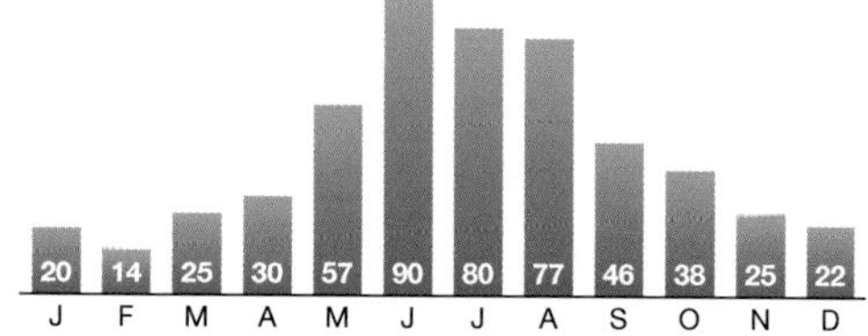

16.1 Manitoba Hydro Place, view from Portage Avenue

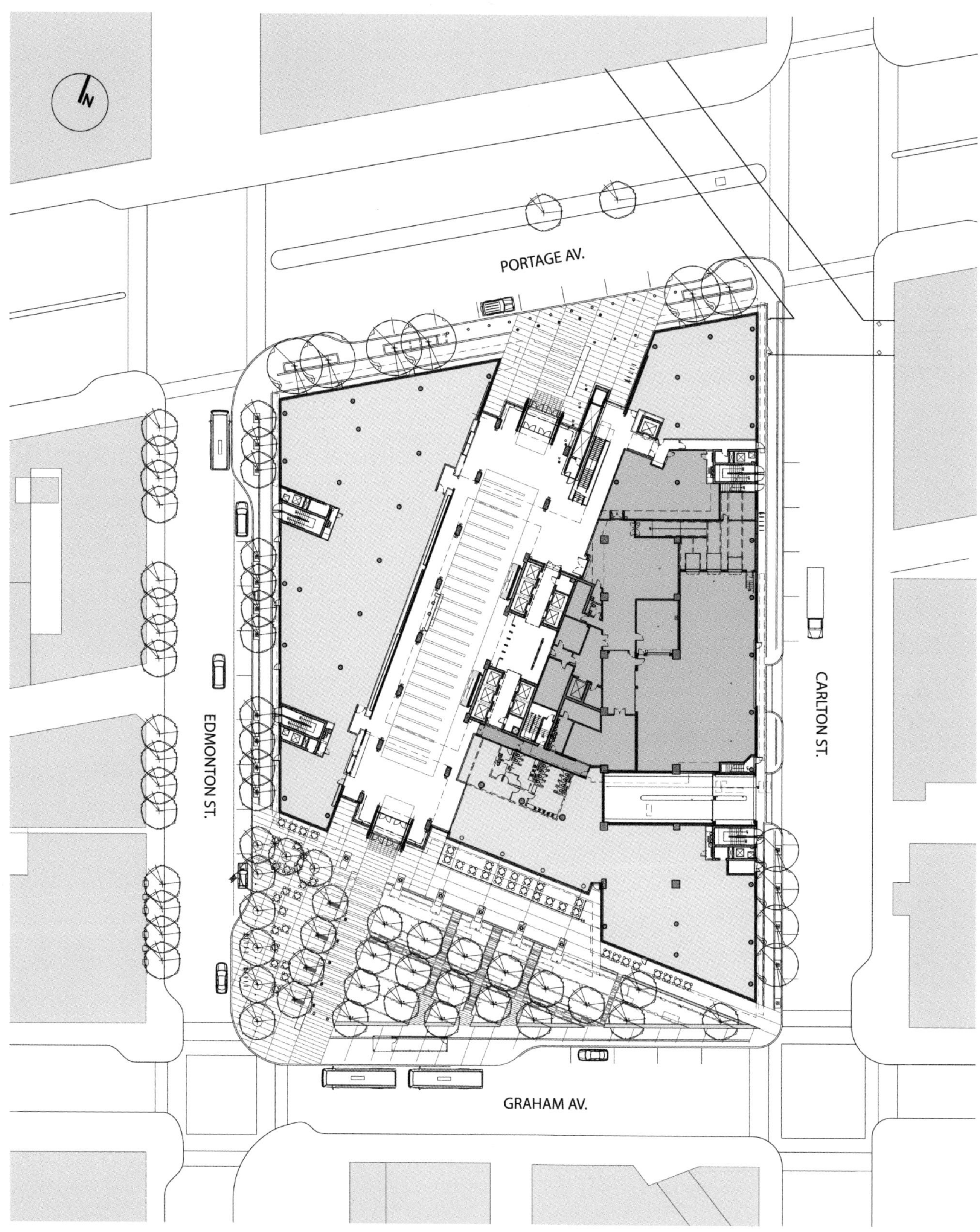

16.2 Manitoba Hydro Place, site diagram with typical office floor and view of roof gardens below

16.3 Manitoba Hydro Place, view from the south

THE CHICAGO OF THE NORTH

With a range of 90° C from the lowest and the highest measured ambient air temperatures, Winnipeg, Manitoba, is one of the coldest large cities on the planet. The city lies at the edge of the open prairie, a location that exposes the area to severe weather systems, including blizzards and cold Arctic high pressure systems.

In the heart of this city, the utility company Manitoba Hydro found a site where they decided to consolidate office space from 19 locations in the metropolitan area. The site has excellent access by public transportation, by bicycle and by car. On this site the new headquarters were built, named Manitoba Hydro Place.

Snow cover season in Winnipeg lasts for 132 days in a typical meteorological year, but the city is also blessed with an abundance of sunshine, with 306 days of measurable sunshine. At 50 degrees Northern latitude, winter sun angles are low.

Responding to this challenging location and climate, the design team created a tower which adopts an A-type footprint. The tower sits on a podium that addresses the streets on all four sides, but the tower itself breaks off of the city grid and aligns itself to the cardinal directions.

PASSIVE SOLAR HEATING

Three 6-story tall sunspaces facing due south work in tandem with a tall solar chimney pointing north to maximize the use of winter solar gain and minimize the use of fan power for fresh air supply.

Fresh air supply is provided by a long air intake grille at the bottom of each sunspace. Here, the air is pre-conditioned by heating coils placed in a low bench along the window wall, supplementing the solar gain. Conditioned air is then supplied to the office lofts through a raised floor plenum, which takes in the air through the sunspaces.

BUOYANCY-DRIVEN AIRFLOW

As the pre-conditioned air enters the sunspace through a warming chamber integral to the window seat, heat is also picked up from the direct gain solar aperture: the exterior glazed wall. A plate ceiling fan prevents heat from building up at the upper regions of the space, thus allowing for an even temperature distribution among the six floors.

Water falls down through the space, adhering to bundles of 4mm-wide Mylar ribbons suspended 24 meters from floor to ceiling. In the summer, chilled water causes water vapor in the warm and humid air to condense on the water surface, thus dehumidifying the air. In the winter, the air surrounding the water is colder and drier, causing the falling water to humidify the space through evaporation (see Figure 16.4).

The method of supping air to the office lofts through a raised floor cavity allowed the design team to eliminate the traditional suspended ceiling, which in turn allows the exposed undersides of

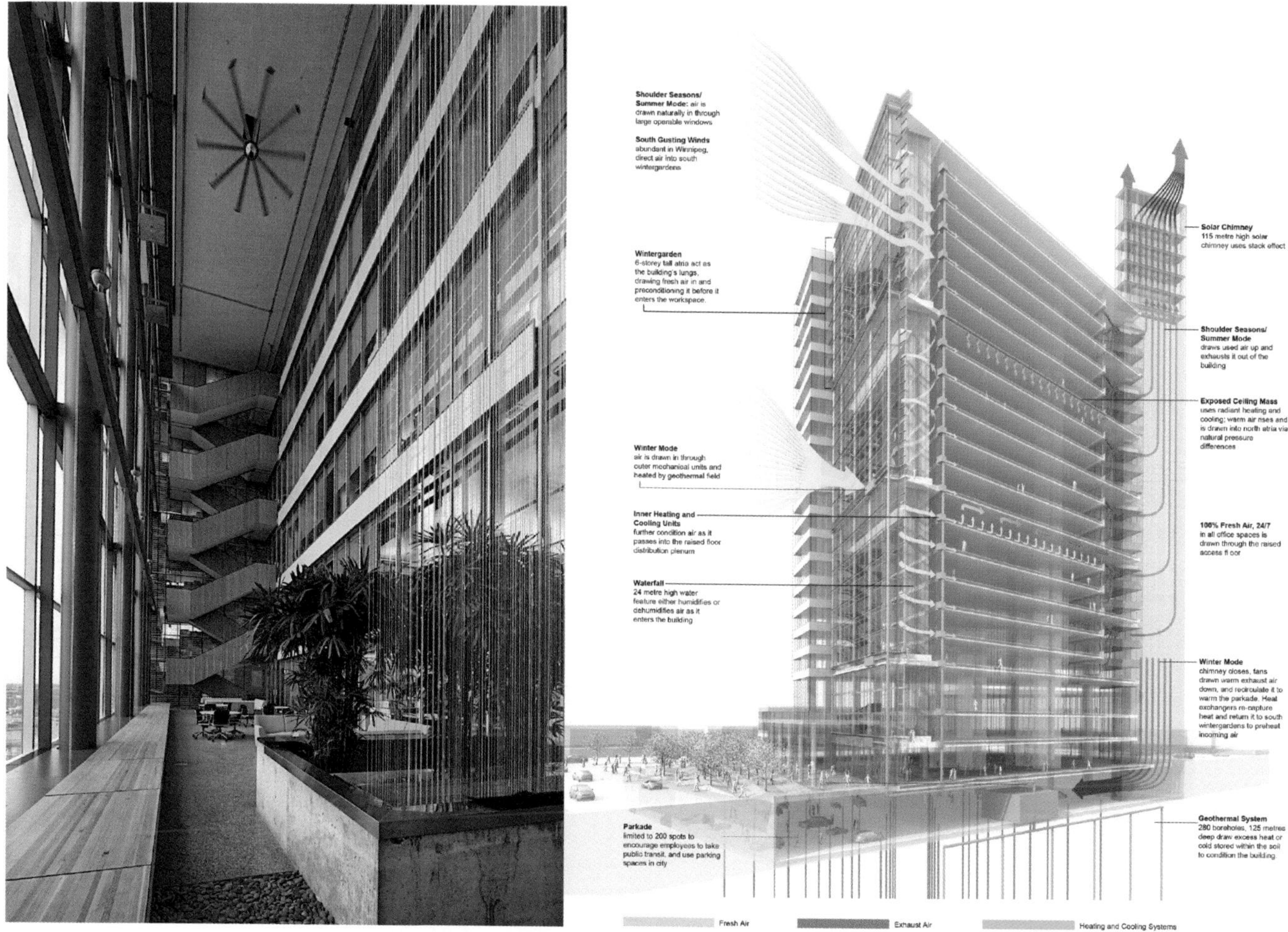

16.4 Manitoba Hydro Place, view of sun space (left), environmental diagram (right)

the concrete slabs to act as thermal mass, absorbing and releasing energy in a diurnal cycle. Return air from the lofts flows freely towards air exhaust grilles in the solar chimney, as seen in Figure 16.4.

As with most of the assemblies and systems in the building, the solar chimney operates in more than one mode. In the summer, air flows up the chimney, exhausting at the top. In this mode, air flow is mainly driven by buoyancy. The building inhales and exhales in a natural manner, only assisted by mechanical fan power. In the winter, the directional flow inside the tower is reversed. Fan power is now used to pull the air down into the underground parking garage where a hydronic loop recovers heat from the exhaust air. Residual warm air tempers the garage.

A BIODYNAMIC FAÇADE: A TEMPERED BUFFER

In cold climate locations at high latitudes, solar gain is sometimes useful from east- and west-facing façades. Contrary to the general rule to protect the east and west sides of a building from solar exposure, the situation for a site-specific building in a city like Winnipeg is more complex. In a successful low energy building, east- and west-facing double-skin façades, therefore, must be biodynamic: performing as a thermal buffer against heat loss in the winter, utilizing solar gains in spring and fall, and protecting the building from overheating in the summer.

The double-skin façade is typically sealed on cold winter days, acting as a thermal buffer much like a thermos flask. In spring and fall, the building's control system open up the operable windows to allow fresh air to enter the wall cavity and eventually enter the office lofts. The façade can also be ventilated through grilles and dampers at each end, allowing fresh air to be pre-conditioned passively by solar gain when conditions are optimal.

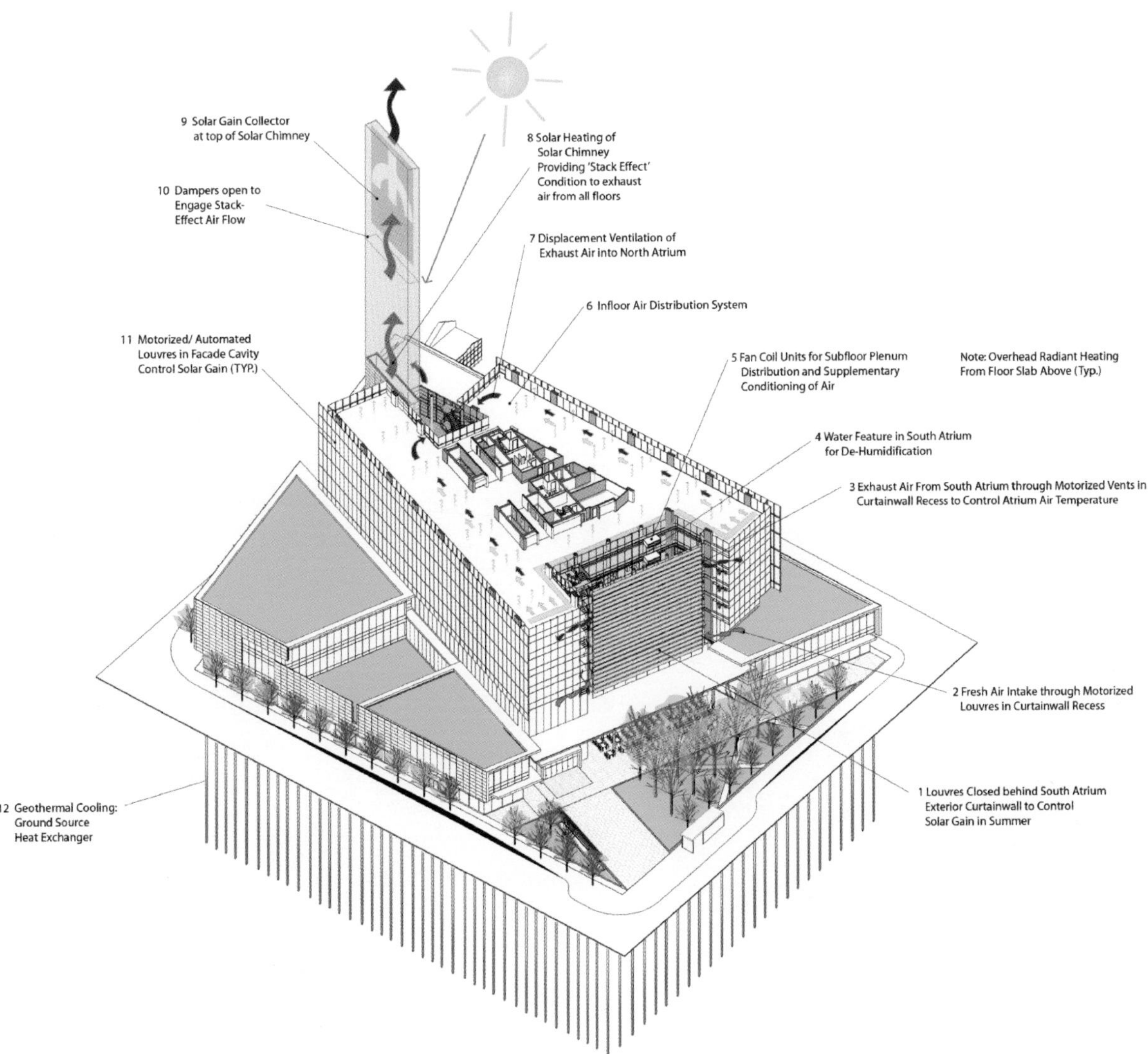

16.5 Manitoba Hydro Place, typical airflow diagram, summer operation

Summer days in Winnipeg can be warm but are usually not too humid. Summer nights are cool. The double-skin façade, therefore, can be used to remove heat from the building through natural ventilative cooling with thermal mass.

With its sophisticated system of blinds, operable windows, external and internal grilles and dampers, occupant-controlled and operated by a computerized energy management system, the double skin is in many ways the twenty-first-century version of the *Fortochka* found at the Winter Palace (see Chapter 3).

DAYLIGHT AND ELECTRIC LIGHT

The combined effect of a transparent façade, narrow 11.5-meter-deep floor plates, and high office loft ceilings allows 85 percent of the building to be sufficiently lit by natural light. Sensors in the electric light fixtures allow dimming down to 10 percent of maximum power level. The result is an office building where the occupants enjoy exposure to daylight and views during the majority of their work hours.

The lighting scheme as designed achieves a high degree of energy efficiency. There are, however, components of the lighting design that are not entirely satisfactory in practical use. The light fixtures cannot be turned off to 0 percent power level. Having all lights operate at 10 percent when there is an abundance of

16.6 Manitoba Hydro Place, winter morning view of double skin façade

16.7 Manitoba Hydro Place, interior view and energy savings diagram. Sculpture by Kevin McKenzie: "Resurrection II" (2006)

daylight in the space represents a significant amount of energy on an annual basis in a building that otherwise shows high performance on all fronts. Lights in elevator lobbies and core circulation spaces are on 24/7 for safety reasons. Here, an occupancy responsive system could present additional savings.

Besides its functional aspects, electric lighting also has a psychological effect, particularly in cold climates with short, dimly lit days. The need for an "energy boost" from electric lights sometimes causes occupants to demand electric lights, even if the daylight levels in the space are sufficient for the task at hand. In this situation, adding LED task lighting could potentially save energy, if used in tandem with dimmers that could shut off the general lighting system entirely.

ENERGY EFFICIENCY 2.0

At the onset of the design process, the team of architects and engineers were targeting an Energy Use Intensity (EUI) of 100 kWh/m^2-Y, already an ambitious goal for a tall office building in an extremely cold climate. Towards the end of the design process, when the energy modeling simulations were perfected, they were looking at an EUI of 88 kWh/m^2-Y, coming in below 30 kWh/ft^2-Y, a significant improvement relative to the already lofty goal.

This impressive level of energy performance was achieved after applying a multitude of passive and active environmental design strategies, including geothermal heat pumps exchanging energy with the ground deep below the building.

As the building became operational, however, it did not perform as well as expected. The team therefore initiated a thorough examination of how the building was performing. Energy use data broken down to a high degree of detail were used in comparison with energy modeling to investigate and search for discrepancies. In an attempt called "Energy Efficiency v. 2.0," pumps and motor controls were tuned, boilers were balanced against heat pumps and a multitude of tweaks and small improvements were made to the systems operations. The result (diagram in Figure 16.7) was a building that now performs better than the most ambitious goals, possibly the most energy-efficient tall office building in North America (Akerstream *et al.*, 2013).

33°N

17

Tempe Transportation Center

LOCATION: TEMPE, ARIZONA, USA

BUILT: 2009

ARCHITECT: ARCHITEKTON

LEED NC 2.1 PLATINUM

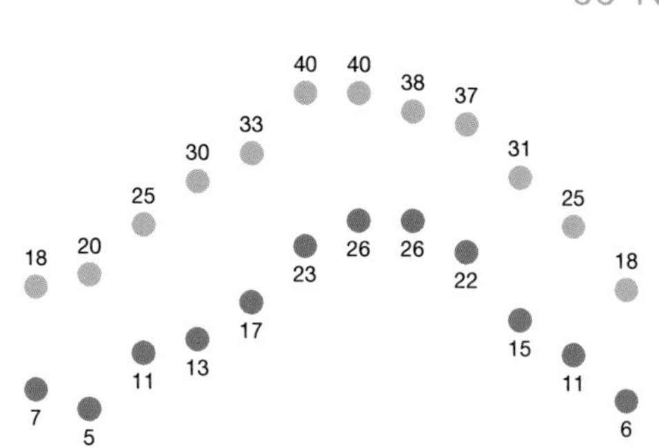

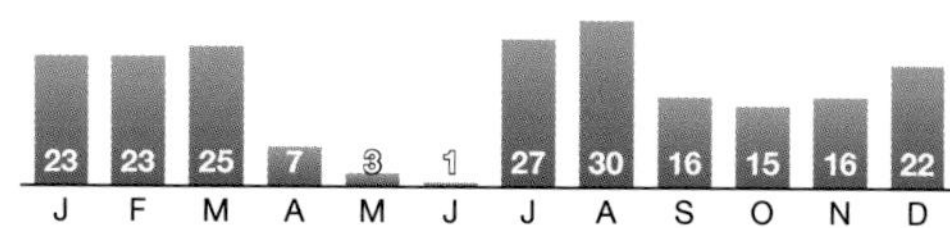

17.1 Tempe Transportation Center, view towards Tempe Butte

17.2 Light rail stop at Tempe Transportation Center

HIKE, BIKE, RIDE

Tempe Transportation Center is located near a trailhead at the foot of Tempe Butte. Hikers who ascend the trails to the top of the butte get a panoramic view of the Phoenix metropolitan area: the Valley of the Sun. From this vantage point one also gets the best view of a notable feature of the Transportation Center: its green roof.

Unlike most of the world's deserts, the Sonoran Desert is blessed with a unique biological diversity, where plants and animals have adapted to the predominantly hot and dry climate of the lower Arizona desert. As the name of the "valley" suggests, sun plays a dominant role among the environmental forces that plants, animals, people and buildings must relate to.

Rainfall is minimal and unreliable. While some months are almost entirely lacking precipitation, the "monsoon" may drop an inch of rain in less than a hour.

Basic considerations for any desert design, therefore, are concerned with sun, light and water: How to take advantage of solar radiation for space heating in the winter and how to create the shade needed to avoid unwanted solar gain in the summer. How to make the most efficient use of water, how to harvest water, to retain it and to recycle it in a desert environment.

Besides offering a good starting point for a hike up the butte, Tempe Transportation Center is a real transportation hub. Inside is a bike service shop with amenities for bike parking. The building connects to a light rail station on its north side. To the east lies the bus and shuttle terminal, which also accommodates ZipCar parking. There is ample public parking facilities for cars nearby.

Whether you hike, bike or ride a bus, a shuttle, a car or a tram, Tempe Transportation Center is where you switch among multiple modes of transportation.

WHERE IS THE SUN?

With the sun as a dominating environmental factor, it becomes necessary for a high performance building design to respond appropriately to the sun's diurnal and seasonal movement across

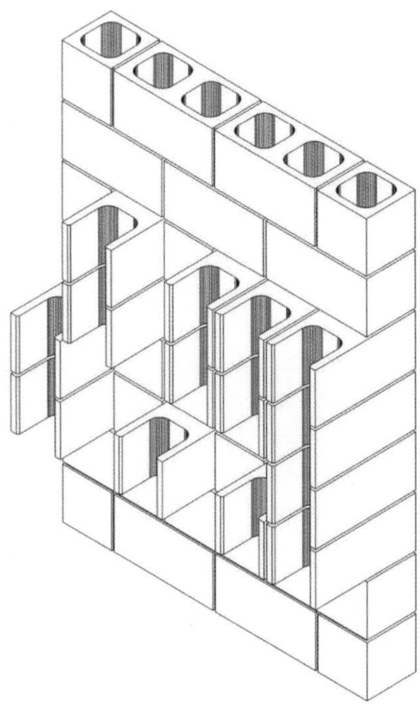

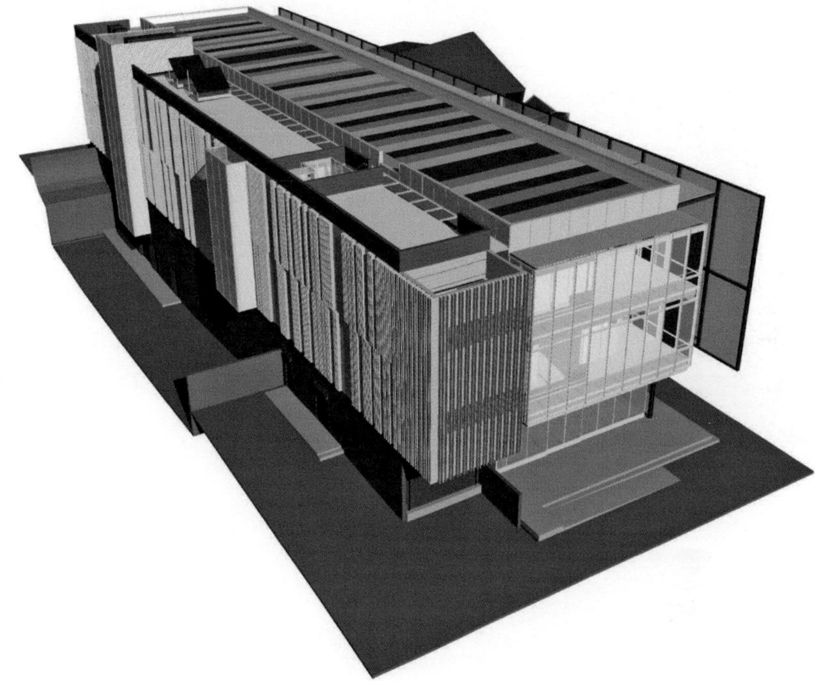

17.3 Isometric detail of west-facing wall, perspective with desert landscaping on the roof

the sky dome. The Tempe Transportation Center design clearly exhibits how climate-responsive design can be executed in such a hot and dry climate.

The overall organization of the floor plates into zones, as well as the façade treatment, exemplifies a unique design solution to each orientation: the ground below, the roof above, and the east, south, west and north façades.

Functional building elements and mechanical system components traditionally found in the central core of a building, such as air handlers and stairs, were organized in a re-configured core along the entire west face of the building. This buffer zone protects the building from unwanted solar gain on a hot afternoon. An inventive exterior wall assembly design using cut-up concrete blocks creates a shading effect resembling the ribs on a Saguaro cactus.

On the south side, the sun is controlled by deep overhangs, extending out from a curtain wall that is pulled back from the face of the building. This arrangement creates a porch-like extension of the conditioned space, sunny in the winter and fully shaded in the summer.

Two innovative and very different strategies were employed for the roof and the east-facing wall.

A DYNAMIC FAÇADE

The long axis of the building is oriented north–south, as determined by site conditions and zoning regulations, with a roughly 15 degrees clockwise rotation. The east side, therefore, is bathed in sun until one hour past noon. To address this challenge, the

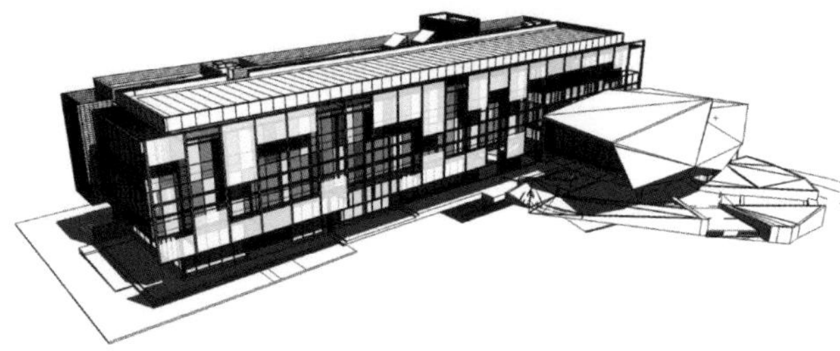

17.4 Early morning view of the east-facing façade, isometric diagram of dynamic shading

design team introduced a movable screen for sun control in front of a mostly glazed exterior wall facing the bus terminal.

The screen wall is constructed as a steel framework where adjustable and fully retractable blinds are installed. During the early morning hours, the blinds are fully engaged, as seen in Figure 17.4 (top). Then, as the sun climbs higher in the sky and changes its azimuth towards the south, the blinds can be partially pulled up, as seen in the lower image (Figure 17.4, bottom). After 1 p.m. the blinds can be pulled up along the entire façade, allowing more daylight to enter the office floors and opening up views to the outside.

RECYCLING AND UPCYCLING

A novel and unexpected approach to recycling is seen in the interiors and on the grounds under and around the building. One example is the signage (Figure 17.5, right) announcing room names and numbers and providing a small pad where a room schedule may be placed for shared meeting rooms. Scraps from galvanized steel studs and metal sheets were re-used on site to produce the signage, which appropriately takes on an industrial esthetic.

Outside, low gabion walls are used as landscaping elements, partially extending in under the elevated assembly space. Instead of commonly used crushed concrete or river rocks, the gabions are filled with glass "rocks" coming straight out of a glass recycling plant. The glass comes in many different shades and colors, adding beauty to a roughly designed functional object in public space.

GREEN ROOF IN THE DESERT

Early in the design process, the design team discussed which solutions to select for the roof. Since the roof sees the highest intensity of solar radiation during the hot desert summer, the team was looking for an effective way to prevent it from overheating and consequently transfer heat to the interior of the building. An additional design criterion was to find a solution that could add beauty to the building, as seen from Tempe Butte, while making a statement about how to design and build in harmony with nature.

A green vegetated roof was identified as one possible solution, but could a green roof survive in the desert? A green roof on a mid-size public building was not a new idea, but could it work here?

The team approached the School of Architecture at Arizona State University with this question. To find the answer, a research project was established, with faculty and graduate students building test units on the school's Solar Roof Laboratory.

After performing an experimental evaluation of several combinations of plant species, plant densities, soil types and irrigation schemes, the research team came to a conclusion. As seen in

17.5 Gabions filled with recycled glass, used as landscaping walls (left), recycled construction waste used as room signs (right)

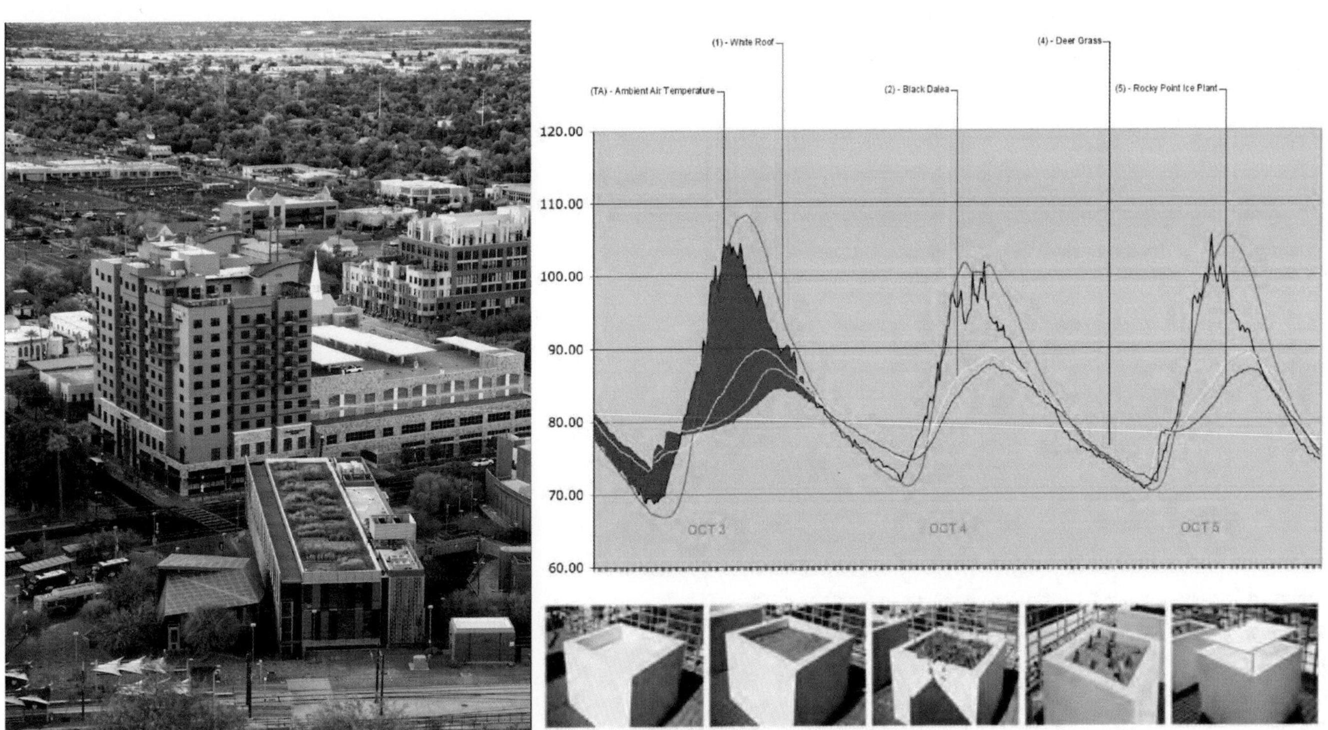

17.6 View from Tempe Butte of the vegetated roof (left), chart illustrated findings from research project (right)

Figure 17.6, the best performing green roof assembly would lead to a more stable temperature on the top of the roof membrane (under the plant material), which otherwise would see very large surface temperature swings. The cooling effect represented by significantly lower daytime temperatures would more than compensate for the slightly higher roof membrane temperatures at night (Lerum, 2005).

The research team made it clear, however, that a green roof would not survive in a desert climate without some form of irrigation. Therefore, the implemented green roof design incorporates irrigation using recycled water from the building.

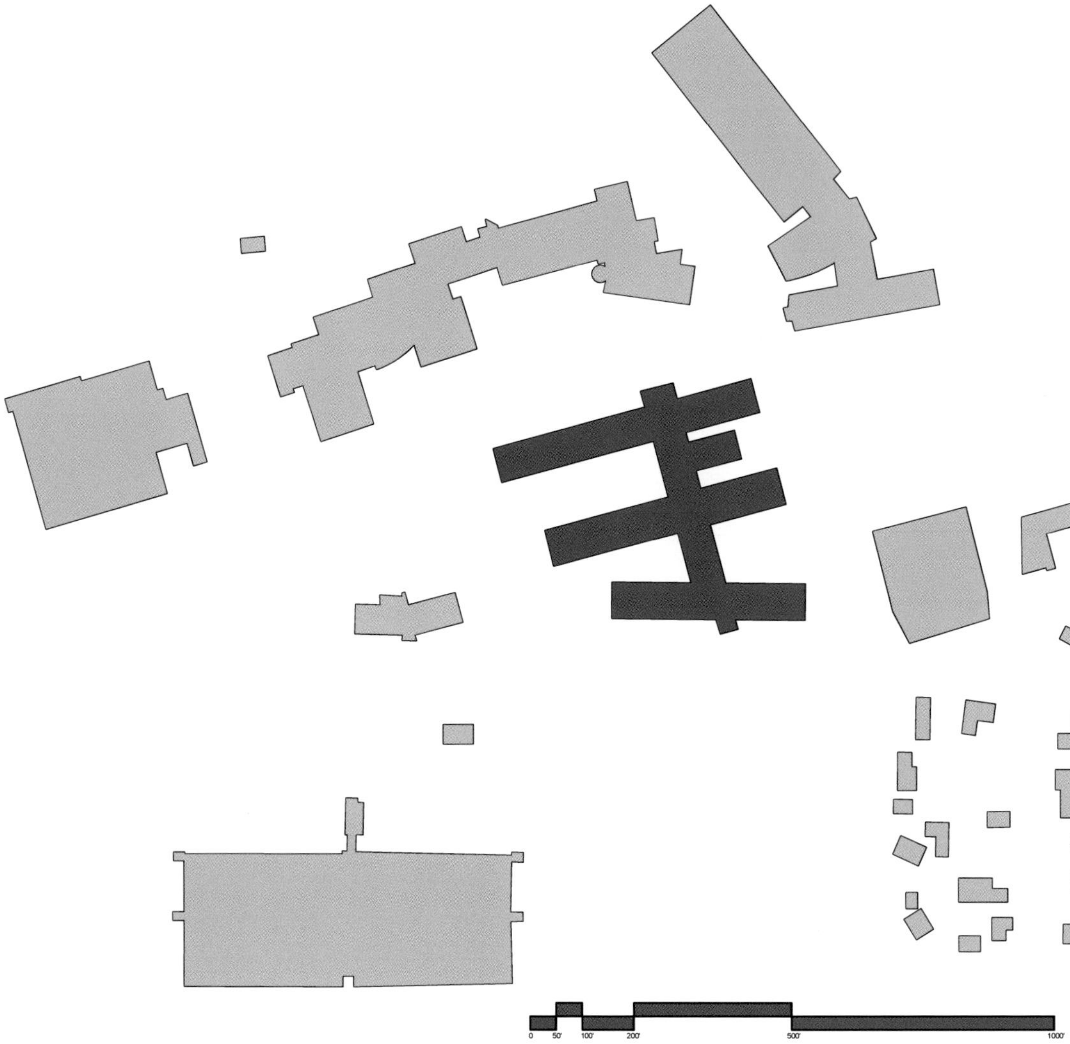

18

NREL Research Support Facility

LOCATION: GOLDEN, COLORADO, USA

BUILT: 2010

DESIGN-BUILD: RNL AND HASELDEN CONSTRUCTION

LEED-NC PLATINUM CERTIFIED

NET ZERO SITE ENERGY

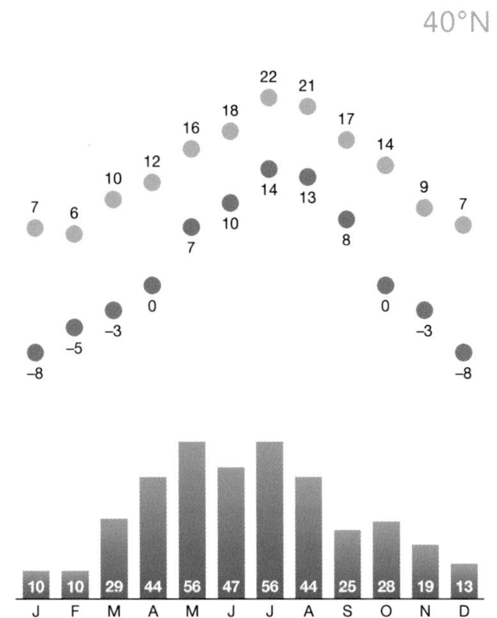

18.1 NREL Research Support Facility, view from the east

TRANSPIRED

The Research Support Facility at the National Renewable Energy Laboratory (NREL) in Golden, Colorado, was designed not only as a functional and comfortable work environment. There was also a vision to use the 360,000 square feet (33,445 m^2) three-story building to showcase best practices in the application of sustainable, energy efficient and innovative technologies and solutions.

Implementing and showcasing a variety of the latest and greatest technologies made the new facility into a laboratory in and of itself. Real-time monitoring of performance parameters at a small physical scale and at small time intervals generates big data that NREL can use to analyze and, if necessary, improve solutions and technologies at the forefront of high performance building design. Some of the implemented technologies were invented at NREL, such as the transpired façade integrated solar collectors installed on the south side (Figure 18.2) and the electrochromic glass installed on the west-facing window walls.

Located in a semi-arid continental climate zone, the NREL campus enjoys 300 days of sunshine in a typical year. Winter nights can be quite cold and summer days hot and dry. These are environmental conditions that invite the use of passive design strategies for heating, cooling and daylighting, as a first step on the road to net zero energy use.

18.2 NREL Research Support Facility, view of south-facing transpired solar collector

BACK TO THE FUTURE

In many ways, the final design scheme for the Research Support Facility (RSF) looks to the past before looking into the future. Passive strategies, tried and tested through centuries, were applied in an attempt to minimize auxiliary energy use before implementing new high tech products and solutions.

The three-story building is divided into three parallel bars, each 40 feet wide, with their long sides facing south and north. South-facing windows coupled with thermal mass walls and slabs act as devices for direct solar gain in the winter. In the summer, when the sun is high in the southern sky, architecturally integrated overhangs and side fins effectively shade the glass, while optical louvers allow filtered daylight to enter the office interiors.

Operable windows on the north and south façades help create a comfortable and enjoyable work environment responding to diurnal and seasonal swings. On a cool night followed by a hot and sunny day, the building is purged as high mass night ventilation cooling is applied. On a comfortable day in spring or fall, the building is naturally ventilated.

The transpired solar collectors heat fresh air as it is pulled in behind the perforated, corrugated steel panels. The warmed air is circulated through a concrete labyrinth in the crawlspace under

18.3 NREL Research Support Facility, south façade

18.4 NREL Research Support Facility, exposed radiant floor system

the building, thus reducing the energy required to precondition ventilation air when the building is in closed/winter mode.

A three-layer assembly is used for the prefabricated exterior wall elements. Two inches (50 mm) of rigid insulation is sandwiched between a 3-inch (75 mm) exterior concrete layer and a 6-inch (150 mm) interior concrete wall, combining the advantages of thermal resistance, thermal lag and thermal storage capacity.

By taking advantage of climate responsive passive design strategies, the energy demand for space conditioning, ventilation and proper workspace lighting is dramatically reduced.

HYBRID SYSTEMS

A significant portion of energy savings in office buildings is related to methodically and analytically separating space conditioning systems from systems required for heating and cooling of ventilation air. At the NREL Research Support Facility, 70 miles (113 km) of piping and tubing were used to install hydronic heating and cooling embedded in the floor slabs and the steel and concrete roof. Radiant ceilings, therefore, heat and cool the office floors independent of the air system.

A dedicated outside air displacement ventilation system supplies fresh air through grilles in the raised floor. This quiet, energy-efficient, low velocity air supply system maintains indoor air quality when the building is in closed mode (summer and winter). When conditions are favorable, natural ventilation takes over the task of providing fresh air, and high mass night ventilation cooling takes over the task of removing heat. While chilled water is primarily supplied through evaporative cooling, high efficiency chillers are used for back-up.

An innovative cooling system developed for the large data center plays an important role in achieving the overall energy performance of the research support facility. Outside air is pulled down an air intake tower where additional cooling is provided by evaporative cooling devices or chillers, as needed. Inside the data center, heat is contained in the bays. Hot air is pulled back into the labyrinth below the building (or exhausted to the outside) as cool air is brought in from the tower. With a measured power usage effectiveness (PUE) of 1.1, the RSF can showcase one of the most efficient data centers in the world.

BEETLE KILL PINE

Beetle-killed pine harvested from Western forests is used extensively as interior wall surfaces throughout the building. This warm and beautiful material is also used to form sculptural elements, such as the two-story-tall back wall in the main lobby.

The project exhibits other creative ways of using recycled or reclaimed products, minimizing the depletion of natural resources:

- Crushed concrete from the demolition of the old Denver airport was used as aggregate in foundations and site-built concrete floor slabs.
- Structural steel columns were made from reclaimed natural gas pipelines.
- Countertops are made with sunflower seed hulls.
- A network of basins and canals forms an integral part of a storm water management plan, leading surface water to retention areas where the water is discharged back into the ground. Crushed, recycled glass is used in the basins to create subsurface pathways, thus reducing loss of water to evaporation.

18.5 NREL Research Support Facility, interior wall clad with "beetle-killed" pine

18.6 Design strategies for daylight distribution at the Research Support Facility (left) and the Energy Systems Integration Facility (right)

HOW ARE WE DOING?

Starting with a design target Energy Use Intensity of 25 kBtu/ft^2-Y (79 kWh/m^2-Y), the project landed an EUI of 34.4 kBtu/ft^2-Y (108 kWh/m^2-Y), including heating, cooling, lighting, plug loads and the large data center. The increase from design target to real-world performance reflects various improvements in user comfort implemented during the design process.

With a total occupied floor area (including the data center) of 360,000 square feet (33,445 m^2), the annual energy use comes in at around 3.6 million kWh. A 2.5 MWp photovoltaic system was built to offset the annual energy demand, effectively bringing the balance in at net zero site energy.

Panels installed on the roofs of the three wings account for 868 kWp of photovoltaic peak capacity. The remaining 1,670 kWp arrays are installed as shading canopies over a guest parking lot and a staff parking structure.

NREL found that up to 30 percent of energy savings in office buildings depends on occupancy behavior. Without actively engaging the users, a significant portion of the achievements reached through all the hard design phase work could be compromised.

At the RSF, users are reminded by notes popping up on their screens when it is time to shut off task lighting or open the windows. Significant savings were achieved by eliminating individual space heaters and personal printers. When daylighting is insufficient, 25W T8 fluorescent light fixtures provide 30-foot candles (300 LUX) on work surfaces.

Plug loads associated with one work station were reduced to 56 W: one 18 W display, a 30 W laptop computer, a 6 W task light and a 2 W VOIP telephone.

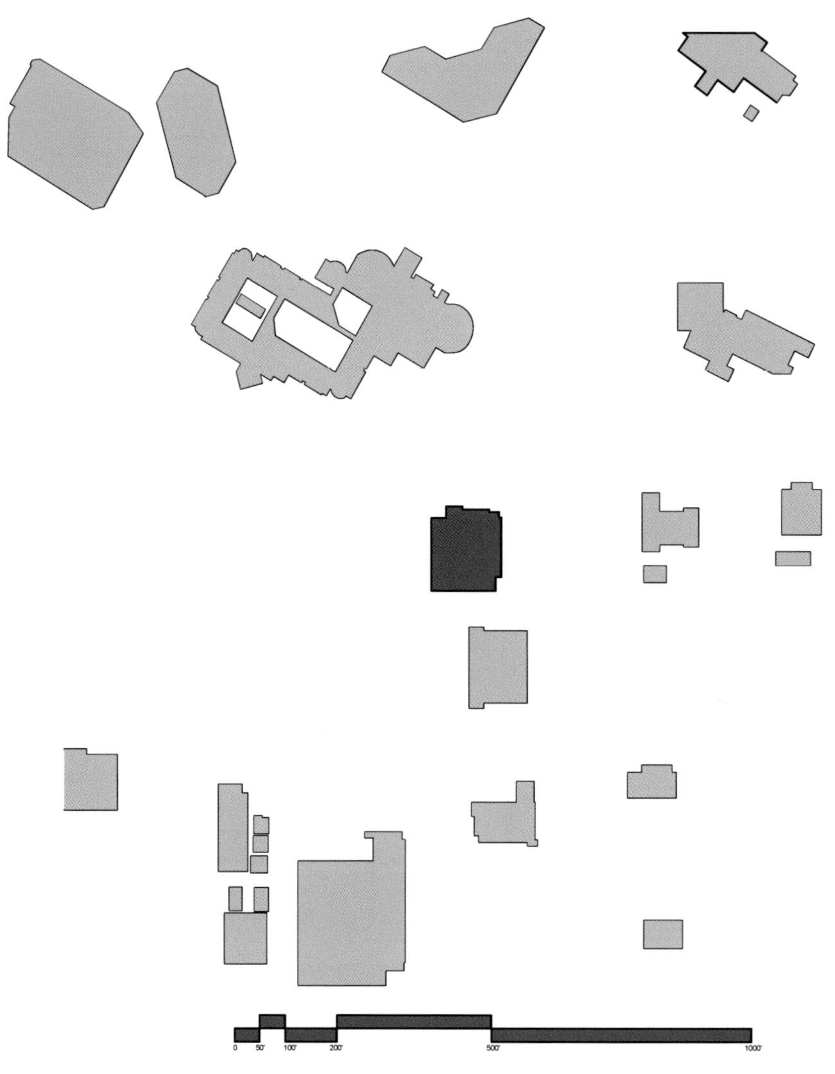

33°N

19

DPR Construction

LOCATION: PHOENIX, ARIZONA, USA

BUILT: 2011

ARCHITECT: SMITHGROUPJJR

SBIC BEYOND GREEN AWARD

LIVING BUILDING CHALLENGE 2.1 CERTIFIED

LEED PLATINUM CERTIFIED

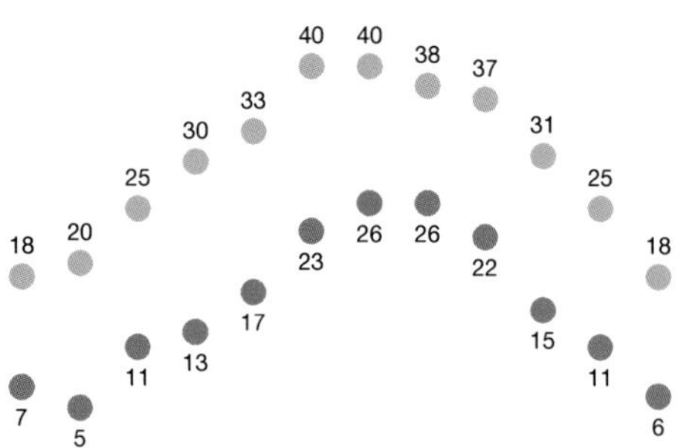

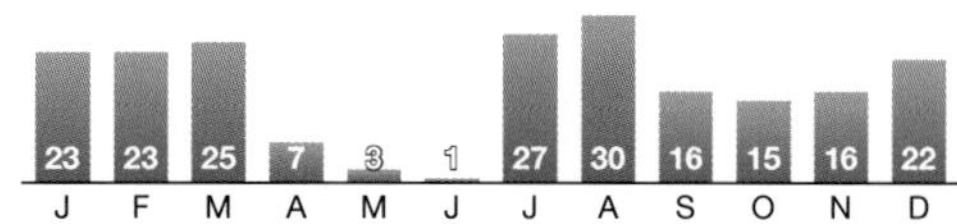

19.1 DPR Construction Phoenix Regional Office, main entrance

19.2 The building before renovation, view of east façade

REUSE, RENEW, REVITALIZE

In 2010, approaching the end of the lease period for their office space in the Camelback Corridor, DPR Construction looked at an urban renewal zone in search of a new home for their Phoenix Regional Office. They found a windowless building formerly used as a paint store and later turned into an adult bookstore (Figure 19.2).

The structurally sound one-story building was pushed up against the property line to the south and west, leaving the corner lot developed with parking towards 44th Street to the east and Van Buren Street to the north. Reusing and modernizing a building on a developed site helped the project team meet the first of many sustainable design criteria. Passing the Limit to Growth requirement established by the International Living Future Institute, the project also contributes to a much-needed revitalization in an urban renewal zone.

The centrally located site promises easy access to the building by car on busy surface streets, by bike, along paths running parallel to the canal network and by the new light rail system which also connects directly to the Phoenix Sky Harbor airport terminals.

PHOENIX: A BUILDING REBORN

After a design and construction period of only ten months, the dilapidated windowless building was reborn as a modern net zero energy office building (Figure 19.3). While leaving most of the existing building shell intact, a vast transformation had taken place.

Program elements commonly associated with the core of a building, such as bathrooms, server room, central printing facilities and storage rooms, were located along the south and west edges of the floor plate, leaving exterior walls on these two sides with only a few small window openings. Accepting a penalty for

19.3 DPR Construction Phoenix Regional Office, view from north-east

not taking advantage of passive solar heating during a short winter, the L-shaped perimeter core acts as a buffer against unwanted solar heat gains during a summer that typically comes with a hundred days with temperatures above 100° F.

The north and east façades were opened up with large, glazed panels and operable overhead doors, protected by a "green screen."

DESIGN STRATEGIES

Opening up the building with large expanses of transparent exterior walls to the north and east provides access to views of the outside (Figure 19.4). The green screens along these two sides of the building filter sunlight and create a connection to nature, transforming views towards harder, automobile-dominated surfaces beyond the screen.

Windows and glazed overhead doors are shaded by translucent panels. In contrast to the massive buffer zone towards the south and west, the rusted steel-supported green screen and translucent shading create a habitable indoor-outdoor space, a comfortable environment on the doorstep between a desert city climate and climate-controlled work spaces inside.

Operable windows are used for natural ventilation and ventilative cooling. A building dashboard publishes real-time climate and performance information, encouraging the users to open the windows when beneficial to comfort and energy efficiency.

A grid of more than 80 solar tubes piercing through the roof supplement natural light entering the office from the side. This hybrid daylighting scheme covers near 100 percent of the work stations, allowing the responsive control system to turn off electric lights during daytime work hours. High output fluorescent tube fixtures cut down on the energy use when daylight levels are insufficient.

19.4 DPR Construction Phoenix Regional Office, indoor/outdoor connections

A building that comes alive as its envelope and its systems respond to changing environmental conditions in real time will ultimately change the way users interact with and react to climate conditions inside. By adopting an expanded comfort zone definition, additional savings in energy use are achieved. From a winter morning to a summer afternoon, the indoor air temperature fluctuates between 68° F (20° C) and 82° F (28° C).

At the end of the work day, a "vampire switch" is activated to shut off phantom plug loads, leading to a reduction of about one-third of the energy allocated to computers, printers and the like.

FOUR SHOWER TOWERS AND A SOLAR CHIMNEY

In the hot and dry desert climate of Phoenix, Arizona, summer comes with unbearably hot days. As the ambient temperature climbs towards 120° F (50° C) in the afternoon, the following night may not offer much relief. With a coincident minimum air temperature of around 30° C, continuous mechanical cooling is unavoidable for days and weeks on end. Focusing on these extremes, however, can take attention away from seasons when the outdoor conditions are more favorable.

In March, with a design dry bulb temperature of 32° C (90° F) and a mean coincident wet bulb temperature of 15° C (60° F), the relative humidity is around 12 percent. Under such climatic conditions, an efficient evaporative cooling device could lower the air temperature to below 20° C (68° F), approaching 18° C (65° F) during the hottest hours of the day.

Four shower towers located on the east side of the building work in tandem with an 80-ft-long solar chimney on the roof of the building (Figure 19.5). The zinc-clad solar chimney creates a negative pressure, pulling air out of the building. At the top of the shower towers, misters create a spray, causing water to evaporate in the dry air. Colder air with higher density falls down the chimney and is allowed to enter the habitable space through grilles with motorized, automated dampers.

This alternative, mainly passive, cooling system is controlled by a building energy management system using live weather data to activate the shower towers, reducing the hours of operation in mechanical cooling mode by 24 percent.

19.5 DPR Construction Phoenix Regional Office, view of one of the shower towers

MATERIALS

When a suspended ceiling with inadequate thermal insulation was removed, a beautiful wood structure came into view (Figure 19.6). Additional insulation was added on top of the roof before installing a new white membrane. Most of the new wood used during construction came from sources certified by the Forest Stewardship Council (FSC). Space-defining interior panels were made from FSC-certified fast growing bamboo.

Depletion of natural resources was limited in many ways. Since the new office building was furnished with work stations recycled from DPR's previous location in Phoenix, only a few new work stations had to be built.

19.6 DPR Construction Phoenix Regional Office, interior

19.7 DPR Construction Phoenix Regional Office, view of east façade with PV canopy above parking area

THE PATH TOWARDS NET ZERO

Implementing strategies for water reuse in a desert city office building is challenged by limited access to rainwater and graywater. During the three first months in 2014, the rainfall in Phoenix totaled 32 mm (1.26 inches). Therefore, the design team focused on water-saving measures.

Waterless urinals and high efficiency plumbing fixtures installed throughout the building contribute to a reduction in indoor water use of 40 percent as compared to the LEED 2009 baseline. Landscaping with drip-irrigated drought-tolerant plants reduced outdoor potable water use by 75 percent over the same baseline. Water captured from condensation on cooling coils inside the roof-mounted heat pumps is used as replacement water for the evaporative cool towers, which offsets some of the tower water use.

A 4.5 kW closed loop solar thermal system with two solar collectors on the roof and a 85-gallon storage tank supplies a modest demand for hot water to sinks and showers.

Several innovative and carefully executed energy-saving techniques led to a considerable decrease in the annual energy demand for heating, cooling, lighting and plugged-in devices. Based on measured and documented energy used in the building and energy produced on the site, the project was one of the first office buildings to be certified as a Net Zero Energy building by the International Living Future Institute.

With an annual output of 142,000 kWh, the 79 kWp photovoltaic system on the roof of the parking area (Figure 19.7) more than offsets the energy used by the building. An annual energy use of less than 135,000 kWh divided by a floor area of just above 1500 m^2 results in an Energy Use Intensity (EUI) of 88 kWh/m^2-Y or 28 kBtu/ft^2-Y.

34°N

20

Morphosis Studio

LOCATION: CULVER CITY, CALIFORNIA, USA

BUILT: 2011

ARCHITECT: MORPHOSIS

TARGETING NET ZERO ENERGY

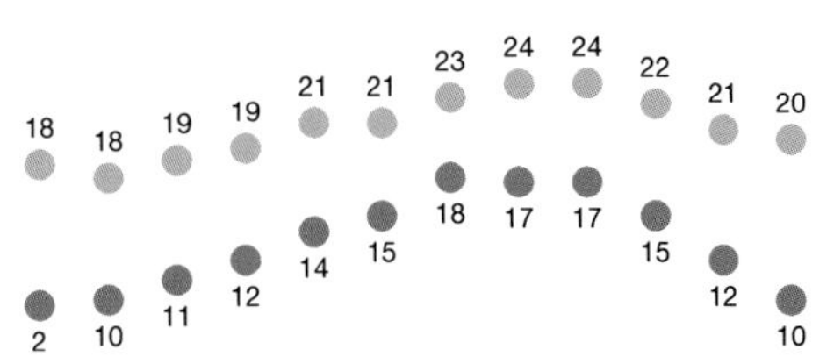

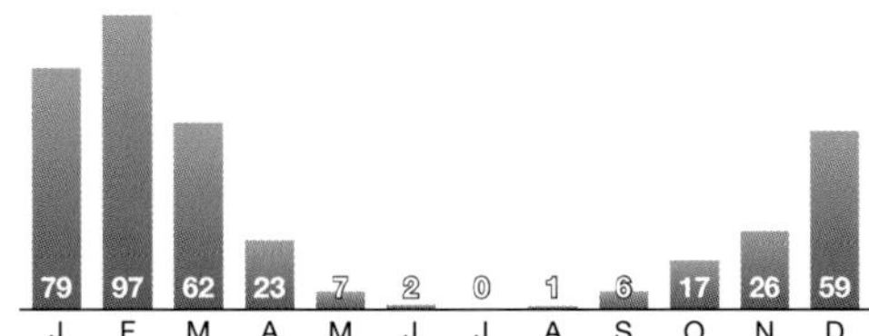

20.1 Morphosis Studio, exterior wall used for full-scale testing of façade systems

AT THE EXPO LINE

When Morphosis was ready to move out of their workshop and offices in Santa Monica, California, they found an irregularly shaped vacant lot in Culver City for their new home. Located just north of the light rail Expo Line, the site is connected to Downtown Los Angeles, and eventually Santa Monica, by public transportation.

The building pushes up against the site boundary with masonry walls facing south and east, uninterrupted by any openings. A long roof slopes gently towards the south, protected by a layer of white corrugated steel panels. It is towards the south-west that the building opens up, with large glass panels facing a secluded courtyard. A steel structure filters the low afternoon sun. Along with mature trees, it provides shelter for the patio, creating a pleasant connection of the interior spaces to the outdoors.

Los Angeles enjoys a mild climate with average day maximum temperatures ranging from 16° C in February to 24° C in August. Average minimum temperatures are below 15° C for nine months out of the year, and well below 20° C during the three warmest summer months. In this climate type, it becomes evident that a building targeting net zero energy use must respond to its natural setting by allowing and controlling solar radiation, daylight and outside air.

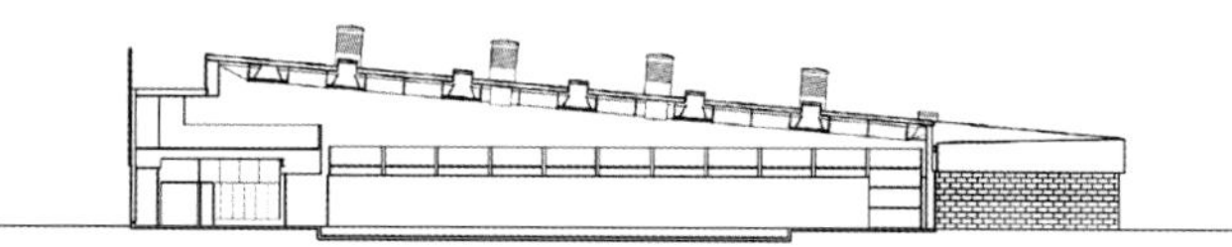

20.2 Morphosis Studio, section through double-height space showing skylights and wind catchers in sloping roof

TEMPORAL MODALITY: TIME AND MOVEMENT

The Morphosis Studio building was designed to change its properties in response to variations in the ambient conditions. This temporal modality reflects the building's ability to negotiate internal and external swings through diurnal and seasonal cycles.

The long sliding window wall facing the patio is shaded by the building in the morning hours. Then, as the sun moves to a high position at noon, opaque glass overhangs create necessary shade. In the afternoon, as the sun moves lower towards the west, mature trees work with a steel structure to filter the light (Figure 20.3).

It is this intimate and dynamic relationship between the studio and the patio that lets the building breathe horizontally. Vertically, the high bay studio space breathes through the wind catchers on the roof (see Figure 20.4). It is also through the roof that the studio receives most of the daylight that fills the interior from dawn to dusk.

CATCHING AIR: FILTERING LIGHT

For centuries, wind catchers have been used to improve comfort in buildings. In arid climate zones wind catchers were used along with inventive courtyard designs to pull fresh air down into evaporation chambers before the cooled air was allowed to pass through the building interiors before escaping out onto the patio.

The twenty-first-century version installed on the roof of the Morphosis Studio is a monodraught wind catcher that exchanges outside air with the building's interiors within one device. Damper blades inside the unit allow the air to move in and down on one side while escaping up and out on the opposite side. Damper positions are controlled by motors powered by photovoltaic cells on the south-sloping top of the unit, responding to sensors registering ambient air parameters.

When conditions are favorable, the wind catchers can naturally ventilate the interiors during daytime for comfort and improved air quality. Measurements show a CO_2 concentration around 650 ppm, well below the accepted maximum of 8–900 ppm CO_2.

On a cool summer night the interior air temperature can be lowered 4–5° F. In this scenario, the wind catchers work with the thermal mass in masonry walls and concrete floors to generate a

20.3 Morphosis Studio, sliding glass panels open up to a patio shaded by mature trees

20.4 Morphosis Studio, skylights and wind catchers protrude the roof, bringing light to and exchanging air with the double height studio space

capacity to provide free cooling by absorbing heat from the interior and storing it until the next diurnal cycle begins.

Eighteen square skylights in the main roof allow daylight to filter into the studio below. Fluorescent tube light fixtures integrated into the light wells are equipped with dimmers and daylight sensors. Levels of natural light at the work surface have been measured as high as 80 lumbers per square foot, above 850 Lux. The recommended light level for office work with computer monitors ranges from 300 to 500 Lux.

DESIGN LABORATORY

The Morphosis Studio is not only a sustainable work environment for the production of architectural services. It is also a design laboratory. The north-west façade, facing the covered parking, extends into a steel structure suitable for testing components and assemblies proposed for projects the firm is currently involved in.

20.5 Morphosis Studio, exterior wall extension used for full-scale testing of façade systems, while defining and protecting the patio

20.6 Morphosis Studio, tandem parking arrangement protected by photovoltaic panels for onsite electricity generation

The opaque, insulated part of the wall can be used to test windows and other exterior wall assemblies, while the steel structure extension is used for exterior panels and shading devices.

Figure 20.5 shows a section of exterior shading panels proposed for the new Emerson College building in Hollywood.

TARGETING NET ZERO

Parking is organized in a tandem arrangement along the northwest edge of the lot. A canopy of photovoltaic panels covers the two-car deep parking bay (Figure 20.6). With an annual electricity production of 62,000 kWh, the PV system offsets about half the total gross annual energy demand.

According to the energy consultants Buro Happol, the Energy Use Intensity (measured) is 16.3 kBtu/ft^2-Y. Further improvements in energy efficiency, along with the possibility of extending the PV array, will bring the building closer to a target EUI where the annual energy use will match the on-site energy production.

POST OCCUPANCY EVALUATION

To further document and analyze how the building performs, a comprehensive post-occupancy evaluation project aims at generating a database of metrics that will be used to fine-tune the comfort system operations, the building itself and how it is used. While smart meters and sub-metering are used to collect building and systems performance data, sense-cams and other wearable devices will register comfort parameters and biometrics, as experienced by the people who use the building on a daily basis.

Rayner Banham wrote extensively about buildings as comfortable "environments fit for human activities" (Banham, 1984). Advanced post-occupancy evaluation procedures, including high technology measuring devices, will help designers approach that definition in a scientific manner.

20.7 Morphosis Studio, sliding entrance gate, design by Tom Farage

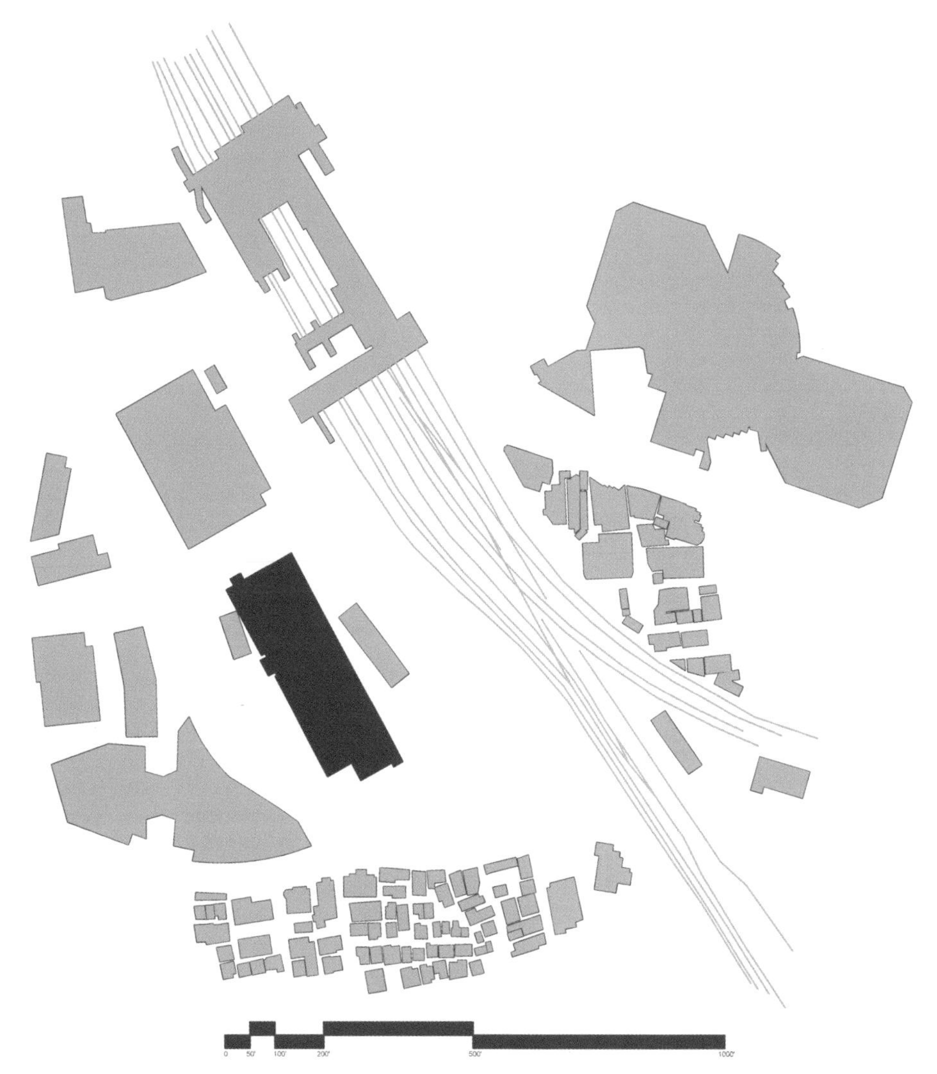

21

36°N

The Sony Osaki Building

LOCATION: SHINAGAWA-KU, TOKYO, JAPAN

BUILT: 2011

ARCHITECT: NIKKEN SEKKEI

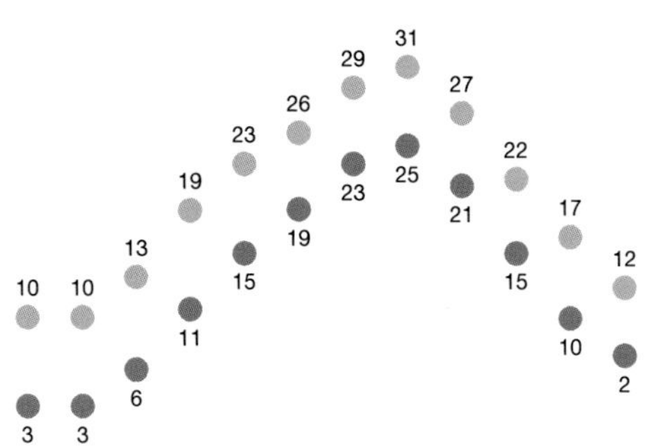

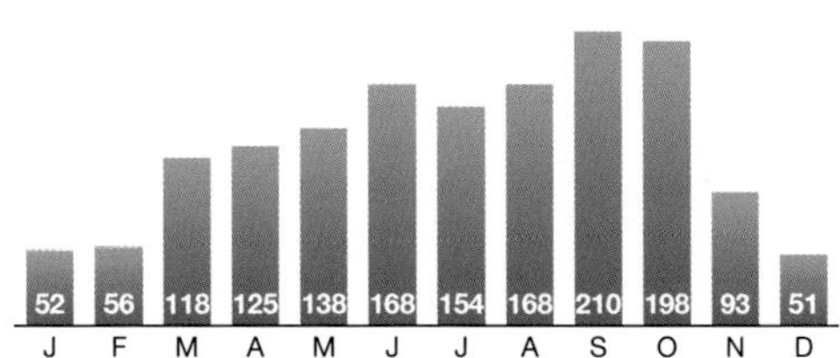

21.1 Sony Osaki Building, view from the east

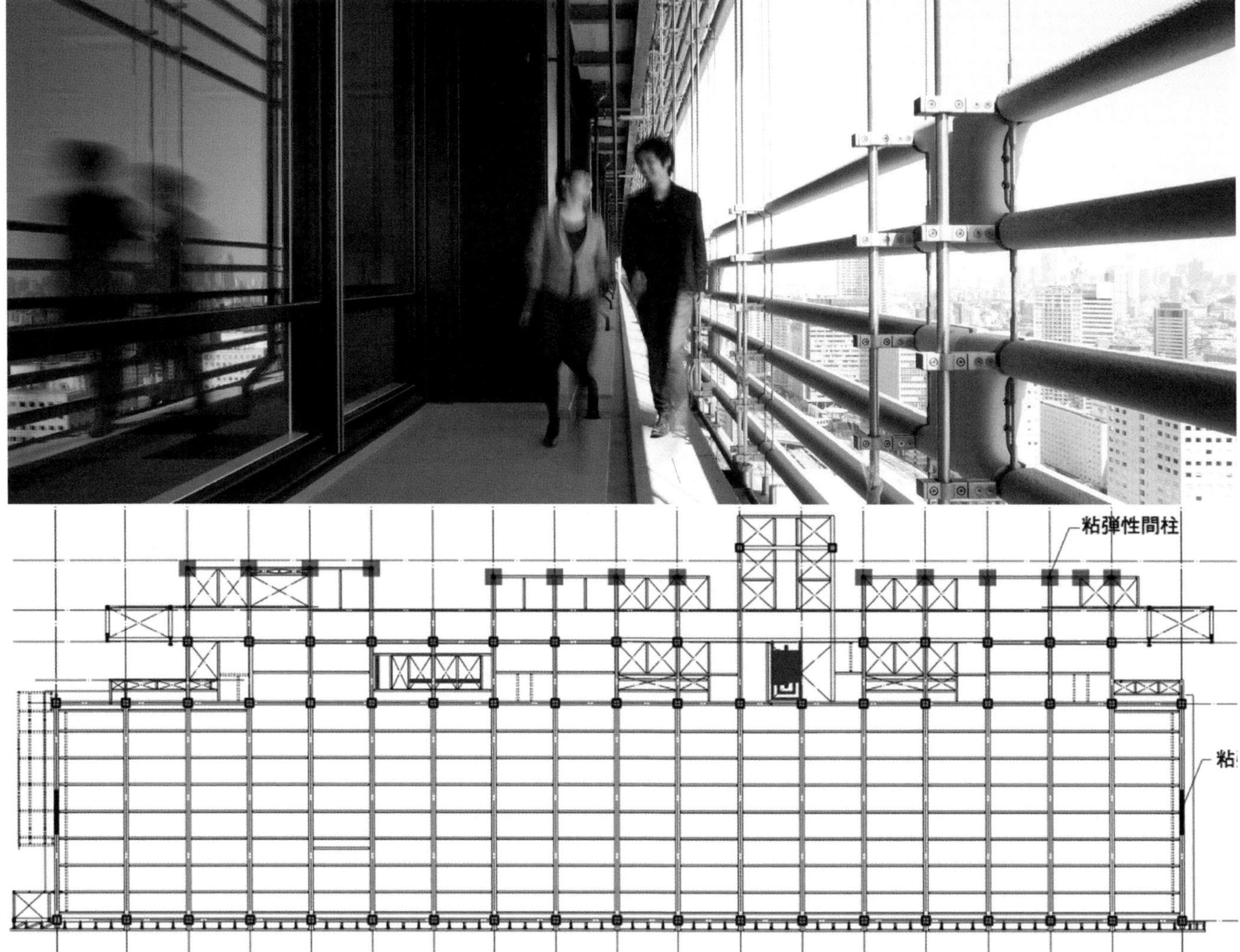

21.2 Sony Osaki Building, exterior balcony with ceramic tube evaporative cooling system

AT THE STATION

You get off the train at Osaki station as one of more than 100,000 other users that day and the Sony building immediately comes into view. Two minutes later, you find yourself on a landscaped plaza in front of the main entrance at the foot of the 133-meter-tall building, housing 5000 employees at Sony's Research and Development department.

Oriented with its long sides along the north–south axis and rotated 30 degrees counter-clockwise, the building's façades exhibit unique architectural responses to climate and location. While the fully glazed east side is protected from the sun's rays by a screen made of ceramic tubes providing evaporative cooling, the mostly opaque west side is shielded by shiny steel panels with narrow, tall windows interspersed sparingly on the 23-story-tall façade.

Exterior balconies along the entire east façade continue around to the short ends of the building. Acting as building-integrated shading devices, the balconies also serve other functions: as emergency escape routes and as easy maintenance access for window cleaning and for servicing the ceramic screen.

EVAPORATIVE CERAMICS

The evaporative screen design was inspired by the ancient technique of using porous clay vessels filled with water as means of cooling the surrounding air. Horizontally mounted ceramic tubes are joined together into one large water drainage system running down the entire east façade (Figure 21.3). The vertical spacing of the tubes varies in response to the screen's functions:

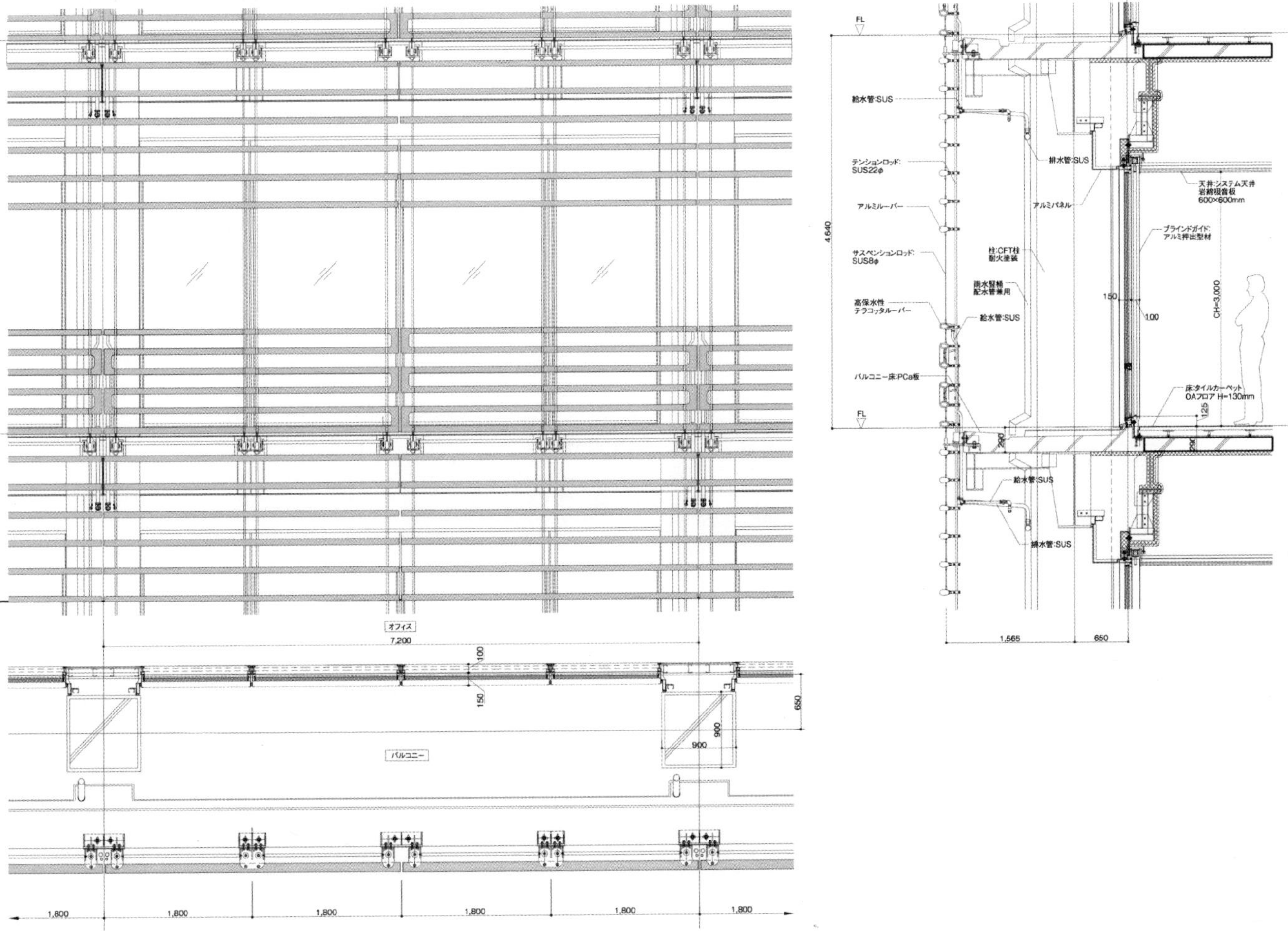

21.3 Sony Osaki Building, plan, elevation and section of façade screen with ceramic tube evaporative cooling system

In addition to cooling the façade, the screen also filters daylight (the upper portion), leaves openings for views to the urban landscape (the mid-section) and forms the balcony railing.

The tubes channel rainwater collected from the roof of the building and filtered before feeding the evaporative process. Reservoirs beneath the building are used to collect water on rainy days. The water is pumped back into the ceramic screen during periods of hot and dry weather.

A seemingly simple idea of utilizing heat removal associated with evaporating water to cool the building required extensive engineering and product development before the concept could materialize as a functioning façade assembly. To make that happen, the design team found a partner in Toto, one of the world's leading makers of ceramics for bathrooms.

IN RESPONSE TO CLIMATE

The final form for the ceramic tube cross-section is an elongated rectangle with rounded ends. A glazed ceramic material was used for the lower portion of the cross-section, preventing dripping from the tubes as water is running down the façade inside them. The remaining portion of the cross-section is made from a porous ceramic material, allowing the evaporative process to take place as the tubes are heated by solar radiation. The entire 23-story-tall screen, therefore, acts as a gigantic evaporative cooler.

On a warm day in the early summer, the design dry bulb temperature could reach 26° C with a mean coincident wet bulb temperature of 18.4° C (*ASHRAE Handbook*, 2005). Under these conditions, the screen could lower the air temperature by as much as 6 degrees C. Decreasing the temperature of the air adjacent to the glazed façade from 26 to 20 degrees would represent a significant cooling load reduction.

21.4 Sony Osaki Building, computational fluid dynamic simulation diagram shows cooling effect of the ceramic tube façade screen

21.5 Sony Osaki Building, view of the west-facing façade

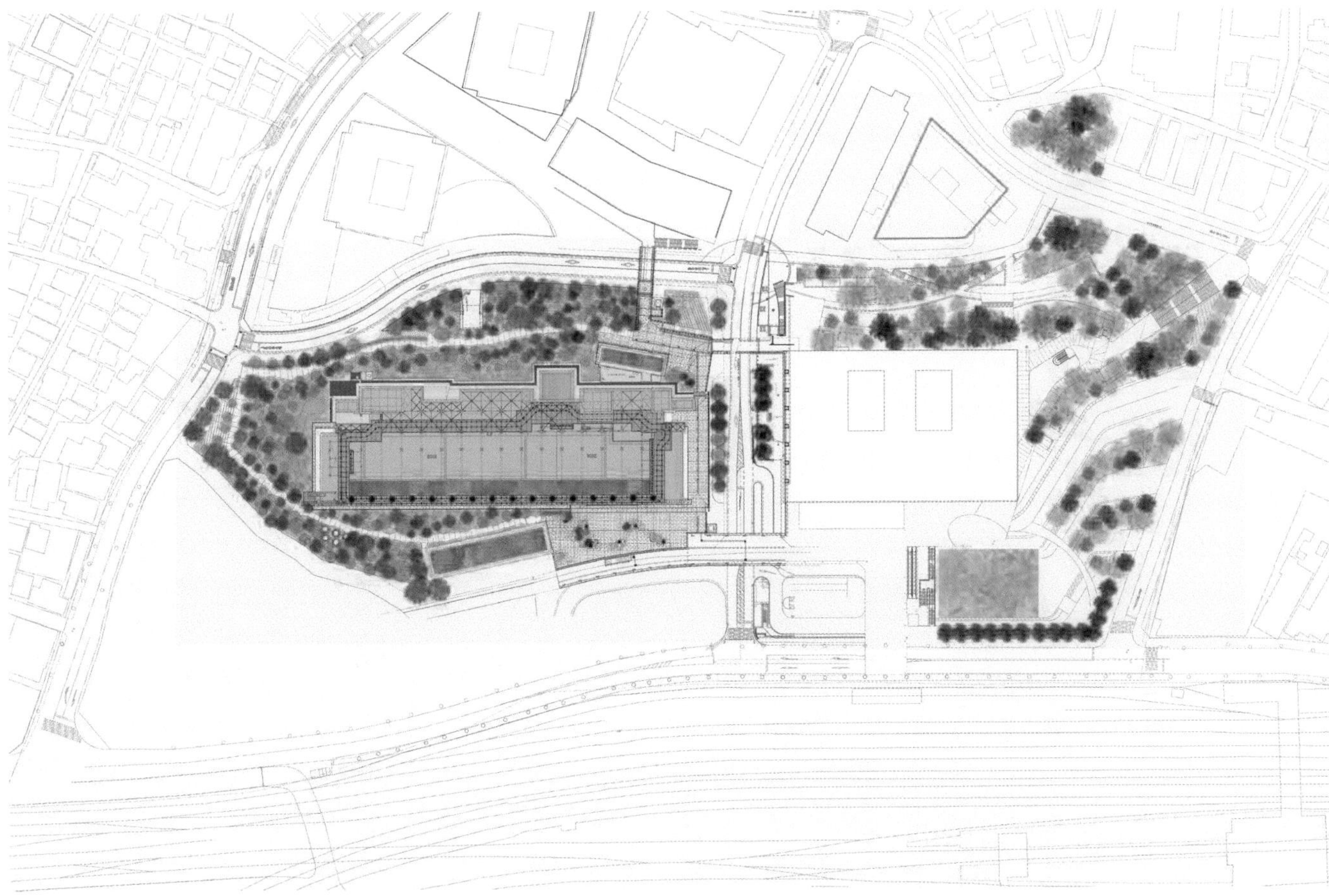

21.6 Sony Osaki Building, landscaping plan

Since the power of the evaporative cooling effect increases with rising ambient air temperatures and decreasing humidity, the thermal performance of the screen will fluctuate diurnally and seasonally. Figure 21.4, generated from computational fluid dynamic simulations, illustrates the general performance pattern: cooler air surrounding the tubes slowly descends towards the entrance plaza and garden.

THE SUN SHIELD

With all core functions moved towards the west side of the floor plate, the building offers 24-meters-deep free-span office floors, uninterrupted by servant spaces or columns. The considerable floor plate depth defines the limit to how consistently the building may take advantage of natural light to illuminate its interiors. This limitation, however, is offset by improved flexibility and space efficiency, which could greatly extend the building's life expectancy in a city known for its rapid transformation in the built environment.

Architecturally, the placement of core functions along the entire west side offers an opportunity for a unique façade expression, where the shiny, mostly opaque metal skin takes on sculptural properties, modestly perforated with narrow glazed vertical openings. In contrast to the cool, light-filtering evaporative grille on the front side, the back façade stands tall as a piece of minimalist art (Figure 21.5).

BIODIVERSITY

As the design team developed a detailed plan for landscaping the grounds around the building, advanced computer simulations were used to generate scenarios showing how plants could grow and interact. Available data on plant properties, such as growth rate, soil requirements and adaptation to sun and shade, were entered into the computer model (Figure 21.6). This method aided the designers in making decisions regarding the age and maturity of the great variety of species to be planted. The end result is a garden showcasing biodiversity in a man-made ecological system inspired by the natural growth, aging and renewal of lands less impacted by human interaction.

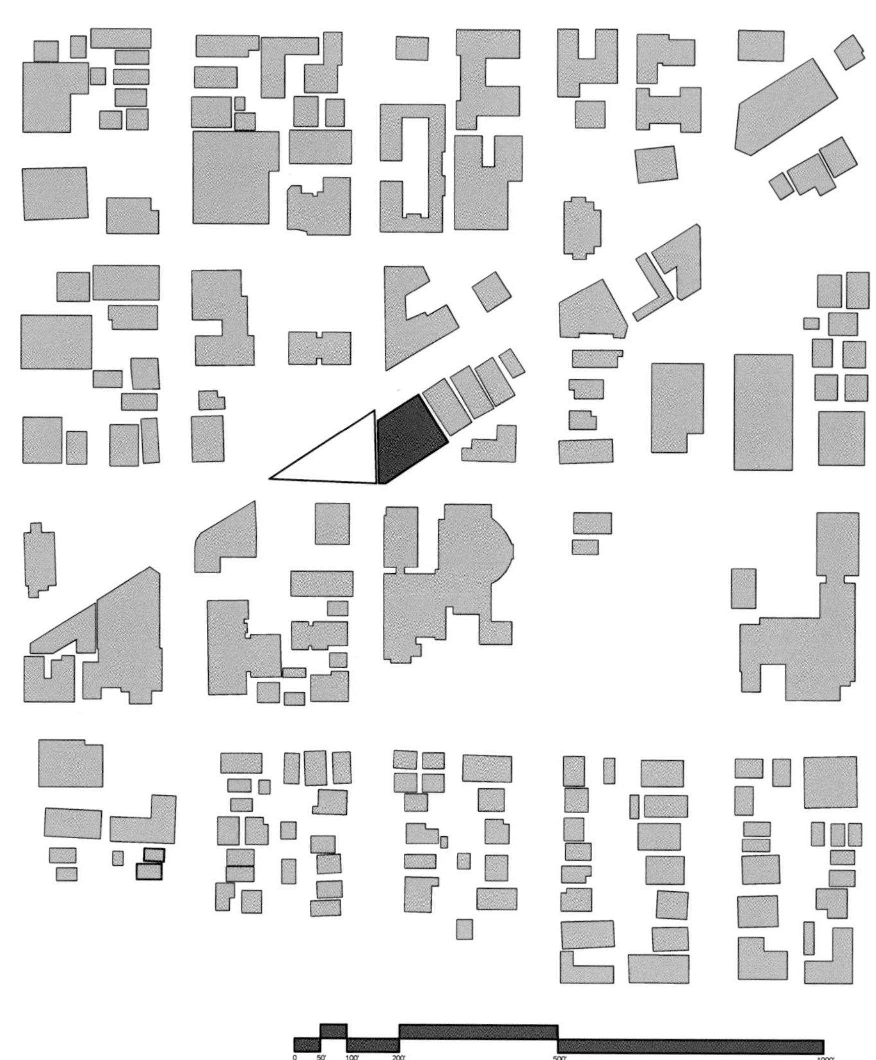

48°N

22
The Bullitt Center

LOCATION: SEATTLE, WA, USA

BUILT: 2010

ARCHITECT: THE MILLER HULL PARTNERSHIP

TARGETING LIVING BUILDING CHALLENGE CERTIFICATION

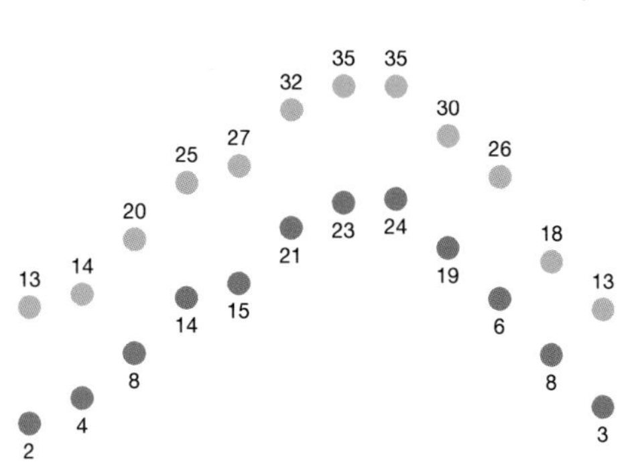

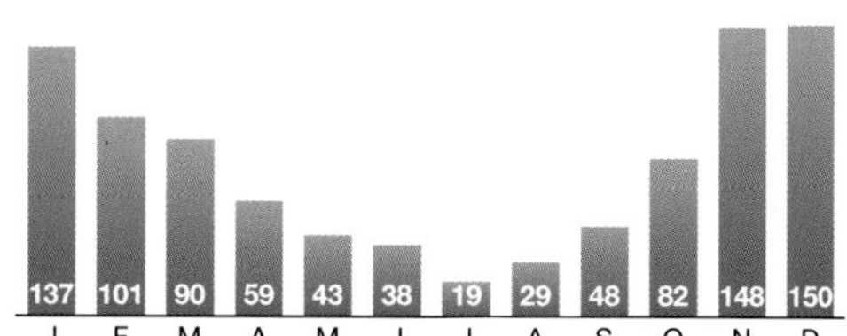

22.1 Bullitt Center, view from East Pike Street

22.2 Bullitt Center, photovoltaic roof canopy

A LIVING BUILDING

To build a five-story net zero office building on a tight lot in a Pacific North-West city might, at first, seem like a daunting task. With no extra room outside the building footprint to generate energy on-site, the energy demand required on an annual basis would have to be supplied by integrated systems on the building itself. How could that be done in the city of Seattle with an average 266 cloudy days in a typical meteorological year?

This was one of the major challenges facing the client and the design team. As they took steps beyond energy performance, the client asked the team to design a building that was functional, beautiful, sustainable, net zero energy and net zero water. In other words, the Bullitt Center was targeting Living Building Challenge certification.

Located on the south side of East Madison Street, which runs at an angle to the orthogonal grid, the building has one façade facing directly west, one façade blocked by a neighboring building, and the remaining two façades facing north-west and south-east. Immediately to the west, there is a grove of tall, mature trees in a small triangular city park. This grove of trees presented themselves as an opportunity for some shade and a wonderful view of their canopies.

THE PATH TOWARDS NET ZERO

During the early stages of the design process, the client and the design team worked with researchers, educators, consultants and advisors to generate several design schemes for analysis and critical evaluation.

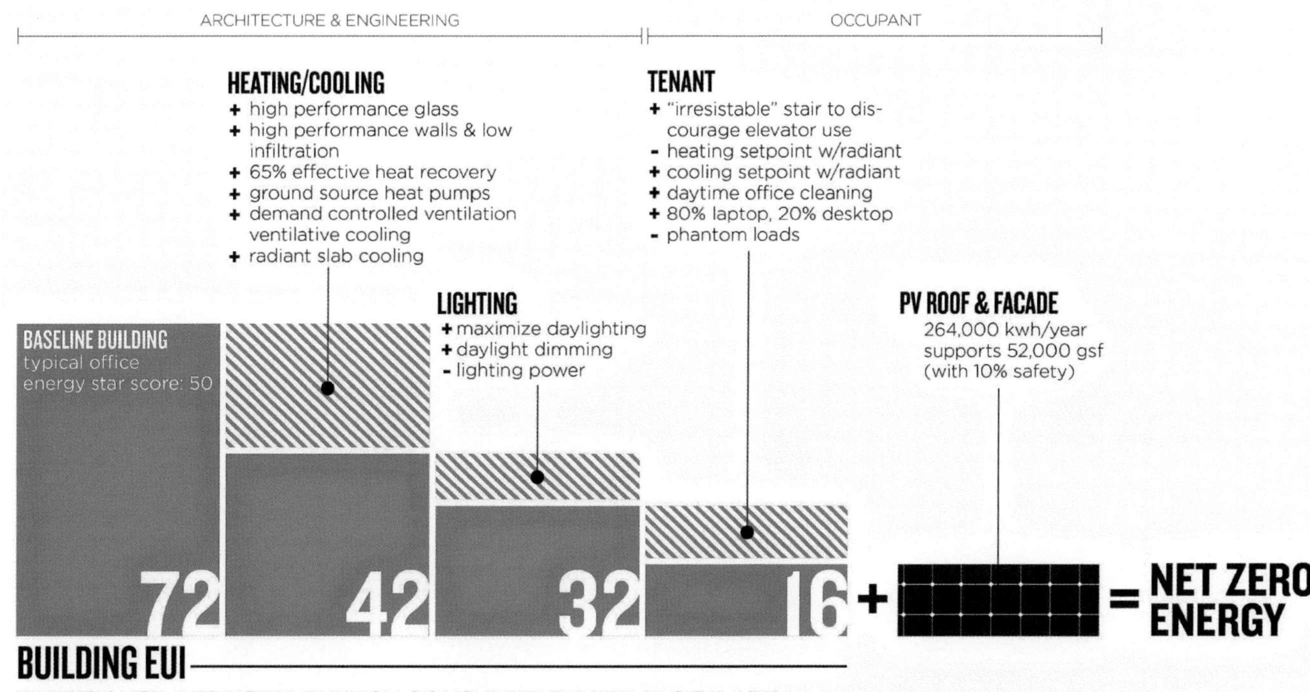

22.3 Bullitt Center, design strategies for net zero energy, decreasing energy use intensity

Since the need to provide access to daylight was a given, floor plans with light wells and atria were taken into consideration. The end result of this exploration, however, was to eliminate any light well or atrium. Carefully placing the core in the middle of a 70-ft-wide floor plate made it possible to reach 82 percent daylight coverage while achieving a favorable ratio of rentable space over total floor area.

With the overall footprint of the building in place, the team set out to solve the energy equation. How low could one possibly make the energy demand side of the equation, and how could that demand be supplied by electric energy produced on the building itself?

The team decided to approach this question by calculating backwards: While keeping an eye on how to minimize energy demand, they set out to find out how to maximize the annual electric energy production from building integrated photovoltaic panels. The ideal orientation and tilt of a photovoltaic roof canopy were found to be a sloping surface facing due south at a 25 degree altitude angle. But such a roof surface could not be implemented without asking the city for a variance from the building height zoning limitation.

The team found that if a record low Energy Use Intensity of 16–20 kBtu/ft^2-Y could be achieved, the building would still use roughly 250,000 kWh electric energy per year. Simulations showed that a 14,000 ft^2 photovoltaic array facing south at a 10 degree tilt angle could meet that demand. Since the building footprint was less than 14,000 ft^2, the team decided to ask the city for permission to extend a PV canopy out over sidewalks and setbacks, as an alternative to applying for a variance from the height limit.

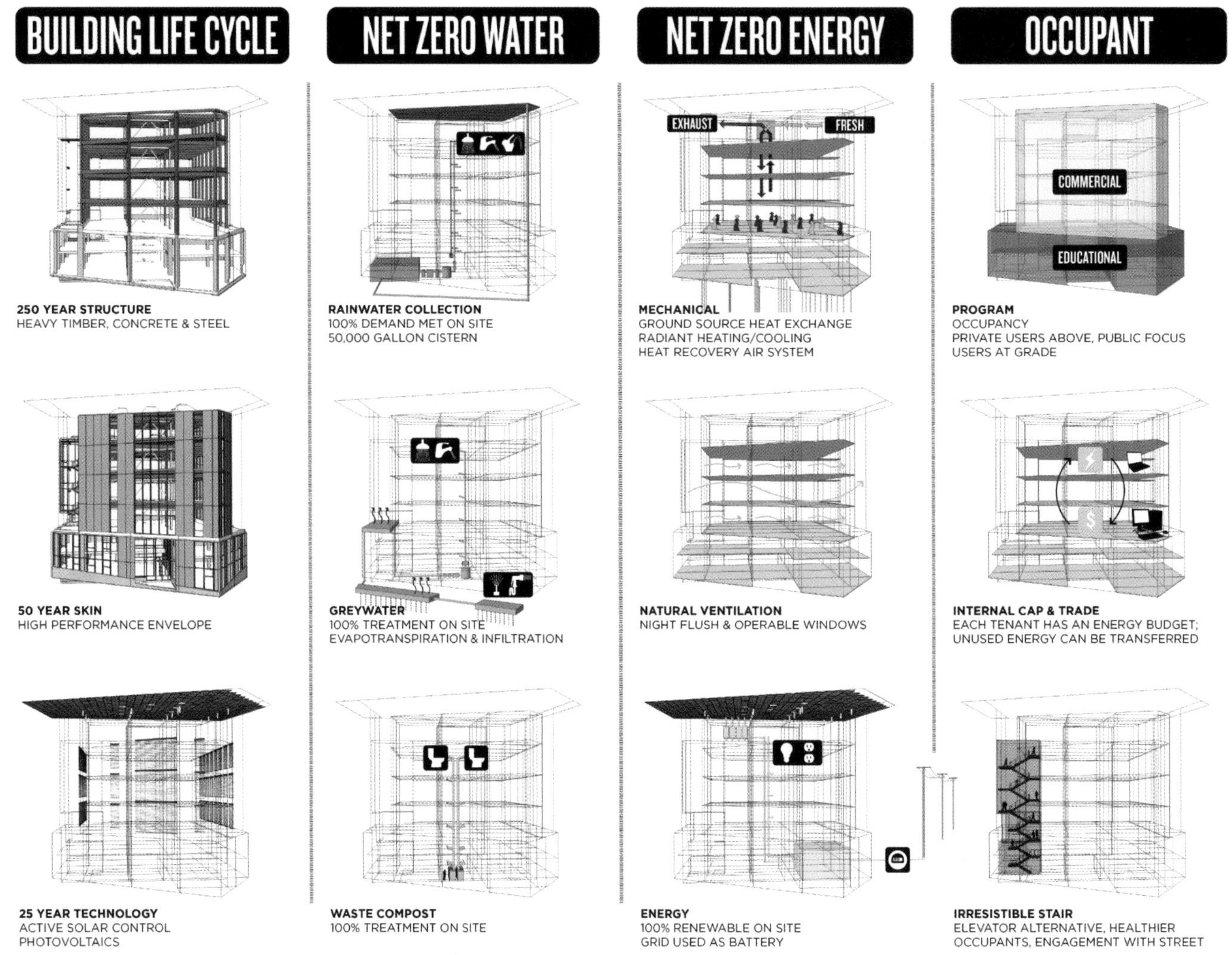

BUILDING LIFE CYCLE

250 YEAR STRUCTURE
HEAVY TIMBER, CONCRETE & STEEL

50 YEAR SKIN
HIGH PERFORMANCE ENVELOPE

25 YEAR TECHNOLOGY
ACTIVE SOLAR CONTROL
PHOTOVOLTAICS

NET ZERO WATER

RAINWATER COLLECTION
100% DEMAND MET ON SITE
50,000 GALLON CISTERN

GREYWATER
100% TREATMENT ON SITE
EVAPOTRANSPIRATION & INFILTRATION

WASTE COMPOST
100% TREATMENT ON SITE

NET ZERO ENERGY

EXHAUST
FRESH

MECHANICAL
GROUND SOURCE HEAT EXCHANGE
RADIANT HEATING/COOLING
HEAT RECOVERY AIR SYSTEM

NATURAL VENTILATION
NIGHT FLUSH & OPERABLE WINDOWS

ENERGY
100% RENEWABLE ON SITE
GRID USED AS BATTERY

OCCUPANT

COMMERCIAL
EDUCATIONAL

PROGRAM
OCCUPANCY
PRIVATE USERS ABOVE, PUBLIC FOCUS
USERS AT GRADE

INTERNAL CAP & TRADE
EACH TENANT HAS AN ENERGY BUDGET;
UNUSED ENERGY CAN BE TRANSFERRED

IRRESISTIBLE STAIR
ELEVATOR ALTERNATIVE, HEALTHIER
OCCUPANTS, ENGAGEMENT WITH STREET

22.4 Bullitt Center, design strategies for a net zero energy building

With deep cuts in energy demand for heating, cooling, lighting and occupancy loads, an extended PV canopy could balance the energy equation at a target EUI of 16 kBtu/ft^2-Y or 50 kWh/m^2-Y (Figure 22.3).

DESIGN STRATEGIES

A sustainable building targeting the requirements of the Living Building Challenge is not only a performance-driven net zero energy and net zero water building. It is also a building that is designed to have a long life, serving its users through generations, offering a functional, healthy, and beautiful work environment.

The promise of a long life comes with a well-crafted building that is flexible and requires minimum maintenance. All parts of a building, however, do not have the same life expectancy. Therefore, main building assemblies and systems are integrated, but at the same time separable. While the structural wood, concrete and steel systems may last for 250 years, the building envelope has a 50-year design life, while active sun control devices and photovoltaic panels may need to be replaced after 25 years.

To achieve net zero water use, rainwater is collected and stored, graywater is treated on site and waste from toilets is composted.

A high performance envelope combined with ground source heat pumps, hydronic heating and cooling, natural ventilation, efficient lighting and daylight design reduce the energy demand.

In the end, a living building will depend on its users to reach a level of high performance. An "irresistible" stair encourages occupants to skip the elevator and walk up the building. An internal "cap and trade" system lets users buy and sell energy units while staying within the overall energy budget for the building as a whole.

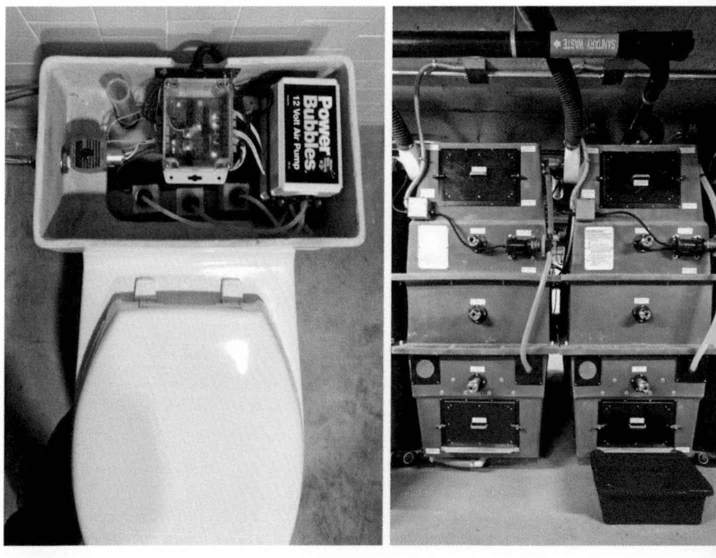

22.5 Bullitt Center, waterless toilet (left), sanitary waste digesters (right)

WATER AND WASTE

Rainwater collected from the roof below the photovoltaic canopy is stored in a 56,000-gallon cistern in the basement. The generous size of the water storage tank ensures that 100 percent of the clean water requirement is met. Water harvested on site is used for showers and lavatories in the building and to irrigate green roofs and exterior landscaping. Potable water delivered to the site is only used for drinking and cooking.

All graywater from the building is treated on site. Vegetated roofs and infiltration beds below ground transform the water, turning it back into a useful resource. Processed graywater feeds back to nature by evapotranspiration to the atmosphere and by infiltration into the earth, replenishing groundwater and restoring the predevelopment hygroscopic balance of the site.

Waterless toilets and urinals use foam and vacuum pumps to transport waste into an array of composting digesters placed in the basement (Figure 22.5). Sawdust is added to the mix. Eventually the processed waste will be transported offsite and used as fertilizer.

LIGHT AND AIR

Core elements are placed at the center of the floor plate and pushed up against a windowless wall towards the neighboring building on the north-east side. This leaves the rentable portion of a typical office floor with ample access to daylight, views to the outdoors and fresh air through operable windows. The windows predominantly take on a portrait format, reaching to the ceiling. The high-performing window system incorporates thermally broken aluminum frames and an opening mechanism that moves the large glass panes out horizontally, always leaving the face of the glass in a vertical position.

22.6 Bullitt Center, the large sliding glass panel provides natural ventilation and a view towards the park

The windows are controlled by the building energy management system. When ambient air conditions are favorable, the system responds to indoor air parameters. The building comes alive, changing its property with nature, using cool night air to remove heat from the structure after a warm summer day, improving indoor air quality at no cost through natural ventilation.

Large sliding glass panels on the west façade opens up to let the users enjoy a close connection to the canopies of mature park trees (Figure 22.6).

22.7 Bullitt Center, typical office floor

MATERIALS

Above a podium built with reinforced concrete, the main structure is entirely made from certified wood from sustainable harvests. This structural system of laminated floor slabs and heavy timber columns and beams is complemented by one steel frame for lateral bracing at each floor (Figure 22.7).

To avoid using massive heavy timber construction from large mature trees, all components of the wood structure were made from smaller size wood, laminated with non-toxic glue.

Tubing for the hydronic heating and cooling system is embedded in a layer of concrete poured on top of the laminated wood slabs. To help reduce carbon emissions associated with traditional reinforced concrete structures, fly-ash was used to replace most of the Portland cement in the mix. Roughly 95 percent of the reinforcement bars came from post-consumer recycled steel.

Hydronic heating and cooling embedded in the structure, combined with a sophisticated natural ventilation and cooling scheme, reduce the load on the mechanical forced air system to a minimum. Forced air is used primarily to ensure indoor air quality when the building is in closed mode and for cooling and dehumidification on the hottest summer days.

Integrated design decisions involving structure, materials and comfort systems render the offices with exposed concrete floors in a loft-like environment where the warmth and beauty of wood play a dominant role.

BIOPHILIA AND THE IRRESISTIBLE STAIRCASE

The new Bullitt Center building is capable of establishing a connection to nature and maintaining a comfortable work environment while balancing heating, cooling, ventilation and sun control. But the center would not qualify as a living building without actively engaging its users. The irresistible staircase occupies prime real estate on East Madison Street (Figure 22.8), inviting the users to save energy and improve health by not using the elevator.

According to the biologist E. O. Wilson, "biophilia" is described as an innate and genetically determined affinity of human beings with the natural world. By enabling its occupants to form connections to nature, living buildings could promote health and well-being, ultimately leading to improved productivity.

While the irresistible staircase at the Bullitt Center stands as the symbol of a green, living building, connections among humans, man-made structures and nature go deeper and broader, pointing towards future sustainable designs for the built environment.

22.8 Bullitt Center, view from East Madison Street, with "irresistible" stairs

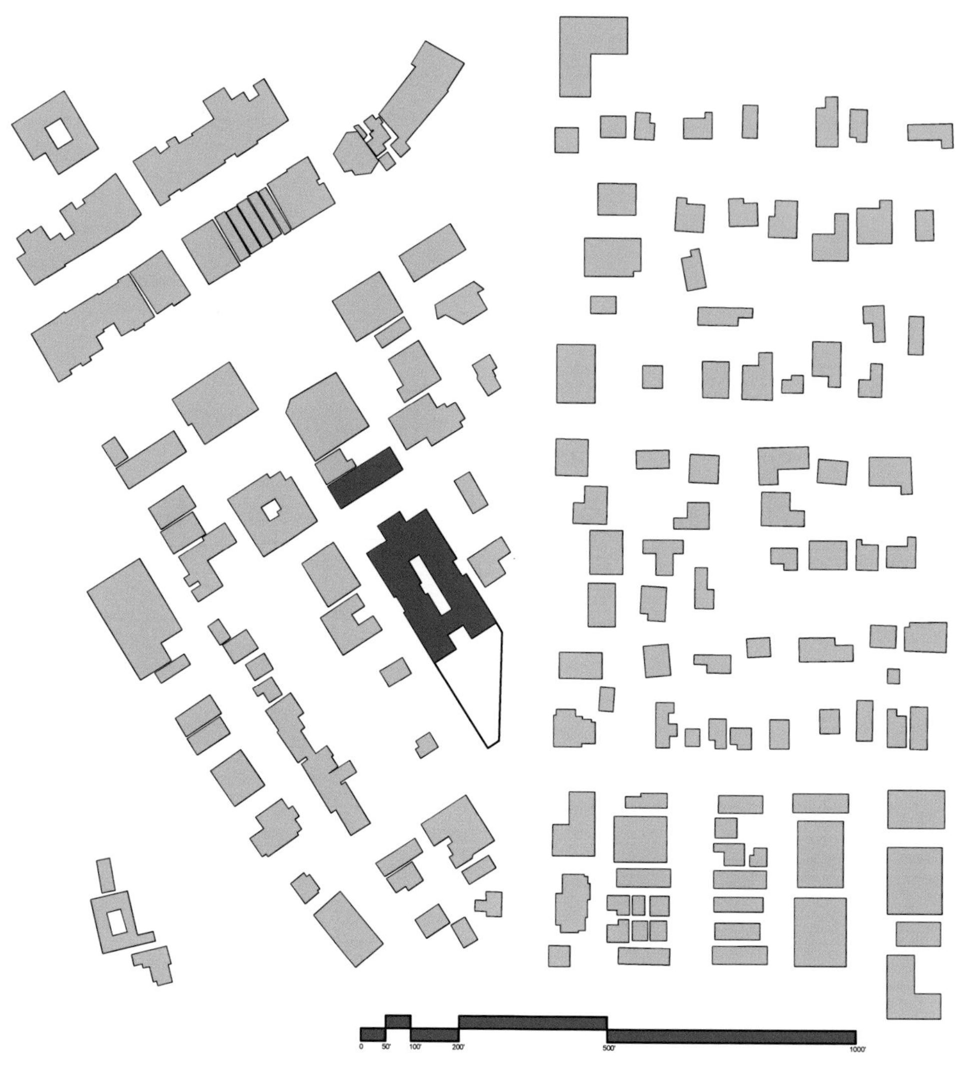

23

The Packard Foundation Headquarters

LOCATION: LOS ALTOS, CALIFORNIA, USA

BUILT: 2012

ARCHITECT: EHDD ARCHITECTURE

ENVIRONMENTAL ENGINEERING: INTEGRAL GROUP

LIVING BUILDING CHALLENGE CERTIFIED

LEED PLATINUM CERTIFIED

WINNER OF THE BEST PROJECT AWARD

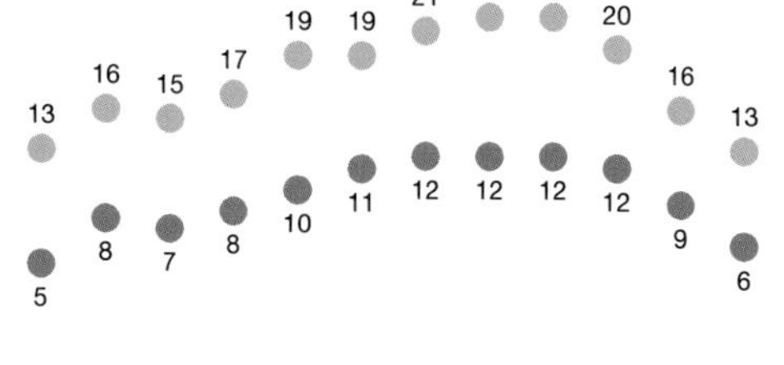

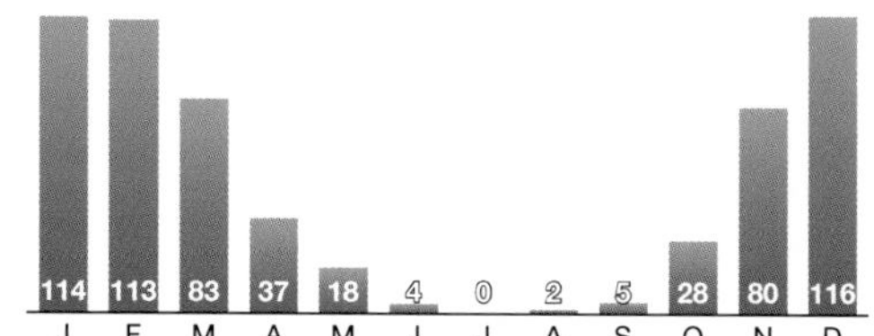

23.1 Packard Foundation Headquarters, view of main entrance, from South San Antonio Road

MISSION

When the Packard Foundation was looking for a place to construct a new headquarters building near downtown Los Altos, one of their goals was to consolidate several office locations under one roof. With this project, the Foundation asked the architects and engineers to design a building that was not only functional, comfortable and beautiful. The new development should in many ways come to reflect the Foundation's mission: conserving resources, protecting the planet and improving people's lives.

The beautiful landscaping, the user-controlled windows and sliding doors, multiple indoor-outdoor connections, the extensive use of sustainably harvested natural materials, these all come together in a design that responds positively to the philosophy of biophilia: the instinctive bond between humans and other living systems. "For decades, the Foundation has focused on conserving and preserving the Earth's ecosystems by promoting renewable energy, reducing carbon emissions, and through energy efficiency" (Azevedo, 2012).

SITE

The Packard Foundation Headquarters, centrally located in Los Altos, California, was built on a 1.5 acre, previously developed site. Waste from deconstructing existing structures on the site was salvaged, with a 96 percent recycling rate.

23.2 Packard Foundation Headquarters, landscaping

23.3 Packard Foundation Headquarters, storm water management along South San Antonio Road

A constructed wetlands area at the southern end of the site is part of a comprehensive storm management plan. Along with narrow rain gardens interspersed between the side walks and the street, storm water is used to irrigate mature urban trees before replenishing the groundwater source (Figure 23.3).

Rainwater captured on sloping roofs is fed into a 20,000-gallon underground cistern, reducing potable water demand by 69 percent.

An alternative transportation mode program made it possible to reduce parking demand to 67 spaces, from 160 required by code.

BIO-CLIMATIC DESIGN STRATEGIES

Considering the size and shape of the lot, an initial design approach might have been to place one long building centered on the site, parallel to 2nd Street. Instead, the architects split that footprint into two 40-ft-wide office wings. By moving the wings apart and engaging the street, a courtyard was created in the middle.

This design concept made it possible to let natural light into the office floors. Additional daylight is provided at the top floors through centrally placed skylights. When interiors are served by natural light, the energy demand for electric lighting decreases, which in turn leads to lower internal heat load and lower demand for cooling. Findings from several research projects indicate that productivity and well-being increase in work environments with access to natural light and views of the outdoors.

To avoid cooling load penalties from east- and west-facing windows, several shading strategies were employed. While sunshades, overhangs, balconies and trellises create hard, controllable shade, mature trees provide additional shading by filtering sunlight. The combined effect of constructed shading devices and mature trees creates a play of light on and around the building, changing seasonally and with time of day.

A well-insulated, tight envelope with triple pane glazing helps reduce heat loss and heat gain by reducing conduction to a minimum.

23.4 Packard Foundation Headquarters, typical office floor

INNOVATIVE SYSTEMS APPROACH

With the implementation of bio-climatic design strategies, the first step was taken towards reducing energy demand. The next step was to introduce energy-efficient mechanical systems for heating, cooling and ventilation.

23.5 Packard Foundation Headquarters, large sliding glass panels open up to the inner courtyard

23.6 Packard Foundation Headquarters, façade facing the inner courtyard

Ceiling-mounted induction units, sometimes incorrectly described as "active chilled beams," were used to condition the air inside the building. While supplying fresh air, the units also circulate air in each space by induction. Since the air supply ducts feeding the induction units serve only to deliver fresh air to maintain indoor air quality, the space, materials and costs for ductwork, as well as energy use for fan operation, were reduced by 75 percent as compared to a traditional forced air system.

Chilled water is primarily produced by two cooling towers and stored in two 25,000-gallon underground reservoirs. A high efficiency chiller is used as a back-up system, needed only at extreme climate conditions with low wet bulb depression and high cooling loads. Chilled water is stored at 55° F (13° C) in the summer and 60° F (15.5° C) in the winter.

With very low auxiliary heating demand, the induction units can be used as combined heating and cooling devices. Air source heat pumps deliver hot water to the coils inside the induction units.

The end result is a highly efficient mechanical system that works with the building-integrated passive strategies as a hybrid system providing comfort uniquely tailored to each zone.

Operable windows and large sliding glass doors encourage the use of natural ventilation to maintain indoor air quality and make use of free cooling when climate conditions are favorable (Figure 23.5).

MATERIALS

The materials used on exterior surfaces are generally warm in color and feel. The contemporary nature of glass surfaces and dark steel framing is contrasted by the beauty of natural materials on the building and in the grounds: wood, stone, copper, trees, bushes and flowers. A green roof on a horizontal portion of the building comes into view as one ascends to the second floor.

All wood used in the project came from Forest Stewardship Council (FSC) certified sources. Exterior wood panels are made from Western Red Cedar, while wood veneers used for interior finishes were sourced from eucalyptus trees harvested during the San Francisco Doyle Drive project.

Mt. Moriah stone was quarried in the Utah/Nevada border region, less than 500 miles from the site. Copper used from exterior cladding is 75 percent recycled, installed with integral finish.

REAL-WORLD PERFORMANCE

To offset the total building and site energy demand, photovoltaic arrays were installed on the sloping roofs of the building and on a canopy covering guest parking (Figure 23.7). More than nine hundred panels, with a total peak power output of 291 kWp, were estimated to produce 305,000 kWh of on-site renewable energy annually. The actual electric energy produced and metered over a 12-month period exceeded that estimate.

The first-year actual annual energy use was 298,193 kWh, which made the building perform beyond net zero. With a conditioned floor area between 46,000 and 47,000 square feet (4,334 m^2), the documented Energy Use Intensity (EUI) comes in at 21.8 kBtu/ft^2-Y or 68.8 kWh/m^2-Y.

23.7 Packard Foundation Headquarters, guest parking, with canopy generating electricity from photovoltaic panels

24

Kimbell Art Museum Extension

LOCATION: DALLAS, TEXAS, USA

BUILT: 2013

ARCHITECT: RENZO PIANO BUILDING WORKSHOP

ENVIRONMENTAL ENGINEERING: ARUP

33°N

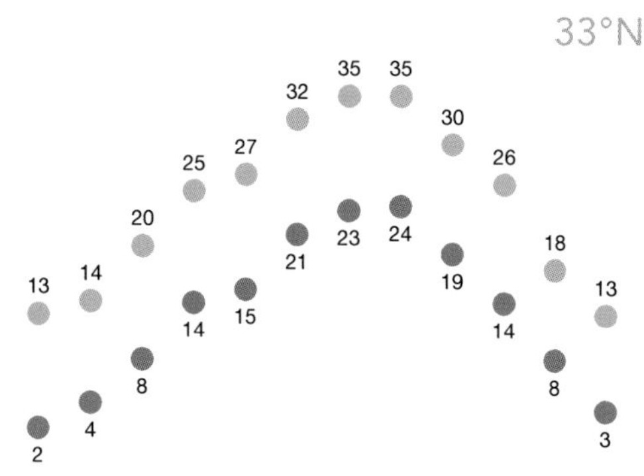

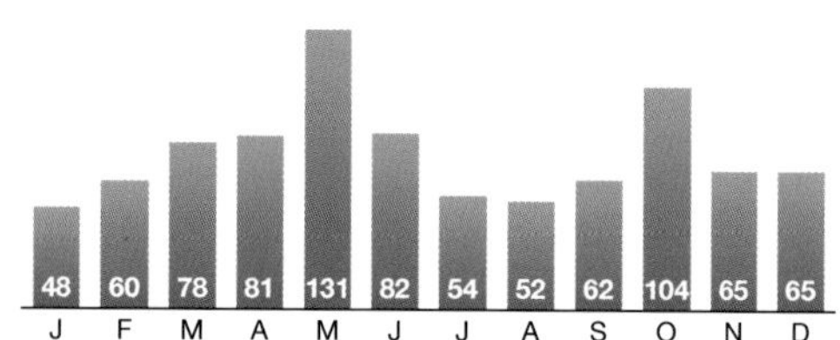

24.1 Kimbell Art Museum Extension, south façade

CONVERSATIONS WITH KAHN

Not unlike other Renzo Piano museum designs for the Menil Collection, the Bayeler Foundation Museum, the Nasher Sculpture Center and the Cy Twombley Pavilion, the Kimbell Art Museum Extension presents itself as a freestanding, single-story museum building, intimate in scale. Not surprisingly, the Kimbell Art Museum extension has been named the Piano Pavilion. The key to creating the appearance of a light, unimposing counterpart to the Kahn building lies in the sectional (vertical) organization of the building program. The western half of the new extension holds a third gallery, a library, an auditorium, an education center and storage and mechanical rooms, placed on two floors below a landscaped green roof.

24.2 Kimbell Art Museum, light and shade at noon on a winter day

Seen as a roof plan diagram, the eastern half (the Pavilion) is the mirror image of the first Kimbell Art Museum building, designed by Louis Kahn and completed in 1972. The two buildings are situated 60 meters apart, looking at each other across the park, each with 90-meter façade divided into three: a central transparent entrance wall protected by a portico and flanked by windowless side wings. Piano explains how he came to a conclusion about the right distance between the two buildings:

> When you are in a dialog with another person, you put yourself at the right distance. If you are too close to the person, it becomes ridiculous. If you stay too far away, it's wrong. You have to choose the right distance. So, it's the same thing for buildings.
>
> (Piano, Kimbell Art Museum video, 2014)

PROPORTIONS AND SCALE

Geometrically, the main body of Kahn's building consists of 24 vaulted concrete roofs, each 20 x 100 feet (6 x 30 meters). Piano plans his building on a structural grid defined by double wooden beams set 3 meters apart and spanning 30 meters. Recognizing Kahn as one of his mentors, Piano speaks about the influence Kahn's work has had on his design:

> Kahn's Kimbell Art museum building has been always in the middle of this, and not really because of the language, because it is not my language, it is more about scale, it is more about construction as well because that building is extremely well done.
>
> (Kimbell Art Museum video, 2014)

A new underground parking garage was built under the park between the two buildings. This design move made it possible, for the first time, for visitors to enter the Kahn building from the west side into the main floor. Piano says:

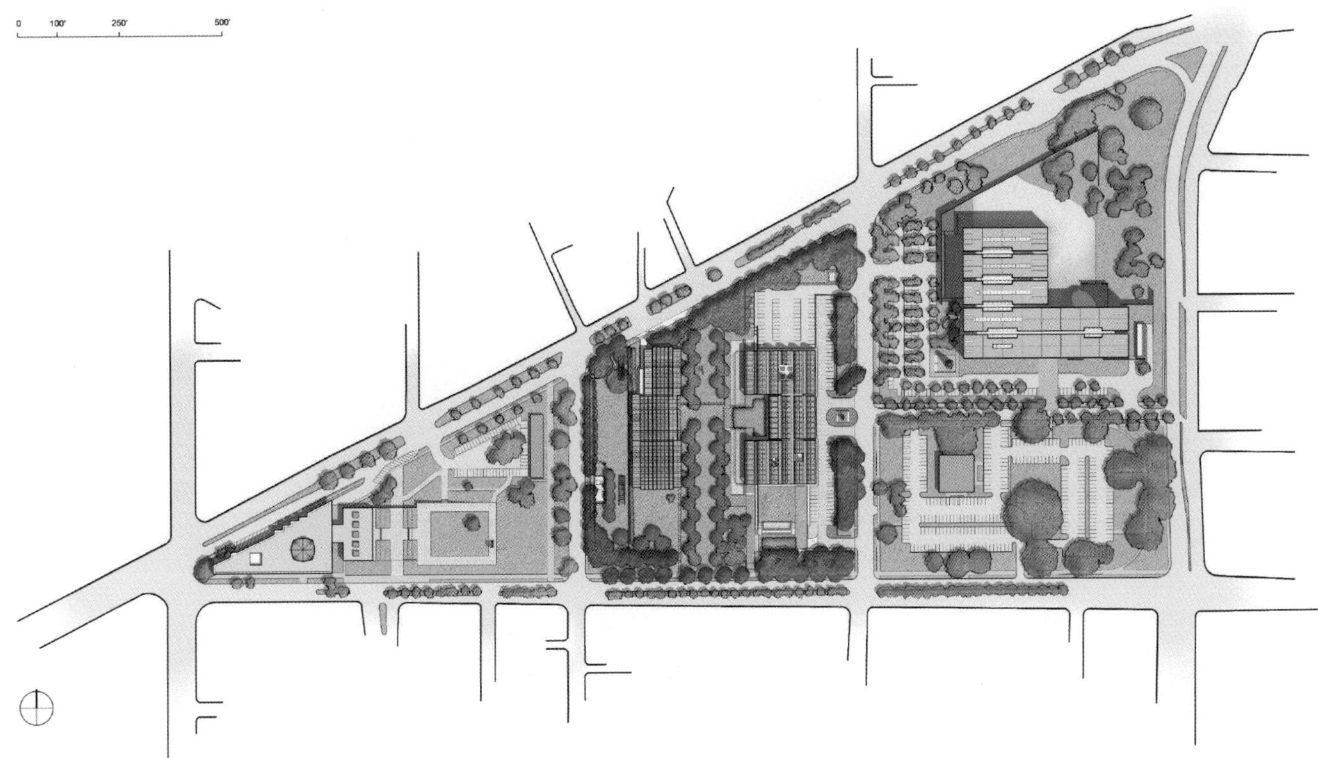

24.3 Kimbell Art Museum Extension, site plan

> Since the Kahn building was built, everybody enters from the wrong side. Kahn didn't drive. He didn't get a driver's license. He did not think about Texas as a place you go by car. Of course, you go by car. I decided to close the back door to the Kahn building and there start the intervention. I always thought that some day we should make this right. Now you come up the elevator from the parking garage and you arrive in front of the Kahn building – as it should be.
>
> (ibid.)

TOPOS: CONCRETE, WOOD, STEEL, GLASS

Piano sees the column as coming out of the ground. With a reference to the Greek "topos," he sees the column grid organizing the ground plane of the site:

> The beam comes flying in and it touches the column. It's not different from ships entering the harbor of Genova. You bring yourself and your heritage into the job. I am an Italian and there is very little I can do about that.
>
> (ibid.)

24.4 Kimbell Art Museum Extension, south-east corner

24.5 Kimbell Art Museum Extension, south gallery

Piano's attention to detail is not limited to the building elements and the materials they are constructed with. Even more important is the way the elements come together, how they join. Square concrete columns seem to grow out of the ground. On top of the columns rest steel connectors that reach up in between the double laminated wood beams, a joining element that leaves the beams hovering above the columns. A similar concept drives the design of the steel frame supporting a glass roof with louvers seemingly floating above the building.

BREATHING FLOORS

> When the building is finished, you will love the idea of seeing a sculpture against a wall of concrete. I am not saying "against" in the sense of touching the wall, but the concrete will act beautifully as a background for a piece of art.
>
> (ibid.)

A visitor entering one of the galleries for the first time is absorbed by the art objects exhibited there. The architectural space is what makes the enjoyment of the art possible. The space may be seen as art in itself, but it is never imposing. Piano uses the diffuse natural light from the roof and combines it with controlled light from one glazed wall (Figure 24.5). He then uses the color and the materiality of concrete walls and white oak floors to temper the light. There is nothing about the architecture that is screaming for attention.

The air in the main gallery spaces is conditioned by a fan-powered low velocity plenum system working with buoyancy, the tendency of warmer air to rise. At first glance, there is no ductwork and no visible grilles, except for the air supply vents at the base of the glazed exterior wall. Air is supplied through portions of the wood floor where the floor planks are mounted with narrow gaps, allowing the air to heat, cool and ventilate the room through floor "diffusers" from a plenum below.

The galleries are separated from the lobby spaces by a 2-meter-wide concrete wall. On closer inspection, one finds that these thick walls encapsulate vertical downdraft return plenums. Vitiated air is returned to an energy recovery unit in the mechanical room below, entering through concealed air intakes at the top of the walls, below the glass roof.

24.6 Kimbell Art Museum Extension, view of the roof at night

A FLOATING ROOF

An array of curved glass panels mounted on a steel frame constitutes the weather protection portion of the layered roof system. Light is controlled by exterior louvers and filtered in two stages: through a translucent layer in the glass roof and through fabric screens below the glass.

The curved skylights are built with insulated glass units with laminated glass on both sides of a Krypton-filled cavity. The U-value of the glass units is 1.8 W/m^2-K (SI), which translates to R 3.15 (IP).

There are 2,403 louvers above the skylight, installed with a single axis tracking mechanism. With 12 photovoltaic cells per louver, a total of 28,836 PV cells amounts to 702 m^2 of photovoltaics, with an estimated capacity of 188.3 kWp. The louver system performs three functions: (1) allowing natural light to enter the space below from the north; (2) protecting the glass roof from unwanted solar heat gain; and (3) producing electric energy from the integrated photovoltaic cells. Electricity produced by the PV arrays on the roof is estimated to offset up to 70 percent of the energy used for lighting and air conditioning the three galleries.

THE GREEN BLANKET

The lightness and transparency of the eastern half of the new building are contrasted by the western half being concealed by a protecting green roof (Figure 24.7). The landscaping of the vegetated roof is designed to erase any distinction between the building itself and the park it sits below. Like an ancient burial ground, this part of the building is hardly more than a slight curvature in the landscape, but unlike a burial ground, however, the building is not experienced as a basement or underground vault.

The secret to achieving a feeling of openness in a building submerged in the landscape can be found in two strategic design moves. The east and west halves of the building are separated by long and narrow courtyards along the north–south axis, only

24.7 Kimbell Art Museum Extension, green roof above south-west gallery

24.8 Kimbell Art Museum Extension, south-west gallery

traversed by two glass connectors. The western edge of the building faces a two-story-deep light well.

By placing more than half of the building under a landscaped green blanket, the entire building now appears as an intimately scaled pavilion paying respect to the Kahn building, while greatly improving the energy performance of the building as a whole.

LIGHT AND SHADE

> The idea of space is not made by the wall, the floor, the ceiling, but by the untouchable, like light. Architecture is about people, it's about society, is about science, invention, technology, is about history, is about art, the art of building.
>
> (Piano, Kimbell Art Museum video, 2014)

Kahn had said that an art museum should embrace daylight because objects of art are best seen in natural light. While this may be true for the majority of the art on display, some objects of art must be protected by limiting the light levels in the space. The south-west gallery provides a protective exhibition space of this kind. Placed under the opaque green roof, this gallery is the ideal space to exhibit art that is sensitive to light, such as the many five-hundred-year-old pieces of Asian art made with ink and mineral pigments on silk and paper.

Even in this low light gallery, Piano provides two apertures of natural light. Natural light enters the space through a south-facing window facing a light well and through the glass "connector" to the south-east gallery. There is also light entering indirectly from the brightly lit auditorium lobby. These carefully controlled points of natural light act as references as one navigates the museum's interiors, moving from the brightness of the outdoors through the diffuse light of the east galleries to the shades of darkness in the west gallery.

PERFORMANCE

Fort Worth enjoys a semi-arid climate with plenty of sunshine. Considerable seasonal and diurnal swings in the ambient air temperature tend to take attention away from the fact that the annual average temperature is 18° C (65° F), at the lower end of the comfort zone. Twenty feet below ground, diurnal swings are eliminated and seasonal swings are moderately centered around the annual average air temperature.

By submerging more than half of the building program into the ground, the western part of the building sits in thermal equilibrium with the ground, only experiencing moderate heat gain from internal loads and the windows facing the light wells. In assessing the energy performance of the whole building, one cannot avoid considering the possibility of a trade-off between the transparent eastern half and the protected western half.

There is evidence of a similar trade-off potential in the pavilion itself. Thermal insulation is sandwiched between the interior and the exterior layers of the high mass, thick concrete walls, creating an assembly that, with a U-value of 0.036 (SI) or R 22 (IP) tends to offset the lesser heat transfer properties of the roof.

With an estimated net Energy Use Intensity of 120 kWh/m^2-Y, based on total occupied floor area, the reduced annual CO_2 emissions are about 55 kg CO_2/m^2, half of the total CO_2 emissions of the Kahn building.

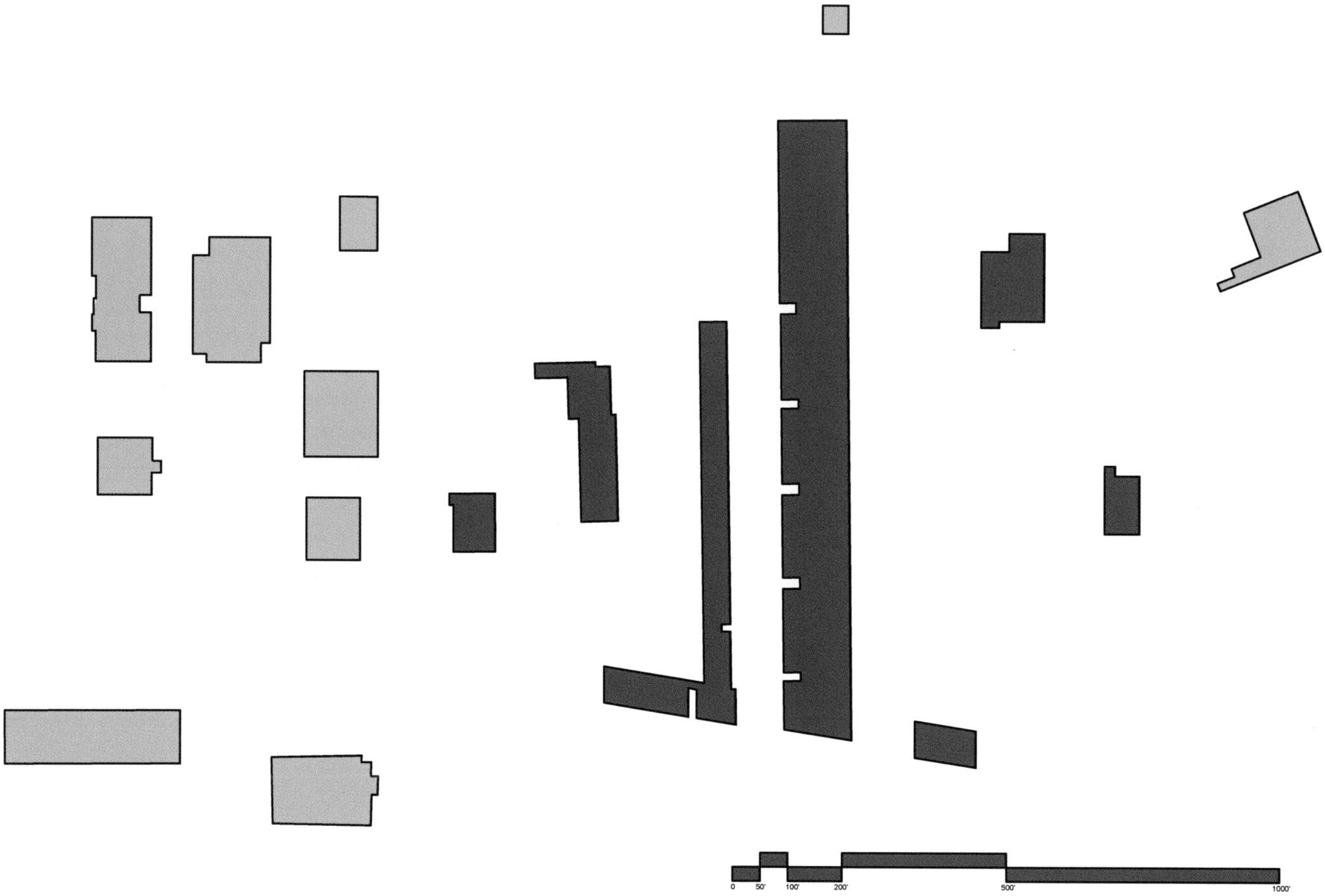

25

Mariposa Land Port of Entry

LOCATION: NOGALES, ARIZONA, USA

BUILT: 2014

ARCHITECT: JONES STUDIO

LEED NC 2.2 GOLD

31°N

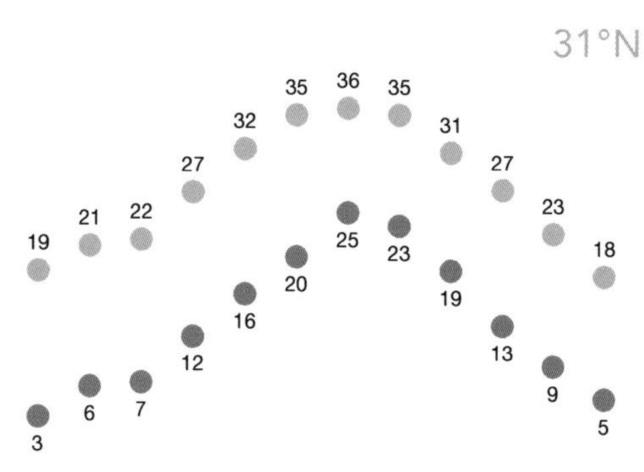

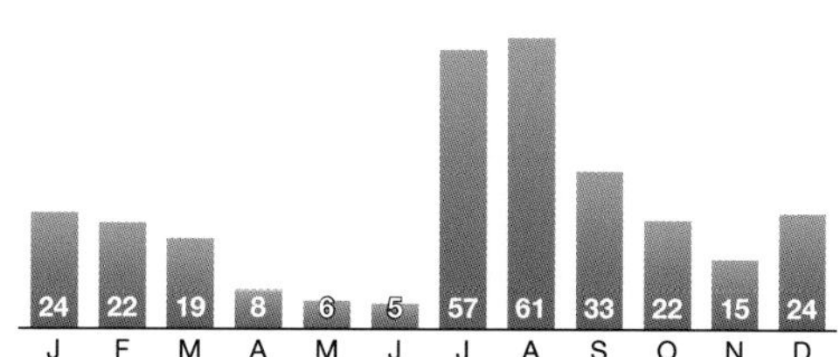

25.1 Mariposa Land Port of Entry, view of the desert oasis

25.2 Mariposa Land Port of Entry, circular windows to offices behind west-facing concrete wall

BORDER LINES

In his essay "Border Lines," the architect Eddie Jones makes a reference to a poem with the same title by Alberto Rios, which ends: "Together, let us turn the map until we see clearly: The border is what joins us, not what separates us" (Rios, 2003). Jones continues: "Rios reminds us of our responsibility to each other, despite and because of, the invisible borders we draw around ourselves" (Jones, 2011).

Mariposa Land Port of Entry was reconstructed in stages while in continuous operation as one of the busiest ports of entry to the US. Included in the Design Excellence Program, which mandates new federal buildings to represent democracy and dignity, the new facility is emerging as a peaceful and friendly oasis in the desert, alleviating the fear and stress often experienced when crossing a border between nations.

Addressing these border conditions, where anxiety associated with crossing a border is compounded by a harsh physical

25.3 Mariposa Land Port of Entry, aerial view and campus plan

environment in an extreme climate, the design team aspired to alleviate discomfort with expressions of respect and extensive modulated shade.

The sense of dignity and respect emerging from a campus of buildings set upon a 57-acre man-made plateau is at the same time a welcoming gesture, an outstretched hand inviting you to enter a gateway to America.

DESERT OASIS

Since water in an arid climate evaporates rather quickly, the romantic notion of an oasis or garden in the desert is often associated with a constant and reliable source of water emerging out of the earth. Since there is no such abundance of groundwater flowing to the surface at the Nogales border crossing, a man-made oasis, therefore, would have to rely on rainwater. But is there enough precipitation at the site to sustain an oasis with hundreds of newly planted trees? Jones says: "Although we strived to create an oasis in the desert, offering a welcoming respite from the extreme heat, a man-made oasis in an arid climate would be irresponsible unless it was self-reliant."

Contrary to common belief, the Sonoran Desert is not as dry as the name suggests. Saguaro cacti, Palo Verde trees and creosote bushes enjoy up to 11 inches of rainfall in a typical meteorological year, but 1 inch of rain may fall in less than an hour on a stormy monsoon day. Unless carefully managed by natural ecosystems or man-made constructions, most of the rainwater is lost to flooding and evaporation.

A PRECIOUS RESOURCE

The design team response was to develop a water harvesting and management plan (Figure 25.4). Water is collected from 276,000 square feet of roof surfaces and other non-permeable pavements, channeled through architecturally articulated scuppers and downspouts into collection wells (Figure 25.5). From there, the water is filtered and piped into an underground reservoir located on the south side of the plateau. By October 2013, when the facility was still under construction, the reservoir was filled with one million gallons of storm water that had been collected.

Two elongated buildings define the spine of the oasis: a fully landscaped outdoor space taking on the dimensions of a small town main street. The carefully managed movement of the water is expressed by rusted steel scuppers, pouring water into troughs connected with underground filtering wells. Drought-tolerant bushes and trees are planted in the troughs, soaking up water as

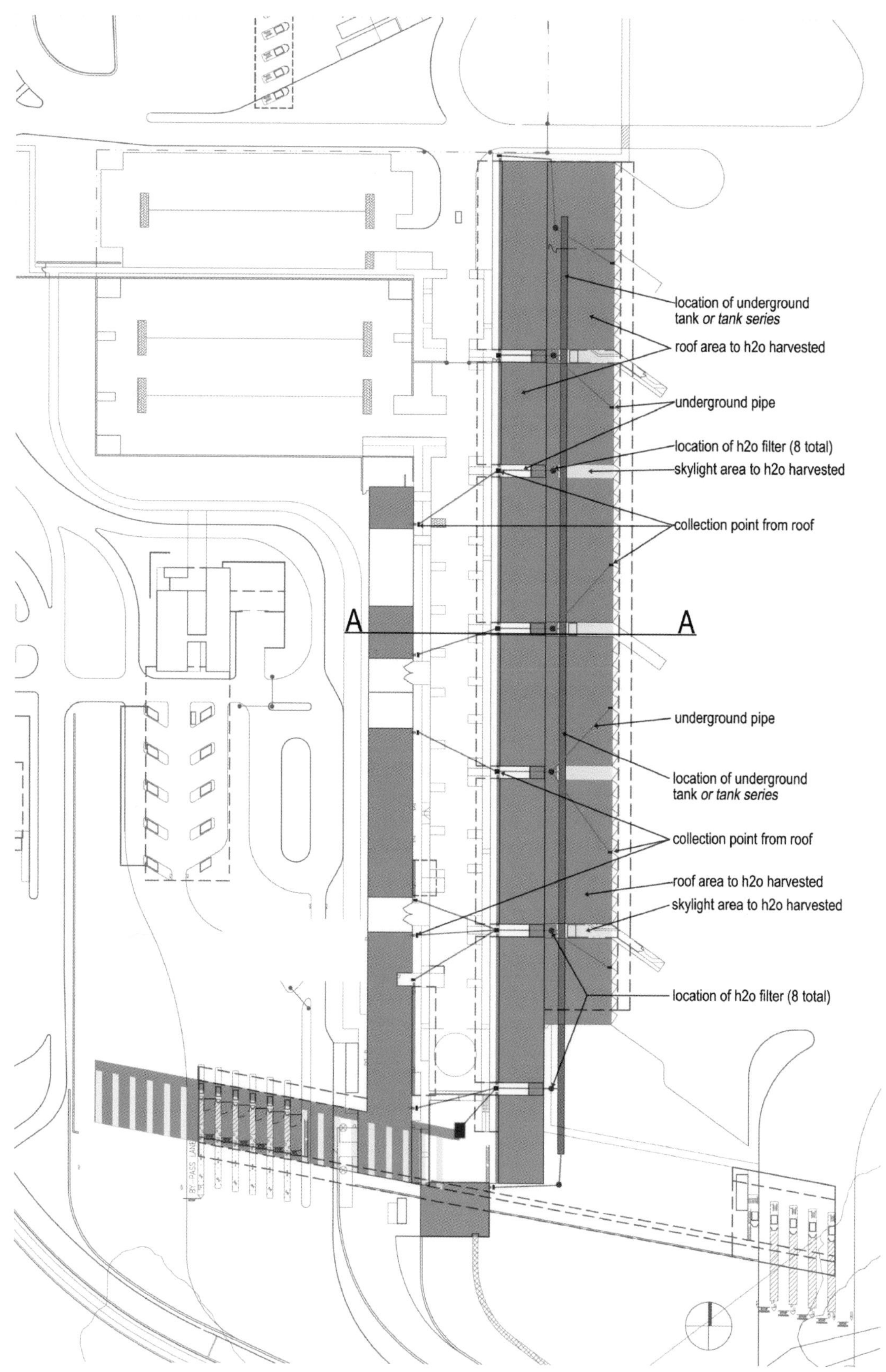

25.4 Mariposa Land Port of Entry, water harvesting diagram

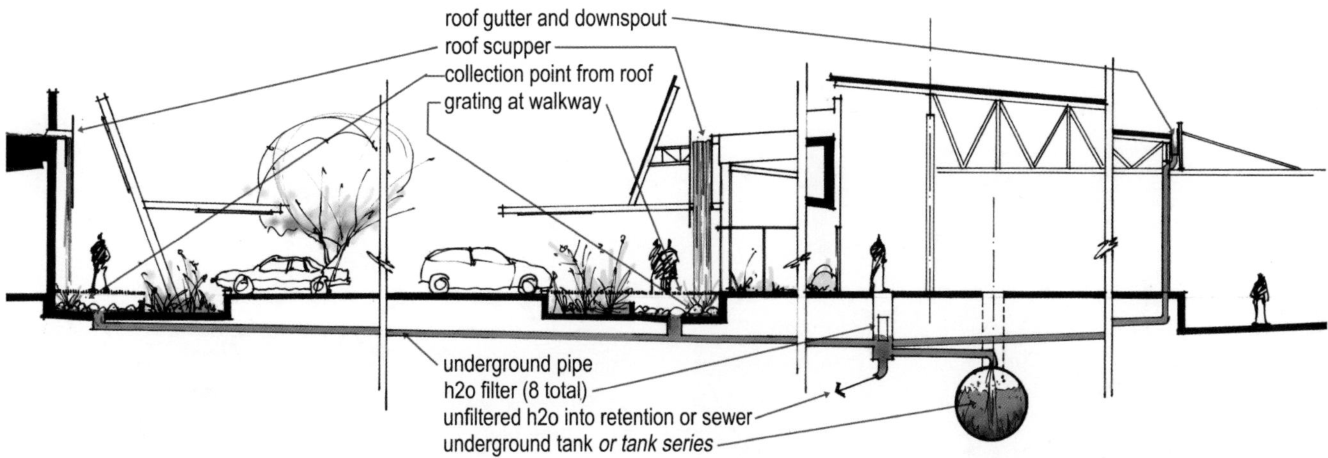

25.5 Mariposa Land Port of Entry, storm water management and water harvesting scheme

it flows towards the underground man-made reservoir. Unfiltered water can be led to retention ponds.

In between gentle winter rains and monsoon flash floods, the Sonoran Desert frequently experiences long periods with no significant precipitation. Water stored underground can then be pumped back up to irrigate the newly planted trees, which will depend on some degree of irrigation until they are established.

BALANCING LIGHT

Light in the desert is abundant. With most days dominated by clear skies and harsh light, the need for shade is inevitable. Access to daylight is still a necessary component to maintain a comfortable and productive work environment. Controlling light, therefore, becomes a balancing act between bringing daylight deep into the building's interiors while preventing sunlight from creating glare and also delivering heat when cooling is in demand.

A typical office floor, as seen in Figure 25.6, opens up to the main street at the center of the oasis with access to lights and view to the outdoors. Large floor-to-ceiling windows are protected by deep overhanging canopies. Clerestory windows above the canopies are protected by panels installed at an angle, allowing diffuse natural light to reflect onto the ceiling.

25.6 Mariposa Land Port of Entry, typical east pavilion office floor

25.7 Mariposa Land Port of Entry, shaded inspection area, with industrial ceiling fan

Energy-efficient artificial lighting systems are equipped with controls to dim electric lights in response to increasing availability of daylight.

DESIGN STRATEGIES

All new buildings at the Mariposa Land Port of Entry are built with a high performance envelope, including well-insulated roofs and "Thermomass" walls. Along with extensive canopies and shading devices, insulated glass units with high visible transmittance and low heat gain coefficient contribute to an overall decrease in energy demand for heating and cooling.

Specific site conditions and functional requirements related to traffic flow and logistics determined the general layout with buildings oriented with their long sides facing east and west, an arrangement that does not lend itself to passive solar heating. The design of each building type on the campus responds uniquely to this challenge by keeping large transparent wall sections protected by canopies. Exposed west-facing walls are mostly opaque, only punctuated by small circular windows (see Figure 25.2).

Functional outdoor spaces are protected from the sun by the same type of canopies and trellises used to create shade for the open office floors. Large ceiling-mounted propeller fans create local breezes for an improved sense of thermal comfort (Figure 25.7).

A proposed photovoltaic (PV) shading structure covering the large central parking lot is targeting 1000 kWp. With an expected annual electric energy production from solar energy on site at approximately 1.8 million kWh, the PV alone could offset around 50 percent of the total annual energy use.

ENERGY PERFORMANCE

In hot and dry climates, soils are often sandy and dry. With the absence of humidity in the earth, implementation of ground source heat pumps is not a viable solution. Likewise, there are no large bodies of water nearby where heat could be dissipated. The dryness of the ambient air, however, means that heat can be exchanged with the environment through evaporation.

To take advantage of this condition, high efficiency water-cooled chillers deliver heat from the building to two 250-ton cooling towers. Condensing water from cooling coils in the air handlers is reclaimed. Water from on-site harvesting can be used to replenish the cooling towers.

A variable air volume heating and cooling system uses air contamination sensors to determine the minimum amount of outside air required to maintain the indoor air quality. Hot water for space heating and forced air re-heat is provided by high efficiency gas-fired boilers. A solar hot water system installed in each building supplies sinks and showers.

Energy modeling showed that a central forced air system would provide improved energy efficiency, compared to packaged units installed on each building. While central air conditioning is expected to reduce electric energy use, there is a penalty associated with using natural gas-fired boilers to supply VAV units with hot water re-heat.

The nature of a port of entry with 24/7 operations and high use of electricity for security lighting on the entire site leads to a baseline EUI that is relatively high. Building energy simulations predict an Energy Use Intensity for this specific project of 130 kBtu/ft^2-Y, well below the modeled baseline at 156 kBtu/ft^2-Y.

MATERIALS

Raw untreated materials such as concrete and rusted steel are used throughout the project. This approach is not only cost-effective, but also a strategy for avoiding possible sources of emissions of volatile organic compounds to the interior. The use of raw concrete and rusted steel is also conducive to a "desert aesthetic," responding to the rough and sometimes uninviting character of rocky soils, spiny cacti and waterless riverbeds.

Long stretches of retaining walls had to be built when the original site was extended. The walls holding in place a 57-acre plateau are made with gabions filled with crushed concrete recycled from sidewalks, terraces and demolished buildings (Figure 25.8).

Like the plants and creatures of the Sonoran Desert, this material palette may at first seem hostile to a newly arrived visitor. But like the desert, over time, it reveals a sense of calming timelessness.

25.8 Mariposa Land Port of Entry, recycled concrete-filled caisson landscaping wall, with raw steel storm water drainage

26

Billings Public Library

LOCATION: BILLINGS, MONTANA, USA

BUILT: 2014

ARCHITECT: WILL BRUDER + WORKSBUREAU

LEED GOLD

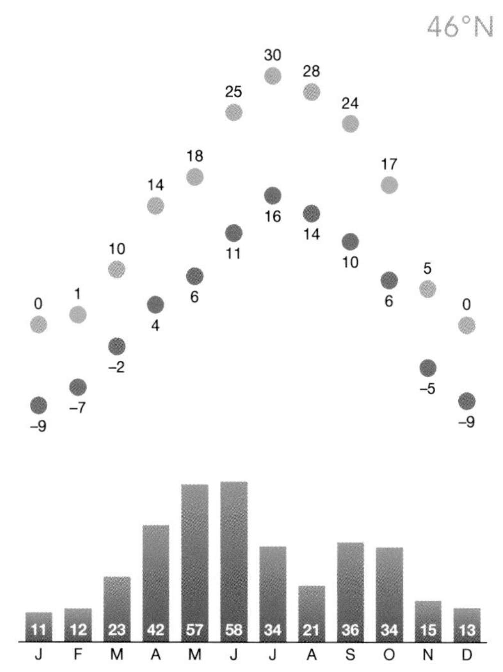

26.1 Billings Public Library, great reading room facing North 28th Street

26.2 Billings Public Library, view from 6th Avenue North

CROWD IS ALL SMILES

On January 6, 2014, the day of the "soft opening" of the new Billings Public Library, Jaci Webb of the *Billings Gazette* reported that by noon, five hundred people had already strolled through the new library building, "most of them wide-eyed and grinning." As with other libraries designed by Will Bruder, like the Phoenix Public Library (Lerum, 2008), the Billings Library won the hearts of the patrons from day one. A favorite space, particularly for children, is the "story tower," a cone-shaped, elliptical space flowing through two floors to a skylight above.

The new library lines the street edges on the corner of 6th Avenue and 28th Street, centrally located in a section of Billings where the grid is rotated almost 45 degrees relative to the cardinal directions. This rotation presented the architects with a challenge when protecting transparent portions of the exterior walls from unwanted summer solar gains while opening up the interiors to light and views.

The building takes on a simple rectangular form with the short ends facing NE and SW. The long sides are protected from low morning and evening summer sun angles by a perforated screen made from corrugated steel panels. The north-east end is protected by vertical fins, making a prominent appearance in front of the grand reading room above the public spaces at street level. The south-west end of the building is almost entirely opaque, with only a narrow window band delivering daylight to offices and servant spaces.

A CIVIC BUILDING

Despite its simple form and a structure inspired by pole barns, and its lone presence on a city block, the Billings Public Library is indeed conceived as a city building with citizens in mind.

The main floor of the building is devoted to its users. At the north-east end facing the city, one finds the open stacks for popular literature conveniently located near the street entrance and the entrance from the landscaped parking lot. The children's area is moved towards the back, surrounding the story tower. Café and services are found in between, with a meeting room on the south-east side.

On the second floor, directly above the popular books collection, lies the grand reading room with more open stacks, reading

26.3 Billings Public Library, great reading room (top), plan of second floor (below)

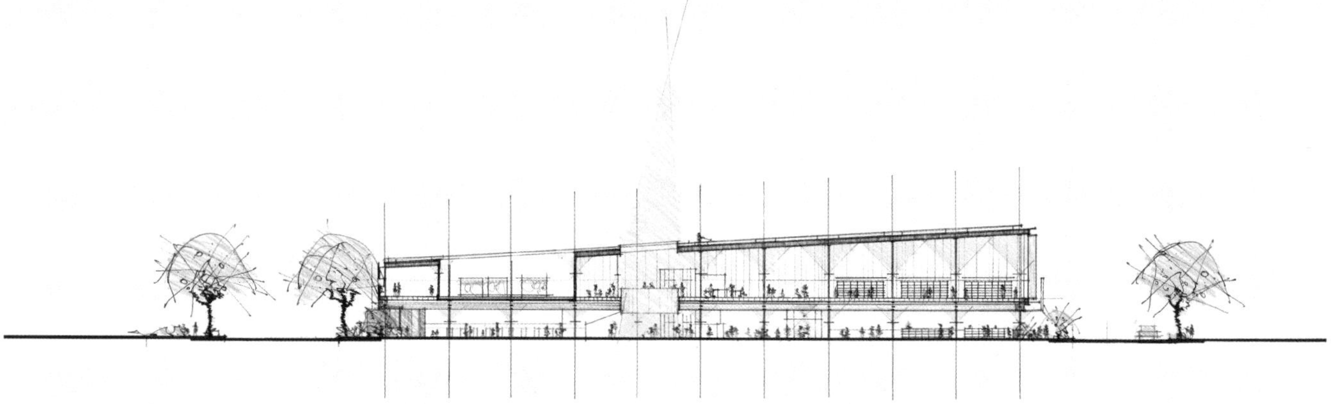

26.4 Billings Public Library, model and longitudinal section

26.5 Billings Public Library, white roof with on site electricity generating photovoltaic panels

nooks for teens and computer stations. A fully glazed end wall at the tallest end of the building section opens up to a magnificent view of mature tree canopies with the characteristic rock outcroppings in the background.

SEEKING THE SUN, HARVESTING WATER

The clear rectangular footprint combined with a gently sloping roof lays the ground for cost savings through efficiency of construction. The white roof slopes in one direction without any major ridges, valleys, gutters or drains. Rainwater is collected in a deep built-in gutter along the lower short end, which drains into oversized downspouts at two corners to an underground reservoir.

The new library was built adjacent to an old library building of brick construction, which included a full height basement. When demolishing the old building, masonry walls and other recyclable materials suited for landfill will be placed in the basement and covered by landscaping, thus providing a large cistern for on-site storm water management. This approach to the end-of-life for the old building also prevents brick and mortar from ending up in a landfill.

A 30 kWp photovoltaic array is designed to be mounted above the white roof membrane. Energy production from the PV system is expected to contribute to more than 5 percent annual electricity cost savings.

ENERGY PERFORMANCE

The building is expected to demonstrate an Energy Use Intensity (EUI) of 55 kBtu/ft^2-Y, which translates to roughly 173 kWh/m^2-Y. Measured against a code-compliant building design (ASHRAE 90.1 2007), energy simulations show a 46 percent savings potential, earning 15 points towards LEED Gold certification. This level of energy efficiency was achieved through a coordinated effort, including envelope design, high performance lighting and energy-efficient mechanical systems design.

26.6 Billings Public Library, stainless steel ventilation aperture integrated with interior wood paneling recycled from snow fences

The window-to-wall ratio has been optimized, while honoring the need for daylight and views. The envelope features vision glass, fritted glass and well-insulated opaque walls. The shade scrim on the long sides of the building facing NW and SE was designed in response to climate and solar geometry.

Low velocity displacement ventilation provides improved thermal comfort while utilizing outside air for natural cooling. Reduced fan power requirement leads to additional energy savings.

SYSTEMS INTEGRATION AND RECYCLED SNOW FENCES

Low velocity air distribution systems often require air supply apertures with larger surfaces than high velocity air supply grilles. The architect took this challenge as an opportunity. Wall panels made up of recycled wood from abandoned Wyoming snow fences were used to create beautiful interior wall surfaces where vertically mounted perforated steel diffusers seamlessly blend into the mix, while maintaining a contrasting effect between the old and the new (Figure 26.6). While the untreated weathered wood passively responds to and helps regulate humidity levels in the space, the active air system steps in to assist in maintaining indoor air quality and thermal comfort.

Other types of recycled wood paneling are used throughout the interiors, accentuating and giving identity to the most precious spaces.

PART FOUR

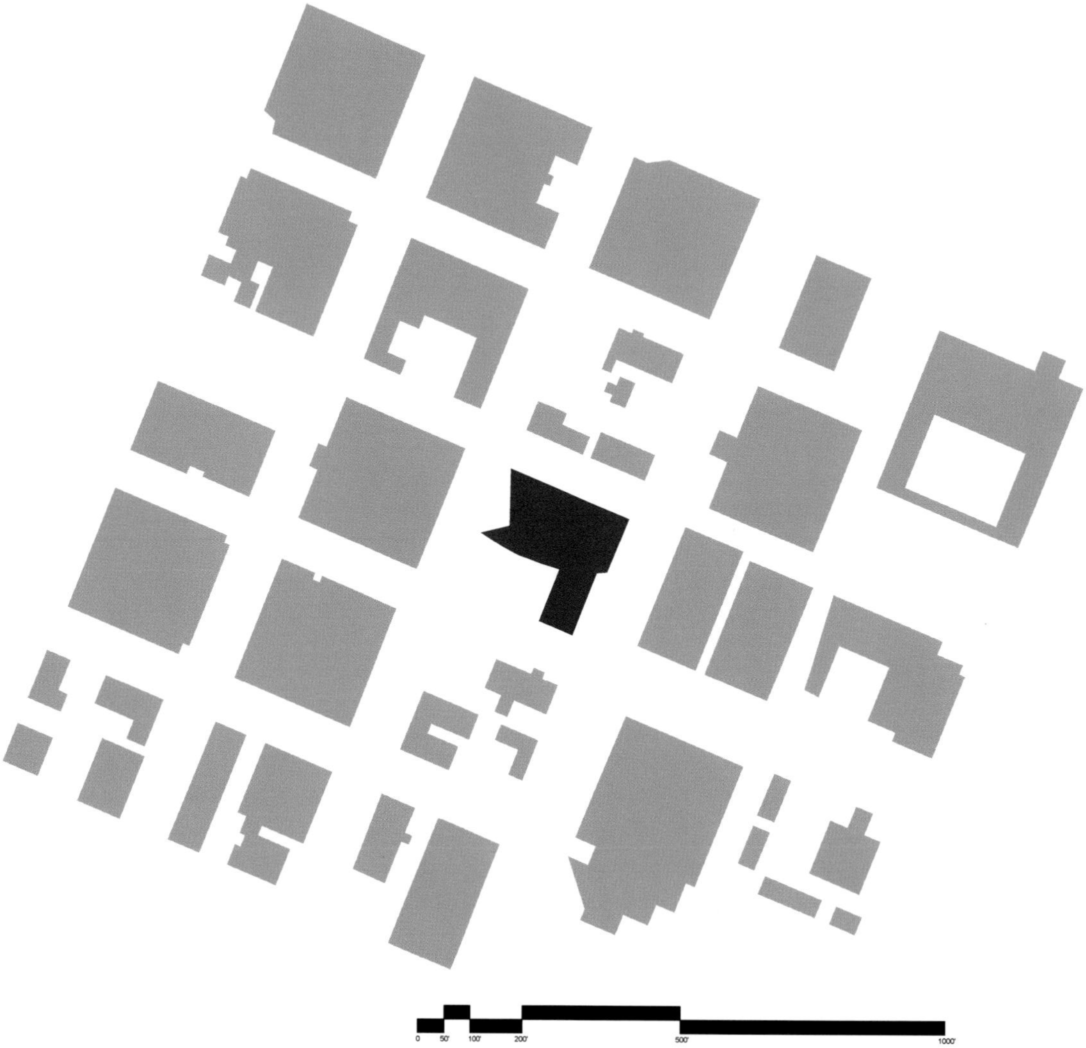

0 50' 100' 200' 500' 1000'

27

Oregon Sustainability Center

LOCATION: PORTLAND, OREGON, USA

PROJECT TERMINATED 2012

ARCHITECT: SERA/GBD ARCHITECTS

TARGETING LIVING BUILDING CHALLENGE CERTIFICATION

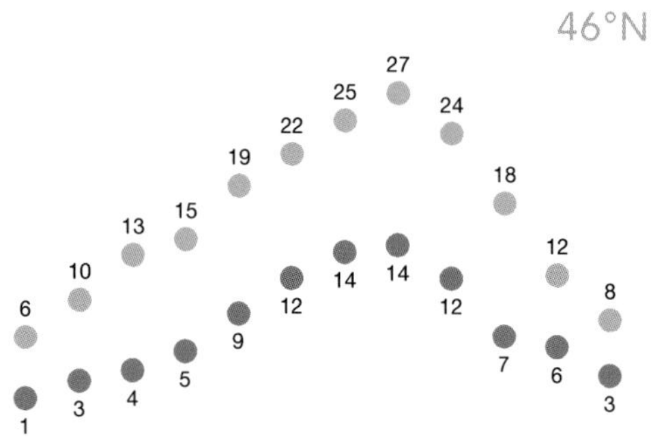

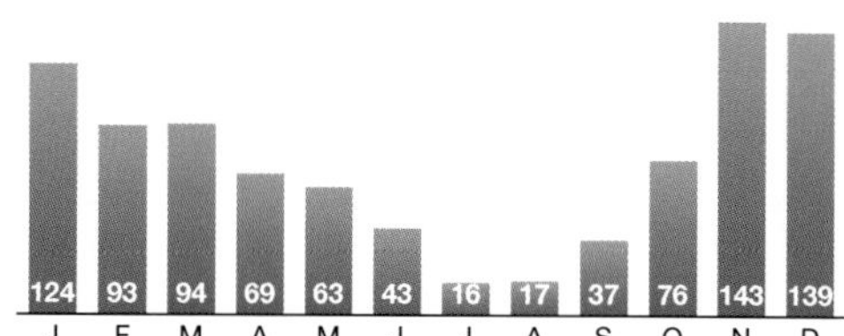

27.1 Oregon Sustainability Center, view from the north-west

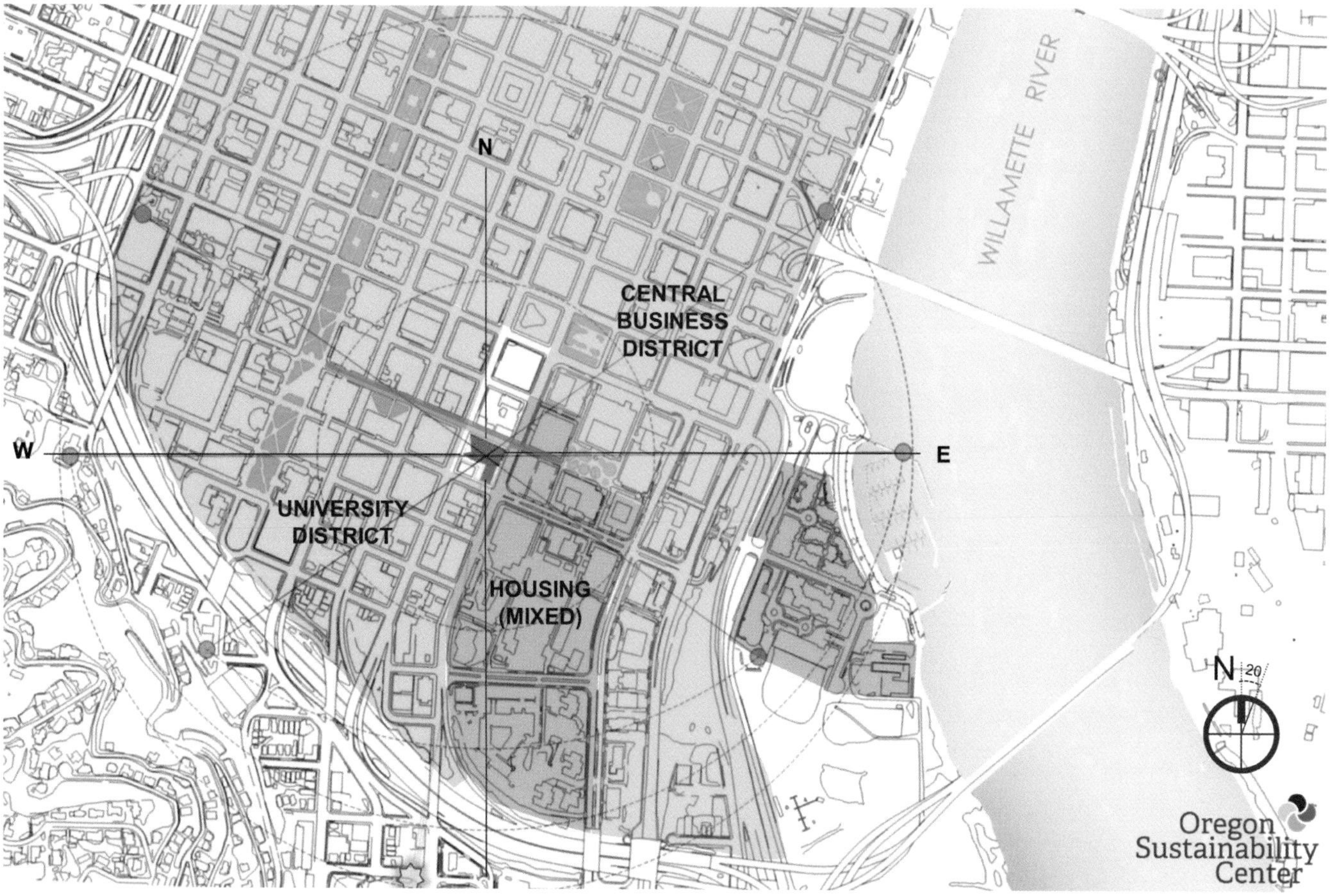

27.2 Oregon Sustainability Center, orientation and urban context

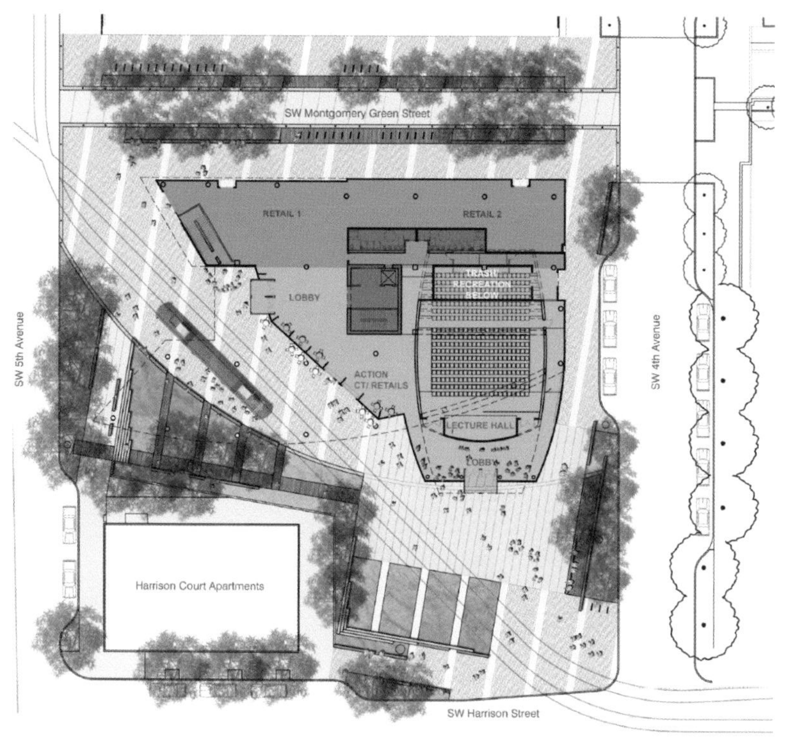

27.3 Oregon Sustainability Center, site plan

ZERO, ZERO, ZERO

The Oregon Sustainability Center was to be developed as a beacon for communities and organizations promoting sustainability in the Portland, Oregon, area. Designed within the framework of the Living Building Challenge, the Center would become home to sustainability-oriented businesses, non-profit organizations, higher education and research facilities, and public agencies.

Design goals were set high: to achieve net zero energy use and net zero water use, with all wastewater managed on site. At the time of its conception, the Center was the largest project to take on the Living Building Challenge, both in square footage and height.

To reach these ambitious design goals, the following strategies were employed: a high performance envelope, high efficiency active systems, passive systems design including daylighting and night ventilation of thermal mass, and optimal use of "free" ambient sources of energy. The design team further recognized a need to actively engage future occupants in keeping the energy use from equipment at a minimum (Lerum, 2013).

A centrally located site was selected at the edge of the university district, near the central business district in Portland. Since light rail lines cross the city block at a diagonal, the building was designed to embrace public transportation by reaching over the tracks, allowing free passage for rail cars across a public plaza under the building.

THE ENERGY CHALLENGE

A net zero building designed to harvest on-site energy mainly from the roof is by definition limited in height. The ratio between the collector area and the total occupied floor area sets the target for the building's Energy Use Intensity (EUI). Therefore, the building can only go up (increase its number of floors) as much as the projected EUI goes down.

Figure 27.4 shows a comparison of the Oregon Sustainability Center target EUI (16 kBtu/ft^2-Y) to other high performance buildings, and to the national average EUI for a typical office building (94 kBtu/ft^2-Y). Taking the location and climate of Portland into

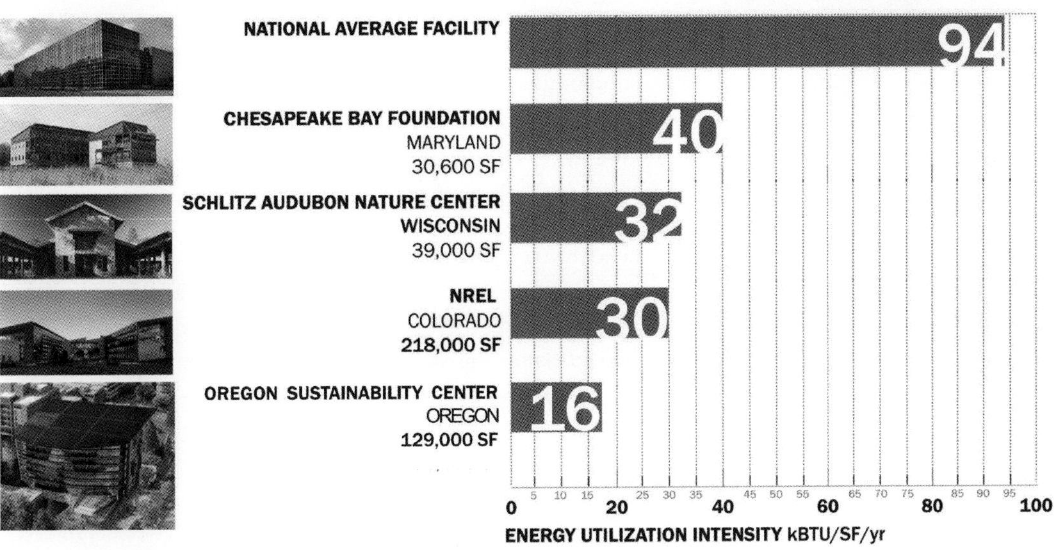

27.4 Oregon Sustainability Center, energy use intensity comparison chart

account, the design team found that an EUI of 16 kBtu/ft^2-Y or 50 kWh/m^2-Y could support five or six floors of rentable space in a net zero energy building, harvesting energy predominantly from a photovoltaic roof covering 100 percent of the building's footprint.

SOLVING THE ENERGY EQUATION

Once a direct relationship between the rentable floor area and the amount of predicted annual energy production was established, the design team looked for ways to decrease the energy demand while increasing the on-site energy production.

In addition to the 381 kWp mono-crystalline photovoltaic panels on the roof (blue in Figure 27.5), PV-covered horizontal sun shading devices (shown in red) account for an additional 114 kWp of installed PV panels generating electricity from light. Two fields of bifocal photovoltaic cells account for 67 kWp, bringing the total installed power at peak performance to 562 kWp. This system could produce an estimated 658,567 kWh in a typical year.

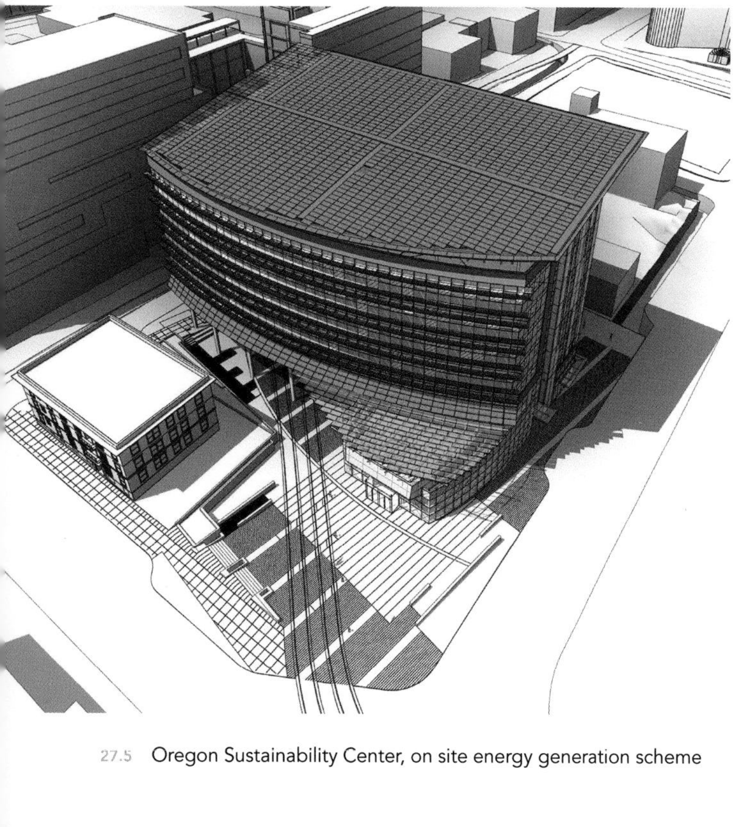

27.5 Oregon Sustainability Center, on site energy generation scheme

Once the estimated maximum amount of annual on-site energy production is established, the focus shifts to the demand side of the equation. Orientation, window sizing, daylighting design and thermal insulation properties of the envelope are "passive" architectural strategies for lowering the demand. These strategies were employed in parallel with high efficiency equipment for heating and cooling, such as geothermal heat pumps exchanging energy with the ground deep below the building where the temperature is fairly constant at 60° F (15–16° C).

The design team found that a low velocity underfloor air supply system, combined with hydronic heating and cooling in exposed concrete slabs (as ceilings), was the most efficient way to maintain indoor air quality and thermal comfort.

THE WATER CYCLE

After the energy equation was solved, the design team approached the next challenge: to achieve net zero water use and on-site wastewater management. Figure 27.6 explains how the large photovoltaic roof could duplicate as a rainwater harvesting device. An oversized gutter along the lower edge of the sloping roof collects the rainwater, which would be stored in a large underground rainwater storage tank. Treated rainwater turned into potable water was to be supplied to sinks and showers.

Wastewater from toilets and other non-potable points of use would be treated in an eco-machine-type treatment system in tandem with a bryophyte wall with tree-moss and other non-vascular plants. Treated wastewater would then be used to supply the non-potable water fixtures.

Emergency connections to the city water main and sewer system should only be used when the on-site systems were down for maintenance or in case of system failure.

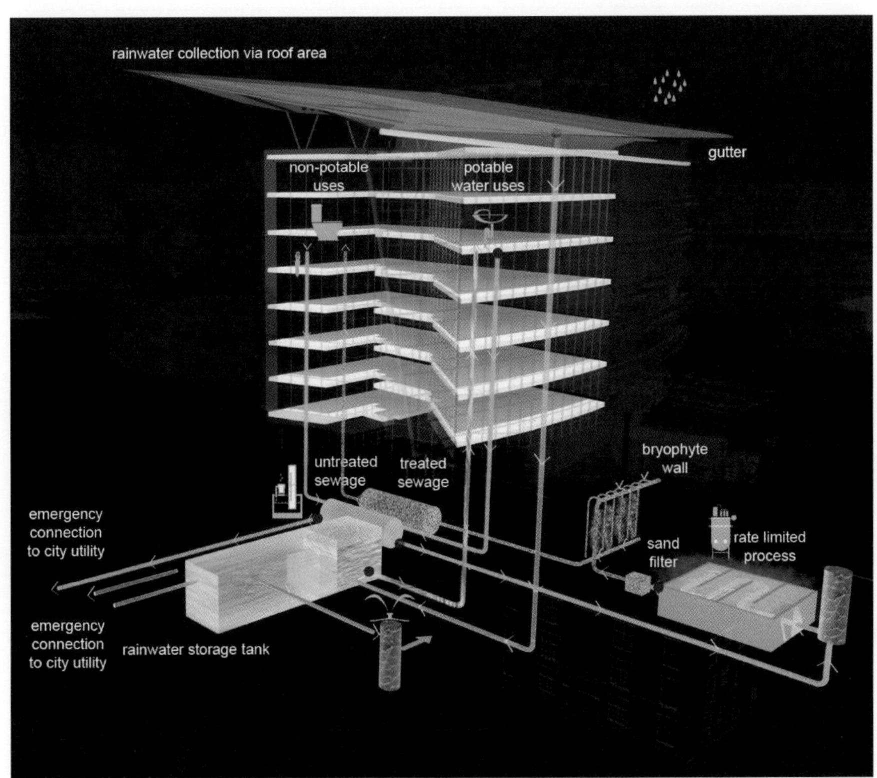

27.6 Oregon Sustainability Center, water harvesting and recycling diagram

As with the concept of net zero energy, net zero water use and on-site wastewater management do not necessarily mean that the building should go off the grid. Instead, a high performance urban building should be seen as self-sustaining, but grid-connected. By alternating between delivering to the grid and drawing from the grid, a sustainable building is able to balance the use of energy and water with the amount of energy or water harvested over the course of a typical meteorological year.

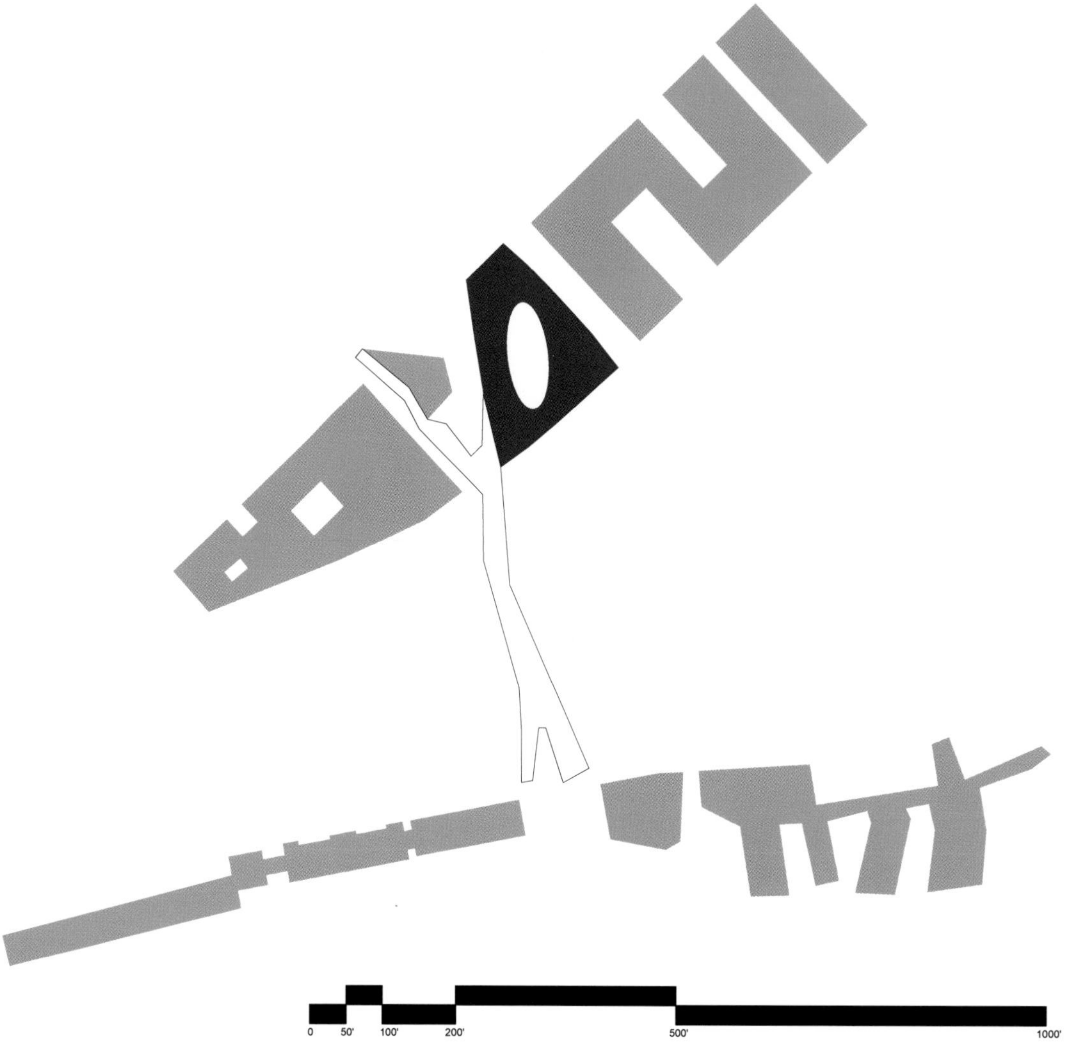

0 50' 100' 200' 500' 1000'

28

Powerhouse One

LOCATION: TRONDHEIM, NORWAY

ARCHITECT: SNØHETTA

TARGETING BREEAM OUTSTANDING

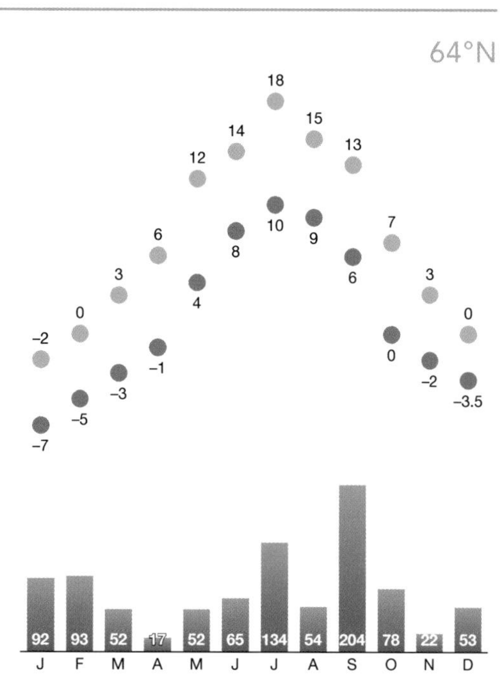

28.1 Powerhouse One, view towards the Trondheim fjord

28.2 Powerhouse One, view towards the east

FORM FOLLOWS ENVIRONMENT

Powerhouse One is the name chosen for the development of a Norwegian experimental office building project. Promoted by leading entities from the research community, the construction industry and governmental funding programs, the project design team is headed by Snøhetta Architects in cooperation with their consulting engineers.

The site for the Powerhouse One project was found by the water's edge at the heart of Trondheim, the technology capital of Norway. At 64 degrees Northern Latitude, Trondheim lies just below the Arctic Circle, as far north as Fairbanks, Alaska. The proximity to the Trondheim fjord, and by extension the North Sea, causes air and water temperatures to be tempered by the Gulf Stream, which makes the climate less severe than one would expect at such a high latitude. The seasons, however, are as much characterized by light as they are by temperature. While daylight is present almost all day and night at mid-summer, winter daylight is dim and lasts only a few hours.

At this climatically challenging location, the goal was set high: not only to reach a net zero energy building, but to surpass that target and enter the territory of a plus design: a building that during its lifetime would generate enough energy to support its operation and, in addition, would generate enough energy to pay back the energy used to produce the building and to ultimately demolish and recycle it.

CATCHING THE SUN AT 64 DEGREES NORTH

Starting with a globe set into a 3D digital model of the site, energy simulation software was used to identify the tilt and orientation of a plane that would receive the most solar radiation over the course of a typical meteorological year (TMY). This plane was then conceived as the roof plane of the building. The tilt and orientation of this conceptual plane could also prove beneficial in a wind-harvesting scheme, with micro wind turbines placed along the sharp northern edge (Figure 28.3).

Taking the maximum allowed built volume, according to the zoning plan, as the starting point for the next step in developing a conceptual design, the footprint was modified from a rectangle to a plan shaped like a polygon with a shorter north perimeter line and a longer south-facing street edge. The footprint was modified further in response to a desire to extend one of the major sight lines in Trondheim all the way to the water's edge.

The third step in the design process was to intersect the optimal sun harvesting plane with the massing derived from a modified zoning footprint. The intersection was tuned to produce

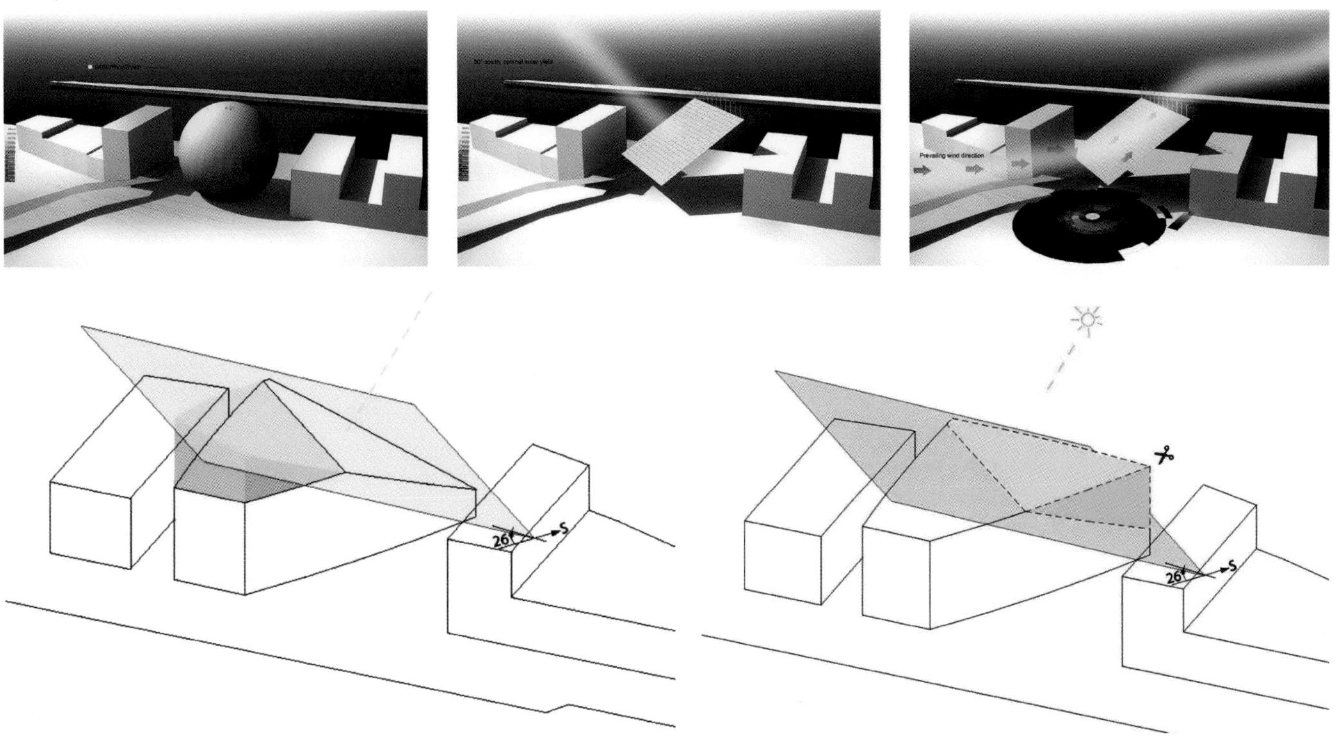

28.3 Powerhouse One, form follows the environment

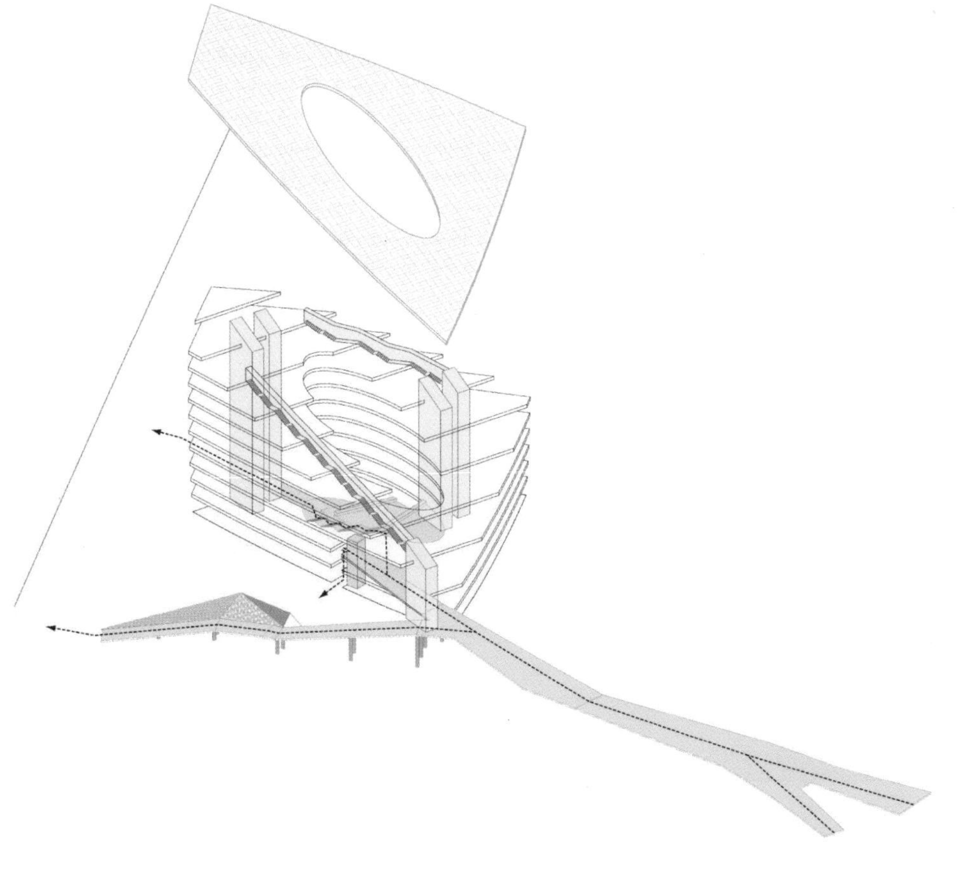

28.4 Powerhouse One, horizontal circulation diagram

a balance in volume between what would be subtracted (green in Figure 28.3) and what would be added (orange in Figure 28.3). Now, with the overall massing in place, it became evident that a variance from the zoning plan was needed. A building design targeting a level of performance beyond net zero could not fit the rectilinear boxy flat roof formal language of a Modernist era zoning plan.

28.5 Powerhouse One, view from the north

BRING IN THE LIGHT

Once the overall massing was determined, the architects decided to cut a piece out of the core of the building. This void became the vertical atrium, oval in footprint and going up through the building from the base to the roof. Pedestrians, whether occupants, visitors or passers-by, enter from the street side through the southwest corner of the building, pass through the atrium and continue to exit to the north, on the dock side.

Natural light is allowed to flow down into the atrium, thus providing all major office floors with daylight from two sides. The resulting massing scheme offers floor plates that are narrow enough for work stations to occupy the inside and outside perimeter, with access to air, light and views through operable windows.

ENVELOPE CONCEPT

All five envelope surfaces, including the roof, are conceived of as intelligent double-skin assemblies. The inside of the façade is a super-insulated opaque wall with double pane operable windows. The outer layer is a single pane of glass that comes in three flavors: transparent, semi-transparent with embedded see-through photovoltaic cells and mostly opaque with near 100 percent photovoltaic coverage. The transparent panels correspond to view windows in the inner section of the exterior wall. The semi-transparent panels correspond to windows primarily for daylight.

The ratio of transparent to semi-transparent to opaque exterior panels varies from one building surface to the next, and within each orientation, responding to the amount of solar energy each surface is expected to receive in a typical year.

The cavity between the exterior single pane of glass and the interior double pane window can be used for sun control made possible by automated, motorized blinds. The roof cavity can be used for airflow as a seasonal strategy for ventilation and heat recovery.

SLOW MOVING AIR

In a high performance building design where each minute possibility for energy saving is scrutinized, air must be moved with the least possible assistance from mechanical devices. Energy used for air-moving fans is reduced primarily by two strategies: minimize the pressure drop at each point in the system, and reduce the velocity. To achieve this goal, Powerhouse One makes use of a bundle of technological features, some well known, others inventive and on the cutting edge.

The energy-efficient form, the daylighting strategy, the super-insulated envelope, and the use of thermal mass in exposed concrete ceilings, all contribute to minimizing the demand on the air system to heat and cool the building. The air system's primary task, therefore, is to maintain indoor air quality.

Air is supplied through a pressurized built-up floor with low velocity air supply grilles. The air is allowed to pass through overflow openings into shared spaces. Stair towers are used as plenums to extract the air, thus taking advantage of buoyancy-driven air movement.

During the colder months of the year, when heat recovery from exhaust air is beneficial, the air is pulled down the stair towers to heat the recovery units below. In summer mode, when heat recovery is not required, air flows freely up the stair towers and out through openings in the roof.

Reversing the direction of the air flow in the stair towers seasonally is a technique similar to the approach applied to the solar chimney at Manitoba Hydro Place (see Chapter 16), but the idea of using stairwells as conduits for air circulations was actively used much earlier, as is evident in Manchester Town Hall, designed by Alfred Waterhouse in the late nineteenth century (see Chapter 10).

FJORD ENERGY

The building sits in an urban transition zone, negotiating movements from city to water's edge, from street to dockside. Powerhouse One interacts with the city and the water, not only in an urban sense, but also by technological means.

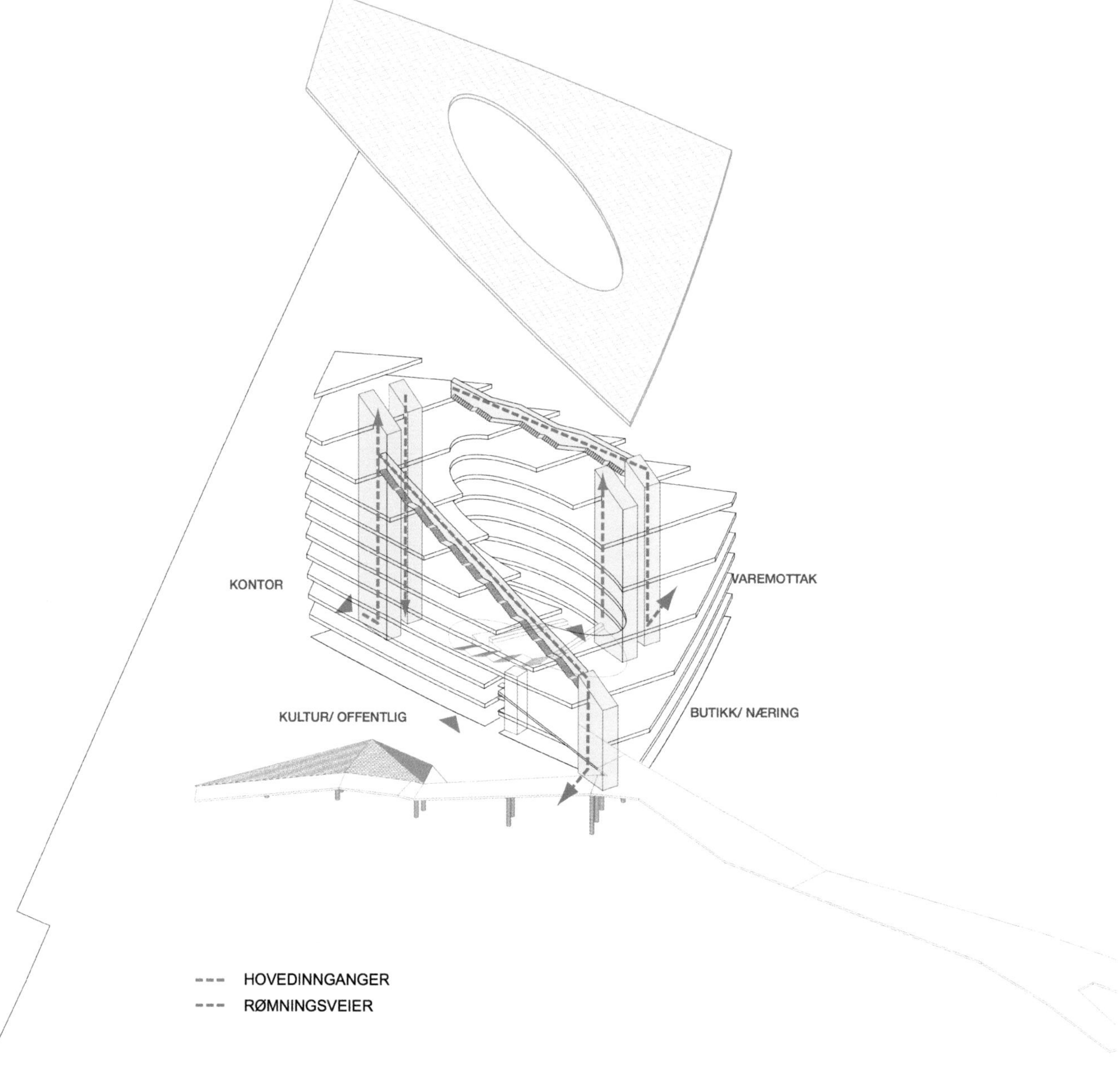

28.6 Powerhouse One, vertical circulation diagram

28.7 Powerhouse One, view across the channel

The water temperature in the Trondheim Fjord is rather constant at 8–12° C when reaching depths of 20 meters or more. Water from the fjord can be used as a primary source for cooling, if needed, by heat exchange between closed freshwater loops in the building and the fjord. Water source heat pumps will be used to provide energy for space heating, pulling heat out of the fjord.

As with geothermal heat pumps, water source heat pumps connected to a large body of water produce a higher output of energy for space heating or cooling relative to the energy input required to drive the equipment. Using a large body of water as a heat source or a heat dump is advantageous because of the excellent heat transfer characteristics of water and the fact that a building will not manage to significantly change the temperature of the source, thus avoiding the reduction in efficiency sometimes experienced in ground source heat pumps when the earth temperature surrounding the wells reaches a low in late winter.

BEYOND NET ZERO

The designers, researchers, and developers involved in the Powerhouse One project set out to reach an energy performance goal above and beyond net zero (see Figure 28.8). Taking into account the highest possible estimate for how much of the sun's energy can be harvested from the sloping roof, they found that a super-insulated, well-designed building could possibly reach a balance between demand and supply if the entire roof was covered with high output photovoltaic cells. Therefore, in order to go beyond that line, an intelligent façade had to be developed, implementing an optimized mix of transparent, semi-transparent and opaque façade panels, using walls as complementary energy suppliers to the roof as the main on-site energy source.

It is worth noting that at a high latitude location, such as Trondheim, east-, west- and north-facing exterior wall surfaces can generate a significant amount of energy during the summer months when the sun rises an hour or two after midnight and sets after ten in the evening.

In these cold climate high latitude locations, solar heat gain is not a threat to the energy balance, provided the building is intelligently designed with the goal of finding a balance in the relationship and interaction between the environment and the built form. Powerhouse One seeks to find that balance.

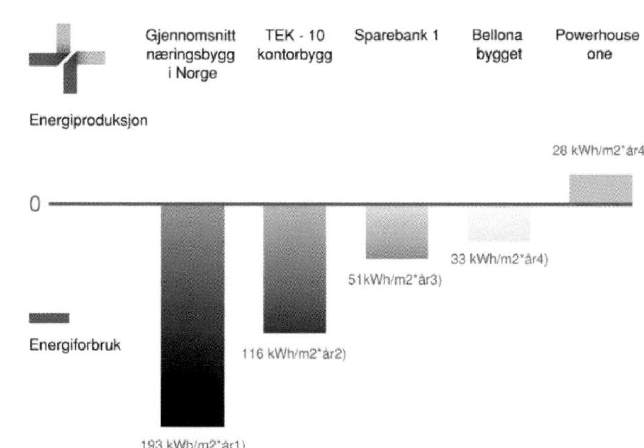

28.8 Powerhouse One, energy use intensity comparison diagram

Illustration Credits

1.1 Image from: Drysdale and Hayward, *Health and Comfort in House Building*, 1876, London: F.N. Spon.

1.2, 2.2, 2.5, 2.6, 2.7, 2.8, 3.1, 3.2, 3.3, 3.4, 3.5, 3.6, 3.8, 3.10, 4.1, 4.3, 4.4, 4.5, 4.7, 5.1, 5.2, 5.3, 5.4, 5.6, 5.7, 6.1, 6.5, 7.1, 7.4, 7.6, 7.7, 7.8, 8.1, 8.5, 9.1, 9.4, 9.8, 10.1, 10.3, 10.4, 10.5, 10.7, 10.8, 10.9, 11.1, 11.2, 11.3, 11.4, 11.8, 11.9, 12.1, 12.4, 12.5, 12.7, 13.1, 13.2, 13.5, 14.1, 14.3, 15.1, 15.3, 15.4, 15.5, 16.1, 16.4, 16.6, 16.7, 17.1, 17.2, 17.4, 17.5, 17.6, 18.1, 18.2, 18.3, 18.4, 18.5, 18.6, 19.1, 20.1, 20.3, 20.4, 20.5, 20.6, 20.7, 21.5, 22.1, 22.5, 22.6, 22.7, 22.8, 23.1, 23.2, 23.3, 23.4, 23.5, 23.6, 23.7, 24.1, 24.2, 24.4, 24.5, 24.6, 24.7, 24.8, 25.1, 25.2, 25.6, 25.7, 26.3, 26.5, 26.6 Vidar Lerum

1.3 *Encyclopèdie de l'architecture et de la construction* (1888: 467).

1.4 The Glasgow School of Art

1.5 US Patent 2117416. Inventor: Harold F. Hagren.

1.6 Section redrawn from copy of drawing by John W. Simpson and E. J. Milner Allen, 1894, obtained from The Mitchell Library, Glasgow.

2.1 Copyright (C) reserved, RIBA Library Drawings & Archives Collections.

2.3 Copyright Renzo Piano Building Workshop (RPBW).

2.4 Copyright Renzo Piano Building Workshop (RPBW).

2.8. Portal Spas images by Worksbureau.

3.2 Bernoulli, D., *Hydrodynamics*, 1738 (book cover, left image).

3.6 Diagram redrawn from a psychrometric chart (Carrier Corporation).

3.7 Basement plan redrawn from a plan diagram obtained from the State Hermitage Museum, St Petersburg, Russia.

3.9 Section diagram based on image reproduced in Matsenkov (2011: 81).

4.2 Sir John Soane's Museum.

4.6 Sir John Soane's Museum.

5.5 Sun angle diagram based on a drawing reproduced in the journal *Building Budget* (1899).

6.2 Parliamentary Archives, House of Lords, Westminster, London. Contains Parliamentary information licensed under the Open Parliament Licence v1.0.

6.3 David Boswell Reid (1844: 305).

6.4 Parliamentary Archives, House of Lords, Westminster, London. Contains Parliamentary information licensed under the Open Parliament Licence v1.0.

6.5 Drawing: Parliamentary Archives, House of Lords, Westminster, London. Contains Parliamentary information licensed under the Open Parliament Licence v1.0.

6.6 Parliamentary Archives, House of Lords, Westminster, London. Contains Parliamentary information licensed under the Open Parliament Licence v1.0.

7.2 Copyright (C) reserved, RIBA Library Drawings & Archives Collections.

7.3 Copyright (C) reserved, RIBA Library Drawings & Archives Collections.

7.5 David Boswell Reid (1855), Dg. 37.

8.2 © Illustrated London News Ltd/Mary Evans.

8.3 *The Builder*, 1850. Panizzi's sketch reproduced from Harris (1910).

8.4 *The American Architect and Building News*, October 18, 1884.

9.2 *The Builder*, 1870, Dec 3.

9.3 University of Glasgow, Archive Services.

9.4 The Mitchell Library (drawing).

9.5 From: Minutes of Proceedings of The Institution of Civil Engineers, Vol. LV, Session 1878.

9.6 University of Glasgow, Archive Services.

9.7 University of Glasgow, Archive Services.

10.2 Copyright (C) reserved, RIBA Library Drawings & Archives Collections.

10.6 Copyright (C) reserved, RIBA Library Drawings & Archives Collections.

11.5 Copyright (C) reserved, RIBA Library Drawings & Archives Collections.

11.6 Copyright (C) reserved, RIBA Library Drawings & Archives Collections.

11.7 Copyright (C) reserved, RIBA Library Drawings & Archives Collections.

12.2 Illustration from Inland Architect, 1897. Ryerson & Burnham Archives, Ryerson & Burnham Libraries, The Art Institute of Chicago.

12.3 Birmingham Children's Hospital, Estates & Facilities.

12.6 Birmingham Children's Hospital, Estates & Facilities.
12.8 Birmingham Children's Hospital, Estates & Facilities.
13.3 © The Kubala Washatko, Architects, Inc. (left), Vidar Lerum (right).
13.4 © The Kubala Washatko, Architects, Inc.
14.2 Courtesy: Perkins+Will.
14.4 © Lucie Marusin/Courtesy: Perkins+Will.
14.5 © Don F. Wong/Courtesy: Perkins+Will.
14.6 Courtesy: Perkins+Will.
15.2 Weber Thompson.
15.5 Weber Thompson (right), Vidar Lerum (left).
15.6 Weber Thompson.
16.2 KPMB Architects (Design Architects), Smith Carter Architects & Engineers (Executive Architect), Transsolar (Specialist Energy/Climate Engineer), Prairie Architects Inc. (Advocate Architect).
16.3 © Gerry Kopelow/Gerry Kopelow Photographics, Inc.
16.4 KPMB Architects (Design Architects), Smith Carter Architects & Engineers (Executive Architect), Transsolar (Specialist Energy/Climate Engineer), Prairie Architects Inc. (Advocate Architect), illustration by Bryan Christie (right), photo: Vidar Lerum (left).
16.5 KPMB Architects (Design Architects), Smith Carter Architects & Engineers (Executive Architect), Transsolar (Specialist Energy/Climate Engineer), Prairie Architects Inc. (Advocate Architect).
16.7 Mark Pauls, Manitoba Hydro (chart). Sculpture by Kevin McKenzie: "Resurrection II" (2006), Acrylic on steel and plexiglass base, with LED lighting, photo: Vidar Lerum.
17.3 Architekton.
17.4 Architekton (diagram), Vidar Lerum (photo).
19.2 Photo by Gregg Mastorakos, courtesy DPR Construction and SmithGroupJJR.
19.3 Photo by Gregg Mastorakos, courtesy DPR Construction and SmithGroupJJR.
19.4 Photo by Gregg Mastorakos, courtesy DPR Construction and SmithGroupJJR.
19.5 Photo by Gregg Mastorakos, courtesy DPR Construction and SmithGroupJJR.
19.6 Photo by Gregg Mastorakos, courtesy DPR Construction and SmithGroupJJR.
19.7 Photo by Gregg Mastorakos, courtesy DPR Construction and SmithGroupJJR.
20.2. Morphosis.
21.1 Nikken Sekkei LTD.
21.2 Nikken Sekkei LTD.
21.3 Nikken Sekkei LTD.
21.4 Nikken Sekkei LTD.
21.6 Nikken Sekkei LTD.
22.2 Benjamin Benschneider.
22.3 The Miller Hull Partnership.
22.4 The Miller Hull Partnership.
24.3 Copyright Renzo Piano Building Workshop (RPBW).
25.3 Courtesy: Jones Studio, Inc.
25.4 Courtesy: Jones Studio, Inc.
25.5 Courtesy: Jones Studio, Inc.
25.6 Photo © Bill Timmermann, courtesy Jones Studio, Inc.
26.1 Courtesy: Will Bruder + Partners Ltd with O2 Architects.
26.2 Courtesy: Will Bruder + Partners Ltd with O2 Architects.
26.3 Plan drawing: courtesy Will Bruder + Partners Ltd with O2 Architects, photo: Vidar Lerum.
26.4 Courtesy Will Bruder + Partners Ltd with O2 Architects.
27.1 Portland Development Commission, Gerding Edlin Development, GBD Architects, SERA Architects, Interface Engineers, PAE Consulting Engineers, kpff, Nevue Ngan, Otak, and Skanska US Building.
27.2 Portland Development Commission, Gerding Edlin Development, GBD Architects, SERA Architects, Interface Engineers, PAE Consulting Engineers, kpff, Nevue Ngan, Otak, and Skanska US Building.
27.3 Portland Development Commission, Gerding Edlin Development, GBD Architects, SERA Architects, Interface Engineers, PAE Consulting Engineers, kpff, Nevue Ngan, Otak, and Skanska US Building.
27.4 Portland Development Commission, Gerding Edlin Development, GBD Architects, SERA Architects, Interface Engineers, PAE Consulting Engineers, kpff, Nevue Ngan, Otak, and Skanska US Building.
27.5 Portland Development Commission, Gerding Edlin Development, GBD Architects, SERA Architects, Interface Engineers, PAE Consulting Engineers, kpff, Nevue Ngan, Otak, and Skanska US Building.

27.6 Portland Development Commission, Gerding Edlin Development, GBD Architects, SERA Architects, Interface Engineers, PAE Consulting Engineers, kpff, Nevue Ngan, Otak, and Skanska US Building.

28.1 Snøhetta/MIR.

28.2 Snøhetta/MIR.

28.3 Snøhetta.

28.4 Snøhetta.

28.5 Snøhetta/MIR.

28.6 Snøhetta.

28.7 Snøhetta/MIR.

28.8 Snøhetta.

Bibliography

Addis, W. (2007) *Building: 3000 Years Of Design Engineering And Construction*. London; New York, Phaidon Press.

Anon (1850) "Professor Hosking's Project." *The Builder* VIII(385): 2.

Anon (1855) "British Museum: Plan of New Reading-Room in Quadrangle." *The Builder* 2.

Anon (1857) "The New Reading-Room of the British Museum." *The Times*, p. 1.

Anon (1884) Plan showing the arrangement of the library of reference in the reading room of the British museum. London.

Anon (1888) "Bibliothèque." *Encyclopèdie de l'architecture*: 2.

Anon (1894) "The New Birmingham Hospital." *The Times*, p. 1.

Anon (1897) "The New General Hospital: Princess Christian In Birmingham." *The Times*. London. Issue 35520: 1.

Anon (1905) "Natural History Museum." *Architect & Contract Reporter* 74.

Anon (1913) "Children's Hospital, Birmingham." *Architects' and Builders' Journal* 21(37): 545.

Anon (1916) "Obituary." *Royal Institute of British Architects Journal* 24: 223–224.

Anon (1960) "Natural History Museum, London, SW 7." *Architectural Design* 30: 408-408.

Anon (2011) "Nikken Sekkei: Sony City Osaki, Tokyo, 2007-11." *GA Japan: environmental design* (112): 94-103.

Archer, J. H. G. (1982) "A civic achievement: the building of Manchester Town Hall: part one: the commissioning." *Lancashire and Cheshire Antiquarian Society Transactions* 81.

Aristotle, P.H. Wicksteed, and Francis Macdonald Cornford. (1929) *Aristotle, the Physics*. London: W. Heinemann; G.P. Putnam's Sons.

ASHRAE Handbook (2005) Available at: www.ashrae.org

Azevedo, M. A. (2012) *Packard Foundation: Do As We Do*. www.theregistrysf.com. Retrieved July 9, 2015.

Baldwin, W. J. (1899) *An Outline of Ventilation and Warming*. New York: The author.

Banham, R. (1980) *Theory and Design in the First Machine Age*. Cambridge, Mass.: MIT Press.

Banham, R. (1984) *The Architecture of the Well-Tempered Environment*. London: Architectural Press.

Banham, R., S. Bayley and Open University. (1975) *Mechanical Services* / prepared by Reyner Banham The modern flat / prepared by Stephen Bayley. Milton Keynes: Open University Press.

Barry, Alfred. (1867) *The Life and Works of Sir Charles Barry*. London: John Murray.

Becket, P. (2006) "Terracotta tales: The Natural History Museum, London - who was Monsieur Dujardin?" *Glazed Expressions / Tiles & Architectural Ceramics Society*(57): 9-9.

Bell, E. I. (1881) "The new Natural History Museum." *American Magazine of Art* 4: 358.

Bernal, J. D. (1953) *Science and Industry in the Nineteenth Century*. London: Routledge & Paul.

Bernoulli, D. (1738) *Danielis Bernoulli . . . Hydrodynamica, sive De viribus et motibus fluidorum commentarii. Opus academicum ab auctore, dum Petropoli ageret, congestum. Argentorati: sumptibus J.R. Dulseckeri*.

Blackall, C. H. (1884) "Heating and ventilation of the British Museum." *The American Architect and Building* News: 2.

Bullen, J. B. (1989) "Refurbishment of Alfred Waterhouse's Romanesque "Temple of Nature": the Natural History Museum, London." *Building* 10(254): 3–56.

Bullen, J. B. (2006) "Alfred Waterhouse's Romanesque 'Temple of Nature': the Natural History Museum, London." *Architectural History* 49: 257–285.

Butti, K. and J. Perlin, (1980) *A Golden Thread: 2500 Years of Solar Architecture and Technology*. Palo Alto, CA: Cheshire Books.

Caine, T. H. and D. Cruickshank (1882) "The Manchester mural paintings: Civic pride [Manchester Town Hall]." *American Magazine of Art* 5(213): 114–115.

Carroon, J. (2010) *Sustainable Preservation: Greening Existing Buildings*. Hoboken, N.J., Wiley.

Chabannes, J.-F. d. (1818) On conducting air by forced ventilation, and regulating the temperature in dwelling, with a description of the application of the principles as establshed in Covent Garden Theatre and Lloyd's Subscription Rooms, and a short account of different patent apparatus for warming and cooling air and liquids. London.

Chabannes, J.-F. d. and Making of the Modern World (1801) A short essay on the composition of oeconomical fuel and of various mixtures that may be used with coal, to produce a clear saving of one-third part of the expence of keeping up fires in general. Lambeth, Printed by S. Tibson,: vii, 42 p.

Chabannes, J.-F. d. and Making of the Modern World (1815) Explanation of a new method for warming and purifying the air in private houses and public buildings for totally destroying smoke, for purifying the air in stables, and every kind of building in which animals are lodged. S.l., s.n.,: 25 p.

Chambers, R. (2007) "St. George's Hall, Liverpool: a review of the recent work." *Journal of Architectural Conservation* 13: [37]-56.

Chawner, T., H. Rhodes, M. H. Port, National Archives (Great Britain) and London Topographical Society (2011) The Palace of Westminster surveyed on the eve of the conflagration, 1834. London Topographical Society publication no 171. London, London Topographical Society.

Cook, J. (1998) "Designing ventilation with heating: Natural History Museum in 1873 London." *ASHRAE Journal* 40(4): 44.

Cook, J. and T. Hinchcliffe (1995) "Designing the well-tempered institution of 1873." *Arq: architectural research quarterly* 1(2): 70-78.

Cook, J. and T. Hinchcliffe (1996) "Delivering the well-tempered institution of 1873." *Arq: architectural research quarterly* 2(1): 66-75.

Cruickshank, D. (2001) "Civic pride [Manchester Town Hall]." *Architects' Journal* 1(213): [28-43.

Cunningham, C. (1873) "The proposed history museum, South Kensington. The Waterhouse Collection of the RIBA and the workings of a nineteenth-century office." *American Builder* 8-9: 170-171.

Cunningham, C. (2006) "The Waterhouse Collection of the RIBA and the workings of a nineteenth-century office." *Architectural History* 49: 287-316.

Cunningham, C. and A. Waterhouse (2001) *The Terracotta Designs of Alfred Waterhouse*. London: The Natural History Museum in association with Wiley-Academy.

Cunningham, C. and P. Waterhouse (1992) *Alfred Waterhouse, 1830–1905: Biography of a Practice*. Oxford: Clarendon Press.

Curl, J. S. (1974) *Victorian Architecture: Its Practical Aspects*. Cranbury, NJ: Fairleigh Dickinson University Press.

Curl, J. S. (1990) *Victorian Architecture*. Newton Abbot: David & Charles.

Curl, J. S. (2007) *Victorian Architecture: Diversity & Invention*. Reading: Spire.

Daniels, K. (1997) *The Technology of Ecological Building: Basic Principles and Measures, Examples and Ideas*. Basel: Birkhäuser Verlag.

Daniels, K. (1998) Low-tech Light-tech High-tech: Building in the Information Age. Basel; Boston: Birkäuser.

Daniels, K. and R. E. Hammann (2009) *Energy Design for Tomorrow = Energy Design für morgen*. Stuttgart: Edition Axel Menges.

Darley, G. (1999) *John Soane: An Accidental Romantic*. New Haven CT: Yale University Press.

De Beer, G. R. (1953) "A storehouse of natural history." *Country life* 113: 1966-1968.

Drysdale, J. J. and J.W. Hayward (1876) *Health and Comfort in House Building*. London: F. N. Spon.

Ducamp, E., M. F. Korshunova, T. a. n. B. Bushmina, T. a. n. B. Semionova and Gosudarstvennyĭ Ėrmitazh (Russia) (1995) *The Winter Palace, Saint Petersburg*. Paris; Saint Petersburg: Alain de Gourcuff; State Hermitage Museum.

Fawcett, J. (1976) *Seven Victorian Architects*. London: Thames and Hudson.

Girouard, M. (1981) *Alfred Waterhouse and the Natural History Museum*. New Haven: Yale University Press in association with the British Museum (Natural History).

Disraeli, Benjamin, J. A. W. Gunn, & Wiebe, M. G. (1982) *Benjamin Disraeli Letters*. Toronto; Buffalo: University of Toronto Press.

Fulcrum, Mott MacDonald. (2011) Natural History Museum Waterhouse Building Ventilation Improvements. London: Mott McDonald Fulcrum.

Hamilton, G. H. (1954) *The Art and Architecture of Russia*. Baltimore: Penguin Books.

Harris, P. R. (1979) *The Reading Room*. Library. London: British Library.

Harris, P. R. (1991) *The Library of the British Museum: Retrospective Essays on the Department of Printed Books*. London: British Library.

Harris, P. R. (1998) *A History of the British Museum Library, 1753-1973*. London: British Library.

Hawkes, D. (1996) *The Environmental Tradition: Studies in the Architecture Of Environment*. London: E&FN Spon.

Hawkes, D. (2008) *The Environmental Imagination: Technics and Poetics of the Architectural Environment*. New York: Routledge.

Hawkes, D. (2012) *Architecture and Climate: An Environmental History of British Architecture, 1600–2000*. New York: Routledge.

Hawkes, D. and W. Forster (2002) *Energy efficient buildings: architecture, engineering, and environment*. New York: W.W. Norton & Co.

Hawkes, D., J. McDonald and K. Steemers (2002) *The Selective Environment*. London; New York: Spon Press.

Henman, W. (1896) "Construction of hospitals." *Royal Institute of British Architects Journal* 4: 333–343.

Henman, W. (1904a) "Notes on the plenum system of ventilation." *Royal Institute of British Architects Journal* 11: 427–442.

Henman, W. (1904b) "The Plenum System of Ventilation." *The Builder* 6.

Henman, W. and H. Lea (1903) "Royal Victoria Hospital, Belfast: Its Initiation, Design, and Equipment." *Journal of the Royal Institute of British Architects*, June 11, pp. 89–113.

Hepplewhite, P., N. Tonge, N. Pritchard, K. Banham, J. Lane and J. Bottomley (1995) *Victorian Britain*. Leamington Spa: Scholastic Publications Ltd.

MacKenzie, William (1863) "On the Mechanical Ventilation and Warming of St. George's Hall, Liverpool. In: Institution of Mechanical Engineers. *Proceedings*. Birmingham: Institution of Mechanical Engineers, p. 194.

Jenkins, F. (1967) "The making of a municipal palace: Manchester Town Hall." *Country Life* 141: 336–339.

Jones, E. (2011) "Border lines." *Forward* 111.

Kimbell Art Museum (Producer) (2014, April 25, 2015) Kahn: Piano - The Piano Pavilion at the Kimbell Art Museum. [Video]. https://youtu.be/tx6R_4zCTUU.

King, A. (1966) "Hospital planning: revised thoughts on the origin of the pavilion principle in England." *Medical History* 10(4): 360–373.

King, G. (2006) *The Court of the Last Tsar: Pomp, Power, and Pageantry in the Reign of Nicholas II*. Hoboken, NJ: John Wiley & Sons, Inc.

Le Camus de Mézières, N. ([1780] 1992) *The Genius of Architecture, or, The Analogy of That Art with Our Sensations*. Chicago: Getty Center for the History of Art and the Humanities.

Le Corbusier (1923) *Towards a New Architecture*. London: Architectural Press.

Leopold, A. (1949) *A Sand County Almanac, and Sketches Here and There*. New York: Oxford University Press.

Leopold, A. and A. Brooks (1933) *Game Management*. New York, London: C. Scribner's Sons.

Leopold, A., J. B. Callicott and E. T. Freyfogle (1999) *For the Health of the Land: Previously Unpublished Essays and Other Writings*. Washington, DC: Island Press.

Lerum, V. (2008) *High-Performance Building*. Hoboken, NJ: John Wiley & Sons, Inc.

Lerum, V. (2013) *Clark Brockman Interview*. Notes. Portland, OR.

Loukomski, G. K. (1928) "Rastrelli, architecte (1700–1771)." *Amour de l'art* 9: 25–29.

Making of the Modern World and J.-F. d. Chabannes (1820) Appendix to the Marquis de Chabannes' publication on conducting air by forced ventilation and equalizing the temperature of dwellings published in 1818: being a continuation of the description of the patent apparatus for warming and cooling air and liquid, and containing an account of the new water calorifere, and other apparatus, and also of the manner in which the following places have been warmed and ventillated this year . . .: illustrated with copper plate engravings. London, To be had at the Patent Calorifere Fumivore Manufactory and Foundry,: 32 p., 37 folded leaves of plates.

Matsenkov, S. (2011) *The Attic Floor at the Hermitage*. St. Petersburg: The State Hermitage Museum.

Middleton, Robin (1982) *The Beaux-arts and Nineteenth-Century French Architecture*. Cambridge, MA: MIT Press.

Morrison, G. B. (1887) *The Ventilation and Warming of School Buildings*. New York: D. Appleton.

Newton, Isaac, Samuel Smith, and Benjamin Walford. (1704) Opticks, or, A treatise of the reflexions, refractions, inflexions and colours of light: also two treatises of the species and magnitude of curvilinear figures. London: Printed for Sam. Smith, and Benj. Walford, printers to the Royal Society, at the Prince's Arms in St. Paul's Church-yard.

Nicolson, Marjorie Hope. (1946) *Newton Demands The Muse; Newton's Opticks And The Eighteenth Century Poets.* Princeton, NJ: Princeton University Press.

Nightingale, F. and Making of the Modern World (1861) Notes on nursing for the labouring classes. London, Harrison,: 1 online resource (96, 91 p.).

Olley, J. and C. Wilson (1985) "The Natural History Museum: Pioneer of modern museum design: Masters of building (3)." *Architects' Journal* 181(13): 32.

Parker, S. (2010) *Museum of Life.* London: Natural History Museum.

Pass, A. J. (1988) Thomas Worthington: *Victorian Architecture and Social Purpose.* Manchester: Manchester Literary and Philosophical Publications.

Phipson, W. W., J. Forrest and Institution of Civil Engineers (Great Britain) (1879) On the heating and ventilating apparatus of the Glasgow University. London, Printed by William Clowes and Sons.

Port, M. H. and Paul Mellon Centre for Studies in British Art (1976) *The Houses of Parliament.* New Haven: Published for the Paul Mellon Centre for Studies in British Art (London) by Yale University Press.

Porteous, Colin (2002) *The New Eco-architecture: Alternatives from the Modern Movement.* London; New York: Spon Press.

Powell, K. (1996) "Maturing with style." *Architects' Journal* 204(4): 20-21.

Reid, D. B. (1855) Diagrams of the Ventilation of St. George's Hall. London; Document obtained from Nick Sturrock, CIBSE Heritage Group.

Reid, D. B. (1858) Ventilation in American Dwellings. New York.

Reid, D. B. and Making of the Modern World (1844) Illustrations of the theory and practice of ventilation with remarks on warming, exclusive lighting, and the communication of sound. London: Printed for Longman, Brown, Green & Longmans: xx, 451 p., 451 leaf of plates.

Reid, D. B., Making of the Modern World and Great Britain. Commissioners for Inquiring into the State of Large Towns and Populous Districts (1845) Report on the state of Newcastle-upon-Tyne and other towns. London: Printed by W. Clowes and Sons, for H.M.S.O.: 156 p., 121 leaves of plates.

Richardson, C. J. (1856) *A popular treatise on the warming & ventilation of buildings showing the advantage of the improved system of heated water circulation.* London: J. Weale.

Rios, A. (2003) Líneas Fronterizas/Border Lines. Available at: www.vqronline.org/lineas-fronterizas-border-lines.

Robins, E. C. (1883) "Modern Hospital Construction." *The Builder*: 8.

Shvidkovsky, D. O. and A. Orloff (1996) *St. Petersburg: Architecture of the Tsars.* New York: Abbeville Press Publishers.

Rose, W.illiam B. (2005) *Water in Buildings: An Architect's Guide to Moisture and Mold.* Hoboken, NJ: John Wiley & Sons.

Skodock, C. (2006) Barock in Russland: zum œuvre des Hofarchitekten Francesco Bartolomeo Rastrelli: mit Werkkatalog auf CD-ROM. Wiesbaden: Harrassowitz.

Steinbach, S. (2012) *Understanding the Victorians: Politics, Culture, and Society in Nineteenth-century Britain.* New York: Routledge.

Tanner, T., A. Leopold and Soil Conservation Society of America (1987) *Aldo Leopold: The Man and His Legacy.* Ankeny, Iowa: Soil Conservation Society of America.

Tausky, N. Z., L. D. DiStefano, London Regional Art Gallery (Ont.) and Robinson Tracy Durand and Moore (Firm) (1986) *Victorian Architecture in London and Southwestern Ontario: Symbols of Aspiration.* Toronto: University of Toronto Press.

Taylor, J. R. B. (1997) *The Architect and the Pavilion Hospital: Dialogue and Design Creativity in England, 1850–1914.* London; New York: Leicester University Press.

Thompson, P. (1968) "Building of the Year: Manchester Town Hall." *Victorian Studies* 11(3): 401–403.

Van Zanten, David (1987) *Designing Paris: The Architecture of Duban, Labrouste, Duc, and Vaudoyer.* Cambridge, Mass.: MIT Press.

Waterhouse, A. (1876) "Description of the new town hall at Manchester." *Royal Institute of British Architects Papers*: 117–136.

Waterhouse, A. and R. Waite (1915) "Manchester Old Town Hall Description of the new town hall at Manchester First look at £165 million Manchester refurbishment." *Architects and Builders Journal* 19(232): 41.

Willmert, T. (1993) "Heating Methods and Their Impact on Soane's Work: Lincoln's Inn Fields and Dulwich Picture Gallery." *Journal of the Society of Architectural Historians* 52(1): 26–58.

Index